SIX PLAYS OF PLAUTUS

LIONEL CASSON is Professor of Classics at New York University and Director of the summer session of the American Academy in Rome. His chief intellectual interests—the history of the sea in ancient times, and Greek and Roman comedy—are both reflected in his published works. The first produced *The Ancient Mariners;* the second, *Masters of Ancient Comedy, Selected Satires of Lucian,* and now *Six Plays of Plautus.* Dr. Casson has also given more than fifty television lectures on Greek drama, including a course for Sunrise Semester. He is a frequent contributor to literary and scholarly magazines, among them, *Scientific American, The Saturday Review,* and *The New York Times Sunday Book Review.*

Six Plays of Plautus

EDITED AND TRANSLATED BY
LIONEL CASSON

Anchor Books
Doubleday & Company, Inc.
Garden City, New York
1963

Lionel Casson's translation of *The Rope* first appeared in MAS-
TERS OF ANCIENT COMEDY, published by The Macmillan Company in 1960, and is reprinted here by arrangement with The
Macmillan Company. The translation has been slightly revised
for the Anchor Books edition.

Library of Congress Catalog Card Number 63–18038
Copyright © 1960, 1963 by Lionel Casson
All Rights Reserved
Printed in the United States of America
First Edition

To Ernest Hettich, teacher and friend

PREFACE

Plautus wrote upwards of fifty plays, of which twenty have survived more or less in their entirety.[1] In making my choice for this anthology, I tried not only to include his best but to give some idea of his range. His forte was farce, and my selections exemplify at least three of his favorite farcical devices: mistaken identity (*The Menaechmus Twins, Amphitryon*); the lecherous old codger (*Casina*); and the scheming servant (*Pseudolus*). *The Rope* is an example of his more romantic style; the plot is as important to the play as the purely comic scenes, and these, in line with the general tenor of the work, are of a somewhat higher order than the unabashed tomfoolery of the *Pseudolus* or the *Casina*. And, lastly, *The Pot of Gold* reveals what Plautus could do with the subtler humor to be evoked from character.

I have arranged the plays alphabetically, as is traditional in editions of Plautus. In spite of many learned attempts, no one has yet succeeded in demonstrating convincingly the chronological order of his work (see p. xviii).

In these translations I have followed the same principles I did in my *Masters of Ancient Comedy*, and I can do no bet-

[1] I say "more or less" because all but one of the preserved manuscripts of his work derive from a single manuscript of the eighth century A.D. which was, unfortunately, in a mutilated condition, and, as a consequence, there are gaps in the text that range from a few lines (see, e.g., *Casina*, ll. 889, 890) to whole scenes (see, e.g., *Amphitryon*, l. 1035).

ter than repeat what I wrote there (p. viii) to explain what
my procedure has been:

"All Greek and Roman drama was in verse. Moreover, . . .
Plautus [was], in a sense, writing musical comedy: a considerable portion of [his] plays is not dialogue to be spoken
but lyrics to be sung. These by their very nature called for
translation in verse. Everywhere else I have used prose.

"The usual purpose of a verse translation is to retain the
style and spirit of the original at the expense, if necessary, of
literal accuracy; and, of a prose translation, precisely the
opposite. What I have done is to reverse this usual state of
affairs: I have chosen prose in order to retain the spirit, if not
the style, of the original, and my prose is, if anything, more
free than many a translation in verse.

"There have been many periods in the history of drama
when verse was the only accepted vehicle for comedy. Today, of course, playwrights writing in the vein of . . . Plautus
use normal colloquial speech. My aim was to make these
ancient plays sound as much like contemporary comedy as I
could—and still remain a translator and not an adapter. That
meant not only using prose, but prose that reflected the vo-
cabulary and rhythms of contemporary speech. Every line I
translated I subjected to a simple test: I read it aloud and
asked myself whether it sounded the way a person would
express himself in the given situation today. Frequently the
original lent itself to a rendering that satisfied this require-
ment and was at the same time a close translation; more
often, close translation was impossible and I rendered the
general sense of a passage with no attempt to reproduce the
meaning of the individual words; at times I frankly para-
phrased. All references that would make sense only to ancient
audiences or modern scholars I replaced with some sort of
current equivalent. For the ubiquitous oaths and exclamations
that invoke the names of ancient deities I substituted modern
expressions; I converted drachmas and talents into dollars
(allowing for current inflation has made my figures considerably higher than those in earlier translations); I replaced
ancient geographical names with modern equivalents; I doc-

tored the jokes where necessary to make them intelligible to today's audiences. Moreover, in line with my aim to make living theater of these plays, I added full stage directions, just as a modern playwright would."

The lyric portions of the originals are extremely fluid and flexible, characterized by lines of unequal length and by frequent changes of meter. My renderings reproduce only the metrical pace, as it were. Where the mood was comic, I used rhymed verse; where more serious, unrhymed.

Plautus chose the names he assigned his characters with great care. A number are not actually names but pure comic inventions, and for these I used English equivalents (e.g., Sponge, the scrounger in *The Menaechmus Twins,* is in the original *Peniculus,* literally "brush"). For other characters, he (or the author of the Greek original he adapted) used common Greek names which were somehow especially apt, just as a playwright of today will emphasize a female character's nature by giving her a name such as Faith or Grace; in these cases I kept the original name but explained its aptness in the stage directions.

Plautus wrote his plays to be performed without breaks. Subsequently, editors introduced act divisions. Since these have become traditional, and serve a useful purpose as well, I have retained them.

I am indebted to The Macmillan Company of New York for permission to reproduce from *Masters of Ancient Comedy* my translation of *The Rope;* I have corrected some minor errors in the prose portion and redone some of the lyrics in rhymed verse.

As always, I owe a large debt of gratitude to my most careful and helpful critic, my father. The introduction and stage directions have everywhere benefited from his rigorous insistence on accuracy in language, and the dialogue from his keen ear for accuracy in idiom. My wife contributed many a well-turned phrase and gave brightness to many a lackluster line. And I am grateful to the John Simon Guggenheim Memorial Foundation for providing in an indirect way the free time that made this volume possible—in an indirect way because these translations were largely done as daily relaxation after hours of close research on the topic for which I had actually received my fellowship.

Lionel Casson

Rome
September 1962

CONTENTS

INTRODUCTION

Sometime around 250 B.C., in the tiny mountain village of Sarsina high in the Apennines of Umbria, ancient Rome's best-known playwright was born.

We know so little about his life that we're not even sure of his full name; probably—but only probably—it was Titus Maccius Plautus. We can only guess how a backwoods country boy managed to leave his village, to learn Latin so well he achieved effects with it no later writers ever matched (the native tongue of Sarsina was not Latin but Umbrian, a relative of Latin), to learn the literary language of the day, Greek (see below, p. xvii), to crack the world of the theater at the capital, and through it to fight his way to reputation and money. According to one of the stories told about him years after he died, he got his start in the theater as an actor in native farces. This could very well be true: Plautus' plays show unmistakably that their author knew what went on behind the stage as well as on it. Moreover, what easier way was there for a boy with the appropriate talent to escape the shackles of a small town than by joining an itinerant theatrical troupe? Once Plautus achieved fame, he never lost it: when he died, in 184 B.C., he was the dean of Rome's writers of comedy.

Comedy itself was only three centuries or so older than he was. It had achieved definite form where so much else of Western culture had, in Athens of the fifth century B.C.: the first recorded performance of a comedy took place in March 486 B.C., in the Theater of Dionysus on the south slope of Athens' Acropolis.

But the type of comedy that flourished in fifth-century Athens, Greek "Old Comedy" as it has been called, neither lasted very long nor started any important trends. When its best-known exponent, Aristophanes, died, it more or less died with him. Old Comedy was, essentially, topical satire, and Aristophanes' plays, full of withering, uproarious jibes at contemporary Athenian politics and politicos, education and educators, writings and writers, did not interest subsequent generations to whom all this was just so much ancient history, and whose taste in comedy ran in different directions.

Toward the end of his life, however, Aristophanes started to mine a comic vein that, being more universal in appeal, lasted a good deal longer, right through Plautus down to our own times, in fact. He shifted the emphasis from satire to humor, and began to write about people as a class, not specific personalities, and to poke fun at men's ways in general, not at their behavior as citizens in a given place at a given time.

By 300 B.C., this form of comedy, Greek "New Comedy" as it has been called, had come to maturity and was providing the principal and preferred theatrical fare of the day. Aristophanes was a thing of the past; audiences jammed the theaters to see the latest works of the masters of New Comedy, of Diphilus, Philemon, Apollodorus of Carystus, and, above all, Menander. They wrote about ordinary people, mocking—Menander gently, the others more boisterously—human foibles and crotchets, the laughable things people are prone to do, the silly behavior certain circumstances almost invariably call forth. The world these playwrights chose to portray is small: they deal almost exclusively with the doings of upper middle-class households. The dramatis personae are equally limited: the father of the household, irascible or stupid as plot requires; his formidable wife; their idler of a son; scheming servants; dull-witted servants; longwinded cooks; gold-digging courtesans; famished hangers-on; flint-hearted pimps. The plot often revolves about, or at the very least includes, a love affair, and there was an unfortunate tendency (we haven't overcome it to this day) to tell—with variations, to be sure—the story of the boy who meets the girl, can't marry her because she has no money or comes from the wrong side of the tracks, but ends up living happily ever after since she turns out to be the rich neighbor's long-lost daughter.

According to the ancient critics, Menander and the other great names in Greek New Comedy wrote consummate masterpieces. We today are in no position either to confirm or contest this judgment for, of the hundreds of these works that were staged, all that has survived is one complete play and that a rather poor specimen, half of another, and one third each of two more.[1]

New Comedy was immensely popular. The latest productions of Diphilus and Menander, after opening in Athens, went to theaters all over the Greek-speaking world, in Asia Minor, on the Aegean Isles, along the coast of North Africa, and—most important for comedy's subsequent history —in South Italy.

As early as 700 B.C., the lower part of Italy, from Naples south through Sicily, had been largely taken over by Greeks. The area was dotted with their populous and well-to-do cities, each of which by 300 B.C. had its theater where not only local farces and skits were put on but also the latest imports of New Comedy from Athens.

To the north lay Rome. Until just a few decades before Plautus was born, Rome was relatively obscure and provincial, with no pretensions to culture, a nation of hard-fisted farmers and hard-fighting soldiers. However, by the time Plautus was an adult, she had extended her power southward and was the acknowledged mistress of the Greek cities of southern Italy. Her soldiers, statesmen, and merchants came into contact with, and got eye-filling glimpses of, a new, far more sophisticated and gracious way of life. Among other things, they were exposed to the delights of the Greek stage

[1] For translations of these, see my *Masters of Ancient Comedy*, pp. 65–175.

and, in no time at all, developed a healthy appetite for it. This was a milestone in the history of comedy: it was responsible for the creation of Latin comedy, and Latin comedy is the direct ancestor of much of the comedy of later Western literature.

The Romans, to be sure, had some theatrical fare of their own. Their village fiestas featured several types of short, boisterous farce, including one in which song and dance played an important part; if Plautus actually did start his career as an actor, it must have been in pieces of this kind. But it was all rather primitive stuff. In 240 B.C., a Greek named Livius Andronicus translated and adapted a Greek New Comedy for a Roman audience and immediately started a vogue; he had filled a need. Latin versions of Greek plays quickly found a place on programs alongside the local fare, and, in larger communities, easily outstripped it in popularity. Livius was followed by Gnaeus Naevius (ca. 270–201 B.C.), Rome's first native playwright, who, in addition to adapting Greek works, inaugurated true Roman comedy by writing original plays in Latin. He apparently was a talented author, but unfortunately only fragments of his work have been preserved. The distinction of having produced the earliest Latin plays to survive goes to his gifted younger contemporary, Plautus.

Plautus, in a very real sense, faced the same problems as a writer for Broadway today. He had to turn out pieces that would please a motley, more or less undiscriminating audience, and he had to sell them to tough, business-minded producers.

In the ancient world, plays were put on as part of the general entertainment given at public festivals. During Plautus' lifetime, Rome had four great annual festivals whose programs included drama, and special events such as the funerals of great men or victory celebrations provided still further opportunities for the playwright. Plays were never lone features on these occasions; they shared the program with chariot races, horse races, boxing matches, and other similar entertainments. The theatrical troupes, small groups of five or six actors usually of Greek extraction, were managed by a *dominus gregis* or "leader of the troupe." He was producer and director combined: he entered into a contract with the officials in charge of a given festival to supply a certain number of performances, and, when the time came, staged them. The officials payed him a lump sum and furnished the facilities: for the actors a temporary wooden structure which was nothing more than a long, low, narrow stage with a backdrop showing two or three house fronts, and for the audience temporary wooden bleachers. It was the job of the *dominus* to find his troupe likely scripts, which he either bought himself or recommended for purchase to the officials.

These were the men Plautus had to deal with: the *domini*, the festival officials, and on occasion a Roman aristocrat who was footing the bill for a special event. For one reason above all others he had no trouble peddling his plays: he knew what his audiences wanted, and he gave it to them.

Plautus as a playwright is not original in the strictest sense. In writing a play, he began, following in the footsteps of Livius, with a Greek original, a work by one of the writers of New Comedy. But he quickly parts company with Livius, who more or less faithfully rendered his originals into Latin. Since a close translation of a play by, for example, Menander would have little appeal for the crowds at a Roman festival, Plautus generally took from the Greek only the outline of the plot, the characters, and selected segments of the dialogue, and then stepped out on his own. In a sense he worked the way playwrights of today do when they convert a "legitimate" comedy into a musical. Along with revamping the dialogue, he replaced the relatively simple metrical pattern of the original with one more complex and, perhaps as a carry-over from his youthful days as an actor in native farce, introduced frequent scenes in song and dance (the music and dance that accompanied these have disappeared without trace; we are left with only the bare lyrics). Furthermore, since he was writing not for intellectuals but for the people who patronized sporting events and circuses, and since his listeners were there to be amused, he did his level best to make them laugh from the belly. Without a second thought he would interrupt the flow of the action for a scene of pure slapstick or for a series of lowbrow jokes; he made up broadly comic names to label his characters; he explained every turn of the plot to make sure the slowest wits could follow it; he even explained the jokes to make sure everyone got them. At all costs he kept the pot of the action boiling, the stream of gags and puns and comic alliterations flowing. It is of no avail to find fault with him for not providing real endings for his plays, for introducing characters and then abruptly dropping them, for making, in a word, the most elementary blunders in playwrighting. He did not care—the play was not the thing, the laughs were.

None of the Greek plays he adapted has survived, and we consequently cannot be certain of the exact extent of his changes, but there cannot be much doubt that they were far-reaching. *The Rope*, for example, very likely has much less in common with the play by Diphilus from which it was taken than, say, *My Fair Lady* has with Shaw's *Pygmalion*.

Much scholarly effort has been expended in trying to work out the chronological order of Plautus' comedies and thereby trace his development as a playwright, but without much success. However, we can be fairly certain that the six included here belong to his mature years. Moreover, we know definitely that the *Pseudolus* was one of his latest works, and very likely the *Casina* was too; it seems pretty clear that, as Plautus grew older, he tended to increase the length of the lyric portions, and of all his plays the *Casina* has the largest proportion of these.

Plautus has been as popular after death as he was during his lifetime. If he owes a debt to his Greek predecessors, later playwrights of the highest stature have evened the account by being indebted to him, from Shakespeare in the sixteenth century (*The Comedy of Errors* is based on *The Menaechmus Twins*) through Molière in the seventeenth (e.g., *l'Avare* is based on *The Pot of Gold*) to Giraudoux in the twentieth (*Amphitryon 38* is an adaptation of the *Amphitryon*). Along with his younger contemporary, Terence, Plautus kept the spirit of Greek New Comedy alive and enabled it to make its great contributions to later literature. Dickens' Sam Weller, Wodehouse's Jeeves, the girls in the movies who come from the wrong side of the tracks and then turn out to be the long-lost daughters of eminently eligible parents—these and countless others are the lineal descendants of Pseudolus, Trachalio, Palaestra, and others of Plautus' dramatis personae. Nor is he merely a disembodied literary influence; he is still living theater. At this moment he is represented on the Broadway stage (*A Funny Thing Happened on the Way to the Forum* is a pastiche of Pseudolus, Casina, et al.), and not too many years ago the last of a long line of adaptations of *The Menaechmus Twins*, Richard Rodgers' and Lorenz Hart's *The Boys from Syracuse*, was a smash hit as a musical comedy and a motion picture. Probably no other single writer has had so profound and continuing an influence on the history of comedy.

BIBLIOGRAPHICAL NOTE

For anyone interested in studying further Plautus' plays and their influence, or any phase of Roman comedy, George Duckworth's monumental *The Nature of Roman Comedy* (Princeton University Press, 1952) provides a useful starting point. It covers, with extensive bibliography, just about every phase of the subject.

SIX PLAYS OF PLAUTUS

AMPHITRYON

DRAMATIS PERSONAE

MERCURY

SOSIA, *servant of Amphitryon (slave)*

JOVE

ALCMENA, *wife of Amphitryon*

AMPHITRYON, *Alcmena's husband, commander in chief of the Theban army*

BLEPHARO, *captain of Amphitryon's ship*

BROMIA, *maid of Alcmena (slave)*

[THESSALA, *maid of Alcmena (slave)*]

SCENE

In front of Amphitryon's house in Thebes.

PROLOGUE

(*The door of Amphitryon's house opens, and a figure emerges, to all outward appearances a typical slave of the comic stage: short, slight, bearded, and with a countenance that reveals equal parts of wiliness and self-interest. Besides the standard servant's garb, he has on his head the broad-brimmed hat the Greeks wore against the sun when traveling. He walks downstage and addresses the audience.*)

PROLOGUE   Do you want me to be bighearted and see that your business transactions, all your buying and selling, make money? Do you want my help in general? Do you want me to expedite your business speculations, foreign and domestic, at present in operation or scheduled for the future, and have them produce steady, fat profits? Do you want me to see that you and all friends and relatives get only good news, and to deliver only messages that will best promote the public welfare? (*Importantly*) I hardly need remind you that the other gods have assigned *me* the responsibility for handling all messages and profits. (*Resuming his former tone*) So, if you want me to aid and abet the pouring of perennial profits into your pockets, please, all of you, don't make any noise during this performance and be fair and honest critics after it's over.

Now let me tell you who ordered me to come here and why, and at the same time give you my name: the orders come from Jove, and my name is Mercury. The reason my father's sent me here is to ask a favor of you. Of course, he's perfectly aware that you'll take whatever he tells you as an order, since he knows you respect and fear the name of Jove, as you should. Nevertheless, he specifically instructed me to put this to you as a request, in nice, polite language. (*Confidentially, gesturing toward the dressing room*) After all, the Jove who told me to come here is just as much afraid of getting into trouble as any of you: his mother was flesh and blood and so was his father, so it's

no wonder that he worries about his own skin. The same
goes for me: I'm Jove's son and, if he should get in trouble,
I'm afraid of catching the disease.

So, that being the case, I come to you in peace, and I
bring a peaceful message. The favor I want to ask is simple and perfectly proper: I'm here as a proper person to
put a proper request to proper people. After all, it's not
proper to ask for improper things from proper people, and
it's stupid to ask for proper things from improper people—
they're a criminal bunch who don't know what right is
and don't hold by it.

Now, please, all of you, pay attention to what I'm going
to say. Our wish should be your command—we deserve
this from you and the nation, Father and I. In tragedies
I've seen all the others—Father Neptune, Lady Virtue,
Lady Victory, Lord Mars, Lady War—reel off all the favors
they've done for you, but do I really have to give you a
list of the good that my father, King of Heaven, has de-
signed and constructed for all of you? And Father's never
been one to nag good people about the good he's done
them. He takes it for granted you're all grateful for it.

Now then, first I'll tell you the favor I've come here to
ask, and then I'll explain the plot of this tragedy. (*As if
taken aback*) What are these frowns for? (*As if a light has
suddenly dawned*) Because I said the play was going to
be a tragedy? (*Airily*) I'm a god—I'll have everything
changed. If you want, I'll turn it from a tragedy to a comedy
without altering a line. Well, do you want me to or not?
(*Suddenly grinning foolishly*) How stupid of me! I'm a
god! I know what you want, I understand your feelings in
the matter perfectly. I'll make it into a comedy with some
tragedy mixed in. After all, with kings and gods appearing
in it, I don't think it would be right to make it pure comedy. But, let's face it, a servant *does* play an important
part. So, as I said just before, I'll make it a tragicomedy.

But to get back to the favor Jove instructed me to ask of
you. He wants detectives to go through every seat in every
row of the house. If they spot a claque working for any

actor, they're to strip each offender of his coat, right here in the house, and hold it as bail. (*Mimicking the manner of a court clerk*) If anyone tries to fix the awarding of prizes for the actors or other artists, either in writing or in person or through third parties, or if the government officials in charge do the fixing themselves, Jove hereby rules that the guilty parties be sentenced under the statute applicable had said parties been convicted of malfeasance in seeking public office. (*Indignantly*) Victors survive struggles through strength not sneakiness and subterfuge; why shouldn't an actor be liable to the same legal penalties as holders of our highest office? Men ought to compete on the basis of character not claques. Good, honest performances will create their own claques—*if* the men who do the judging are honest.

Here's another order I've received: detectives are to be assigned to actors, too. Any actor who arranges for a claque to applaud for himself, or who arranges to cut down on a competitor's applause, is to get the whip till it makes tatters of his hide along with his costume. Now, don't be surprised that Jove is taking such good care of actors today. Nothing to be surprised about: Jove himself is going to act in this play. (*Pauses and looks over the whole audience*) What are you so surprised about? As if we're introducing anything new in having Jove on the stage! Why, just last year, right in this theater, the actors prayed to Jove, and he came down on stage to rescue them.[1] And then, of course, he's always appearing in tragedy. So, as I say, he'll act in the play today, and I will too. And now your attention please, while I explain the plot of this comedy.

(*Gesturing toward the backdrop*) The city here is Thebes. (*Pointing to Amphitryon's house*) In that house there, lives Amphitryon; he was actually born at Argos, the son of a citizen of Argos. He's married to Alcmena, King Electryon's daughter. At the moment Amphitryon is

---

[1] Apparently last year's play ended with a *deus ex machina*.

on active duty as commander in chief of the army, since
Thebes is at war with the Teleboans.

When Amphitryon went off to the front his wife was
pregnant. (*Grinning knowingly*) Now, I think you're all
aware by this time of the way my father carries on, the
liberties he allows himself in this sort of thing, what a
lover he can become once his affections have found an
object. He began carrying on an affair with Alcmena behind her husband's back. He borrowed her husband's looks
for himself, made love to her, and made her pregnant on
his own. I want you to be sure to get Alcmena's situation
straight: she's pregnant by the both of them, by her husband and by almighty Jove. (*Gesturing toward the house*)
Father's inside there right now in bed with her. That's why
tonight's running longer than usual: it'll go on till he's had
his pleasure from where he wants it. He's doing all this, of
course, disguised to look like Amphitryon. Incidentally,
don't be surprised at this get-up I'm wearing, at the way
I've come here dressed like a servant. I'm introducing you
to an age-old story, but in a new garb—that's why I've
come here (*pointing to his costume*) in this new get-up.

All right. Father's inside there at this very moment; yes,
Jove himself right there. He's changed himself into the
image of Amphitryon, and all the servants who see him
think that that's who he is. (*Smiling*) He can be a real
quick-change artist when the spirit moves him. I've changed
myself to look like Sosia, Amphitryon's servant, who's off
at the front with his master. This way I can be Father's
servant during his affair, and the household won't want to
know who I am when they see me running around the
place all day. They'll think I'm a servant, one of themselves, and won't question who I am or what I'm here for.

(*Confidentially*) Father's inside now, (*rapturously*) loll-
ing in the lap of the lovely lady he loves. He's busy telling
Alcmena all about what happened to Amphitryon at the
front. There she is, in the arms of her seducer, and she
thinks she's with her husband! Right now he's telling her
how Amphitryon routed the enemy's troops and was given

a pile of presents as reward. (*As if telling a secret*) We've absconded with all the gifts he got out there. (*Airily*) Father can do whatever he wants to, with no trouble at all.

Now, today Amphitryon's coming home from the front along with the servant whose looks I'm using. (*Taking out a cluster of feathers and sticking them in his hat*) To make it easier for you to tell us apart, I'll always have these little feathers in my hat, while Father, under his hat, will have a little gold tassel, which Amphitryon won't have. None of the household here will be able to see these marks of identification, but you will.

(*His attention caught, looks toward the wings, stage right.*) There's Amphitryon's servant Sosia now, carrying a lantern. He's just come from the waterfront. As soon as he gets to the house, I'll drive him away. You pay attention: it'll be well worth your while to see Jove and Mercury do an act!

(*He steps back and hides in the shadows near the door of the house.*)

ACT I

(*Enter Sosia carrying a lantern. He is the spitting image of the disguised Mercury except for the telltale feathers in the hat.*)

SONG

SOSIA

For guts and nerve no man alive comes close to me right now.

I'm walking alone this time of night though I know damned well just how

Young kids carry on. Or the cops might see me and clap me into jail.

And then next morning I'd be sprung—to report to the whipping detail!

With no chance to plead my case in court, and the master not around,

They'll all be absolutely convinced the case against me is sound;

Eight bruisers then will make me an anvil and pound me full of dents.

Arriving home from overseas, I'll be welcomed at public expense!

(*Shaking his head mournfully*)

The sweat my master was in! I had to go
From the dock this time of night though I said no.

(*Bitterly*)

He couldn't wait till day to send me from there!
No easy job, this serving a millionaire;
A rich man's servant leads a lousy life.
All his nights and days it's just a constant strife
To keep up with the errands and jobs he has to do,
With never a moment's peace or rest for you.
What wealthy master's done work himself? Not one!

So whatever a man can think up, he thinks can be
   done.
"It's all right," he thinks, and never thinks how long
The job may be. But whether the order's all *wrong*
And *not* all right, will never enter his mind.
So a slave runs into wrongs of every kind.
You have to sweat—and shrug and be resigned.

MERCURY (*to the audience*)

Hey, I'm the one who should complain that way!
Till Pappa pressed me into service today
I'd no idea what slavery meant.
Now, *he's* been used to being a slave
Since birth—and listen to him rave!

SOSIA (*working himself up*)

I'm a stupid slob of a slave, I am! I got the idea too soon
To pray to the gods on my safe return, and thank them for
   the boon.
If the gods should ever return the thanks in the way that I
   deserve,
They'd commission a guy to welcome my face as a private
   punching preserve.

(*Shaking his head bitterly*)

That safe return they blessed me with, like an ingrate I
   upset!

MERCURY (*to the audience*)

Not many are like this fellow here—he knows just what he
   should get.

SOSIA

No Theban thought, and neither did I, that things would
   turn out the way
They did turn out: that, safe and sound, we'd make it
   home one day.
Our conquering army's conquered the foe, and now we're
   home again;
A bitter battle's been fought and won, and all the enemy
   slain.

Our men by their morale and might have stormed and won
  the town
Of the nation that so often cruelly cut our people down.
We owe it most to Amphitryon, who led us like a wonder:
He's brought to all his countrymen new lands, renown,
  and plunder,
And Creon he's put upon the throne as king of Thebes for
  life.
Now me he's sent ahead from the dock to go home and
  tell his wife
How, by leading, guiding, ordering, her husband served
  the state.

(*Thoughtfully*)

Now, how to tell her once I'm there—just let me concentrate.
I can, of course, just think up lies, the way I usually do,
Since, when the fight was at its height, my running speed
  was, too.

(*Shrugging*)

I'll simply pretend that I was there and tell her things I've
  heard.
But to figure a way to spin this yarn and think up every
  word
Is what I want to work out first.

(*After a moment's deep thought, brightly*)

                              I'll say that this occurred.

(*In a burlesque of the tragic stage, Sosia clears his throat
resoundingly, strikes a histrionic pose, and launches into a
dramatic recitative à la grand opera.*)

When we first arrived at the enemy's land, the minute we
  came ashore,
Amphitryon at once picked out the leaders on his staff,
And these he sent to the Teleboans to make his position
  clear:
If they were willing to come to terms and, avoiding violence,

Would apprehend and deliver up the bandits with their
    booty,
Would give us back what they'd carried off, he'd start for
    home at once,
He'd lead his forces out of the land and leave the foe in
    peace.
But if they intended otherwise, and refused what he was
    asking,
Then with all the might and men he had, he'd attack and
    storm their town.
The delegates Amphitryon sent repeated this word for
    word.
The Teleboan people, though, brave men with confidence
In both their fighting spirit and strength, got very arrogant
And proceeded to tell our delegates off in no uncertain
    terms:
They answered that, when it came to war, they could well
    defend themselves,
So Thebes had better leave their land, get the army out,
    and fast.
The minute this word was brought to him, Amphitryon
    drew up
His whole great force in front of the camp; the enemy like-
    wise
Mobilized his men in front of the town, magnificently
    armed.

(*Working himself up*)

Once the armies were out in full force on each side,
All the men took their stations, the ranks were drawn up.
We deployed our platoons as we usually do,
And the enemy lined up his forces against us.
Then both the commanders, advancing into
No man's land, held a parley away from the ranks.
Whichever side lost in the fight, they agreed,
Would surrender their city, their temples, their fields,
Their houses, their hearths, their own bodies and souls.

Once agreed, they went back, and the trumpets blared
    forth.
The earth echoed the sound. From each side came a yell.
Each commander, both their man and ours, said his
    prayers
To great Jove, and exhorted his soldiers to fight.

(*With great excitement*)

In the struggle each man gave his all.
Swords clanged; lances broke; and the shouts
Of the men rose as high as the sky.
And an actual cloud floated up
From the breath given off as they gasped.
Scores of soldiers succumbed to their wounds.
Then at last, as we hoped for, our men
See that victory's coming their way.
More and more of the enemy fall.
In we charge to drive home the attack.
Like furies we fight—and they crack!

(*Pauses, then resumes with great feeling*)

Yet not one of the foe turned to flee from the field.
They kept standing their ground, never breaking the
    lines.
Sooner die than abandon their posts, was their thought.
Each fell where he stood; the very corpses kept ranks.

(*Excitedly again*)

When Amphitryon notices this,
He immediately orders a charge
Of his cavalry on the right flank.
Like a flash they obey the command.
With a terrible yell they attack,
At a gallop they charge on the right,
And they shatter and trample the foe.
The enemy yields all along—
A triumph of right over wrong!

(*Sosia stands immobile, transfixed by his own eloquence.*)

MERCURY

Not a word he's said so far is false, every bit of it is true.

For I was there when the fight was fought, and Father was
   there too.

SOSIA

The Teleboans took to their heels, and we got added
   courage.

We fired away at the fleeing foe, and filled their bodies
   with darts.

And Pterelas, their king, was killed by Amphitryon's own
   hand.

The fight we fought out there that day went on from dawn
   to night.

(I remember because, the whole day long, I hadn't had a
   bite.)

The dark at last separated us, and broke the fighting off.

Next day their leaders, bathed in tears, came from town to
   us in camp.

They beg, with olive branch outstretched, our pardon for
   their sins.

They surrender unconditionally: they, each and every one,

Give up to Thebes to treat as it will their city, children,
   homes.

Amphitryon, for his bravery, was awarded the golden cup

That Pterelas their king once used.

(*Nodding with great satisfaction*)

                              I'll tell all this to his spouse.

(*Abruptly turns and walks toward the door*)

Now to carry out the master's orders. Forward march and
   into the house!

(*The following speeches are all asides: each speaker,
though at times he seems to address the other, actually talks
to the audience.*)

MERCURY   Aha! He's heading this way. I'll get going and head him off. I'm not letting him get anywhere near this house today. We look exactly alike, so I'll play a game with him, that's what I'll do. As a matter of fact, since I took his face and figure, it's only right to give myself his character. And that means I have to be canny, tricky, and nasty, and use his own medicine, some nasty trick, to get him away from the door. (*Turning away to look at Sosia*) What's going on? He's looking up at the sky! I'll keep an eye on him and see what he's after.

SOSIA   (*staring at the sky, puzzled*)   I swear to god, if there's one thing in this world I'm convinced of beyond any doubt, it's that tonight the Patron God of Night got tight and is sleeping it off. The Big Dipper hasn't budged in the sky, and the moon's in exactly the same place it was when it rose. Orion, Vesper, the Pleiades—none of them has set. All the stars are standing in the same spot; tonight's not moving aside for tomorrow anywhere.

MERCURY   (*to the heavens*)   Keep it up, Night. Do what Daddy wants. Do what you might with all your might for the almighty. Best investment you could make.

SOSIA   (*as before*)   I don't think I've ever seen a longer night than this. Well, maybe just once, when I got flogged and strung up from dusk till dawn. But, I swear, even that night wasn't as long as this one. If you ask me, the sun's sleeping off a drunk. Did a little overindulging at dinner last night, probably.

MERCURY   Is that so? You stinker, you think gods are like you? Damn you, I'll fix you for such talk—*and* for your bad habits! Just step over here and you'll get what you're not going to like.

SOSIA   (*grinning*)   Where are those woman chasers who can't stand going to bed alone? What a chance to give a workout to a high-priced whore who charges by the night!

MERCURY   Judging by what this fellow says, Father's doing the best and smartest thing. He's lying in bed with Alcmena making love, doing what he likes doing most.

SOSIA Well, I'll go in and give Alcmena the report the master ordered me to. (*Starts walking toward the door, catches sight of the figure of Mercury, and comes to an abrupt halt.*) Hey—who's that I see standing in front of the house? At this time of night? I don't like this!

MERCURY (*with a contemptuous gesture in Sosia's direction*) Nobody scares as easily as this one here.

SOSIA (*nervously*) I get it: here I am all dressed up—and he wants to dress me down!

MERCURY (*grinning*) He's scared stiff. I'll have some fun with him.

SOSIA (*as before*) I'm a goner! My jaw has that pre-sock sensation. He's going to greet the homecomer with a kiss from a fist, I know it. He probably feels sorry for me: because my master made me stay awake last night, his knuckles will see to it I get some sleep today. I'm a goner, an absolute goner! I ask you now, look at the size of that bruiser!

MERCURY (*confidentially*) I'll talk out loud in front of him. He'll hear what I say, and get even more scared. (*Loudly*) Come on, fists, it's been ages since you've given me something to slug away in the stomach. That last time—was it only yesterday? Seems like ages ago! You laid four men out. Knocked them stiff.

SOSIA I'm scared he's going to make a change in my family: here I am, an only child, and he's going to make me a quintuplet! He says he knocked out four men; I'm afraid I'm going to raise the figure.

MERCURY (*rolling up his sleeves and taking a boxer's stance, with satisfaction*) There, that's more like it.

SOSIA He's rolling up his sleeves—getting ready for the kill!

MERCURY (*between his teeth*) He's not going to get away from here without a good licking.

SOSIA Who isn't?

MERCURY (*promptly*) Whoever comes this way—he'll eat knuckles!

SOSIA (*hurriedly*) Not me. I don't like eating this late. I already had dinner. Why don't you be smart and serve that dish to people who are hungry?

MERCURY (*caressing one of his fists, with satisfaction*) Real weight in this here fist.

SOSIA Figuring the poundage in his punch! Poor me!

MERCURY (*thoughtfully*) What if I put him to sleep with a soft, slow sock on the jaw?

SOSIA You'll save my life—I haven't been to bed for three nights running.

MERCURY (*throwing a practice haymaker, disgustedly*) Awful! We're not doing well at all. These knuckles just won't learn how to sock a jaw. One tap with this fist, and I should be able to change a man's looks.

SOSIA He's like the fellows who fix up statues! He's going to make me a new face!

MERCURY (*to his fist*) If you really hit a man, you should knock every bone out of his head.

SOSIA Say, maybe he's thinking of filleting my face like a fish! Keep me from a fellow who fillets folks! If he catches sight of me, I'm done for!

MERCURY (*elaborately sniffing the air*) I smell someone—and he'll be sorry!

SOSIA Oh, my god, did he get a whiff of me?

MERCURY (*with more intensive sniffing*) He was far away before, but he can't be very far now.

SOSIA (*flabbergasted*) This guy's a magician!

MERCURY (*throwing a series of fast jabs*) These fists are bucking like a bronco.

SOSIA If you're going to give them a workout on me, please break them in on the wall first!

MERCURY (*suddenly stops his shadow boxing and stands still, cocking an ear; burlesquing the style of grand opera*) Somebody's words have winged their way to mine ears!

SOSIA   What rotten luck! Why didn't I clip its wings? *I* have to have a voice like a bird!

MERCURY *(snarling)*   He's going to get it from me. I'll fix his wagon.

SOSIA *(promptly)*   I haven't got a wagon.

MERCURY *(as before)*   I'll give him a load of fist.

SOSIA *(resentfully)*   I'm all worn out from the trip back on the boat, I'm still seasick, I can barely walk *without* carrying anything, so don't get the idea I can take any loads.

MERCURY   No question about it—I hear somebody talking.

SOSIA   Saved! He doesn't see me. He says Somebody's talking. One thing I know: my name's Sosia, not Somebody.

MERCURY *(turning toward Sosia, burlesquing the style of grand opera)*   Here from the right, methinks a voice strikes mine ears.

SOSIA *(despondently)*   My voice struck him, eh? I'm afraid *I'll* get struck to even the score. *(Takes a tentative step away.)*

MERCURY *(ironically)*   He's coming my way. Perfect.

SOSIA *(stopping dead in his tracks)*   I'm so scared, I'm numb all over! I swear, I couldn't tell you where in the world I am right now, if you asked me. I'm so scared I can't even move! This is it: this is the end of the master's orders—and Sosia along with them. *(Eyes Mercury uncertainly, notices that he is not moving, and screws up his courage.)* All right. My mind's made up: I'll talk back to him. That way I'll look like someone with guts, and he'll keep his hands off me.

(Sosia, swinging his lantern jauntily, swaggers up to the door. The two now address each other instead of the audience.)

MERCURY *(in his grand opera style)*   Whither away, O stranger with Vulcan's fire in that piece of horn?

SOSIA *(belligerently)*   What do you want to know for, O stranger who fillets faces with his fists?

MERCURY (*menacingly*)   Are you a slave or not?

SOSIA (*shrugging*)   Whichever I like.

MERCURY (*arms akimbo, jaw out*)   Is that so?

SOSIA (*arms akimbo, jaw out*)   Yeah, that's so.

MERCURY (*contemptuously*)   You deserve a good licking.

SOSIA   That's a lie!

MERCURY (*rolling up his sleeves and making other ominous preparations*)   You're going to tell me it's the truth. I'll see to that right now.

SOSIA (*his courage rapidly becoming unscrewed*)   Now, why do you have to do that?

MERCURY (*ominously*)   I want to know where you're going, who you belong to, and what you came for. How about it?

SOSIA (*blandly*)   I came here, and I'm my master's servant. Any the wiser now?

MERCURY (*as before*)   Damn you, I'll stop that mouth of yours!

SOSIA (*girlishly fluttering his eyes, and demurely putting his hands over his lips*)   Oh sir, you can't! It's a very proper mouth, and I take good care of it.

MERCURY (*grimly*)   More nonsense out of you? What are you doing around this house?

SOSIA   What are *you* doing here?

MERCURY   Orders from King Creon. One man stands guard all night every night.

SOSIA (*grandly*)   Very nice of him. Takes good care of the house because he knows we're away. (*Taking a step forward and airily waving Mercury aside*) You can leave now. Tell him the family's back.

MERCURY (*blocking the way*)   I don't know how you can belong to this family. And, "family man," unless you take off this minute, you're not going to get treated like one of the family!

SOSIA (*stubbornly*)   I tell you I live here. I'm a servant here.

MERCURY   Do you know what's going to happen to you? If you don't get out of here, I'm going to make you into a real aristocrat.

SOSIA   How's that?

MERCURY   Once I get my hands on a club, you won't walk away from here, you'll be carried.

SOSIA (*desperately*)   But I tell you I'm one of the family! A family servant.

MERCURY   You're not leaving this minute? Then kindly figure out how soon you want your licking.

SOSIA   You think you're going to keep me out of this house after I came all the way here from overseas?

MERCURY (*incredulously*)   This is your house?

SOSIA   Of course.

MERCURY   Then who's your master?

SOSIA   Amphitryon. He's off now commanding the Theban army. Alcmena's his wife.

MERCURY   Tell me, what's your name?

SOSIA (*drawing himself up; in the grand opera style*)   Men call me Sosia. Sprung from the loins of Davus am I.[2]

MERCURY (*eying him distastefully*)   You've got a nerve! You'll pay for this. Coming here this way with a pack of lies, and dirty schemes on foot!

SOSIA (*reproachfully*)   I came here with my shoes on foot, not dirty schemes.

MERCURY (*promptly*)   Still lying—you came here with your feet on shoes. (*Roars at his joke.*)

SOSIA (*deciding it would be politic to acknowledge this sally, roaring too*)   You're absolutely right.

MERCURY (*suddenly switching off the laughter*)   Then you're absolutely going to get a beating for telling lies.

SOSIA   But I absolutely don't want one.

[2] "Men call me Joe. Sprung from the loins of Mike, etc." will give some idea of the joke.

MERCURY   But you're absolutely going to get one, whether you want it or not. When I say "absolutely," my mind's made up; there's no room for discussion. (*Starts clobbering Sosia.*)

SOSIA   Don't! Please! I beg you!

MERCURY   (*continuing the clobbering*)   Where do you get the nerve to say you're Sosia when I'm Sosia?

SOSIA   He's murdering me!

MERCURY   Murder isn't anything compared with what's coming. Who's your master?

SOSIA   (*hurriedly*)   You are. Those fists of yours have given you right of possession. (*At the top of his lungs*) Men of Thebes! Help!

MERCURY   (*silencing him with a punch*)   So you'll yell, will you, you stinker! Now speak up! What did you come here for?

SOSIA   (*bitterly*)   So you could have somebody to beat to a pulp.

MERCURY   Who's your master?

SOSIA   (*doggedly*)   Amphitryon. I'm his servant Sosia.

MERCURY   That means you're going to get beaten up even more for talking nonsense. *I'm* Sosia, not you.

SOSIA   (*muttering to himself*)   God, do I wish it! You be me, and then I'll beat *you* up.

MERCURY   (*snarling*)   What are you muttering about?

SOSIA   (*hurriedly*)   I'll keep quiet.

MERCURY   Who's your master?

SOSIA   Whoever you say.

MERCURY   Now tell me this: what's your name?

SOSIA   Whatever name you say.

MERCURY   (*glowering*)   You told me you were Amphitryon's Sosia.

SOSIA   I made a mistake. I meant to say I was Amphitryon's *associate*.

MERCURY (*nodding satisfiedly*) I knew darn well the family had only one Sosia—me. You dropped the ball there.

SOSIA (*aside*) I wish to god you'd do that with those fists!

MERCURY (*emphatically*) I'm the Sosia you were trying to tell me a minute ago you were.

SOSIA (*in desperation*) Will you do me a favor? Will you *please* let me talk to you in peace, without getting beaten up?

MERCURY No peace—just a temporary truce, if there's something you want to say.

SOSIA (*quickly*) I don't talk without a treaty of peace—you're stronger than I am, you can lick me.

MERCURY (*with an air of magnanimity*) Say what you want. I won't hurt you.

SOSIA You give me your word?

MERCURY Word of honor.

SOSIA (*suspiciously*) What if you go back on it?

MERCURY (*in his grand opera style*) Then may the wrath of Mercury fall upon Sosia!

SOSIA (*suddenly regaining his aplomb*) Well, now that I can say what I want to, you listen here: *I'm* Amphitryon's servant Sosia.

MERCURY (*advancing on him menacingly*) What, again?

SOSIA (*doggedly*) We made peace, we signed a treaty, so I'm telling you the truth.

MERCURY I'm going to beat you up!

SOSIA (*as before*) You can do whatever you like with me, because you're stronger than I am, you can lick me. (*At the top of his lungs*) But, no matter what you do to me, this is one thing, damn it all, I'm not going to keep quiet about!

MERCURY (*grimly*) You're not going to stop me from being Sosia, not as long as you live.

SOSIA And, damn it all, you're not going to make me be

somebody different from myself. I'm the only servant Sosia we've got in the family. I'm the fellow who went off with Amphitryon to the front.

MERCURY (*to the world at large*) This fellow's out of his mind!

SOSIA That's what's wrong with you, not me! (*To himself*) What the devil! Ain't I Amphitryon's servant Sosia? Didn't our ship arrive just tonight from the port of the Teleboans with me aboard? Didn't my own master send me here? Ain't I standing in front of my own house right this minute? Don't I have a lantern in my hand? Ain't I talking? Ain't I awake? Didn't this fellow here just now beat me up? (*Groaning*) He sure did! My jaw still aches. (*Resolutely*) What am I waiting for? Why don't I go right into my house?

MERCURY What do you mean, *your* house?

SOSIA (*doggedly*) That's what I said.

MERCURY Oh no. Every word you just said is a lie. *I'm* Amphitryon's Sosia. Tonight our ship cleared the land of the Teleboans with *me* on board. It was after we stormed and took King Pterelas' town and beat the Teleboan army by some hard fighting, and Amphitryon killed King Pterelas with his own hands during the battle.

SOSIA (*to the audience, flabbergasted*) Even I don't believe I'm me when I hear him say these things! No doubt about it—this fellow's got everything that happened there down pat! (*To Mercury*) Tell me this: what was Amphitryon presented with out of the booty from the Teleboans?

MERCURY (*promptly*) The gold cup King Pterelas used to drink out of.

SOSIA (*to the audience, glumly*) That's the right answer. (*To Mercury*) Where's the cup now?

MERCURY (*as before*) In a chest. Locked and sealed with Amphitryon's seal.

SOSIA What is his seal?

MERCURY   The rising sun in a four-horse chariot. (*Snarling*) You trying to catch me, damn you?

SOSIA (*to the audience, in despair*)   He's convinced me. I'll have to find another name! I don't know where he could have seen all this. (*Stands glumly for a moment, then is electrified by an idea.*) Wait! Now I'll get him. After all, what I did all by myself in the tent, with no one else around, that's something he'll never be able to tell me, *never*. (*To Mercury, brimming with confidence*) Well, if you're Sosia, what were you busy doing in the tent when the fighting was going on fast and furious? You tell me that, and I give up.

MERCURY (*slowly and with great precision*)   There was a keg of wine. I filled a jug from it.

SOSIA (*to the audience, nervously*)   He's on the right track.

MERCURY   Then I put away the whole jugful, neat, just the way it came from mother grape.

SOSIA (*to the audience, dumb struck*)   That's just what happened! I put away a jugful of wine, neat. (*Savagely*) I'll bet he was hiding there inside that jug.

MERCURY   Well? Have I convinced you you're not Sosia?

SOSIA (*belligerently*)   You're telling me I'm not, eh?

MERCURY (*shrugging*)   What else can I tell you, when *I* am?

SOSIA (*with hand over heart*)   I swear by Jove that *I* am, and I swear that's no lie.

MERCURY (*with hand over heart*)   And I swear by Mercury that Jove doesn't believe you. Take my word, he'll sooner believe me without an oath than you with.

SOSIA (*desperately*)   Well then, who am I, if I'm not Sosia? Answer me that!

MERCURY   When I'm done being Sosia, you go right ahead and be Sosia. But right now *I'm* Sosia, so either you beat it or get a beating, Anonymous!

(*Sosia goes up to him, looks him over, and then steps back scratching his head.*)

SOSIA (*to the audience, baffled*) So help me, when I look at him I recognize all my features, there's no doubt about it! I've seen myself in the mirror lots of times, and he's exactly like me. He's got the same hat and clothes. (*Peering harder*) He's my spitting image! Legs, feet, height, haircut, eyes, nose, lips, jaws, chin, beard, neck, everything. What else is there to say? If he's got whip-scars all over his back, no two items in this world could be more alike. (*Clutching his head*) Yet, when I think it over, I'm the same person I've always been, no question about it! I know my master's name, I know our house, I can use my head, and I've got all my senses. (*Plucking up courage*) I won't pay any attention to what he says; I'll knock on the door. (*Starts walking up to the door.*)

MERCURY (*blocking the way*) Where do you think you're going?

SOSIA Home.

MERCURY (*grimly*) You could climb aboard Jove's own magic chariot this minute to try to get away, but it wouldn't do you a bit of good: you're in for trouble and you're going to get it!

SOSIA (*weakly*) Can't I give my mistress the report my master ordered me to?

MERCURY You can give *your* mistress whatever you want. But I'm not letting you get anywhere near mine. (*Thundering*) Now, don't get me sore or you'll be carried out of here with those legs of yours stove in!

SOSIA (*with alacrity*) Oh no! I'm going. (*Raising his eyes to heaven*) God in heaven, please! Where did I lose myself? Where did I get changed over? Where did I drop my looks? Did I forget myself and leave myself at the pier? Because this fellow here's got hold of the exact same looks I used to have. He's my statue—something nobody'll ever give me when I'm dead, I've already got while alive! (*Eyes Mercury standing resolutely in front of the door and shrugs helplessly.*) I'll go back to the pier and tell the master everything that's happened. (*Mournfully*) Maybe he won't recognize me either. (*Brightening*) I hope to god he doesn't! I'll have these slave clothes off me and a free man's on, in no time! (*Dashes off, stage right.*)

MERCURY (*to the audience, with great satisfaction*) This job went off very nicely. *Very* nicely. I got that blamed nuisance away from the door, and (*gesturing toward the house*) Father can stay on in her arms in peace. (*Grinning*) When that fellow gets back there to his master, he'll tell Amphitryon that Sosia the servant drove him away from the door. Amphitryon'll think he's lying and that he disobeyed orders and never even came here. (*Gleefully*) I'll get both of them all mixed up and drive them and Amphitryon's whole household crazy, until Father's had enough of his inamorata. Then, when it's all over, they'll all find out what happened, and Jove at the end will restore Alcmena and her husband to their former married bliss. You see, Amphitryon is going to raise an awful ruckus with his wife and accuse her of adultery, but Father will step in and put down the insurrection.

(*Starts to go toward the door, then suddenly stops, struck by a new idea.*) There's something I didn't mention before about Alcmena. She's going to give birth today to twins, two boys. One will be a full-term baby, the other just a six-month baby. One is Amphitryon's, the other Jove's; the littler baby has the greater father, and vice versa. You all sure you understand the situation?

(*Looks the faces over anxiously and, reassured, continues.*) For the sake of Alcmena's reputation, Father's fixed it so there'll be only one confinement: she'll be done with two birth pangs in one labor. That way no one'll suspect anything illicit, and this clandestine cohabiting will stay a secret. However, as I mentioned before, Amphitryon will be told the whole story. What's the difference? Alcmena's reputation won't be hurt the least little bit. After all, it wouldn't do for a god to let *his* sin and guilt fall on the head of a mortal. (*His attention caught, looks toward the door.*) I'll shut up now—there's a sound at the door. Here comes the fake Amphitryon with Alcmena, the wife he has on loan.

(*The door opens and Jove and Alcmena step out.*
Alcmena, a ravishingly beautiful woman, perhaps in her early thirties, has more than mere good looks: her face shines with a candor and purity that add a special radiance to her loveliness.
Her consort is a strongly built, handsome man in his forties. By the way he carries himself you can sense immediately that he is used to giving, not taking orders. He carries a stick, and is dressed in traveling clothes topped off by a broad-brimmed hat that has a tiny gold tassel dangling down behind.)

JOVE (*holding both her hands, tenderly*) Good-by, Alcmena dear. Take good care of our household, as you're doing. And please take things easy! You can see for yourself that your time is very near now. I've got to run along. (*Gravely*) Whether it's a girl or a boy—I want the child to be brought up.

ALCMENA (*plaintively*) What's come up, dear, to make you leave home so suddenly?

JOVE (*tenderly*) Believe me, it's not because I'm tired either of you or of being home. But, when the commander in chief isn't with his troops, things that don't need doing get done with lots more dispatch than things that do.

MERCURY (*to the audience, gesturing toward Jove*) A smooth operator, this one here. (*Grinning*) And why not? He's *my* father.[3] Watch how he's going to butter the girl up.

ALCMENA (*pouting*) Well! I can certainly see how much *you* care for your wife.

JOVE (*kissing her*) Isn't it enough for you that I love you more than any other woman in the world?

MERCURY (*aside, gesturing toward the sky where presumably*

[3] Mercury was patron god of thieves.

Juno is) If that one up there finds out that you're busy with things like this, believe me, you'll wish you were Amphitryon instead of Jove!

ALCMENA (*as before*) I'd rather find out for myself than be told. Before your place in bed has had time to get warm, you're on your way! You arrived just yesterday in the middle of the night, and now you're leaving. Do you think I like this?

MERCURY (*to the audience*) I'll go up and have a word with her. Play Helpful Henry for Pappa. (*Walking up to Alcmena and addressing her*) So help me, I don't think there's a man on earth who's as mad about his wife as he's mad about you. (*Glances covertly to observe the effect of this on Jove.*)

JOVE (*to Mercury, thundering*) God damn you! Think I don't know what you're up to! Out of my sight! What do you think you're doing, messing into my affairs? What do you think you're doing, opening that big mouth of yours? (*Brandishing his stick*) Why, I'll take this stick and I'll—

ALCMENA (*interrupting in alarm*) Don't, please!

JOVE (*snarling*) Just let him open that big mouth of his!

MERCURY (*to the audience, grinning*) My debut as Helpful Henry was almost a fiasco.

JOVE (*conciliatorily*) But to get back to what you were saying, dear. You really shouldn't be angry with me. I sneaked away from headquarters. I stole this chance to see you, so I could be the first to tell you, and you the first to hear, how I served my country. And now you've heard all about it. Would I do such a thing if I didn't love you very, very much?

MERCURY (*to the audience, chuckling*) Didn't I tell you he'd do this? A little buttering up, and he has the poor girl eating out of his hand.

JOVE And now I've got to sneak back, so the men won't find out and say I think more of my wife than my country.

ALCMENA (*starting to cry*) You have your poor wife in tears by going away like this.

JOVE (*tenderly*) Sh! Don't spoil those pretty eyes. I'll be back very soon.

ALCMENA (*sobbing*) That "very soon" is such a long, long time!

JOVE (*as before*) Believe me, I'm not very happy about going away and leaving you.

ALCMENA (*bitterly*) Oh sure—that's why you're leaving the same night you came. (*She reaches out to hold him by the arm.*)

JOVE (*gently taking her hand away*) You mustn't hold me back. It's getting late. I want to be out of the city before dawn. (*He holds up a box.*) Here's the cup which was awarded to me for gallantry in action. King Pterelas used to own it; I killed him with my own hands. (*Handing it to her*) It's a present for you, Alcmena.

ALCMENA (*smiling radiantly through her tears*) You're always doing things like that! It's a wonderful gift, as wonderful as the giver.

MERCURY (*bowing gallantly*) Say rather a wonderful gift, as wonderful as the *getter*.

JOVE (*turning on him*) Still at it? Damn you, can't I get rid of you!

ALCMENA (*stroking his cheek*) Please Amphitryon, don't be angry at Sosia. For my sake.

JOVE (*grumbling*) Well, anything to please you.

MERCURY (*to the audience, gesturing toward Jove*) What love does to him! So touchy!

JOVE (*kissing her good-by*) Anything you want before I go?

ALCMENA Yes. Love me even though I'm far away—since I'm all yours, even though you're far away.

MERCURY (*impatiently*) Let's go, Amphitryon! It's already getting light.

JOVE   You go ahead, Sosia. I'll be along in a minute. (*Mercury leaves, stage left. Jove kisses Alcmena again.*) Nothing I can do for you?

ALCMENA   Yes—come back soon. (*She waves a last good-by, then swiftly turns and runs into the house.*)

JOVE (*calling after her*)   All right. (*Winking at the audience*) I'll be back sooner than you think! So cheer up.

(*He turns and, raising his head, addresses the sky.*)

Night, you waited very patiently. You're dismissed; make way for Day. Let Day now spread its clear bright light over the earth. And, Night, to even things up I'll make the day shorter by exactly as much time as you were longer than the night before. Go now—let the dark give way to light!

(*To the audience*)

And now I'll go and follow Mercury.

(*He exits, stage left, and the stage is now empty.*)

ACT II

(*It is now some hours later, and day has dawned. Enter,
stage right, Amphitryon, then Sosia, then some porters carrying baggage. Amphitryon is identical in appearance with the
Jove of the last act, save for the telltale tassel.*)

SONG

AMPHITRYON (*impatiently*)
>Come on! Shake a leg and follow me!

SOSIA (*hurrying to keep up*)
>I am, I'm right behind you, see?

AMPHITRYON (*stopping and eying him distastefully*)
>You're a worthless good-for-nothing, I'd say.

SOSIA (*innocently*)
>But why? What makes you feel that way?

AMPHITRYON (*angrily*)
>Because you stand there telling me
>What never was and never will be.

SOSIA (*shaking his head despondently*)
>You see? You're always doing it.
>You won't trust any of us one bit.

AMPHITRYON (*working himself up*)
>Now what do you mean by that! I swear,
>You good-for-nothing, I'm going to tear
>That good-for-nothing tongue of yours out!

SOSIA (*doggedly*)
>I belong to you, so I've no doubt
>You'll do to me what it suits you to.
>But nothing you can possibly do
>Will make me say this isn't true.

AMPHITRYON (*exploding*)
>You're standing here and yet, you louse,
>You've the nerve to tell me you're now in the
>house!

SOSIA (*as before*)
>> That's true.

AMPHITRYON
>>> Well, god will punish you—
>> And, damn it all, *I* will too.

SOSIA (*sulkily*)
>> You're master here. All I do is serve.

AMPHITRYON (*in a towering rage*)
>>> I want to know where you get the nerve
>>>> To play your jokes on me,
>>> To tell me a thing no man has seen,
>>>> A thing which just can't be.
>>> Of all the barefaced impudence!
>>>> Of all the brazen stunts!
>>> To tell me that the selfsame man
>>>> Can be in two places at once!

SOSIA (*as before*)
>> I tell you that's what happened to me.

AMPHITRYON
>> Oh, you be damned!

SOSIA (*reproachfully*)
>>> But I don't see
>> What I've done to earn these threats from you.

AMPHITRYON
>> You dare to ask, you stinker, you,
>> When you stand there laughing in my face?

SOSIA (*doggedly*)
>> If what I'd said was not the case,
>> Then I'd deserve these damns from you.
>> But it's not a lie. Every word is true,
>> I'm giving you the story straight.

AMPHITRYON (*looking at him in disgust*)
>> The fellow's drunk, as sure as fate.

SOSIA (*despairingly*)
>> I wish I were!

AMPHITRYON (*acidly*)

> You wish to do
> What's already done?

SOSIA (*bewildered*)

> Who me?

AMPHITRYON (*icily*)

> Yes you.
> Just where did you find the liquor, pray?

SOSIA

> Me? Nowhere. Haven't touched a drop today.

AMPHITRYON (*to the world at large, throwing up his hands helplessly*)

> What kind of man is this, anyway!

SOSIA (*expostulating, pointing to the house*)

> By now I've said it ten times, I swear.
> Must I holler in your ear?
> I tell you I'm in that house over there,
> And also beside you here.
> You think that now the situation
> Is sufficiently plain and clear?

AMPHITRYON (*shouting*)

> Stand back from me! Why, this is outrageous!

SOSIA

> Why, what's the matter now?

AMPHITRYON (*witheringly*)

> You're contagious—
> You've caught the plague.

SOSIA (*reproachfully*)

> Why say such a thing?
> I'm in the pink, my health's just flourishing!

AMPHITRYON (*snarling*)

> I'll bet it doesn't stay that way!
> You'll get what's coming to you today:
> If I make it home, I guarantee
> You'll live a life of misery!

(He glares at Sosia balefully in silence for a moment, and then resumes.)

(Icily) Follow me, faithful servant who makes a fool of his master by talking drivel, who, on top of neglecting to carry out his master's orders, deliberately comes to laugh in his master's face, who hands his master an impossible story, something no one's ever heard of even through hearsay—AND whose back, believe you me, will pay for every last one of his lies.

SOSIA *(reproachfully)* Amphitryon, I can't tell you how unhappy it makes an honest servant, one who tells his master the honest truth, to see the truth take a beating.

AMPHITRYON *(as before)* Then let's you and I figure it out: how the devil is it possible for you, at this very moment, to be right here and also in the house? That's what I want to know.

SOSIA It's absolutely true: I'm here and I'm there. If this sounds like a miracle, it's just as much a miracle to me as it is to you.

AMPHITRYON How's that?

SOSIA *(grinning)* Since it's no less a miracle to me than to you. *(Becoming serious again)* So help me, at first I didn't believe in my other me, until my other me convinced me to believe in him. He reeled off the whole story, down to the last detail, of what happened at the front. And he stole my looks along with my name: two drops of milk aren't as alike as my other me is to me. *(Thoughtfully)* You see, when you sent me home from the pier before daybreak a little while ago—

AMPHITRYON *(interrupting impatiently)* Well, what about it?

SOSIA *(ignoring the interruption)* —I'd already been standing in front of the house long before I arrived there.

AMPHITRYON *(throwing up his hands)* What the devil is this nonsense! Are you in your right mind?

SOSIA (*glumly*)   See for yourself.

AMPHITRYON (*tapping his temple significantly; to himself, portentously*)   After he left me, he must have seen the evil eye. Had some evil strike him.

SOSIA (*promptly*)   I sure did: I got beaten to a pulp.

AMPHITRYON   Who beat you?

SOSIA (*as before*)   I did myself. (*As Amphitryon looks at him bewildered*) The me who's in the house now.

AMPHITRYON (*with deadly calm*)   Now watch out. I want only answers to my questions, nothing more. First of all— this other Sosia of yours, who is he? That's what I want to know.

SOSIA   Your servant.

AMPHITRYON (*groaning*)   Even one of you is more than I want! (*Pounding his fist into the palm of his hand*) I've owned only one Sosia in all my life, and that's you!

SOSIA (*shaking his head stubbornly*)   I'll tell you right here and now, Amphitryon: I bet you, when you get home, you'll run into another servant Sosia in addition to me in the house. His father's name was Davus just like mine, he looks exactly like me, and he's the same age. To put it in a nutshell, your Sosia's become twins.

AMPHITRYON (*baffled*)   This is a very strange story. (*After a moment's thought*) Did you get to see my wife?

SOSIA   How? I wasn't allowed into the house.

AMPHITRYON   Who stopped you?

SOSIA   The other Sosia I've been telling you about, the one who beat me up.

AMPHITRYON (*thundering*)   Who is that Sosia?

SOSIA   Me, I tell you! How many times must I say it?

AMPHITRYON (*suddenly struck by a thought, eying him suspiciously*)   Say, tell me this—you weren't asleep a little while ago, were you?

SOSIA (*shaking his head vigorously*)   Not the least little bit.

AMPHITRYON   I was wondering whether maybe you had seen
some Sosia in a dream.

SOSIA (*in high dudgeon*)   I am not in the habit of carrying
out my master's orders in a comatose condition. I was wide
awake when I saw him, I'm wide awake now seeing you,
I'm wide awake now telling you this story, and I was wide
awake a little while ago when I got beaten up. He was wide
awake too.

AMPHITRYON   Who was?

SOSIA (*wearily*)   The other Sosia, I tell you. (*Pleadingly*)
Please! Can't you understand?

AMPHITRYON (*helplessly*)   How the devil could anyone understand! You talk such drivel!

SOSIA (*grimly*)   You'll understand soon enough, when you
see that Sosia standing in front of your eyes.

AMPHITRYON (*starting off toward the door, grimly*)   Then
follow me. The first thing I've got to do is look into this
whole business.

(*He strides up to the door and looks it over. Then, with
Sosia and the porters at his heels, he moves away to examine
the rest of the house from the outside. As they do so, the
door opens and, unnoticed by them, Alcmena steps out.*)

SONG

ALCMENA (*to the audience, sadly*)
As we go through life, how rare is happiness
Compared with misery! It's part of life
For everyone, it's heaven's pleasure that
Sorrow travel hand in hand with joy,
That, once some good has happened, on its heels
There follow even more of toil and trouble.
You see, just now I learned this for myself,
I know it from my own experience.
I was given a moment of joy, the chance I had
To see my husband. It lasted just a night;
Before the day had come, he suddenly

Arose and went away. And now I feel
I'm utterly alone, since he whom I
Love best of all no longer is with me.
His leaving brought me more of sorrow than
His coming brought me joy.

(Pauses, and then, her countenance brightening, resumes proudly)

Yet one thing's made me happy: he conquered his foes
And came back home bearing a crown of glory.
This is my consolation; he may always leave
My side if it is to return to me a hero.
The parting will hurt, but I will bear the hurt
With strength and resolution if this one
Reward I get: to see my husband hailed
By all as victor on the field of battle.
For me just this is enough. Our greatest prize
Is courage—courage takes, beyond all doubt,
First place among all things upon this earth.
Our lives, our liberty, safety, all we own,
Our parents, children, homes, and fatherland—
Courage is the guardian of them all.
For courage embraces every good there is;
If a man has courage, every good is his!

(She falls silent. A moment later, Amphitryon and his entourage return from their inspection of the house. Alcmena, unnoticed, remains buried in thought near the door.)

AMPHITRYON *(to Sosia, enthusiastically)* I know my wife will be overjoyed to see me back. *(Smiling happily, half to himself)* We're very much in love with each other. *(To Sosia)* Especially since everything's gone so well—I led the army to victory, I defeated at the first encounter an enemy everyone thought invincible. Yes, I'm sure of it; she simply can't wait to see me back.

SOSIA What about me? You think that lady friend of mine won't be glad to see *me*?

ALCMENA (*her attention caught by the sound of voices, in surprise*)   There's my husband!

AMPHITRYON (*to Sosia, heading for the door*)   Follow me.

ALCMENA (*to herself*)   What's he coming back for? A little while ago he was saying he was in a hurry to get away. (*Puzzled*) Is he deliberately trying to test me? Does he want to see for himself how I miss him when he's away? (*Smiling happily*) Well, I certainly have no objections to having him back!

SOSIA (*suddenly catching sight of Alcmena and stopping in his tracks*)   Amphitryon, we'd better go back to the ship.

AMPHITRYON (*also stopping; puzzled*)   Why?

SOSIA   Because no one's going to give us homecomers breakfast.

AMPHITRYON (*as before*)   Now what put that idea in your head?

SOSIA   We're too late.

AMPHITRYON   How's that?

SOSIA   There's Alcmena in front of the door. And I can see she's got a full belly.

AMPHITRYON (*looking and smiling*)   Oh, she was pregnant when I left.

SOSIA (*groaning*)   My god! That's the end of me!

AMPHITRYON   What's the matter?

SOSIA   If I follow your figuring, she must be in her ninth month. That means I've come home just in time to start hauling water!

AMPHITRYON (*smiling*)   Come on, cheer up.

SOSIA   Cheer up? Oh, sure! (*Savagely*) Just let me get my hands on a bucket. God damn it, never believe a word I say from this minute on if I don't draw the last drop of life out of that damn well once I get started!

AMPHITRYON   Come along. Don't worry; I'll give someone else the job.

ALCMENA (*to herself, excitedly*)   I think I really should run up to meet him.

(*She walks swiftly up to him, holding out her hands. He takes them in his and looks at her, smiling blissfully.*)

AMPHITRYON (*warmly*)   Joyful greetings from Amphitryon to his darling wife—the finest wife in all Thebes, in her husband's considered opinion, and a good woman too, as every husband in Thebes will tell you. (*Drawing her closer, tenderly*) How have you been, dear? Are you glad to see me?

(*There is a moment of silence as Alcmena stares at him uncomprehendingly.*)

SOSIA (*aside, acidly*)   Never saw anybody more glad. Giving him about as warm a greeting as you would a stray mutt!

AMPHITRYON (*as before*)   And to see you pregnant this way and so near your time! I'm simply delighted!

ALCMENA (*bewildered*)   Will you please tell me why you must make fun of me like this with these salutations and greetings? As if you didn't see me just a little while ago! As if you've just this minute come back from the front! (*Curiously*) Why this greeting me as if you hadn't seen me for ages?

AMPHITRYON (*taken aback*)   Why, I haven't laid eyes on you until just now!

ALCMENA (*as before*)   Now what makes you say that?

AMPHITRYON (*as before*)   Because I've learned to tell the truth!

ALCMENA (*annoyed*)   Well, a man who unlearns what he's learned is not behaving well at all! Are you two trying to test my feelings? (*Softening her tone as she notices their genuine bewilderment*) What brings you back so quickly? A bad omen hold you back? The weather keeping you from sailing to the front, as you said you were going to do a little while ago?

AMPHITRYON   "A little while ago?" How little a while ago was this little while ago?

ALCMENA (*resentfully*) You're trying to catch me! (*With a careless wave of the hand, irritably*) Some time ago. Just before.

AMPHITRYON (*throwing up his hands*) Now will you kindly explain how that's possible? (*Mimicking her*) "Some time ago. Just before."

ALCMENA (*acidly*) What do you think? That, because you're making fun of me, I'm making fun of you? Imagine telling me that this is the first I've seen of you when you just left here a little while ago!

AMPHITRYON (*to Sosia, incredulously*) She's talking raving nonsense!

SOSIA (*to Amphitryon, with an I-understand-the-whole-business air*) Just wait a little while, until she sleeps off this dream.

AMPHITRYON   You mean she dreams while she's wide awake?

ALCMENA (*to Amphitryon, sharply*) I most certainly am wide awake, and I'm telling you what happened with these eyes of mine wide open. A little while ago, just before daybreak, I saw both you and (*gesturing contemptuously toward Sosia*) him.

AMPHITRYON   Where?

ALCMENA   Here, in your own house.

AMPHITRYON (*brusquely*) You never did!

SOSIA (*to Amphitryon*) Wait a second. (*Eagerly*) What if the ship brought us from the dock to the door here in our sleep?

AMPHITRYON (*witheringly*) Are you on her side too?

SOSIA (*whispering urgently*) What do you expect? Don't you understand? If you try to say no to a madwoman, you'll make the crazy thing crazier, and she'll keep clobbering you. Say yes to her, and she'll let you off with only one sock.

AMPHITRYON (*to Sosia, grimly*) There's one thing that's going to happen right now: I'm going to give her a piece of my mind for not giving me a greeting on my return home.

SOSIA (*to Amphitryon*) You'll stir up a hornet's nest!

AMPHITRYON (*to Sosia*) Quiet! (*To Alcmena*) Alcmena, I want to ask you something.

ALCMENA (*shrugging*) Go ahead. Anything you like.

AMPHITRYON (*angrily*) Have you had an attack of stupidity? Or an overdose of the feeling that no one's good enough for you?

ALCMENA (*helplessly*) My dear husband, whatever put the idea in your head to ask me a question like that?

AMPHITRYON (*bitterly*) Because, up to now, you always used to come up and greet me the way any decent, loving wife would greet a husband. Now I come home and find you completely changed!

ALCMENA (*earnestly*) But I did! My dear, the very moment you arrived yesterday, I greeted you. I asked how you were, I took your hand, and I kissed you.

SOSIA (*to Alcmena, uncomprehendingly*) You greeted him yesterday?

ALCMENA You too, Sosia.

SOSIA (*to Amphitryon, shaking his head mournfully*) Amphitryon, I had hoped she would bear you a son, but she's not big with child.

AMPHITRYON With what, then?

SOSIA With bats in her belfry!

ALCMENA (*to Sosia, acidly*) I am perfectly sound, and god willing, I'll be safe when I give birth. (*Gesturing toward Amphitryon*) And if he'd only do his duty, you'd get a good smack of the whip! (*Raising her voice*) You'd get what you deserve for putting a jinx like that on me, you jinxer you!

SOSIA (*muttering to himself, sullenly*) Yeah? A pregnant woman should get a good smack—(*catching Alcmena's*

glare and switching abruptly to bright innocence) a snack,
I mean. You know, something to nibble on in case she
starts to feel nauseous.

AMPHITRYON (*to Alcmena*)   You saw me here yesterday?

ALCMENA (*wearily*)   If you must be told for the tenth time,
yes!

AMPHITRYON (*hopefully*)   In a dream, maybe?

ALCMENA (*as before*)   No. I was wide awake, and so were
you.

AMPHITRYON (*to the world at large*)   The troubles I have!

SOSIA   What's the matter?

AMPHITRYON   My wife's gone crazy!

SOSIA (*gloomily, nodding knowledgeably*)   Sudden attack of
manic depression. Nothing like it for driving people mad.

AMPHITRYON (*solicitously*)   When did you first feel this
coming on, Alcmena?

ALCMENA (*preserving an icy calm*)   I tell you, I am *not*
crazy.

AMPHITRYON   Then why do you say you saw me yesterday,
when I only arrived in port last night? I had dinner there,
and I slept all night on board. (*Emphatically*) I haven't
put foot inside this house since the day I left with the army
to fight the Teleboans. And, what's more, defeated them.

ALCMENA (*as before*)   That's not so. You had dinner with
me, and you slept with me.

AMPHITRYON (*roaring*)   What did you say?

ALCMENA (*as before*)   The truth.

AMPHITRYON (*grimly*)   Not about that, it isn't. About anything else, I wouldn't know.

ALCMENA (*as before*)   And, at the crack of dawn, you left
for the front.

AMPHITRYON (*frantically*)   How can this be?

SOSIA (*promptly*)   She's telling it just as she remembers it.
It's a dream she's telling you. (*To Alcmena, shaking his*

head regretfully) But, after you woke up, Alcmena, you should have offered special prayers to Jove. He's our patron god of miracles, you know.

ALCMENA (*disgusted*) Oh, go to the devil!

SOSIA (*muttering to himself*) No, you go—(*catching her glare and switching abruptly to bright innocence*) and take care of those prayers. Do you good.

ALCMENA (*to Amphitryon, grimly*) That's the second time he's insulted me, and you let him get away with it.

AMPHITRYON (*to Sosia*) Shut up! (*To Alcmena*) Now tell me: today, at the crack of dawn, I went away from you, did I?

ALCMENA (*shrugging*) If it wasn't you two, then who told me the story of how the battle went?

AMPHITRYON (*flabbergasted*) You mean to say you know about that?

ALCMENA Of course! I heard from you all about how you stormed and took a great city and how you killed King Pterelas yourself.

AMPHITRYON (*as before*) *I* told you that?

ALCMENA Yes, you. And Sosia was there with us.

AMPHITRYON (*to Sosia*) Did you hear me tell her all this today?

SOSIA (*with a how-silly-can-you-get tone of voice*) Now where would I have heard you?

AMPHITRYON (*to Sosia, throwing up his hands*) Ask *her*, not me.

ALCMENA (*to Amphitryon, witheringly*) Strange, isn't it, that he won't contradict you.

AMPHITRYON Sosia! Look at me.

SOSIA I'm looking.

AMPHITRYON Now, don't just yes me; I want you to tell me the truth. Did you hear me tell her today these things she said I did?

SOSIA (*scornfully*) Please! Are you crazy too? Asking me a question like that! This is the first I've seen of her, just like yourself.

AMPHITRYON (*grimly*) Well, Alcmena? Did you hear him?

ALCMENA (*calmly*) I certainly did—telling lies!

AMPHITRYON So you don't trust either him or your own husband, eh?

ALCMENA (*as before*) Only because I trust myself most of all, and I know that everything happened exactly as I've told it to you.

AMPHITRYON You say that I arrived here yesterday?

ALCMENA You deny that you left here today?

AMPHITRYON (*exploding*) Of course I do! I tell you, this is the first and only time I've been home!

ALCMENA (*tossing her head*) Then I'd like to know whether you're also going to deny that this morning you gave me the gold cup you said you received as an award?

AMPHITRYON (*snorting*) I did not give you that cup, nor did I mention a word about it! I'll admit I had in mind to give it to you, and I still do. (*Doing a double take*) Who told you about it, anyway?

ALCMENA (*coldly*) You told me about it with your own lips and gave it to me with your own hands.

AMPHITRYON (*in desperation*) Wait here. Don't move. Please! (*Turning and whispering to Sosia*) This is incredible, Sosia! How could she have known that I was awarded a gold cup? (*Menacingly*) Unless you met her before and told her the whole story.

SOSIA (*hastily*) I never said a word to her! The first time I laid eyes on her was when you did.

AMPHITRYON (*clutching his head in despair*) What kind of person is she!

ALCMENA (*patiently*) Would you like me to show you the cup?

AMPHITRYON Yes, I would!

ALCMENA   Very well. (*She goes to the door and claps her hands. A moment later a maid appears in the doorway.*) Thessala, go back in and bring out the cup my husband gave me this morning.

AMPHITRYON   (*pulling Sosia off to the side*)   Come over here, Sosia. (*Sotto voce, nervously*) Listen, if she has that cup, that'll be the miracle to end all miracles.

SOSIA   (*sotto voce, incredulously*)   You mean you believe her? (*Pointing to a box in the hands of one of the porters*) But it's in this chest here. Locked and sealed with your own seal.

AMPHITRYON   (*as before*)   Is the seal intact?

SOSIA   (*sotto voce*)   Take a look.

AMPHITRYON   (*doing so; sotto voce, relieved*)   Perfect. Just the way I sealed it.

SOSIA   (*sotto voce*)   Listen, why don't you have her treated for lunacy?

AMPHITRYON   (*sotto voce, gloomily*)   Damn it all, I'll have to. She's crazy as a loon, damn it!

(*The maid reappears carrying a cup which she hands to Alcmena, who turns and calls to Amphitryon.*)

ALCMENA   No need for any more talk. Here's your cup. (*Holding it up*) See?

AMPHITRYON   (*striding over*)   Let's have it.

ALCMENA   (*handing it to him*)   Here you are. And take a good look. Since you insist on denying cold facts, I'll make it as plain as day for you. (*Sternly*) Is this the cup that was awarded to you?

AMPHITRYON   (*dumb struck*)   In the name of Jove! What *is* this I see? It's the cup all right! (*To Sosia, dumbly*) Sosia, I'm a ruined man!

SOSIA   (*grimly*)   Either this woman is the greatest witch that ever lived, or your cup must still be in that box.

AMPHITRYON   (*grimly*)   Then hurry and open that box.

SOSIA (*throwing up his hands*) Why bother? The seal's still intact. (*Wildly*) Everything's working out perfectly: you've produced a second Amphitryon, I've produced a second Sosia, and now, if the cup comes up with a cup, we've all become twins!

AMPHITRYON (*as before*) We're opening that chest and having a look, and that's that!

SOSIA Will you please just check the seal first, so you don't start blaming me afterwards?

AMPHITRYON (*thundering*) Open it! This woman wants to drive us both insane with these stories of hers! (*Sosia starts fumbling with the chest.*)

ALCMENA (*helplessly*) Where would I have gotten it except from you? It was your gift to me!

AMPHITRYON (*grimly*) I've got to look into this business.

SOSIA (*emitting a war whoop*) By Jove! By Jove almighty!

AMPHITRYON (*startled*) What's the matter?

SOSIA (*pointing to the chest, shaking like a leaf*) There's no cup in this chest!

AMPHITRYON What's that you say?

SOSIA The truth!

AMPHITRYON (*between his teeth*) It better turn up, or you'll pay for it with your hide.

ALCMENA (*holding out the cup, calmly*) It has turned up—here.

AMPHITRYON (*to Alcmena, as before*) All right. Who gave it to you?

ALCMENA (*as before*) The man who's asking me the question.

SOSIA (*to Amphitryon, dancing with rage*) Trying to trick me, eh? You sneaked away from the ship, you ran ahead by a different road, you took the cup out, you gave it to her, and then you sneaked the seal back on!

AMPHITRYON (*clutching his head*) Oh, my god! Are you

out to help this madwoman too? (*To Alcmena, wearily*)
So you say we arrived here yesterday?

ALCMENA (*quietly and calmly*) Yes, I do. And the minute
you arrived, you greeted me. I greeted you and gave you a
kiss.

SOSIA (*to the audience, shaking his head dolefully*) Right
away, I don't like the way it begins. Bad stuff, this kiss
business.

AMPHITRYON Go on.

ALCMENA Then you took a bath.

AMPHITRYON And after my bath?

ALCMENA You sat down to table.

SOSIA (*to Amphitryon*) Good! Perfect! Get to the bottom of
this.

AMPHITRYON (*to Sosia, brusquely*) Don't interrupt! (*To
Alcmena*) Go on with your story.

ALCMENA Dinner was served. We ate together. I sat alongside you.

AMPHITRYON On the same couch?

ALCMENA On the same couch.

SOSIA (*shaking his head dolefully*) I don't like the sound of
this dinner party!

AMPHITRYON (*turning on him*) Let her go on with her ex-
planations. (*To Alcmena*) And after we finished dinner?

ALCMENA You said you were sleepy. The table was cleared,
and we went off to bed.

AMPHITRYON Where did you sleep?

ALCMENA With you. In the same room. In the same bed.

AMPHITRYON (*gasping convulsively*) You've done for me!

SOSIA (*in alarm*) What's the matter?

AMPHITRYON This woman's just murdered me!

ALCMENA (*agitated*) What did I do? Please!

AMPHITRYON (*turning his back on her*) Don't you talk to
me!

SOSIA What's the matter?

AMPHITRYON (*dramatically*) I'm ruined! Her honor—while I was away, it was stained!

ALCMENA (*wounded*) God in heaven! My dear husband, how can you say a thing like that about me!

AMPHITRYON (*wildly*) Your husband? I? Don't you call me by that name! False woman, it's a false name!

SOSIA (*to the audience, grinning*) This is a pretty sticky state of affairs if (*gesturing toward Amphitryon*) he's become a woman and isn't her man.

ALCMENA (*helplessly*) What did I do to make you say such things to me?

AMPHITRYON (*in a cold fury*) You've just presented the facts yourself. You have to ask *me* what you did wrong?

ALCMENA (*bewildered*) How could I have done anything wrong, when I was with you, the man I married?

AMPHITRYON (*screaming*) You were with me? (*To the world at large*) There isn't a woman alive as brazen as this one! (*Icily*) If you have no sense of shame, the very least you can do is act as if you did.

ALCMENA (*her eyes flashing*) Neither I nor anyone in my family would ever stoop to the behavior you're accusing me of. Is it your idea to catch me in adultery? You never will!

AMPHITRYON (*throwing up his arms in despair*) Oh, my god in heaven! (*Turning to Sosia*) Sosia, you at least recognize me, don't you?

SOSIA (*looking him over, coolly*) Just about.

AMPHITRYON Didn't I have dinner yesterday aboard ship in port?

ALCMENA (*coldly*) I have witnesses, too, to back up what *I* say.

SOSIA (*to Amphitryon, scratching his head*) I really don't know what to say about this whole business except that, maybe, there's some other Amphitryon who takes over your affairs while you're away and (*delicately, with a glance in*

Alcmena's direction) discharges your duties for you in your absence. If a fake Sosia is a miracle, believe you me, this other Amphitryon of yours is an even bigger one!

AMPHITRYON (*desperately*)   Some witch must have driven her out of her wits.

ALCMENA (*passionately*)   In the name of the supreme god of the heavens, in the name of Our Lady Juno, whom I reverence and worship with all my heart as I should, I swear to you that, outside of yourself, no man's body has touched mine to rob me of my honor!

AMPHITRYON (*dully*)   I only wish it were true.

ALCMENA (*resentfully*)   It *is* true. But that doesn't mean a thing because you don't want to believe it.

AMPHITRYON (*sneering*)   You're a woman, you're quick to swear.

ALCMENA (*proudly*)   A woman who's done no wrong can be quick to swear. She can speak up for herself with confidence and without fear.

AMPHITRYON (*muttering*)   You're quick to swear, all right.

ALCMENA (*as before*)   As any good woman should be!

AMPHITRYON (*as before*)   Good, eh? That's what you *say*.

ALCMENA (*gravely*)   What people generally mean by the word "dowry" is not what I consider my dowry to be. No—mine is decency and honor and self-control; respect for heaven, love for my parents, and good relations with all my family; to carry out your wishes, to give to the good, and to help the honest.

SOSIA   So help me, if everything she says is true, this woman's a paragon of virtue!

AMPHITRYON (*unhappily*)   I'm so mixed up, I don't even know my own name!

SOSIA (*promptly*)   You're Amphitryon, all right. But be careful: the way people have been changing ever since we got back, you might lose your right title to it if you don't watch out.

AMPHITRYON (*wearily*)   Alcmena, I must look into this matter, I can't just drop it.

ALCMENA   I'd be very glad if you would.

AMPHITRYON (*as before*)   Now what do you say to this?
Your cousin Naucrates came over on the same ship with me.
Suppose I bring him here from the dock. If he denies that
things happened as you say they did, what do you think
would be the fair thing to do? Can you give me any good
reason why I shouldn't divorce you?

ALCMENA   None at all—*if* I've done something wrong.

AMPHITRYON   Agreed. (*To Sosia, gesturing toward the porters*)   Take them inside. I'm going back to the ship to get
Naucrates.

(*Amphitryon shuffles off despondently, stage right. Sosia
gestures to the porters, who file into the house. He is about
to follow them when, struck by a thought, he turns back to
Alcmena.*)

SOSIA (*confidentially*)   Look, there's no one around now besides us two. Tell me the honest truth: is there another
Sosia inside who looks exactly like me?

ALCMENA   Oh, get away from me! (*Disgustedly*) Like master, like man!

SOSIA (*grumbling*)   If that's the way you want it, I'll go. (*Enters the house.*)

ALCMENA (*to the audience, shaking her head sadly*)   A
strange way for my husband to be acting. To get pleasure
out of falsely accusing me of misconduct! (*Shrugging*)
Well, whatever it is, I'll find out soon enough from Cousin
Naucrates.

(*She turns and enters the house. The stage is now empty.*)

ACT III

(*Enter Jove, stage left. He walks downstage and addresses the audience.*)

JOVE I'm the Amphitryon with the servant Sosia who turns into Mercury when it's convenient, the Amphitryon who lives in (*pointing toward the sky*) the penthouse and sometimes becomes Jove when the spirit moves him. But the minute I arrive here, quick as a flash I change my clothes and become Amphitryon.

(*With a respectful bow*) This time I'm here for your sakes: I didn't want to leave this comedy only half done. At the same time, I wanted to come to Alcmena's rescue, since her husband, (*gesturing in the general direction of the port*) that Amphitryon, is accusing her of adultery though she's done nothing wrong. After all, I'd be to blame if what I alone was responsible for should fall on the head of poor, innocent Alcmena. (*Grinning*) I'll pass myself off now as Amphitryon, as I did before, and drive the whole household crazy. (*Becoming grave*) However, after it's all over, I'll reveal the secret, and I'll help Alcmena when her time comes: I'll see to it that she delivers both the child her husband conceived and the one I conceived with only one confinement and without any pain.

(*Looking about*) I told Mercury to stand by me immediately in case I had orders for him. (*With a wave of his hand, draws the audience's attention to the door of the house. The next second it opens, and Alcmena appears in the doorway.*) I'll speak to her right now.

(*Alcmena emerges from her house carrying a bag. She slams the door shut behind her and, not noticing Jove, walks downstage and puts down the bag.*)

ALCMENA (*to the audience, in a rage*) I simply can't stay in this house. To have my own husband accuse me this way

of adultery, of shame and dishonor! Things that happened
he shouts to high heaven never happened, and the next
minute accuses me of things that never happened, that
were none of my doing. What's more, he imagines I'll shrug
all this off as just so much water under the bridge. I will
not! He can't falsely accuse me of adultery—I won't stand
for it! Either I leave him, or he gives me full satisfaction,
and, what's more, swears to me that he takes back every
word he's uttered against his wife's innocence!

JOVE (*to the audience*)   I'll have to arrange things the way
she wants if I'm ever to get her to take back her fond lover.
Amphitryon is an innocent victim: my doings have fallen
on his neck, and my love affair let him in for a lot of trouble
a little while ago. But now the tongue-lashing and cursing
she got from him is falling on *my* neck, and *I'm* the innocent
victim! (*Walks up to her.*)

ALCMENA (*to the audience*)   There's the man who's made his
wife miserable by accusing her of shame and dishonor.

(*Turns her back on him as he comes up.*)

JOVE (*tenderly*)   My dear wife, I want to talk to you. Why
do you turn your back on me?

ALCMENA (*furiously*)   It's my nature. I can't stand the sight
of an enemy.

JOVE   Hey, what's this! An enemy?

ALCMENA (*as before*)   Exactly. It's the truth—unless you're
ready to accuse me of calling you by a false name this time
too!

JOVE (*putting his arm about her; meltingly*)   You're so angry!

ALCMENA (*thrusting his arm away*)   You keep your hands
off me! (*Witheringly*) After all, if you had any sense and
were in your right mind, you'd hardly want to hold a conversation, serious or otherwise, with a woman you consider
and call immoral. Not unless you're stupider than the
stupidest!

JOVE (*earnestly*) My calling you so doesn't make you any more so, and I *don't* consider you immoral. I've come here for only one purpose: to apologize to you. I've never felt so badly about anything as I did when I heard you were angry with me. "Why did you say such things?" you'll ask. I'll tell you why. It was not, I swear it, that I thought you were immoral; I was just testing your feelings, what you'd do, how you'd be inclined to take it. What I said to you before wasn't serious—it was all a joke! Just ask Sosia.

ALCMENA (*glaring at him*) You go ahead and bring my Cousin Naucrates, just as you said you were going to do, to be your witness that you hadn't been here before.

JOVE (*reproachfully*) Now, if something's said in a joke, it's not fair to take it seriously.

ALCMENA (*bitterly*) A joke that cut me to the very heart, as I know only too well.

JOVE (*on his knees*) Alcmena, I beg you! On my knees! Please! Forgive me! Pardon me! Don't be angry with me!

ALCMENA (*coldly*) My character makes everything you've said against me simply meaningless. (*Turning from him*) Since I've never had anything to do with immorality in deed, I want nothing to do with it in word. I'm saying good-by now. Keep your part of the property, and arrange to return mine. And now, if you please, send some servants to escort me.

JOVE (*frantically*) Are you in your right mind?

ALCMENA (*picking up her bag, as before*) If you won't send any, I'll go by myself. (*Proudly*) My honor will be my escort! (*Starts walking away.*)

JOVE (*urgently*) Wait! (*As she stops*) I will swear any oath you want that I believe you are a faithful wife. (*Dramatically*) And if I swear falsely, (*raising his eyes to heaven*) Almighty Jove, I call on you to bring heaven's wrath upon Amphitryon for all time!

ALCMENA (*shuddering*) No! Heaven's blessing!

JOVE (*dryly*) I'm sure it will be that, because that was no

false oath I gave you. (*Taking her gently by the arm*)
Now, are you still angry with me?

ALCMENA (*reluctantly*)   No.

JOVE   Good! (*Gently*) You know, in life things like this happen all the time. We have our joys, and then again our
sorrows. We have fights, and then we make up again. Yet,
whenever we have fights of this kind and make up again,
we're twice as good friends as we were before.

ALCMENA (*reproachfully*)   You should have been careful
and not said such a thing in the first place. (*Smiling
at him*) But, since you've apologized completely for everything, well, I'll let it go.

(*They embrace and stand for a moment smiling happily at
each other.*)

JOVE (*as if suddenly remembering something*)   Listen, you
must have the ritual utensils made ready for me. When I
was at the front I made some vows about what I'd do if I
returned safe and sound, and I want to carry them out.

ALCMENA   I'll take care of it. (*Claps her hands, and two maid
servants appear at the door.*)

JOVE (*to the servants*)   Call Sosia out here. (*They re-enter
the house. He turns to Alcmena.*) I want him to bring
Blepharo—he was captain of my ship—here to have lunch
with me. (*To the audience, grinning*) Blepharo is not only
going to get no lunch—he's going to be one surprised man
when I haul Amphitryon out of here by the neck!

ALCMENA (*to the audience*)   I wonder what he's up to, talking to himself like that? (*Her attention caught, glances toward the door*) Someone's coming out. It's Sosia.

(*Sosia emerges from the house and walks up to Jove.*)

SOSIA (*to Jove, seriously*)   Here I am, Amphitryon. Anything
to be done, just say the word and I'll do it.

JOVE   Sosia, you've come just at the right time.

SOSIA (*looking from the one to the other*)   Have you two

made peace? (*Breaking into a smile*) Well, I'm delighted! It's a pleasure to see you two relaxed! (*Seriously again*) The system a good servant should follow is this: whatever your owners do, you do, you take your expression from them. If they're sad, you be sad; if they're gay, you be gay. (*Switching on the smile again*) So, tell me: you've made up, have you?

JOVE (*eying him piercingly*) What are you making jokes for? You know very well everything I said a while back was just in fun.

SOSIA (*bewildered*) Just in fun was it? I thought you were dead serious!

JOVE (*smiling at Alcmena*) I've apologized for everything, and now there's peace between us.

SOSIA Fine!

JOVE And now I want to go in and take care of those vows I made.

SOSIA Good idea.

JOVE You go to the pier and invite Captain Blepharo to lunch for me. We'll eat just as soon as I'm done with my prayers.

SOSIA (*over his shoulder as he dashes off, stage right*) By the time you think I've just arrived there, I'll already be back here.

JOVE (*calling after him*) Just hurry back.

ALCMENA You don't want me for anything, do you? Then I'll go in and get ready whatever you need.

JOVE You run along and get everything set up as quickly as you can.

ALCMENA You can come in whenever you want. I'll see to it there are no delays.

JOVE (*kissing her tenderly*) That's the way an attentive wife should talk. (*She goes into the house, and he turns to the audience.*) I fooled them both, mistress and servant. They think I'm Amphitryon—are they ever wrong! (*Looking upward*) Hey there! You, the immortal Sosia! Put in an appearance here. You hear what I say even though you're not here in the flesh. When Amphitryon gets back, keep him away from the house. Use any trick you can think of. I want you to play around with him till I've had my pleasure with this wife of his I'm borrowing. Now, please see that you do all this just the way you know I want it done. And I want you to stand by and help while I (*grinning*) offer up prayers to myself!

(*He enters the house. A moment later Mercury dashes in at top speed, stage left.*)

SONG

MERCURY (*yelling*)

Hey, gangway everyone, clear the road! Out of my way, I say!

No man alive better have the nerve to stand and block my way!

(*Pulling up, in normal tones*)

Why shouldn't the right to threaten the public be given gods, like me,

When two-bit slaves do it all the time, in every comedy?

They rush to yell, "The boat's come in! Your father's home, and mad!"

But *I'm* obeying Jove himself; I'm here on orders from Dad.

So *I've* an even greater right to holler "Clear the way"—

My father calls and, quick, I run; one word, and I obey.

With Jove I'm just as dutiful as any father's pet.

When he's in love, I'm Helpful Henry; I aid, advise, abet,

And share his joys—the times he's happy are when I'm happiest.

He has affairs. That's good. He's smart: he does as he likes best.

And everyone of you should too—of course, with moderation.

Now, Father wants Amphitryon fooled. You'll see a presentation,

A spectacle for spectators, of fooling at its height.
I'll put a garland on my head, and make believe I'm tight,
Then climb to the roof and, when he comes, get rid of him from there:
Though he hasn't had a drop to drink, he'll end up soused for fair.

(*Chuckling*)

And then his servant Sosia will pay for what I've done—
Amphitryon will demonstrate that *he's* the guilty one.
What's that to me? My job is Jove, to be at his beck and call.

(*His attention caught, he looks off, stage right*)

Well, look who's here—Amphitryon. May I kindly ask you all
To give me your attention while I take him for a ride.
It involves my acting out a part, so now I'll go inside
And fix myself to look as though I'd tied one on somewhere.
Then up I go to the top of the roof to drive him off from there.

(*Mercury dashes inside. A moment later Amphitryon enters, shuffling along disconsolately.*)

AMPHITRYON (*to the audience, irritably*) I went to get Naucrates, but I couldn't. He wasn't on the ship, he wasn't at home, and I wasn't able to find a soul in town who had seen him. I've been all over: up and down every street, in the gyms, in the drugstores, the bazaar, the market, the athletic field, the main square, all the doctors' offices, all the barbers', every temple in town—I'm worn out with looking, and I can't find him any place.

(*Falls silent a moment, shaking his head bitterly. Then, resolutely*) I'll go home, get Alcmena, and go further into this matter of who it was who made her disgrace herself. I'm going to get to the bottom of this business or die in the attempt!

(*Strides up to the door, tries it, and steps back in sur-*

prise) The door's bolted! (*Bitterly*) Great! Just like everything else that's been going on around here. Well, I'll just bang on it. (*Pounding away*) Open up! Hey, isn't anyone going to open this door?

(*Mercury suddenly appears on the roof, a garland sitting askew on his head, and leans over.*)

MERCURY (*as if drunk*)   Who'z 'at at the door?

AMPHITRYON (*shouting*)   I am.

MERCURY (*with drunken incomprehension*)   Wha' d'ya mean, "I am?"

AMPHITRYON (*snarling*)   You heard me!

MERCURY (*waggling a finger at him, playfully reproachful*) Breaking down doors this way! God will punish you.

AMPHITRYON (*taken aback, incredulously*)   What's that?

MERCURY (*piously*)   It's that He'll make you unhappy your whole life long.

AMPHITRYON (*recognizing the face, in a voice of thunder*) Sosia!

MERCURY (*brightly*)   That's right. I'm Sosia. (*Belligerently*) Think I'd forgotten it? What do you want?

AMPHITRYON (*dancing with rage*)   You good-for-nothing, you have to *ask* me what I want?

MERCURY (*belligerently*)   Sure, I'm asking. You almost banged that door off its hinges, dumbbell. You think the government supplies us with doors? What are you looking at me for, stupid? What do you want? Who are you, anyway?

AMPHITRYON (*between his teeth*)   God damn you, you'll be the death of every whip I own! Asking me who I am! I'll warm your god-damned hide for you for talking like that!

MERCURY (*sadly*)   You must have been a bad boy when you were young.

AMPHITRYON   How so?

MERCURY Because, in your old age, you're begging for a beating.

(*Roars at his own joke.*)

AMPHITRYON (*between his teeth*) I'll torture the life out of you for those words.

MERCURY (*piously*) I'm going to pray for you.

AMPHITRYON How's that?

MERCURY I'm going to pray you come to a bad end.

[At this point there was a large gap, perhaps three hundred verses, in the lost manuscript from which all our surviving copies of the *Amphitryon* derive. However, from some twenty random lines cited in ancient grammars and similar works, we can reconstruct what took place. Mercury dumps a bucket of water on Amphitryon, and the slapstick between them continues until the noise draws Alcmena out of the house; whereupon she and Amphitryon renew their quarrel. At some point Sosia enters; he had carried out Jove's orders, and has Captain Blepharo in tow. Amphitryon, of course, immediately wades into Sosia, but Jove appears on the scene, disguised as Amphitryon, and wades into *him,* accusing him of lechery and seduction. The argument between them grows hot and heavy, each claiming that he is the real thing and the other an impostor, until both agree to put the problem in Blepharo's hands: he is to test them and decide. Blepharo makes a number of attempts, gets nowhere, and, at the point where he admits defeat, the text resumes. Jove, Amphitryon, and Blepharo are on stage; we are now in Act IV.]

BLEPHARO Look—you two divide yourselves up by yourselves. I'm leaving, I've got things to do. (*Shaking his head*) I don't think I've ever seen anything as queer as all this anywhere.

AMPHITRYON (*desperately*) Blepharo, I beg you: stand by me; don't go away!

BLEPHARO (*resolutely*) Good-by! What's the good of my

standing by if I can't tell which one of you to stand by?
(*Leaves, stage right, still shaking his head.*)

JOVE (*to the audience, excitedly*)   I'm going into the house.
Alcmena's giving birth! (*Turns and rushes inside.*)

AMPHITRYON (*to the audience, watching Blepharo go off and
not noticing Jove's departure*)   Oh, my god! Now what do
I do? My friends and allies have all run out on me!
(*Grimly*) By god, he's not going to make a fool of me like
this and get away with it, whoever he is! I'm going straight
to King Creon this minute and tell him about the whole
business. I'll get even on that witch doctor who's turned
my whole household into lunatics. (*Turning to carry out his
threat and seeing no one; startled*) Where is he? By god,
I'll bet he's inside, with my wife! (*Clutching his head*) I'll
swear, not another man in all Thebes has such misery! Now
what do I do? Nobody knows who I am. Everybody plays
any joke he feels like on me. (*Wildly*) I'll break into the
house, that's what I'll do. Anyone I lay eyes on—maid or
servant, wife or seducer, my own father or grandfather—
I'll cut their throats right there in the house! All the gods
in heaven, including Jove himself, can't stop me even if
they want to. I've made up my mind and I'm going to do
it! Here I go into the house!

(*He makes a mad dash for the door but a sudden tremendous clap of thunder and blinding flash of lightning stop him
dead in his tracks; he falls flat on the ground, unconscious.*)

ACT V

(*Amphitryon is still unconscious, sprawled full length on the ground in front of his house. The thunder and lightning continue for a few moments and then gradually cease. Suddenly the door flies open, and Bromia, Alcmena's maid, her hair disheveled and her clothes in disarray, bursts out. Without noticing Amphitryon, she rushes downstage and addresses the audience.*)

SONG

BROMIA (*hysterically*)

My mind has given up the thought that I've any chance to survive,

My heart's abandoned every hope—I'll never stay alive!

It seems to me that everything—the earth, the air, the sky—

Have all conspired against my life, have willed to see me die.

The strangest things went on in the house! God knows what I should do!

(*Gasping for breath*)

Oh, god! I'm sick! Some water, please! My end is near, I'm through!

My head aches so, my hearing's gone, my vision's not what it should be.

No other woman's this miserable, no other ever *could* be!

(*Stops, gets hold of herself, and resumes much more calmly.*)

It's what Alcmena had happen to her. Once in labor, she prayed to god.

Then, bang and crash! Thunder and lightning! So sudden, so near, so hard!

The sound knocked over all of us; we fell in our tracks, struck dumb.

And then a mighty voice called out, "Alcmena, help has come!

Don't fear! A god from heaven's on hand to shed his favor
   on thee."
"And rise, all you," it said to us, "who fell through fear of
   me."
I rose, since I had fallen too. The lightning gleamed so, I
Was sure our house had caught on fire. Then I heard
   Alcmena's cry.
For a moment, horror held me fast—but fear for her won
   out.
I ran to see what she'd called me for. Amazed, I look about:
She'd given birth to twins, two boys. It was all a mystery,
A birth none saw or had foreseen.

(*Suddenly noticing Amphitryon*)

                              My god, what's this I see?
Who is the gentleman stretched out here, before our very
   door!
Some victim of Jove's thunderbolt? By Jove, he looks it, for
He's laid out there as if he's dead. I think I'd better run
And check. Perhaps I know the man.

(*Rushing up to Amphitryon and taking a look; startled*)

                              My master, Amphitryon!

(*Shouting in his ear*)

Amphitryon!

AMPHITRYON (*groaning*)
   I'm dead.

BROMIA
                  Get up!

AMPHITRYON (*as before*)
                  A corpse.

BROMIA (*reaching out and taking his hand*)
                  Here, let me have your hand.

AMPHITRYON (*feebly*)
   Who's holding me?

BROMIA
                  Your Bromia.

(*She hauls mightily and succeeds in pulling him to his feet.*)

AMPHITRYON (*holding his head, his eyes closed; dazedly*)

But *I* don't understand—
That crack from Jove has me numb with fear. I feel as if I died
And have just come back from the underworld.

(*Finally pulling out of his stupor and looking at her curiously*)

But what brings *you* outside?

BROMIA (*nervously*)

The same fear and dread gripped all of us.

(*Pointing to the door; dramatically*)

In there, the house where you dwell,
I saw such a wonder I'm still unnerved.

(*Covering her face, hysterically*)

Amphitryon, it's hell!

AMPHITRYON (*pulling her hands from her face and forcing her to look at him*)

Now answer this: am I your master? Am I Amphitryon?

BROMIA

Of course you are.

AMPHITRYON

No, look again.

BROMIA (*as before*)

Of course you're Amphitryon.

AMPHITRYON (*to the world at large, bitterly*)

The only one of my household here who's preserved her sanity.

BROMIA (*reproachfully*)

No sir, we're all completely sane.

AMPHITRYON (*as before*)

There's one exception—me.
The shameful conduct of my wife has driven *me* insane.

BROMIA (*passionately*)

But you, yourself, will admit you're wrong as soon as I explain!

(*Stops for a moment to make sure he is willing to listen, then continues gently*) Yes, you'll realize that your wife is a decent and honorable woman. It will take me only a moment to tell you some things that will prove it beyond any doubt.

(*She pauses, then begins again, observing him keenly to note the effect of her words.*) To begin with, Alcmena has just given birth to twins, two boys.

AMPHITRYON (*blankly*)   Twins, you say?

BROMIA   Twins.

AMPHITRYON (*hopelessly*)   God help me!

BROMIA (*impatiently*)   Please let me go on—I want to show you that god *is* helping both you and your wife.

AMPHITRYON   Go on.

BROMIA (*excitedly*)   When her time came, and she went into labor, your wife, as women in childbirth always do, washed her hands, covered her head, and prayed to god to help her. The next second, there was a mighty clap of thunder. At first we all thought your house would come crashing down; the lightning gleamed so, the whole place looked as though it were made of gold.

AMPHITRYON (*savagely*)   Will you kindly let me go as soon as you're through having fun with me? (*Shrugs as Bromia gestures helplessly and falls silent*) All right, what happened next?

BROMIA (*resuming excitedly*)   During all this, not one of us heard your wife utter a groan or a cry. It was a completely painless delivery.

AMPHITRYON (*grudgingly*)   Well, I'm glad to hear that—in spite of all she's done to me.

BROMIA (*impatiently*)   Forget all that and just listen to what I'm going to tell you. (*Resuming her excited narrative tone*) When it was all over, she told us to wash the babies down.

We started right in. Well, I can't tell you how big and strong the baby was that I was bathing! There wasn't one of us who could pin the diapers and clothes around him.

AMPHITRYON (*scratching his head*) This is an incredible story. If it's true, my wife certainly received a lot of help from heaven.

BROMIA (*eagerly*) Believe me, what comes next you'll say is even more incredible. (*Resuming her narrative tone*) I had just put him in his cradle when there slithered down through the skylight two serpents with crests, both of them simply enormous. The next minute, there they were, the two of them, with heads raised looking about.

AMPHITRYON (*shuddering*) Oh, my god!

BROMIA (*reassuringly*) Nothing to be afraid about. (*Resuming her narrative tone*) The serpents eyed everyone there. As soon as they spotted the children, they made a rush for them. I pulled the cradles back and steered them away; I was frightened for myself but even more afraid for the babies. The snakes followed after, fiercer than ever. Then that child, the one I had bathed, saw them. He jumped right out of his cradle, went straight for them, and, in a flash, had one gripped in each hand.

AMPHITRYON Incredible! This is a very dangerous deed you've described! Just hearing about it gives me the shudders! What then? Go on?

BROMIA The baby strangled both those serpents. And, while he was doing it, a mighty voice was heard calling to Alcmena—

AMPHITRYON (*interrupting angrily*) Who was the man?

BROMIA Man? It was the lord of men and of gods, almighty Jove! He announced that he had had intercourse with Alcmena in secret and that the child that had killed the snakes was his. (*As an afterthought*) The other, he said was yours.

(*For a full moment Amphitryon stands buried in thought.*)

AMPHITRYON (*suddenly his old vibrant self*) Well, I certainly have no cause for complaint when I'm given the chance to share my goods with Jove. Go inside and have the ritual utensils made ready for me right away. I want to pray hard and long, and beg almighty Jove for peace. And I'll call in Tiresias, the prophet, and ask what he thinks I should do. At the same time I'll tell him how this whole business happened. (*A tremendous clap of thunder is heard.*) What's that? Thunder—but so loud! (*Falling to his knees*) Oh god, help me, please!

VOICE FROM OFF STAGE (*slowly and impressively*) Take heart, Amphitryon. I am here to help you and your family. There is nothing to be afraid of. Prophets, fortune tellers—don't bother with any of them. I will tell you both the future and the past much better than they, for I am Jove.

To begin with, I borrowed your Alcmena's body, slept with her, and conceived a son by her. You too conceived a son, when you left to go to the front. She has brought forth both together, in one birth. The one sprung from my seed will do deeds that will make your name great forever. Go back now to Alcmena and live with her in the harmony you two have always known. She deserves no reproaches; *I* forced her to do what she did. And now I must return to the heavens.

AMPHITRYON I'll do as you command—but I beg you: don't forget your promises. I'll go inside now to my wife, and I won't bother with Tiresias. (*He rises from his knees, walks downstage and addresses the audience.*) And now, ladies and gentlemen, for Jove's sake, a good loud round of applause!

THE POT OF GOLD

DRAMATIS PERSONAE

EUCLIO, *an elderly gentleman, not very well off, father of Phaedria*

GRAPE (STAPHYLA), *his aged housekeeper (slave)*

EUNOMIA, *an elderly, well-to-do lady, sister of Megadorus and mother of Lyconides*

MEGADORUS, *an elderly, well-to-do gentleman, brother of Eunomia and uncle of Lyconides*

STROBILUS, *his servant (slave)*

EEL (CONGRIO), *a cook (slave)*

CHARCOAL (ANTHRAX), *a cook (slave)*

PYTHODICUS, *a servant belonging to Megadorus' household (slave)*

STROBILUS, *servant of Lyconides*

LYCONIDES, *a young man about town, son of Eunomia and nephew of Megadorus*

[PHRYGIA, *a piper (slave)*]

[ELEUSIUM, *a piper (slave)*]

[PHAEDRIA, *a lovely young girl, daughter of Euclio*]

SERVANTS

SCENE

A street in Athens. Three buildings front on it: the house of Euclio, the house of Megadorus, and the Temple of Trust; the last has an altar in front of it. The exit on stage left leads downtown, that on stage right to the country.

PROLOGUE

(*The door of Euclio's house opens, and a wraithlike little figure flutters out and proceeds downstage to deliver the prologue.*)

SPIRIT OF EUCLIO'S HOUSE In case you're wondering who I am, I'll take a second to explain. (*Gesturing toward Euclio's door*) This house you just saw me come out of—well, I'm the special spirit assigned to the family there. I've been living in the house for years; I took care of it for the grandfather and the father of the man who lives there now.

Now, the grandfather enlisted my help and, without letting a soul know, put in my charge a treasure of gold; he buried it in the middle of the fireplace and begged me to watch over it for him. To his dying day he didn't want his son to know about it; he had such a miserly soul he preferred to leave the poor man a pauper rather than show him where this money was. All he left was some farmland, not very much at that, and, with a lot of hard work, his son managed to make a miserable living out of it.

When he died—I mean the one who put the gold in my charge—I began watching to see whether the son would show more respect for me than his father had. But he took less and less notice of me as time went on, and paid me less and less respect. (*Grinning*) So I returned the favor—and he died too.

He left behind a son, the man living here now, who's the same sort as his father and grandfather. However, he has an only daughter who never fails, every day of the year, to offer me incense, wine, or the like, and set out fresh flowers for me. To repay her for this high regard, I saw to it that Euclio discovered the money. I did it to make it easier for him to get her married if he wanted to.

You see, a boy from one of the best families has seduced her. The boy knows who the girl he seduced is, but she doesn't know who her seducer was—and her father doesn't know she's been seduced!

(*Leaning forward and speaking confidentially*) Today I'll arrange to have (*gesturing towards Megadorus' house*) this old fellow next door ask to marry her. I have a special reason for doing this: (*nodding knowingly*) it's going to make it easier for her seducer to marry her. Now, the old fellow who'll ask for her hand is the uncle of the boy who did her wrong. It all happened in the dark during the all-night festival for Lady Ceres. (*Suddenly angry shouting is heard from inside Euclio's house.*) There's the old man hollering his head off as usual. He's throwing the old hag out of the house so she won't find out his secret. I think he wants to take a look at his gold to make sure it hasn't been stolen.

ACT I

(The shouts from inside grow louder. A second later, the door flies open, and an old woman bursts out with an old man at her heels. As they do, the Spirit slips unobserved back into the house.

The old woman is Grape [Staphyla, literally "grape cluster," presumably so-called because of a weakness for the jug], a wretched old hag who is Euclio's only servant. The old man is Euclio, "good reputation." He is dressed in the simple, threadbare clothes of a poor man. At the moment he is in a rage, but this is the result of an emotional state not something innate in his character; under normal circumstances he is no more irascible than any other poor man.)

EUCLIO *(roaring)* Out! Out, I say! God damn it, I want you out of here, you pry-eyed spy in petticoats, you!

GRAPE *(whining)* What are you beating up a poor old woman like me for?

EUCLIO *(savagely)* To keep you a poor old woman. And to make a worthless slut live the way a worthless slut should.

GRAPE *(helplessly)* But why throw me out of the house now?

EUCLIO So, you damned slut, I'm supposed to give you reasons, am I? *(Pointing to a spot well away from the house)* Over there, away from the door! OVER THERE! *(Impatiently, as the old woman hobbles along)* Look at her dawdle! Do you know what's going to happen to you? I swear to god, if I get a club or a whip in my hands, I'll put some speed in that snail's pace of yours!

GRAPE *(to herself, bitterly)* I wish to god I could be sent to the gallows! Better than slaving for you and having to live like this.

EUCLIO *(to himself, snarling)* Aha! The sneak's whispering secrets to herself. *(To Grape)* So help me I'll gouge the eyes out of your head—that'll keep you from spying on

what I'm doing! (*As Grape stops*) Keep moving! Farther.
Still farther. Whoa—stand there. If you budge the width of
my little finger from that spot, or turn around, until I tell
you to, by god I'll send you to the hangman to learn how
to behave. (*To the audience, nervously*) I swear, never in
all my life have I laid eyes on a worse old hag than this
one. I'm scared stiff of her—she might trap me with some
trick when I'm not on my guard and find out where the
money's hidden. She's got eyes in the back of her head,
damn her. I'll go in now and check whether the money's
where I hid it. (*Tearing his hair*) My god, my god, the
worry that money gives me! (*Goes into the house.*)

GRAPE (*to the audience, shaking her head in perplexity*) My
goodness, I don't know what I can say to explain the terrible
thing that's happened to Euclio, what kind of madness this
is. Imagine—throwing a poor woman out of the house this
way ten times a day! I simply can't understand what this
lunacy is that's come over him. All night long he doesn't
close his eyes, and then, when dawn comes, all day long
he sits in the house like a crippled shoemaker.

   (*Pauses for a second, then throws her arms wide in
desperation.*) And I really don't know what I can do now
to hide his daughter's disgrace—the time for her to have
her baby is getting very near. (*Heaving a sigh*) If you
ask me, the best thing I can do is put a rope around my
neck and hang myself till I become one long, limp capital I!

(*She stops suddenly as the door flies open and Euclio
steps out again. It is immediately apparent that his state of
mind is much improved.*)

EUCLIO (*to the audience*) Finally I can leave the house with
my mind at ease. I've had a look, and everything inside is
safe. (*To Grape*) Go back in the house now and keep an
eye on things inside.

GRAPE (*with heavy sarcasm*) Oh, sure. I'm to keep an eye
on things inside, am I? So nobody will walk off with the
house, I suppose. Because there's nothing else there that

would do a thief any good—all we've got is plenty of nothing and spider webs.

EUCLIO (*with equal sarcasm*) I'm surprised the good lord
doesn't turn me into the Shah of Persia or Alexander the
Great just for your benefit, you old bitch. (*Roaring*) I
want you to keep an eye on those spider webs for me!

(*Glares at her a moment and then resumes more calmly*)
I'm a poor man. I admit it, I put up with it. What god
gives, I bear. Now go inside and keep the door shut; I'll be
back soon. Watch out that you don't let any strangers in
the house. And I want you to put out the fire: someone
may want a light, and I don't want to give them any excuse
to ask you for it. (*Grimly*) If I see that fire still alive, I'll
put out *you*, and fast. If anyone asks for water, tell him
our bucket ran away. Knife, ax, pestle, mortar, the things
neighbors are always asking to borrow—say we had a robbery and everything was stolen. I absolutely forbid a single
soul to be allowed in my house while I'm away. I'm warning you—if Lady Luck herself comes to the door, you're not
to let her in.

GRAPE (*muttering*) If you ask me, she'll take good care not
to come, on her own. She's never visited *our* house, even
when she's been in the neighborhood.

EUCLIO Shut up and go in.

GRAPE (*promptly*) I'm shutting up and going in. (*She goes
inside.*)

EUCLIO (*calling after her*) Shut the door tight and double-
lock it. I'll be back soon.

(*Turning to the audience*) It's sheer torture to leave the
house. Believe me, I hate to go off. But I know what I'm
doing. You see, our ward leader announced that a cash
bonus of ten dollars a man was going to be distributed. If
I pass mine up and don't claim it, I have the feeling everybody will immediately suspect I have money in the house.
Ten dollars isn't much, but people don't expect a poor man
to turn up his nose at it and not bother to collect it. (*Shaking his head worriedly*) As it is, in spite of all I do to keep

everybody from knowing, everybody seems to know. Everybody gives me a much more friendly hello than they used to. They come to me, stop, shake my hand, ask me about my health, what I'm doing, how things are going . . . (*Stands in preoccupied silence for a moment. Then, rousing himself*) Well, I'll be on my way. Afterwards, I'll get myself back home just as fast as I can!

(*He leaves, stage left, and the stage is now empty.*)

ACT II

(Enter Eunomia and Megadorus from Megadorus' house. Megadorus, "big giver," is a pleasant old gentleman, dressed expensively and in good taste, who gives an unmistakable impression of honesty and decency. Eunomia, "proper rules," his older sister, is a proper, serious Athenian matron.)

SONG

EUNOMIA

I do hope, my brother, you'll feel that what I say
To you, I'm saying as a sister should—
My words are from the heart and for your good.
And I don't deceive myself one bit: I know
The name we women have for making trouble.
We're all considered chatterboxes, and
It's true. There's never been, so men impute,
A single case on record of a female mute.
Despite this, brother, keep one thing in mind,
That you are my nearest of kin and I am yours.
And so it's only right for both of us
To think about and advise—I you, you me—
Whatever we feel is best for each other's good,
And not to keep this back or be afraid
To say it. You should share your thoughts with me,
And I no less should share all mine with you.
That's why just now I sneaked you out of doors—
To discuss an important personal matter of yours.

MEGADORUS *(smiling broadly and reaching out his hand)*

My good woman, come here. I want to shake your hand.

EUNOMIA *(with a great show of looking puzzled)*

Where is she? Who *is* this good woman. I don't understand.

MEGADORUS

It's you.

EUNOMIA (*as before*)
> Who, me?

MEGADORUS (*gallantly—but with a mischievous gleam in his eye*)
> > Don't say I'm wrong because
> I'll say that *you're* wrong.

EUNOMIA (*playfully*)
> > Ah, don't break the laws
> Of truth. You see, you can't pick out, dear brother,
> A woman who's good. Each one is worse than the
> other.

MEGADORUS (*nodding vigorously*)
> Rest assured, I'll never contest the point. I agree!

EUNOMIA (*darting a sharp look at him but, reassured by his deadpan serenity, getting down to business*)
> Your attention, please.

MEGADORUS (*promptly*)
> > It's all yours. Just order me,
> And whatever you want, you count on it, I'll do.

EUNOMIA
> There's something that I consider best for you,
> And to talk you into it, is why I'm here.

MEGADORUS (*dryly*)
> You're always doing this for me, my dear.

EUNOMIA (*smugly*)
> I think I should.

MEGADORUS
> > What is it?

EUNOMIA (*enthusiastically*)
> > To guarantee
> A life of joy and raise a family—

MEGADORUS (*interrupting, fervently*)
> God grant it all!

EUNOMIA (*ignoring the interruption*)
> > —I'd like to see
> You take a wife.

MEGADORUS (*clapping a hand to his brow, roaring*)
                    You've murdered me!

EUNOMIA (*alarmed*)
            What's happened?

MEGADORUS
                        You just bashed in my head!
            Those words you said were heavy as lead!

EUNOMIA (*as if addressing a schoolboy*)
            Come, do as sister says.

MEGADORUS
                        You'd like me to?
        All right.

EUNOMIA (*earnestly*)
                I'm sure it's just the thing for you.

MEGADORUS
            And I'd prefer committing suicide.
            Any girl you care to pick I'll make my bride
            Upon these terms: she comes tomorrow for the
                marriage;
            Next day she leaves in the undertaker's carriage.
            With this condition, I'll take the girl you say.
            Let's have her, and you name the wedding day.

EUNOMIA (*blithely ignoring her brother's remonstrances,
thoughtfully*)
            I can give you one whose dowry's huge, but then
            She's rather old, she'll never see fifty again.

        (*Brightly*)
            But if you say to go and ask her for you,
            I assure you, brother, I'm perfectly willing to.

MEGADORUS (*patiently*) Do you mind if I ask you a question?

EUNOMIA (*as before*) Not at all! Ask any you want.

MEGADORUS Let's say a man past middle age takes a middle-
aged wife, and, by some luck, the old gentleman gets the
old girl pregnant. Don't you agree that there's a perfect

name all ready for their offspring—Postumus?[1] (*Stops to observe the reaction and, there being none, continues.*) Now, my sister, I'm going to spare you a lot of this trouble you're going to. Thanks to heaven and the family fortune, I have money enough. I don't need your high and mighty ladies with their big dowries, their shouting, ordering, fancy carriages, silks and satins. They simply spend a husband into slavery.

EUNOMIA (*stiffly*)   Then would you please tell me who it is you would like to marry?

MEGADORUS (*looking her straight in the eye*)   All right, I will. Do you know old Euclio? The neighbor next door, who's not very well off?

EUNOMIA   I do. And a very nice man too, I must say.

MEGADORUS (*as before*)   I'd like to make his daughter my wife. (*As Eunomia opens her mouth*) Not a word! I know what you're going to say: she's a pauper. Well, this particular pauper pleases me.

EUNOMIA (*shrugging*)   God bless the marriage.

MEGADORUS (*cheerfully*)   Just what I hope.

EUNOMIA (*having lost interest*)   I must be off now.

MEGADORUS   Good-by.

EUNOMIA   Good-by. (*Exit, stage left.*)

MEGADORUS (*to himself*)   I'll have a talk with Euclio, if he's home. (*Turns and happens to look toward the wings, stage left.*) Ah, there he is. Must be on his way back from someplace.

(*Enter Euclio stomping along in a foul temper.*)

EUCLIO (*muttering to himself*)   I had the feeling I was going for nothing when I left the house; that's why I hated to go. (*Bitterly*) Not one of the members of the ward council showed up, and neither did the leader, who was supposed

---

[1] A name commonly given to a son born after the father has died.

to distribute the bonus. Now I'm in a hurry to hurry home
—my head's here but my heart's in the house.

MEGADORUS (*effusively*)   Well, Euclio! The very best wishes
to you, my friend!

EUCLIO (*looking up in surprise, warily*)   The very best to
you too, Megadorus.

MEGADORUS (*solicitously*)   Tell me, how're you feeling? All
right? As well as you'd like?

EUCLIO (*to the audience, worried*)   When a rich man's so
nice to somebody poor, there's something behind it. That
fellow knows I've got gold; that's the reason for these extra-
nice greetings I'm getting.

MEGADORUS (*as before*)   You say you're feeling well?

EUCLIO (*looking woebegone*)   When it comes to money, not
well at all, believe me.

MEGADORUS (*heartily*)   Well, if your mind's at peace, you've
got all you need to enjoy life.

EUCLIO (*to the audience, agonized*)   I'll swear the old hag's
tipped him off about the gold! Absolutely no doubt about
it! (*Between his teeth*) Wait till I get back inside! I'll cut
her tongue off and gouge her eyes out!

MEGADORUS (*puzzled*)   What are you talking to yourself
about?

EUCLIO (*quickly resuming his woebegone expression*)   Just
complaining about how poor I am. Here I am with a
grown daughter who hasn't a dime to her dowry and can
never get married. Who could I possibly marry her off to?

MEGADORUS (*clapping him on the back*)   Don't say such
things! Cheer up, Euclio! There'll be a dowry; I'll help you
out. Whatever you need, just say the word. Give me your
orders.

EUCLIO (*to the audience, with a crafty look*)   Promising to
give—which means he's out to get; he's got his mouth
agape to gulp my gold. While one hand holds out a piece
of bread, the other hides a stick. Any rich man who's so

nice and generous to somebody poor, I just don't trust.
He puts out a helping hand—and it leaves a trail of damage.
I know these octopuses. Whatever they touch, they take.

MEGADORUS (*gravely*) Euclio, give me a minute of your
time. There's something I'd like to discuss with you—won't
take long—which should be a good thing for both of us.

EUCLIO (*to the audience, frantically*) Oh my god, I'm done
for! My gold's been snitched! And now he wants to make
a deal with me, I know it! I've got to take a look in the
house. (*Whirls about and heads for his door.*)

MEGADORUS (*calling after him in surprise*) Where are you
going?

EUCLIO (*over his shoulder*) Be right back—something I've
got to see in the house. (*He disappears inside.*)

MEGADORUS (*to himself, worriedly*) Damn, I'm afraid that
the minute I mention marrying his daughter, he'll think
I'm playing a joke on him. Poverty's made him the stingi-
est man alive, bar none.

(*The door opens, and Euclio emerges in a considerably
better frame of mind than he had been in a moment before.*)

EUCLIO (*to the audience*) The good lord's watching over
me: it's safe. By safe I only mean it isn't gone. (*Shaking
his head*) That was a bad scare I had. I almost died before
I got back in the house. (*To Megadorus*) Back again,
Megadorus. Now, do you want me for anything?

MEGADORUS Thank you. (*Gravely*) I hope you don't mind
answering some questions I'd like to ask you.

EUCLIO (*darting a sharp glance at him*) No—providing you
don't ask anything I mind answering.

MEGADORUS Tell me, what's your opinion of my family
background?

EUCLIO Good.

MEGADORUS Of my integrity?

EUCLIO Good.

MEGADORUS   My conduct?

EUCLIO   Not bad. Not dishonest.

MEGADORUS   And you know how old I am.

EUCLIO   Yes. *And* how rich.

MEGADORUS   (*enthusiastically*)   Now, I consider you a fine, upstanding member of the community, and always have.

EUCLIO   (*to the audience, in consternation*)   He's sniffed my gold! (*To Megadorus, coldly*) Just what is it you want from me?

MEGADORUS   You know the kind of man I am, and I know the kind you are. With that clear, I'm asking you for the hand of your daughter—and, god willing, it will mean happiness for me, you, and her. (*Earnestly*) Promise me you'll do it!

EUCLIO   (*bitingly*)   Look here, Megadorus. This conduct does no credit to the way you've conducted yourself in the past. Making fun of a poor old man who's never done any harm to you or your family! I never did, I never said one thing to justify doing to me what you're doing to me now.

MEGADORUS   (*helplessly*)   Good god! I'm not here to make fun of you, and I'm *not* making fun of you. I wouldn't think of such a thing!

EUCLIO   (*suspiciously*)   Then why are you asking to marry my daughter?

MEGADORUS   (*earnestly*)   So you can be better off because of me, and I because of you and your daughter.

EUCLIO   (*coldly*)   Here's something that occurs to me, Megadorus. You're a rich man, one of the upper crust, and I'm poor, poor as they come. Suppose I let you marry my daughter. It occurs to me that we'd be like a bull and a donkey and, when donkey Euclio is hitched up with bull Megadorus and can't pull his share of the load, donkey Euclio is going to go down in the mud, and bull Megadorus is not going to bother looking back; he's going to act as if the donkey never was. I'll find out that you're not going to treat me as an equal, while my own class is going to laugh

at me. And, should there be a divorce, things really will be
unstable—I won't have a stable in either camp: the donkeys
are going to maul me with their teeth and the bulls gore
me with their horns. It's a risky business, this moving up
from the donkeys to the bulls.

MEGADORUS (*earnestly*) Why, the very best thing you could
possibly do is be connected with, and as closely as you can,
the right kind of people. Listen to me—accept my offer, let
me have her.

EUCLIO (*hastily*) But I can't give you a dowry.

MEGADORUS Don't! Let her come with a fine character, and
she'll have dowry enough.

EUCLIO I just brought it up so you wouldn't get the idea
(*forcing a laugh*) I suddenly found a buried treasure.

MEGADORUS (*smiling*) I know, you don't have to tell me.
Just say yes.

EUCLIO Yes. (*Suddenly hearing a clink*) Oh my god in
heaven, is this to be the end of me?

MEGADORUS (*puzzled*) What's the matter with you?

EUCLIO Wasn't there a sound like a shovel just then?
(*Whirls about and dashes into his house.*)

MEGADORUS (*turning to point toward his own house*) It's
from my garden. I gave orders to do some digging there.
(*Turning back and seeing no Euclio, to himself*) Hey,
where *is* the man? Off he goes without letting me know
where I stand! (*Sadly*) He sees I want to be his friend, so
he turns up his nose at me. He's doing just what they all do.
When somebody rich tries to make friends with somebody
poor, the poor man's always afraid to get involved. And his
fears make him lose out because, invariably, after he's
passed up the chance and it's too late, he gets second
thoughts.

(*The door opens, and Euclio comes out again. He turns to
talk to Grape inside.*)

EUCLIO (*through the doorway, snarling*) So help me, if I

don't have that tongue of yours torn out by the roots, I hereby give you full permission to arrange with anyone you want to have me castrated! (*Turns and walks back to Megadorus.*)

MEGADORUS (*angrily*)   It's damned clear to me that, in spite of my gray hairs, and for no good reason at all, you consider me an ideal subject to play games with.

EUCLIO (*hastily*)   Believe me, Megadorus, I'm not playing games. (*Aside, bitterly*)   Not much chance, even if I wanted to!

MEGADORUS (*impatiently*)   Well, what do you say? Do I get to marry your daughter?

EUCLIO   With the understanding she gets the amount of dowry I mentioned.

MEGADORUS (*nodding vigorous assent*)   Then you're giving me your solemn word?

EUCLIO   I'm giving you my solemn word.

MEGADORUS (*beaming*)   God bless us all!

EUCLIO   Amen. (*Sharply*)   Be sure you don't forget our agreement: you don't get a penny of dowry with my daughter.

MEGADORUS   I haven't forgotten.

EUCLIO (*sneering*)   I'm wise to the way you and your kind can mix a man up: it's on, it's off; it's off, it's on—just the way *you* want it.

MEGADORUS (*firmly*)   You'll have no cause to get into any arguments with me. Now, about the wedding. Is there any reason why we shouldn't hold it today?

EUCLIO   None at all. That would be perfect.

MEGADORUS (*promptly*)   Then I'll go and get things ready. Don't need me for anything, do you?

EUCLIO (*promptly*)   Nothing except what you're doing. Run along. Good-by.

MEGADORUS (*rushing to the door of his house and calling*

through the doorway)   Hey, Strobilus! Hurry and follow me to the market. On the double!

(*A slave comes dashing out of the house, and the two race off, stage left.*)

EUCLIO (*to the audience*)   There he goes. Lord in heaven! I tell you, money sure is strong stuff! I'm convinced he's heard I have a fortune in the house and is drooling at the mouth to get at it. That's why he's so set on joining the family. (*Walking to his door and calling through the doorway*) Where's the old hag who's been babbling to all the neighbors that I'm going to give my daughter a dowry? (*Roaring*) Grape! I'm calling you! Are you deaf? (*As she appears at the doorway*) Hurry and wash that handful of dishware we have. I've arranged for my daughter's marriage. I promised her to Megadorus, and the wedding's to be today.

GRAPE   God bless them both! (*Suddenly dismayed*) But it can't be today! That's too soon!

EUCLIO   Shut up and go inside. Make sure everything's taken care of by the time I get back from downtown. And keep the door shut! I'll be back soon. (*Rushes off, stage left.*)

GRAPE (*to the audience, in consternation*)   Now what do I do? This is the end of both of us, me *and* the young mistress! It won't be long before the whole world knows that his daughter's disgraced, that she's going to have a baby. We kept it a deep, dark secret up to now, but we can't any longer. I'll go in now so I'll have all his orders done by the time he gets back. (*Shaking her head ruefully*) I'm scared to death I'll be drinking a double dose of trouble—whip and woe in one!

(*Grape goes into the house. A moment later there enters, stage left, a good-sized retinue: at the head is Megadorus' servant Strobilus, "twister," followed by two cooks, Charcoal [Anthrax] and Eel [Congrio, from conger, "conger eel"], two pipers, and a flock of scullions loaded down with food for the wedding banquet.*)

STROBILUS (*to the assemblage*) After my master finished with the shopping and with hiring you cooks and pipers downtown, his orders to me were to divide everything he had gotten into two.

CHARCOAL Damn it all, you're not going (*making an obscene gesture*) to split me, I tell you that right now. If you want all of me to go somewhere, all right.

EEL (*caustically*) So demure and bashful, this little whore! All anyone has to do is ask you; you're always ready and willing (*repeating the gesture*) to do a split.

STROBILUS (*to Charcoal*) I didn't mean what you're insinuating, Charcoal. The master's having a wedding today—

CHARCOAL (*interrupting*) Whose daughter is he marrying?

STROBILUS (*gesturing toward Euclio's house*) Our next door neighbor, Euclio's. And Euclio's to get half of what was bought, plus one of you cooks and one of the pipers. Master's orders.

CHARCOAL As I get it then, (*pointing to Euclio's house*) half to his house, (*pointing to Megadorus'*) and half to his.

STROBILUS As I get it, you're absolutely right.

CHARCOAL (*gesturing toward Euclio's house*) What's the matter? Can't the old man there pay for his daughter's wedding out of his own pocket?

STROBILUS (*snorting*) Pah!

CHARCOAL What's that mean?

STROBILUS You have to ask? Flint is fluff compared with that old boy!

CHARCOAL You don't say?

EEL You mean that?

STROBILUS Just imagine . . . [a line is lost here] . . . he thinks he's ruined, wiped out. If a puff of smoke comes out of that shack of his, the next minute he's hollering to high heaven. Do you know, when he goes to bed he ties a bag over his mouth!

CHARCOAL   What for?

STROBILUS   So he won't lose any breath while he sleeps.

CHARCOAL (*scornfully*)   Sure, and I suppose he plugs up the pipe at his lower end so he won't lose any wind while he sleeps.

STROBILUS (*offended*)   You believe me, and I'll believe you. That's what I believe is only fair.

CHARCOAL (*hastily*)   Oh no, I believe you.

STROBILUS   Do you know something else? After he washes, it breaks his heart to throw away the water.

CHARCOAL (*grinning*)   You think we can talk the old boy out of fifteen thousand dollars to set us all free?

STROBILUS   He wouldn't even stake you to the chance to starve if you asked him for it. Do you know, the other day when he had his nails manicured at the barber's, he collected all the clippings and took them home with him!

CHARCOAL (*wonderingly*)   Boy, oh boy, this is one stingy man you're talking about!

STROBILUS   Can you imagine a person being that miserly and living that miserably? The other day a buzzard made off with his helping of dinner. He bawled like a baby, went to the judge, and, crying his heart out, asked whether he couldn't have the bird subpoenaed. Oh, I could give you hundreds of stories, if I had the time. (*Getting down to business and looking from Charcoal to Eel*) Now, which of you two is faster? Tell me.

CHARCOAL (*promptly*)   I am. (*Going through a practiced gesture of slipping something into his pocket*) And lots better, too.

STROBILUS (*eying him distastefully*)   I'm talking about a cook, not a crook.

CHARCOAL (*innocently*)   That's what I mean, a cook.

STROBILUS (*to Eel*)   What about you?

EEL (*drawing himself up, importantly*)   See for yourself.

CHARCOAL (*contemptuously*) He's a Sunday cook—it's the only day of the week he gets work.

EEL (*to Charcoal*) Look who's making nasty cracks about *me!* A man who needs only five letters to spell his name— C-R-O-O-K!

CHARCOAL Aah, you're one yourself. A lousy crook!

STROBILUS (*shouting*) Shut up! (*To Charcoal*) Now pick whichever of these two lambs is fatter and take it into my house.

CHARCOAL All right.

STROBILUS (*to Eel*) Eel, take the other one and (*pointing to Euclio's door*) go to that house. (*To one half of the assistants*) You follow him. (*To the others*) The rest of you over there to my house. (*Charcoal leads them into Megadorus' house.*)

EEL (*hollering*) Hey, this division is unfair! Their lamb is fatter!

STROBILUS (*promptly*) But you're getting a fatter piper. (*To one of the pipers*) Phrygia! (*Pointing to Eel*) Follow him. (*To the other*) Eleusium, you go over there into my house. (*Eleusium follows the others into Megadorus' house.*)

EEL (*angrily*) Pretty canny, Strobilus—shoving me off over here with the old skinflint! If I need anything, I'll have to ask till I get hoarse before he'll give it to me.

STROBILUS (*contemptuously*) Stupid! (*Shaking his head in exasperation*) What's the good of doing *you* a good turn? Just a waste of effort!

EEL (*weakly*) A good turn? How?

STROBILUS What a question! In the first place, in the house you're going to, there'll be no fuss and bother around you. Next, if you need anything, you won't waste your breath asking for it, you'll just go get it from home. Over here there's a big household and lots of fuss and bother. Plus furniture, silverware, money, clothes. Over here, if anything disappears—and remember, it's easy to keep hands off where there's nothing to put them on—the next minute they're all hollering (*mimicking*), "The cooks stole it! Arrest 'em, whip 'em, tie 'em up, throw 'em in jail!" None of this is going to happen to you because there's going to be nothing you can make off with. This way. Follow me.

EEL Coming.

(*Strobilus, followed by Eel and the rest of the retinue, walks up to Euclio's door and knocks.*)

STROBILUS (*shouting*) Hey, Grape! Come to the door and open up!

GRAPE (*from inside*) Who is it?

STROBILUS (*shouting*) Strobilus.

GRAPE (*opening the door*) What do you want?

STROBILUS Take these cooks, this piper, and this stuff we bought for the wedding banquet. Megadorus left orders to deliver it all to Euclio.

GRAPE (*eying the bundles; sourly*) You planning to hold a wedding for a water nymph?

STROBILUS Why?

GRAPE I see you haven't brought a drop to drink.

STROBILUS (*reassuringly*) It's coming later, when Megadorus gets back from downtown.

GRAPE (*to Eel, sourly*) We don't have any firewood.

EEL You have rafters, don't you?

GRAPE Of course we have rafters.

EEL Then we have firewood. Don't bother going out to look.

GRAPE (*shrieking*) You filthy good-for-nothing! *You* may be a fire worshiper, but don't ask *us* to burn our house down just to let you cook a dinner and collect a salary!

EEL (*backing down*) I'm not asking you to.

STROBILUS Take them all inside.

GRAPE Follow me.

(*Eel and his party follow Grape into Euclio's house while Strobilus goes into Megadorus' house.*

A moment later, one of Megadorus' household slaves comes out of the door. He turns and talks to the others inside. [This servant, named Pythodicus in the manuscripts, does not reappear. Very likely his whole speech was not written by Plautus but, after his death, was added by some actor or editor.])

SERVANT (*through the doorway*)   Take care of it. I'll go see what the cooks are doing. (*Walking downstage and addressing the audience, grumbling*) That's my biggest headache today, keeping an eye on those cooks. The only other thing I could do is have them make dinner in a dungeon. When it was done we could haul it up in baskets. Then, if they eat up everything they cooked down there, (*grinning*) the lords of hell would be having a feast and those above a famine. But look at me standing around and talking as if I had nothing to do, when we've got all those damned sons of vultures in the house!

(*He turns and rushes back into Megadorus' house. A moment later Euclio stomps in, stage left.*)

EUCLIO (*to the audience*)   In order to do the right thing by my daughter at her wedding, I was willing to take my life in my hands—I went to the market. I asked the price of fish. Dear. Lamb? Dear. Beef? Dear. Veal, tuna, pork? All of them dear. And my having no money made everything even dearer! I left the place hopping mad since I couldn't buy a thing—but I had my fun with that filthy pack of peddlers, I did!

On the way home I began to think things over: splurge on the holidays, I figure, and it's scrimp or go without on the weekdays. I announced this line of reasoning to my belly and heart, and my mind came around to my way of thinking: to marry off my daughter at minimum expense. (*Holding out a tiny packet and some sad-looking garlands*) So I bought this pinch of incense and these garlands; I'll put them in the fireplace for the Spirit of the House and get his blessing on my daughter's union. (*Turning to go into the house)* What's this I see? The door open? And listen to the racket coming from inside! Oh, my god, is this a robbery?

EEL *(from inside)*   Go next door and ask if they've got a bigger pot. This one's small, it doesn't hold enough.

EUCLIO *(to the audience, agonized)*   God in heaven, I'm done for! They're making off with my gold, and they need a bigger pot! *(Raising his eyes to heaven, fervently)* Apollo! I beg you, save me! Help! If you've ever come to the rescue at a time like this, do it now! Shoot your arrows at these crooks—they're treasury thieves![2] *(Clapping a hand to his brow)* What am I waiting here for? Why don't I run in before I'm completely ruined!

(Euclio charges into his house. A moment later Charcoal emerges from Megadorus' house. He turns to speak to his assistants inside.)

CHARCOAL *(through the doorway)*   Sprinter, clean the fish. Cutter, fillet the eels, and make it snappy! I'm going next door to borrow a baking pan from Eel. And, if you're smart, you'll have that chicken plucked smoother than a ballet dancer. *(Starts to go toward Euclio's house when a hullabaloo is suddenly heard coming from it. To himself)* What's all the noise next door? *(Shrugging)* Must be the cooks carrying on the vocal part of their job. I'll run back inside to make sure *we* don't have a ruckus like that.

(Charcoal goes back into Megadorus' house, and the stage is now empty.)

[2] Apollo would theoretically have a fellow sufferer's sympathy: his temples were used as treasuries and were often the targets of plunderers and thieves.

ACT III

(*The din in Euclio's house grows louder and louder. Suddenly the door flies open and Eel, clutching his carving knife, bursts out, followed by his crew, all traveling at top speed.*)

SONG

EEL (*to the world at large*)

Hey, citizens, aliens, women, children, men, hey all of you!

Get off the streets and leave them clear—make way, I'm coming through!

First time I've worked as madhouse cook, and catered to lunatics!

My god, the way they went for us, and beat us up with sticks!

The old boy made me his punching bag, I ache all over, I'm dead.

No wood? There's more in there than any place else, the supply's unlimited!

He laid on us all the wood he could before he sent us out!

(*The door opens, and Euclio appears brandishing a stick.*)

My god, I'm lost! The door's just opened—that lunatic's about!

(*As Euclio spots him and charges*)

He's after me! But I've worked out just what I have to do—

He's taught me the lesson himself, he has: he's running, so I run too!

(*The two race around the stage at top speed.*)

EUCLIO (*screaming*)

Come back! Hey, where are you running? Stop him!

EEL

Dumbbell! Why this shouting?

(*They come to a halt and glare at each other.*)

EUCLIO (*grimly*)

I'm going to give the police your name.

EEL

> And why?

EUCLIO (*pointing*)

> That knife you're flouting.

EEL (*helplessly*)
But I'm a cook!

EUCLIO (*darkly*)

> You threatened me—now tell me why you did it.

EEL (*eying his knife and shaking his head regretfully*)
I'm afraid I goofed. Between your ribs is where I should
have hid it.

EUCLIO (*snarling*)
You're a dirty crook, that's what you are, beyond all human
measure.

There's no one I'd rather do more harm, or do it with
greater pleasure.

EEL (*ruefully*)
No need to tell me, the case is clear—just witness my condition.

With my broken bones, a contortionist couldn't give me
competition.

(*Drawing himself up*)

How dare a beggar like you touch me?

EUCLIO (*sneering*)

> He asks how dare I do it!

(*Brandishing the stick*)

Perhaps you mean I stopped too soon, and you want me to
pursue it?

EEL (*brandishing the knife*)
Lay off, or, I swear, you'll pay for it, while I'm alive and
kicking.

EUCLIO (*caressing his club and grinning malevolently*)
The future I'll not answer for, but right now you sure are
kicking!

(*Sternly*)

While I was away you entered my house without asking
my permission.

What *were* you doing? I want to know!

EEL (*wearily*)

You can stop the inquisition.

We came to cook for the wedding feast.

EUCLIO (*sneering*)

What the hell do *you* care, mister,

If the food I eat is raw or cooked? Since when are you big
sister?

EEL (*as before*)

I want an answer, yes or no: will you let us do our cooking?

EUCLIO

I want an answer: about my things—will they be safe? No
crooking?

EEL (*fervently*)

Just let me get home with the things I brought. I like
them, yours don't attract me.

EUCLIO (*with ponderous irony*)

Oh sure. I know. Don't mention it.

EEL (*puzzled*)

What's the reason you attacked me

So we couldn't cook the dinner inside? Was it something we
did or said there

That wasn't exactly what you wished?

EUCLIO (*exploding*)

You ask, after poking that head there

Into every corner of my house. Your job was by the fire.

You weren't there, so I split your skull; you deserve what
you got, you liar!

And now's the time to make things clear, so you know
what's my position:

You take a single step toward this door without express
permission,

And I make you the saddest man alive. So now you know
  my feeling.

(*Euclio about-faces and starts stalking off toward his
house.*)

EEL (*calling after him, agonized*)

Hey, where are you going? Come back! COME BACK! I
  swear, by our Lady of Stealing,
You hand me back my pots and pans, or a spectacle com-
  mences:
I stand out here and howl and yowl till I drive you out of
  your senses.

(*Euclio storms into the house and slams the door.*)

Now what? My god, what lousy luck that I ever went
  through that door—
My pay for today is just five dollars; my doctor bills will be
  more!

(*A moment later the door opens again, and Euclio comes
out. His arm is pressed to his side to hold a pot hidden under
his coat.*)

EUCLIO (*to the audience*)   So help me, from now on this
  stays with me, I take it wherever I go. I'm not leaving it
  in such mortal danger ever again! (*To Eel and his party*)
  Hey, cooks, pipers, all of you! You can go in now. (*To
  Eel*) Take that gang of slaveys in now, if you want. Go
  ahead—cook, work, run around. Anything you want.

EEL (*glaring at him*)   Fine time to tell me—after splitting
  my skull with that stick!

EUCLIO   Go on in. You were hired for cooking, not looking.

EEL   Listen you, I'm damned well going to collect damages
  from you for this beating. I was hired as a cook, not a
  punching bag.

EUCLIO (*shrugging*)   Go ahead, sue me—but don't bother

me now! Come on, either get that dinner cooked or get away from this house—and go straight to hell.

EEL (*aside, growling*)   Aah, go there yourself. (*He leads his party back into the house.*)

EUCLIO (*watching the last one go in and then turning to the audience*)   He's left. (*Bitterly*) You need a lot of nerve if you're a poor man and you let yourself get involved with the rich. Look what Megadorus is doing. He's going after me in every way he can. He makes believe that he's sending cooks here to show how much he thinks of me, but you know what the real reason is? So they can sneak (*patting the pot*) this away from me! (*With even more bitterness*) My rooster was just as bad; he used to belong to the old hag, and he came damned near destroying me. He began scratching all around where this was buried. Well, it just made my blood boil. So I grabbed a club and brained him. Dirty thief caught in the act! Damn it, if you ask me, those crooks bribed that rooster to reveal where this was. (*Grinning*) The snatchers lost their scratcher—and I was in a cockfight! (*His attention caught, suddenly looks toward the wings, stage left.*) Look who's coming—my in-law Megadorus, back from downtown. I don't dare go by him any longer without stopping and passing the time of day.

(*Enter Megadorus deep in thought. Without noticing Euclio, he makes his way downstage and addresses the audience.*)

MEGADORUS   I told a lot of my friends about my plans and this arrangement I've made. They approved of Euclio's daughter and said I was making a smart and sensible move.

(*Earnestly*) In my opinion, others should do the same thing. If the men who have the money were to go to those who don't, ask for their daughters without dowries, and marry them, there'd be a lot more good feeling in our city. We'd have less envy than we have now, our wives would show us more respect than we're getting now, and we'd spend lots less than we do now. For most of the people it would be the best thing in the world. We'd have a fight on our hands with only a few selfish ones, people who are so grasping and greedy neither the law nor the lash can control them.

(*After a moment's thought*) I suppose someone will want to know who the rich girls with dowries are going to marry if we pass such a law favoring the poor. Well, let them marry whoever they like—providing no dowry goes with them. Under my system, they'll develop some decent traits and bring these as dowry instead of what they bring now. (*Pounding his fist into the palm of his hand*) Why, my system would drop the price of fancy carriage mules— which today cost you more than a horse—below the price of ordinary nags!

EUCLIO (*aside, rapturously*) Believe me, it's a sheer pleasure to listen to him. Marvelous plea for parsimony he's made.

MEGADORUS And then none of our wives will be able to say, (*mimicking a nagging female*) "The dowry I brought you was far more than all the money you had in the world. So I have every right to silks and jewelry and maids and coach mules and coachmen and footmen and errand boys and my own carriages."

EUCLIO (*aside, approvingly*) This man really knows the way our fancy ladies carry on. I'd like to see him appointed Commissioner of Women's Ways.

MEGADORUS (*bitterly*) Nowadays, whatever house in town you go to, you see more vehicles standing around than when you go to a country farm. But these are practically a pleasure compared with the crowds standing around who are after your money. There's the cleaner, the embroiderer, the jeweler, the clothier. Then the salesmen—lace, lingerie, red-dye, violet-dye, yellow-dye, coats, perfume. Add the chemisiers, the shoemakers, the slipper makers, the sandal makers. Plus the dyers. Plus the launderers. Plus the seamstresses. Plus the brassiere makers and corset makers. (*Shakes his head in despair.*)

When you think you finally have them all paid off, in troop another three hundred to start dunning, and your foyer is filled with bagmakers, weavers, fancy-dress makers, cabinetmakers. They're ushered in, they get their money, you think once and for all you have the whole pack paid, and in troop the dyers (yellow-dyers this time)—(*throwing up his hands*) there's always some damned pain-in-the-neck around trying to get something out of you!

EUCLIO (*aside*) I'd go up and talk to him but I'm afraid he'll cut short these wonderful words on the ways of women. So I'll just let him be.

MEGADORUS Then, when you've finally settled accounts with all these rubbish peddlers, at the last minute in comes an old veteran of the wars. He asks for a loan. He steps outside while you check your account with your banker. He waits around, famished, thinking he's going to get his loan. You finish figuring your balance with your banker, and find *you* need a loan! So the soldier has to put off his hopes till some other time. (*Heaving a sigh*) These and plenty of others are the tribulations and expenses, enough to crush a man, that come with large dowries. Now, you take a girl *without* a dowry—a husband can lay down the law to her! But the ones with—(*shaking his head dolefully*) they can drive a poor husband to death with debt and drudgery. (*Turns and catches sight of Euclio.*) Ah, there's my in-law in front of his house. Hello there, Euclio.

EUCLIO (*beaming*) I enjoyed your talk no end. Just ate it up.

MEGADORUS (*surprised*) You heard what I said?

EUCLIO Every word, right from the beginning.

MEGADORUS (*eying Euclio's get-up unhappily*) All the same, I don't think it would be a bad idea if you'd spruce up a bit for your daughter's wedding.

EUCLIO (*putting on his woebegone look*) Family pride is
only for people with the money to dress and the means for
display. Believe me, Megadorus, I and every other poor
man, we're every bit as bad off as people think.

MEGADORUS (*benignly*) No, no. You have all you need, and
may the good lord keep it that way. May he guard and
increase what you have now!

EUCLIO (*abruptly turning away to address the audience,
nervously*) "What you have now"—I don't like that kind
of talk! (*Patting the pot*) He knows as well as I do that I
have this. The old hag told him everything!

MEGADORUS (*jovially*) What's this? Leaving the floor of the
senate for a private confabulation?

EUCLIO (*turning back, in a blind fury*) God damn it, I was
getting ready to accuse you to your face the way you
deserve!

MEGADORUS (*astonished*) What's the matter?

EUCLIO (*as before*) You have to ask? After filling my house,
every corner in it, full of thieves? After sending into my
house five hundred cooks? A bunch of Geryons they were,
each one with six hands! Argus himself couldn't keep an eye
on them, that fellow who was nothing but eyes, the one
who guarded Io for Juno.[3] Then that piper! If Fount
Pirene at Corinth would only gush wine, she could drink
it dry all by herself! And the stuff you bought—

MEGADORUS (*helplessly*) My god, it was enough for an
army! I even sent a lamb over—

EUCLIO (*witheringly*) I don't know of any animal anywhere
more devout than that lamb.

---

[3] One of Hercules' labors involved fighting a monster called
Geryon who, being triple-bodied, had six arms, six legs, and so on.
  Io, one of Jupiter's inamoratas, was turned into a heifer, and
Juno set Argus, who had eyes all over his head and body, to guard-
ing her.

MEGADORUS (*bewildered*) Would you mind telling me just how that lamb is devout?

EUCLIO (*promptly*) Look at all the fasting he's done—he's emaciated, nothing but skin and bones. Hold him up to the light, and you can inspect his entrails while he's still alive. He's like a lantern, he's transparent.

MEGADORUS (*as before*) I paid for having him slaughtered!

EUCLIO Then the best thing for you to do is pay for having him buried instead. Because, if you ask me, by now he's passed away.

MEGADORUS (*deciding to overlook all this as harmless eccentricity, heartily*) Euclio, I want you to have a drink with me today.

EUCLIO (*snarling*) I'm not doing any damned drinking!

MEGADORUS (*dismayed*) But I'm having a whole cask of vintage wine delivered to the house!

EUCLIO None for me. Made a resolution to drink only water.

MEGADORUS (*clapping him on the back*) Well, water-drinker, sure as I'm alive, I'll have you soused before the day is over!

EUCLIO (*to the audience, looking crafty*) I know what he's out to do! Get me dead drunk, that's the tack he's taking. Then, afterwards, this pot I have here will have a change of address. But I'll fix that—I'll hide this somewhere outside the house. Make it all a waste of his wine and time, that's what I'll do.

MEGADORUS (*turning to go*) Well, unless you need me for something, I'll be off. Got to wash up for the ceremony. (*He enters his house.*)

EUCLIO (*holding up his pot*) God in heaven, pot, you and this money you're taking care of have a lot of enemies! The best thing to do now is to take you into the Temple of Trust. I can find a good hiding place for you in there. (*Walking up to the door of the temple*) My Lady of Trust,

you know me and I know you. Just watch out that you
don't change your name if I trust (*slapping the pot*) this
to you. I trust you'll be trustworthy, Trust; that's why I'm
here.

(*He enters the temple, and the stage is now empty.*)

ACT IV

(*Enter, stage left, Lyconides' servant, Strobilus, a smug, swaggering type who, it is immediately apparent, has plenty of time to look after his own interests and is well able to do so.* [*Why he has the same name as Megadorus' servant is hard to explain; it may be the result of ancient tampering with the text.*])

STROBILUS (*to the audience*) What I'm doing now is what all good servants should do: not regard the master's orders as a nuisance and waste of time. A servant who's out to serve the way his master wants him to, should serve the master first and fast, and himself second. If he takes time out to sleep, let him remember in his sleep that he's on call.

(*Pauses to let this sink in, then continues.*) Now, if a servant serves a master who's in love, which is my situation, I consider it said servant's sworn duty, when he sees love getting the upper hand, to save him by holding him back, and never to egg him on in the direction he's heading. It's like boys learning to swim: they're given little reed rafts to help them save their strength and make it easier for them to move their arms and swim; well, my theory is that, when a master's in love, his servant should be his raft, should keep him up and not let him sink to the bottom like a lump of lead.

(*Warming up to his theme*) He should know what the master wants just by reading the look on his face. He should race to carry out orders faster than any race horse. If he does all this, he'll avoid rawhide expressions of disapproval, and he'll never put a shine on a set of shackles with his shins.

(*Stops for a moment, and then continues confidentially.*) Now, my master's in love with the daughter (*gesturing toward Euclio's house*) of this pauper Euclio here. The boy's just gotten word that the girl's engaged to marry (*gesturing toward Megadorus' house*) Megadorus here. So he's sent me to scout the situation and get a line on what's going on. (*Eying the altar in front of the Temple of Trust*) I can take a seat on this altar right here, and no one will suspect a thing. And from here, I can keep an eye on what's doing (*pointing to Euclio's house*) here and (*pointing to Megadorus' house*) here.

(*He sits down. A second later Euclio emerges from the temple. Without noticing that he is being overheard, he turns and addresses the Goddess of Trust.*)

EUCLIO   Lady Trust, take care you don't let a soul know that my money's in there. I'm not afraid of anyone finding it by himself: it's in a good dark corner. (*Waggling a warning finger*) The man who uncovers that potful of gold will make himself a pretty penny, believe you me, so I beg of you, Lady Trust, don't let it happen! I'm going off now to wash. I want to be ready for the ceremony and not hold up my son-in-law: let him take the girl off to his house the minute he comes for her. Look sharp, Lady Trust, and I mean SHARP! I want to be sure to get my pot back from you safe and sound. I'm trusting the money to you—it's in the temple inside your shrine. (*Exits, stage left.*)

STROBILUS   (*springing from his seat and running downstage to address the audience*)   God in heaven! What I just heard that man say! That he hid a whole potful of gold here in the Temple of Trust! (*Turning and addressing the temple*) Please, goddess, don't show *him* more trust than me! (*To the audience*) I think the girl my master's in love with is this man's daughter. Well, while he's busy somewhere else, I'll go in and have a look around the temple to see if I can find the money. (*To the temple*) And, if I do, my lady, I'll ladle you out one full gallon of the best sacramental wine. That's what I'll do for you. (*To the audience, confidentially*) And after I've done it, I'll do something for myself by guzzling it all.

(*Strobilus races into the temple. The next moment Euclio comes rushing back, stage left.*)

EUCLIO (*To the audience, nervously*)   There must be a good reason why a black cat crossed my path just now, and from the left, no less! And all the time, it kept scratching the ground with its claws and yowling and yowling. My heart started right in doing a jig and jumping up into my throat. But why stand here? I've got to run!

(*He races into the temple. Sounds of a scuffle, then, a moment later, out he comes, hauling Strobilus by the ear.*)

EUCLIO (*raging and punching away*)   Outside, you! You must have crawled in there underground, you worm! A minute ago you were nowhere to be seen, and, now that you've appeared, you're going to disappear! God damn it, you'll get it from me, you dirty thief!

STROBILUS (*blustering, as he tries to dodge the shower of blows*)   What the hell's got into you? I've got nothing to do with you, you old goat! What are you hitting me for? What are you hauling me off for? What do you mean by beating me up this way?

EUCLIO (*snarling*)   A born beatable, and he has to ask! You're three times as crooked as any crook, you crook!

STROBILUS (*switching from bluster to high dudgeon*)   What did I ever steal from you?

EUCLIO (*grimly*)   Give it back.

STROBILUS   What do you want me to give back?

EUCLIO   What a question!

STROBILUS (*switching to incredulity*)   You *robbed*? By *me*?

EUCLIO (*snarling*)   *You* robbed. *From* me. Hand it over. (*Getting no response*) Well, what about it?

STROBILUS   What about what?

EUCLIO   You won't get away with it.

STROBILUS   What are you after, anyway?

EUCLIO (*menacingly*)   Give it to me!

STROBILUS   Why, you old goat, you're the one who's always (*with an obscene gesture*) giving it.

EUCLIO   Give it to me, I say! And cut out the jokes. I'm not fooling now.

STROBILUS   (*resentfully*)   What do you want me to give? Why don't you tell me what it is? Believe me, I never in all my life put a hand on anything of yours. Not even a finger!

EUCLIO   Hold out your hands.

STROBILUS   (*promptly doing so*)   I've got 'em out. See?

EUCLIO   (*snarling*)   Yes, I see. (*Baffled*) Better show me that third one you have.

STROBILUS   (*to the world at large*)   This old boy is mad. He's crazy. He's seeing things. (*To Euclio, self-righteously indignant*) You think you're doing the right thing by me?

EUCLIO   Absolutely the wrong thing, I admit it. Hanging's the only right thing, and I'll do it, too, if you don't confess!

STROBILUS   (*as if driven to desperation*)   Confess what!

EUCLIO   (*glaring at him and pointing to the temple*)   What did you steal from there?

STROBILUS   (*hand on heart*)   The good lord strike me dead on the spot if I stole anything of yours—(*aside*) also if I don't!

EUCLIO   Come on, shake out your coat.

STROBILUS   (*promptly doing so, cheerfully*)   Anything you say.

EUCLIO   (*biting his lip*)   Must be under your shirt.

STROBILUS   (*cheerfully*)   Look wherever you like.

EUCLIO   You dirty rat! Being nice just to make me think you didn't steal it! I'm onto your tricks. (*Frisks him, finds nothing, and glares at him. Then, bitterly*) All right, hold out your right hand again.

STROBILUS   (*as before*)   Here you are.

EUCLIO   Now the left one.

STROBILUS   (*holding out both*)   Look, I'll hold out both at the same time.

EUCLIO   (*bitterly*)   All right, no more searching. Just hand it over.

STROBILUS Hand over what?

EUCLIO (*witheringly*) Very funny. (*Snarling*) But I know you've got it!

STROBILUS (*shouting*) Got it? Got *what*!

EUCLIO (*looking crafty*) I won't tell you. You're too anxious to find out. (*Shouting*) Whatever you've got of mine, you hand over!

STROBILUS (*switching to exasperation*) You're out of your mind! You searched me all you wanted, and you didn't find a thing of yours on me. (*Turns and makes as if to walk away.*)

EUCLIO (*suddenly struck by a thought, grabbing him*) Stop, you! (*Pointing to the temple*) Who's in there? Who's the other fellow who was in there with you? (*To the world at large*) Oh my god, I'm a goner! There's another one making trouble in there right now—and if I let go, this one'll run away! (*Suddenly frowning in thought*) But, after all, I just searched him, he hasn't got anything. (*Letting go of him*) All right, you can go.

STROBILUS (*putting a safe distance between him and Euclio*) God damn you to hell and gone!

EUCLIO (*to the audience*) Fine thanks I get! (*To Strobilus, grimly*) Now I'll go in and get that accomplice of yours by the throat and strangle him. Are you going to get out of my sight or not?

STROBILUS (*taking a jump toward the wings, stage left*) I'm going.

EUCLIO Don't let me lay eyes on you again! (*Dashes into the temple.*)

STROBILUS (*to the audience, grimly*) I'd sooner die a slow death than not trap this old boy today! (*Thoughtfully*) He won't dare hide the money here any longer. My guess is he's going to bring it out right now and hide it someplace else. (*Turning to look as he hears the creaking of the door*) Ah—the door! And there's the old boy bringing out his money. I'll just slip back here to this doorway for a little while.

(*He takes his stand in an unobtrusive spot alongside the door of Megadorus' house. A moment later Euclio emerges from the temple with the pot under his coat.*)

EUCLIO (*not noticing Strobilus, to the audience*)   And I thought Lady Trust could be trusted to a T! She came damned near making a monkey out of me! If that cat hadn't come to the rescue, I'd be a dead duck now. I only wish the cat who tipped me off would come along so I could do something nice for it—like saying a few nice words. (*Sternly*) After all, throwing it something to eat would be throwing food away.

(*Meditatively*) Now let me think of a secluded spot to hide this. There's that grove of Lord Sylvanus[4] beyond the city limits; it's all by itself in the middle of a mass of willows. I'll pick a place there. (*Shaking his head ruefully*) Believe me, I'd rather trust Lord Sylvanus than Lady Trust! (*Rushes off, stage right.*)

STROBILUS (*to the audience, jubilantly*)   Well, well! Lady Luck's taking care of me today! Now I'll just run ahead, climb a tree in the forest, and watch from up there where the old man hides the money. My orders are to stay right here, but my mind's made up: I'll go looking for trouble— when it pays off! (*Rushes off after Euclio.*)

(*Enter, stage left, Eunomia and her son, Lyconides, "wolf-son." Lyconides is a good-looking young man in his early twenties, expensively dressed, almost to the point of foppish-ness. Normally he is as satisfied with himself and life as any spoiled only son of an indulgent mother, but at this moment he shows signs of considerable agitation.*)

LYCONIDES (*agitatedly*)   There, I've told you. Now you know everything I do about what happened to Euclio's daugh-

---

[4] Sylvanus was god of the fields and forests.

ter. Mother, I begged you before and now I beg you again,
Mother dear, please, PLEASE talk to Uncle!

EUNOMIA   You know very well that I want to see happen
exactly what you do. And I'm sure I can get my brother
to say yes to this. If it's all as you say it is, that you got
drunk and violated the girl, then you've got every right
to ask.

LYCONIDES   (*reproachfully*) Mother dear! Would I lie to
you? Right to your face?

(*A shriek is suddenly heard from inside Euclio's house.*)

PHAEDRIA   (*from inside*)   Oh, I'm dying! Nurse dear! Please!
Oh, the pain! Oh god, help!

LYCONIDES   (*agonized*)   There you are, Mother! The facts
speak louder than any words. She's screaming! She's giving
birth right now!

EUNOMIA   (*resolutely, walking quickly toward the door of
Megadorus' house*)   Come right inside with me to my
brother. I'll get him to agree to what you want.

LYCONIDES   You go ahead, Mother. I'll follow in a second.
(*To himself, menacingly*) I wonder where that servant of
mine can be? I told him to meet me here! (*After a moment's thought*) But, on second thought, if he's off looking
after my interests, it's wrong for me to blow up at him.
(*Heaving a sigh*) I'll go in and join the jury that's judging
my fate.

(*He enters the house. A moment later Strobilus bounds in,
stage right, clutching the pot.*)

STROBILUS   (*to the audience, ecstatically*)   Here's the one
man in the world richer than the gnomes who live in the
hills of gold! All your famous kings—I won't even bother
mentioning them. (*Snapping his fingers*) Two-bit beggars!
I'm Alexander the Great!

(*Shaking his head wonderingly*) What a day! After I
left here a little while ago, I got there long before he came,

and long before he came I was all set in a tree. From there
I watched where the old man buried the money. When he
left, I got down from my tree, dug up the potful of gold,
and got out of there. I saw the old man on his way back,
but he didn't see me; I kept a little off the road. (*His attention caught, looks toward the wings, stage right.*) Aha!
There he is! Now I'll go and hide this in my house.)

(*Strobilus dashes off, stage left. A moment later Euclio
staggers in, stumbling about blindly as if in a state of shock.*)

SONG

EUCLIO (*to the audience*)
> I'm a goner! I'm finished! I'm through! I can't tell
> > Which direction to take and which not!

(*Shouting*)
> Someone stop him!

(*Bewildered*)
> > > But who? And stop who? I can't see,
> > I walk blindly, my brains are all shot!
> Who knows where I am, who I am, where I'm going?

(*Addressing the spectators in the front row*)
> You must help me, I implore you, you *must*.
> Where's the robber who took it? Please show me, I beg
> > you!

(*To one of them*)
> I say, mister, you're a man I can trust;
> I can tell by your face that you're honest and good.

(*To the whole theater*)
> What's the matter with you? What's so funny?

(*Bitterly*)
> Oh I know what you're like, and I know in these seats
> > There are lots who know how to steal money.
> With fine clothes and clean linen they sit there and look
> > Just like people who'd never stoop low.
> No one here has my pot? Oh, you'll kill me, you will!

(*To a spectator in the first row*)

>   Please tell me—who's got it? Don't know?

(*To the whole audience*)

I'm destitute, derelict, done for, undone;
>   I'm down in the depths of despair.
Oh the misery, mourning, and moans today's brought,
>   Plus starvation, the poorhouse, and care!
I'm the deadest of mortals alive on this earth,
>   I've no need for my life any more.
Oh the gold that I lost, which I'd guarded so well!
>   Oh the comforts and joys I forswore!
And others will now have the pleasure and fun—
>   And who pays for it? I! I can't bear it!

LYCONIDES (*coming out of Megadorus' house*)

Who's this weeping and wailing in front of our house?
>   Is it Euclio? Yes, I could swear it!
Oh my god, I'm a goner! My secret is out!
>   He must know of his daughter's condition.
Do I see him or flee him? Do I stay or go 'way?
>   Oh my god, what an awful position!

EUCLIO (*wheeling about*)   Who's talking there?

LYCONIDES (*coming forward to him*)   I. (*Heaving a sigh*)
An unhappy man.

EUCLIO (*abjectly*)   No, I'm the unhappy man. Miserably unhappy. The trouble, the tragedy that's fallen on me!

LYCONIDES (*not very convincingly*)   Cheer up.

EUCLIO (*miserably*)   I ask you now, how can I possibly?

LYCONIDES (*hanging his head*)   Because the tragedy that's
tormenting you was all my doing. I admit it.

EUCLIO (*unable to believe his ears*)   What did I hear you
say?

LYCONIDES (*as before*)   The truth.

EUCLIO (*trembling with rage*)   Mister, what did I ever do to
you that you should do this to me? Destroy me and my
family this way?

LYCONIDES (*passionately*)   Some evil demon drove me to it, trapped me into doing it!

EUCLIO (*glaring at him*)   How?

LYCONIDES (*abjectly*)   I did wrong, I admit it. I deserve the blame, I know it. What's more, I'm here right now to beg you to be forbearing and forgive me.

EUCLIO (*wildly*)   How could you have had the gall to lay your hands on what wasn't yours to touch!

LYCONIDES (*dumbly*)   What do you want from me? What's done is done; it can't be undone. I think it was heaven's will. Otherwise it couldn't have happened, I know it.

EUCLIO (*snarling*)   And I think it's heaven's will that I take you into my house, throw you in chains, and murder you!

LYCONIDES (*shuddering*)   Don't say such things!

EUCLIO (*thundering*)   What do you mean by putting your hands on what's mine without my permission?

LYCONIDES (*barely audibly*)   It was wine and passion that drove me to do it.

EUCLIO (*as before*)   The colossal nerve of this man! How dare you come to me with that kind of talk? If the law gave the right to plead excuses like that, we could rob old ladies' purses on the street in broad daylight and, if caught, plead we did it because we were drunk and in love! Wine and passion are pretty poor things if they'll let any lush in love do what he likes and get away with it.

LYCONIDES (*humbly*)   I've come to you of my own free will to beg forgiveness for my stupidity.

EUCLIO (*sneering*)   I don't like people who do wrong and then excuse themselves. You know you had no right. You should have kept your hands off!

LYCONIDES   And just because I dared do what I shouldn't, I offer no excuses—(*rapturously*) let me keep this treasure, it's my dearest wish!

EUCLIO (*gasping*)   Keep my treasure? Against my will?

LYCONIDES (*hurriedly*)   Oh, I wouldn't ask to do it against your will. But I do think it would be the right thing to do. (*Earnestly*) I tell you, Euclio, even you'll come to see it's the right thing to do.

EUCLIO (*staring at him uncomprehendingly, then exploding*) God damn it, I'm going to haul you before the judge and bring you up on charges unless you give me back—

LYCONIDES (*interrupting, bewildered*) Give you back what?

EUCLIO What you stole from me.

LYCONIDES (*as before*) I stole something of yours? What? From where?

EUCLIO (*sneering*) Well, god bless you, you don't know!

LYCONIDES Not unless you tell me what you're after.

EUCLIO (*grimly*) I'll tell you. I'm asking you to hand back the pot of gold you confessed you stole from me.

LYCONIDES (*taken aback*) Good god in heaven! I never confessed or did any such thing!

EUCLIO You deny it?

LYCONIDES To my last breath I deny it! I don't know anything about any gold or what this pot of yours is.

EUCLIO It's the one you stole from the grove of Sylvanus. Come on, let's have it. (*In despair, starts wheedling*) Aw, come on, give it back, won't you?

LYCONIDES (*incredulously*) You must be crazy to call me a thief, Euclio. I thought you had found out about something else, something that has to do with me. It's a very important matter, and I'd like to talk it over with you quietly, when you have a quiet moment.

EUCLIO (*looking at him piercingly*) Tell me, on your word of honor: you didn't steal the money?

LYCONIDES (*shaking his head vigorously*) Word of honor.

EUCLIO And you don't know who stole it?

LYCONIDES (*as before*) Word of honor to that too.

EUCLIO And if you find out who stole it, you'll tell me?

LYCONIDES (*nodding*) Right.

EUCLIO And you'll never go after a share of it or hide the thief?

LYCONIDES (*as before*) Agreed.

EUCLIO What if you go back on your word?

LYCONIDES (*raising his right hand and turning his eyes to heaven*) Then may the good lord do with me what he wants.

EUCLIO That's good enough for me. Now say whatever you want to.

LYCONIDES (*importantly*) If you don't happen to know me or my family, (*gesturing toward Megadorus' house*) Megadorus here is my uncle, my father was Antimachus, my mother is Eunomia, and my name is Lyconides.

EUCLIO (*impatiently*) The family I know. What I want to know is: what do you want now?

LYCONIDES (*as before*) You have a daughter—

EUCLIO (*gesturing impatiently toward his house*) Yes, right there in the house.

LYCONIDES She's engaged, I believe, to marry my uncle?

EUCLIO (*wearily*) You know all there is to know.

LYCONIDES Well, my uncle has instructed me to tell you he's breaking the engagement.

EUCLIO (*unable to believe his ears*) Breaking the engagement? Everything's arranged! Everything's ready for the wedding! (*Exploding*) I hope to god he fries in hell! It's because of him that I had the miserable luck to lose all that money today, god damn it!

LYCONIDES (*stoutly*) Cheer up. And don't curse. May it all bring health and happiness to you and your daughter! (*Holding up his hand imperiously as Euclio opens his mouth*) Just say, "I pray to god it will."

EUCLIO (*fervently*) I pray to god it will!

LYCONIDES And I pray to god it will for my sake. Now listen. (*Earnestly*) Even the most worthless good-for-nothing, once he admits he's done wrong, is ashamed and wants to clear himself. So now I implore you, Euclio, if I unintentionally wronged you or your daughter, please forgive me and let me marry her as the law requires. (*Hanging his head*) You see, I have a confession to make: at the last festival for Lady Ceres, I violated your daughter. I was young and wild, and I had had too much to drink. . . .

EUCLIO (*clutching his head and shrieking*)   Ay-ay-ay! What did I hear you say?

LYCONIDES (*deciding it was time to take the offensive, slapping him on the back*)   Why the ay-ay-ay's? You'll be a grandfather when you go to your daughter's wedding, thanks to me! She's having a baby! It's the ninth month; figure it out. That's why my uncle broke off the engagement—it was for my sake. Go inside your house and ask. Find out for yourself whether it isn't just as I say.

EUCLIO (*dumbly*)   I'm ruined! All these troubles on my poor head, one after the other, a whole line of 'em stuck together! Well, I'll go in and find out how much of all this is true. (*Goes into the house.*)

LYCONIDES (*calling after him*)   I'll be right in after you. (*To the audience, happily*) Well, it looks as if I'm finally in safe waters. (*Looking all around*) But I don't see my servant Strobilus. I have no idea where he can be. The only thing I can do is wait around here a little while, and follow the old man in later. In the meantime, I'll be giving him a chance to find out about my affair from the old woman who's the girl's nurse. She knows the whole story.

(*As Lyconides looks off, stage right, Strobilus bursts in, stage left.* [Act V traditionally begins here. To avoid interrupting the action I have not indicated it in the text.])

STROBILUS (*to the world at large, at the top of his lungs*)   God in heaven, what blessings you've showered on me! I have a potful of gold—four pounds of it! Who's richer than I am? Who in this city right now has more of heaven's blessings than I?

LYCONIDES (*dryly*)   I think I heard somebody's voice coming from around here. (*He turns.*)

STROBILUS (*turning and seeing him*)   Is this my master I see?

LYCONIDES   Is this my servant I behold?

STROBILUS (*peering*)   That's who it is.

LYCONIDES (*peering*)   No one else.

STROBILUS (*walking toward him*)   I'll go up to him.

LYCONIDES (*walking toward him*)   I'll go meet him. I suppose he's been to see the old woman, the girl's nurse, as I told him to.

STROBILUS (*stopping; aside*)   Why don't I tell him I found this prize piece of plunder and then ask him to let me go free? I'll go right up and tell him. (*To Lyconides*) I found—

LYCONIDES (*interrupting, impatiently*)   You found what?

STROBILUS (*grinning*)   Not the kind of thing kids holler they find when they open up a bean.

LYCONIDES (*wearily*)   Having fun again as usual, eh? (*Turns as if to go.*)

STROBILUS (*hastily*)   Hey, wait! I'll tell you. Just listen.

LYCONIDES (*reluctantly stopping*)   All right, talk.

STROBILUS (*his eyes shining*)   Today I found a fortune!

LYCONIDES (*disinterestedly*)   Where?

STROBILUS (*ignoring the question, as before*)   A potful of gold, I tell you, four pounds of it!

LYCONIDES (*electrified*)   What's this you say you did?

STROBILUS (*chuckling and gesturing toward Euclio's house*)   I stole it from old man Euclio here.

LYCONIDES   Where is this gold?

STROBILUS   In a chest at home. (*Importantly*) I want you to set me free now.

LYCONIDES (*roaring*)   I set you free? Criminal! Arch-criminal!

STROBILUS (*taken aback, but recovering swiftly and pretend-*

ing to be highly amused) Come off it—I know your game.
Good joke I just played to find out what was in your mind,
wasn't it? You were getting all ready to take the pot away
from me! What would you have done if I had *really* found
one?

LYCONIDES (*grimly*) You're not going to get away with that
nonsense. Come on, hand over the money!

STROBILUS (*as if not believing his ears*) I hand over the
money?

LYCONIDES Hand it over, I tell you, so I can hand it over
(*gesturing toward Euclio's house*) to him.

STROBILUS (*as before*) Money? From where?

LYCONIDES The money you just now admitted was in the
chest.

STROBILUS (*airily*) Oh lord, you know the way I'm always
blabbering a lot of nonsense.

LYCONIDES (*grimly*) You know what's going to happen to
you?

STROBILUS I swear, you can kill me but you'll never get
from me—

[The rest of the play is lost. From some ancient résumés of
the plot that have survived, we know that Lyconides got
Strobilus to return the money and that Euclio not only gave
the boy permission to marry his daughter but threw in the
pot of gold as her dowry.]

CASINA

DRAMATIS PERSONAE

OLYMPIO, *foreman of Lysidamus' farm in the country* (*slave*)

CHALINUS, *servant of Lysidamus on full-time duty as orderly for his son* (*slave*)

CLEOSTRATA, *wife of Lysidamus*

PARDALISCA, *her maid*

MYRRHINA, *wife of Alcesimus, and friend and neighbor of Cleostrata*

LYSIDAMUS, *an elderly gentleman*

ALCESIMUS, *an elderly gentleman, neighbor of Lysidamus*

A COOK

A PIPER

SERVANTS

SCENE

A street in Athens. Two houses front on it: Lysidamus' and Alcesimus'. The exit on stage left leads downtown, that on stage right to the country.

PROLOGUE

(*The speaker of the prologue enters, walks downstage, and addresses the audience.* [The prologue that follows was prepared for some revival put on perhaps three or four decades after the original performance. How much it preserves of the original version is hard to say.])

PROLOGUE (*bowing respectfully*) Greetings, good people who do honor to Honor—and to whom Honor does honor. (*Abruptly raising his head and eying them keenly*) If I've told the truth, please give me a clear sign to let me know right from the beginning that you're all my friends. (*Stops and waits for a round of applause.*)

In my opinion, the people who drink vintage wines are the wise ones—and that goes for the people who like to see vintage plays. Since you all enjoy old-fashioned things and old-fashioned writings, you ought by the same token to have a preference for old-fashioned theater. After all, the new plays coming out nowadays are worth even less than the new coins. Well, once the talk around town put us wise to your yen to see plays by Plautus, we decided to put on an old comedy of his, one you all liked—the old-timers among you, that is; I realize that the youngsters here don't know the piece, but we'll do our best to see to it they do. This play was the hit of the season when it first came out—and that was at a time when the flower of our playwrights were still living, the men who now have passed on to the place we all end up at. But, even though they're no longer with us, they can give us as much enjoyment as if they were.

I beg you, all of you, please give your kind attention to our actors. (*Gaily*) Anyone here worried about his creditors? Forget your debts, drive your cares from your mind. Today's a holiday: the finance companies are out having fun. Everything's quiet; peace profound pervades the financial district. Very logical, our finance companies:

during the holiday they won't dun any of you; once it's over, they won't pay any of you!

(*Stops for a moment, and then raises a hand commandingly for attention.*) If your ears are at leisure, will you please listen? I want to tell you the name of our play. In Greek it's called *Kleroumenoi*, in Latin *Sortientes*. Diphilus wrote it originally in Greek, and Plautus, the fellow with the name that barks, translated it later into Latin.[1]

(*Pointing to Lysidamus' house*) In here lives a married man well on in years. He has a grown son; the boy lives with his father in this same house. There's also a certain servant there who's flat on his back in bad health—correction, flat on his back in bed; I want to stick to the facts.

Well, the servant—now this goes back a good sixteen years—once saw, in the early light of dawn, a woman abandon an infant girl. He rushed up and asked her to let him have the child. She agreed. He carried it off, brought it straight home, gave it to the old fellow's wife, and asked her to take care of it and bring it up. And she did. She brought it up giving it every attention, exactly as she would have given a child of her own.

Once the girl reached an age to interest men, the old fellow fell madly in love with her. But, on the other hand, so did his son. And now, with neither of them knowing it, each is lining up his forces against the other, father against son. The father's commissioned the foreman of his farm to ask to marry the girl; the old boy has hopes, if it goes through, of setting up a love nest somewhere, behind his wife's back. The son's commissioned his orderly to ask to marry the girl; he figures, if it goes through, he'll have the object of his affections right in his own back yard.

The old fellow's wife discovered that her husband was involved in a love affair, and this put her on her son's side. Then the father found out that his son was in love with the

---

[1] Both titles mean "The Drawers of Lots"; apparently the play was dubbed *Casina* by later ages. For Diphilus, see p. xiv. "The name that barks," because *plautus* is the Latin for a breed of dog.

same girl he was and was standing in his way, so he packed the boy off abroad. But the wife saw through it, and she's looking after her son's interests even though he's not around. Now don't look for him to come back today during this play. He won't. Plautus didn't want it that way; he collapsed one of the bridges on the route.

(*Nodding knowingly*) I suppose some of you are saying to each other this very minute, "I ask you—what's going on here? Weddings between servants? Since when do slaves get engaged or get married? That's something new they've started, something you'll see nowhere on earth." Well, I tell you you will, in Greece, at Carthage, and right here in our own country, in Apulia. Why, there the slaves' weddings are usually even bigger affairs than the masters'! It's the truth, and I'll bet whoever is willing one bowl of good wine—providing the judge comes from Carthage, or even Greece, or, for my sake particularly, Apulia. Well? No one here to take me up? Oh, I get it—no one here feels like a drink.

But let me get back to that girl who was foundlingized, the one that that pair of slaves are yearning to marry. It's going to turn out that she's a respectable, freeborn Athenian girl. As a matter of fact, she'll behave like a thoroughly decent girl all through the play. But, believe me, once it's over, I suspect she'll be perfectly willing to play bride without benefit of clergy to whoever offers her the cash.

That's about it. Good-by and good luck, be brave and win all your battles just as you always have.

ACT I

(Enter Olympio, stage right, with Chalinus at his heels. Olympio is foreman of Lysidamus' farm, and his clothes, personal hygiene, and general demeanor make it immediately apparent that he is rather more at home on a manure pile than in a bridal bed. His name suggests the Olympian gods; by the same token we call a 250-pounder "Tiny."

The other is Lysidamus' son's orderly. Chalinus—the name means "bit" (of a bridle); an orderly doubles as groom, and this particular one eventually "bridles" Lysidamus—is the precise opposite of Olympio: immaculate, sophisticated, unmistakably a product of the city.)

OLYMPIO *(angrily)* Can't you leave me alone? Can't I say and think what I want about my own affairs without always having you around? What the devil are you following me for?

CHALINUS Because I made up my mind to. To follow you like a shadow wherever you go. So help me, even if you've got a mind to mount the gallows, I'm going along and that's that. So you can just figure from this whether you'll be able to pull any of your tricks on me and sneak Casina off to be your wife the way you're counting on.

OLYMPIO *(acting as if puzzled)* What business is it of yours what I do?

CHALINUS You've got a nerve! You just tell me what a two-bit hick like you is doing sneaking around town here.

OLYMPIO *(shrugging)* I feel like it.

CHALINUS *(contemptuously)* Why aren't you at your headquarters—in the country. Why aren't you taking care of your official duties and keeping your nose out of things here in town? Back to the farm, you. Back to your dominions, Governor, straight back.

OLYMPIO *(loftily)* I haven't forgotten my responsibilities, Chalinus. I put someone in charge of the farm who'll take

good care while I'm away. I came to the city to ask if I
could marry that fellow slave of yours, that cutey beauty
Casina, the girl you're so madly in love with. And if I do,
once I take her off to the farm with me, I'll stay put in
my headquarters as still as a hen hatching eggs.

CHALINUS (*exploding*) *You* marry her? God damn it, you
can hang me till I'm dead before you'll ever get *her* in your
clutches.

OLYMPIO (*as before*) Then step right up and put the neck
in the noose. Because she's my baby.

CHALINUS Listen, you discard from the dung heap, she's
your baby, is she?

OLYMPIO (*smugly*) It's the truth. You'll find out.

CHALINUS Drop dead!

OLYMPIO (*gleefully*) The things I'm going to do to you at
my wedding! As sure as I'm alive, I'll make you miserable!

CHALINUS (*truculently*) And just what will you do to me?

OLYMPIO What will I do to you? I'll start off by having you
carry the torch for my new bride. Next, I'll hand you one
single jug, and point out eight casks, a copper basin, and
one single path to one single fountain. And if that basin
and those casks aren't full to the brim every minute of the
day, I'll fill that hide of yours full of welts. I'll have such
a beautiful crook in your spine from hauling water we'll
be able to use you for a yoke. Then, once we're out at the
farm, if you ask for something to eat, either you'll chomp
hay or you'll eat dirt like the worms—because, if you don't,
I'll have you hungrier than the patron saint of starvation
on a fast day! Last of all, when you're all fagged out and
famished, I'll see to it you get the rest you deserve during
the night.

CHALINUS What'll you do?

OLYMPIO I'll wedge you in the window where you can hear
me kiss her and hear her say, (*switching to falsetto*)
"Olympio, my darling, my honey, my joy, my life—sweetheart, let me kiss those sweet little eyes! Oh, you're so

lovely, let me love you to death, light of my life, dickey-
bird, turtledove, bunnykins!" And, all the time she's talking like this, you, god damn you, will be stuck in the middle
of the wall like a rat in its hole. (*Abruptly turning away*)
And now, to keep you from getting ideas about answering
me back, I'm going inside. I'm sick and tired of your talk.
(*Stalks into Lysidamus' house.*)

CHALINUS (*grimly*)   And I'm following. Not a chance of your
doing anything here without me around.

(*Chalinus hurries in after Olympio, and the stage is now
empty.*)

ACT II

(*The door of Lysidamus' house opens revealing Cleostrata and Pardalisca. Cleostrata steps past, and Pardalisca waits on the threshold.*

Cleostrata, Lysidamus' wife and the benefactress of the foundling Casina, is a woman in her forties, whose look and manner reveal at a glance that she is no meek, simple hausfrau. Pardalisca, her maid, gives every indication of being an able assistant to a keen and able mistress.)

SONG

CLEOSTRATA (*through the doorway, to her servants inside*)
Now lock the cupboards and bring me the key.
I'm going to step across to see
My next door neighbor. Come and get
Me there, if my husband asks for me.

PARDALISCA (*handing her the key, surprised*)
He told us to get his dinner ready.

CLEOSTRATA (*grimly*)
Say no more! You run along. You can bet he
Will get no dinner today from *me*.
That living disgrace! He's out to defy
Both me and his son, just to satisfy
That lust of his. But I'll make him pay.
I'll even the score with that old roué—
      No food or drink,
      Just fag and nag;
      I'll dish it out
      Till I see him gag.
      It's going to be
      Exactly the life
      He deserves, and he
      Can thank his wife!
      That oversexed antiquity!
      That cesspool of iniquity!

(Pardalisca disappears inside, and Cleostrata turns and starts walking toward Alcesimus' house.)

> Well, now I'll go to weep upon
> My neighbor's shoulder. Oh, dear!
> Her door's just opened and she's coming out—
> Bad time I picked to come here!

(Out of the house steps Myrrhina, Alcesimus' wife, a woman the same age as Cleostrata and dressed much like her. Once over the threshold, she turns to call to her servants inside.)

MYRRHINA *(through the doorway)*

> Now I'm going next door, so you follow this way.[2]
> Listen, you! Doesn't anyone hear what I say?
> I'll be there if my husband or someone should call.

(Muttering to herself as she waits impatiently)

> When alone in the house, I'm so drowsy things fall
> From my hands.

(Calling through the doorway in exasperation)

>   I told you to bring me out here
> The big strainer.

CLEOSTRATA *(calling)*

>   Oh, Myrrhina!

MYRRHINA *(in pleased surprise)*

>   Cleostrata, dear!

(Switching suddenly to a tone of concern)

> You poor thing! What's the matter? You're looking so sad!

CLEOSTRATA *(bitterly)*

> I'm like any poor woman whose marriage went bad.
> It's nothing but trouble whatever you do.
> That's why I was headed this way. To see you.

MYRRHINA

> And *I* was about to come over to you.

---

[2] It was infra dig for a matron to be on the streets alone, even just to cross to visit a neighbor.

What's the trouble? What's got you so heartsick this
time?

Any trouble of yours is a trouble of mine.

CLEOSTRATA (*impulsively kissing her*)

I believe you, I do! There's no friend I love more—
And no friend that deserves it as much. I'd adore
To be like you in so many ways!

MYRRHINA (*kissing her*)

You're a dear.
Now I want to be told all your troubles, you hear?

CLEOSTRATA (*sobbing*)

My husband's disgraced me. The worst *possible* way!

MYRRHINA (*looking blank*)

I don't get it.

CLEOSTRATA (*surprised*)

Get what?

MYRRHINA

May I ask you to say
It again? It's a complaint that I can't get quite clear.

CLEOSTRATA (*slowly and bitterly*)

My husband's disgraced me
The worst way that he could,
And I'm left with no right
To claim rights that I should.

MYRRHINA

Very strange if it's so,
Since in most of our lives
It's the husbands who can't
Claim their rights from the wives!

CLEOSTRATA

Why, he wants to walk off
With my sweet little maid!
And she's mine! It was I
Who raised her and paid

All expenses. He says
That he wants her as bride
For his foreman. But *he*
Wants to sleep at her side!

MYRRHINA (*whispering worriedly*)
Don't say such things!

CLEOSTRATA (*looking around and shrugging*)
         We're safe here now. It's just we two.

MYRRHINA

                     That's so.

(*Overcome by curiosity*)
But how did you ever get that girl? It's hardly *comme il
faut—*
A wife, behind her husband's back, having money of her
own!
And if she has, she never got it by methods I'd condone:
By stealing from the household cash or acting like our
whores.
It's my opinion that all you have is your husband's, dear,
not yours.

CLEOSTRATA (*shocked*)
And you're my friend! From all you've said, you'd think
we're enemies!

MYRRHINA (*confidentially*)
Be quiet, silly, and listen to me. Don't go against him,
please!
Let him do what he likes, let him have his affair.

(*Smiling knowingly*)
                   You lack for nothing, you know.

CLEOSTRATA (*aghast*)
You'd argue against your own best interests? Your mind's
beginning to go!

MYRRHINA *(sharply)*
Now don't be stupid!

(Waggling a warning finger)
                    Don't ever let, in all your intercourse,
Your husband say a certain phrase.

CLEOSTRATA
                                   What's that?

MYRRHINA
                                   "I'm suing for divorce."

CLEOSTRATA *(in a tone of alarm)*
Hush up!

MYRRHINA
        What's up?

CLEOSTRATA *(pointing to the wings, stage left)*
        Just look over there.

MYRRHINA
                    Well, who do you think you see?

CLEOSTRATA
My husband. Look! You'd better go. Quick inside, my dear.

MYRRHINA
                                   I agree.

CLEOSTRATA
            As soon as we have some time,
            Both you and I,
            I'll talk to you again—
            But now, good-by!

MYRRHINA
Good-by!

*(Myrrhina dashes into her house and Cleostrata moves off
to the side.*
*A second later Lysidamus enters. He is a spry old fellow,
feeble enough to have to lean on a stick but determined to
show as few signs of age as possible: his gray hair is pomaded
and curled, he is dressed as flashily as a teenage dandy, and,
from the look in his eye, no young girl could possibly pass
him without getting her bottom pinched.*

He scuttles downstage and, without noticing his wife, addresses the audience.)

LYSIDAMUS (*gaily*)

My feeling is that love outdoes almost every pleasing
    pleasure.

There's nothing I can mention which can offer such a
    measure

Of the charm and spice of life. I wonder at our chefs'
    devices

To season food—they never use the best of all the spices!

A dash of love, and a dish, I feel, will satisfy any eater.

But leave out love, and it's flat, it gets no sourer or sweeter.

Why, love will turn bitter gall to honey, a sourpuss mild
    and mellow.

I base all this on what happened to me, not on talk from
    any fellow.

(*Ostentatiously smoothing his hair and adjusting his
clothes*)

The more I'm smitten with Casina's charms, the better
    grows my humor:

I'm a snappier dish than a fashion plate, a trial to every
    perfumer.

Whenever I find a nice perfume, I smear it till I'm reeking

To stir her passions—(*leering*) and, I think, I've got what
    I've been seeking.

(*The leer suddenly fades and Lysidamus visibly droops.*)

        But my greatest torment is my wife.

        The way that woman clings to life!

(*Shakes his head mournfully—and does a double take as he
catches sight of Cleostrata.*)

        Why, there she is! And no picture of joy.

        Better butter the old bitch up, old boy!

(*Goes up to her and starts to put his arm about her.*)

        Well, how's my darling wife today?

CLEOSTRATA (*between her teeth*)

        Take your hands off me and go away!

LYSIDAMUS (*still holding her by the hand*)
>   I wish my darling Juno were
>   More happy to see her Jupiter.

   (*As Cleostrata tries to twist from his grasp*)
>   Hey, where are you going?

CLEOSTRATA (*twisting free and stepping away*)
>   You let me go!

LYSIDAMUS
>   Hey, wait!

CLEOSTRATA
>   I will not.

LYSIDAMUS (*like a coy lover*)
>   I'll follow, you know.

CLEOSTRATA (*stopping and eying him distastefully*)
>   Are you mad?

LYSIDAMUS (*passionately*)
>   Yes. Mad with love for you.

CLEOSTRATA (*acidly*)
>   Well, *I* would rather do without it.

LYSIDAMUS (*his hand over his heart*)
>   There's nothing can be done about it!

CLEOSTRATA (*exasperated*)
>   You'll be the death of me, someday.

LYSIDAMUS (*under his breath*)
>   How I hope and pray for what you say!

CLEOSTRATA (*overhearing*)
>   Now *that* I'll believe!

LYSIDAMUS (*abjectly, as she turns away*)
>   Turn around, ma chérie!

CLEOSTRATA (*witheringly*)
>   I'm as much your chérie as you're mine, believe me.

   (*Sniffing*)
>   And from whence comes this smell of perfume, eh,
>   chéri?

LYSIDAMUS (*clapping a hand to his brow, aside*)
  Oh, my god! I'm a goner! She's got me red-handed!
  (*Starts inching away unobtrusively*)
    Now to wipe off my head with my coat's what's de-
  manded.
  God damn that perfumer who sold me this stuff!

CLEOSTRATA (*hauling him back*)
  Why, you white-bearded worthless old weasel! Enough!
  I can hardly hold in certain things I should tell you.
  A creature your age to parade with that smell you
  Have on through the streets! You old lecher!

LYSIDAMUS (*lamely*)
                                              But I
  Was just helping a friend buy perfume.

CLEOSTRATA (*to the world at large*)
                                    Hear him lie?
  And how quickly he does it!
  (*To Lysidamus, with biting contempt*)
                              Simply *no* sense of shame!

LYSIDAMUS (*eagerly*)
  But I'll get some. All you want.

CLEOSTRATA (*as before*)
                              You've been wallowing in sin
  At the brothels. Which ones?

LYSIDAMUS (*promptly*)
                              You mean me? never been
  To one.

CLEOSTRATA
    Yes? I know more than you think!

LYSIDAMUS (*nervously*)
                                        Is that so?
  Tell me what.

CLEOSTRATA (*with arms on hips, and her nose against his*)
                  In your dotage you've fallen so low
  Not another old geezer could possibly come

Within range, no not one. Well, where were you, you
bum?

Where's the dive you were at, where you whored and
got tight?

Oh, you're soused! Why, just look at those clothes!
They're a sight!

LYSIDAMUS (*hand on heart*)

May the lord strike the both of us dead if I've touched
One drop of the stuff today.

CLEOSTRATA (*in a tone of finality*)

Oh, go do what you like. Go gorge and get drunk.
Go throw all your money away.

LYSIDAMUS (*giving up his act*)   Enough, woman! Shut your
mouth. You've got my ears ringing. Save a little breath for
arguing with me tomorrow. (*Switching to a tone of lordly
authority*) What about it? Have you learned to control
your temper? To see that you do what your husband wants
done and not go against him?

CLEOSTRATA (*curtly*)   What about what?

LYSIDAMUS   What a question! About your maid Casina.
About letting her marry a fine fellow like our foreman and
be where she'll have plenty of firewood, food, hot water,
clothes, and can bear children and bring them up. And *not*
letting her marry that worthless good-for-nothing of an orderly who to this day hasn't managed to put aside a
plugged nickel.

CLEOSTRATA (*icily*)   It's incredible how, at your time of life,
you still forget to stick to your own business.

LYSIDAMUS   What do you mean?

CLEOSTRATA   If you did things the right way and the best
way, you'd let *me* care for the maids, since they're in my
care.

LYSIDAMUS (*testily*)   Why the devil do you want to give her
to that two-bit shield-hauler?

CLEOSTRATA (*loftily*) Because both of us should do what we can to help our only son.

LYSIDAMUS (*exasperated*) All right, so he is my only son. But I'm as much his only father as he's my only son. He ought to give in to what I want rather than I give in to him.

CLEOSTRATA But you're up to no good, take my word for it. I smell it. I feel it.

LYSIDAMUS W-w-who? Me?

CLEOSTRATA Yes, you! What are you stuttering for? Just what *is* this that your heart's so set on?

LYSIDAMUS (*self-righteously*) To give the girl to a fine, decent servant rather than a good-for-nothing.

CLEOSTRATA Suppose I speak with our foreman and get him to agree, as a special favor to me, to let the other fellow marry her?

LYSIDAMUS And suppose *I* speak with the orderly and get *him* to agree to let the other fellow marry her? (*To himself, tight-lipped*) And I'm pretty sure he'll do what I ask.

CLEOSTRATA Agreed. Do you want me to tell Chalinus for you to step out here? You put it to him, and I'll put it to the foreman.

LYSIDAMUS Fine with me.

CLEOSTRATA He'll be right out. Now we'll find out which of us is the smoother talker. (*She goes into the house.*)

LYSIDAMUS (*the minute the door closes behind her*) Finally I can say what I like: (*at the top of his lungs*) god damn that woman to hell and gone! (*Shaking his head mournfully*) Here I am in the tortures of love—and she's putting obstacles in my way! And it looks as if it's all on purpose. She's got wind of what I'm trying to fix up. (*The door opens and Chalinus steps out.*) That's why she's helping that orderly—it's on purpose, god damn him, GOD DAMN—

CHALINUS YOU— (*in normal tones*) wanted to see me, your wife said.

LYSIDAMUS (*tight-lipped*)   Yes, I wanted to see you.

CHALINUS (*sauntering over toward him, insolently*)   What do you want to tell me? Say it.

LYSIDAMUS (*as before*)   The first thing I want is for you to look civil when you talk to me. It's downright stupid to frown at a man who's got you in his power. (*Chalinus wipes the frown off, and Lysidamus hangs a smile on.*) Well, up to now I've considered you a fine, upstanding fellow.

CHALINUS (*snickering*)   Oh, I know. And if that's the way you feel, why don't you set me free?

LYSIDAMUS (*beaming at him*)   Oh, I want to. But my wanting to do it won't do any good unless *you* do something to help.

CHALINUS (*suspiciously*)   Well, I'd just like to know what you want done.

LYSIDAMUS   Listen, I'll tell you. (*Taking him by the arm, confidentially*)   I gave my word to our foreman that he could marry Casina.

CHALINUS   But your wife and son gave *me* their word.

LYSIDAMUS   I know. (*Eying him narrowly*)   Would you rather be an unmarried free man or a married slave—all your life, both you and any children you have? It's up to you. Pick whichever side of the proposition you want.

CHALINUS (*shrugging*)   If I'm set free, I'll have to live at my own expense. Now I live at yours. (*Sticking his jaw out*)   And about Casina—my mind's made up: I'm not giving her up to any man on earth.

(*They eye each other balefully in dead silence for a few seconds.*)

LYSIDAMUS (*as if suddenly making up his mind*)   Go inside and call my wife out here in front of the house this minute. And bring a jug of water with you and a pair of markers for lots.

CHALINUS (*amused*) Not a bad idea.

LYSIDAMUS (*grimly*) Damn it all, I'll put a spoke in your wheel one way or another. If I can't get anywhere by asking, at least we'll draw lots. That's the way I'll get even with you and those backers of yours.

CHALINUS (*grinning*) But I'm going to win.

LYSIDAMUS (*roaring*) Damn it all, you'll win a slow death by strangling, that's what you'll win.

CHALINUS (*smugly*) Try all the tricks you want. She'll still marry me.

LYSIDAMUS (*as before*) Get out of my sight!

CHALINUS Don't like my looks, eh? (*Shrugging*) I'll live. (*He stalks into the house.*)

LYSIDAMUS (*to the audience, moaning*) What a poor devil I am! Is everything against me? Now I'm worried that that wife of mine will talk Olympio out of marrying Casina. And, if that happens, here's one old man it's all over with. But, if she doesn't talk him out of it, there's still a spark of hope in drawing lots. Then, if the draw lets me down, I'll set up a sword for a mattress and stretch out on it. (*The door opens and Olympio appears in the doorway.*) Sh, here comes Olympio. Couldn't have timed it better.

OLYMPIO (*through the doorway to Cleostrata inside, passionately*) So help me, ma'am, I'd as soon have you put me in a hot oven and brown me till I'm the color of toast as say yes to what you're asking.

LYSIDAMUS (*to the audience*) Saved! From what I can hear, there's still hope.

OLYMPIO (*loftily*) How come you're trying to scare me with those threats of yours about freedom? Why, even if you and your son are against it, even if neither of you want it, even if both of you say no, I can still become free and it won't cost me a cent. (*The door slams in his face. He shrugs and walks downstage.*)

LYSIDAMUS What's the matter, Olympio? Who were you arguing with?

OLYMPIO   Same one you always are.

LYSIDAMUS   My wife?

OLYMPIO   What do you mean, wife? You practically live like a professional hunter: spend twenty-four hours a day with a baying bitch.

LYSIDAMUS   What's she up to? What did she say to you?

OLYMPIO   She's pleading with me, she's begging me not to marry Casina.

LYSIDAMUS (*anxiously*)   And what did you say?

OLYMPIO   I said, if Jupiter himself asked for her, I still wouldn't give her up even to him.

LYSIDAMUS   God bless you!

OLYMPIO   She's boiling now. She's so mad at me she could burst.

LYSIDAMUS   And, boy, do I hope she does! Right in the middle.

OLYMPIO (*with an obscene gesture*)   If you were any good as a husband, that's where she would. (*Disgustedly*) I'm fed up with this love affair of yours. Your wife's against me, your son's against me, the whole household's against me.

LYSIDAMUS   What do you care? (*Tapping his breast importantly*) So long as Jupiter here is on your side, that's all you need, you can snap your fingers at that small fry.

OLYMPIO (*hotly*)   That's a lot of nonsense! You know yourself how fast flesh and blood Jupiters die off. Furthermore, Jupiter, when you die, and the throne passes to the small fry, would you mind telling me who's going to guard my back and shins and head?

LYSIDAMUS   Things will be better for you than you think—*if* we can fix it up so I get to sleep with Casina.

OLYMPIO (*shaking his head*)   Oh lord, I don't think there's a chance. Your wife's dead set against my getting her.

LYSIDAMUS (*grimly*)   What I'm going to do is this. I'm putting two lots in a jug, and you and Chalinus will hold a drawing. Here's my estimate of the situation: (*melodramatically*) we have to draw swords and fight it out!

OLYMPIO What if the drawing doesn't turn out the way you want?

LYSIDAMUS (*shuddering*) Don't say such things! I trust in god. We'll put our hope in heaven.

OLYMPIO (*witheringly*) You can't sell *me* that idea for a plugged nickel. Every man alive has faith in god, and yet I've seen an awful lot of the faithful fooled.

LYSIDAMUS (*putting his fingers to his lips*) Quiet a second!

OLYMPIO What's up?

LYSIDAMUS Look! Chalinus is coming out with the jug and lots. We'll be joining battle soon to fight it out!

(*Chalinus and Cleostrata come out of the house. Chalinus is holding, in one hand a deep and narrow-necked jug full of water, and in the other a pair of heavy markers. Lysidamus is not content merely to pick lots out of a hat; he intends a full-dress, official drawing in which the lots are plucked from the bottom of a jug of water.*)

CLEOSTRATA (*to Chalinus*) Tell me what my husband wants from me.

CHALINUS To see you going up in smoke in the city crematorium.

CLEOSTRATA I dare say he would.

CHALINUS I don't dare say. I know.

LYSIDAMUS (*to Olympio, gesturing toward Chalinus*) There are more experts in the family than I thought—I keep a professional mind reader in the house! What do you say we break camp and march out to meet them? Follow me. (*Walking up to them, affably*) Well, how are you two doing?

CHALINUS Here's everything you asked for: wife, jug, markers, and myself.

OLYMPIO (*sourly*) You're one item I could do without.

CHALINUS (*grinning*) I'll bet you feel that way. I'm your personal needler. I get under your skin. (*Contemptuously*) Stinker! You're so scared, you're starting to sweat.

LYSIDAMUS Shut up, Chalinus.

CHALINUS (*to Lysidamus, loftily, gesturing toward Olympio*) Why don't you take him in hand?

OLYMPIO (*to Lysidamus, making an obscene gesture*) No, him—he's the one who knows how to put it in hand.

LYSIDAMUS (*to Chalinus, pointing to the ground in front of him*) Put the jug down here and give me the lots. (*To the two servants*) Now pay attention. (*Turning away from them to Cleostrata; with gentle reproach*) You know, my dear, I still have the feeling I've had all along, that I can get you to agree to let me marry Casina.

CLEOSTRATA (*blankly*) Let her marry *you?*

LYSIDAMUS Of course, me. (*A light dawning*) No, no, no—I didn't mean that. I meant to say "me" but I said "him." As a matter of fact, all the time it was for me I wanted— (*throwing up his hands helplessly*) Oh my god! I'm saying things all wrong!

CLEOSTRATA (*eying him distastefully*) You certainly are. And doing them wrong too.

LYSIDAMUS (*frantically*) Him—no, me— (*stopping and almost visibly pulling himself together*) Ah, now I'm back on the right track.

CLEOSTRATA (*as before*) You get off it pretty often, believe me.

LYSIDAMUS (*reproachfully*) That always happens when a person wants something very badly. (*Gravely*) Now, Olympio and I recognize your rights, and we both beg you.

CLEOSTRATA For what?

LYSIDAMUS (*in dulcet tones*) I'll explain, honeybunch. We beg you to do our foreman here a favor in this Casina matter.

CLEOSTRATA (*promptly*) I will not. I wouldn't think of it.

LYSIDAMUS (*grimly*) In that case, the two of them will draw lots.

CLEOSTRATA (*shrugging*) Who's stopping them?

LYSIDAMUS (*pontifically*) My legal opinion is that legally this is the best and fairest way. If our side winds up with what we want, we'll be very happy. If not, we won't let it get us down. (*To Olympio*) Pick a lot and see what's written on it.

OLYMPIO (*taking one and looking it over*) Number one.

CHALINUS (*bursting out*) That's not fair! You let him get his before me!

LYSIDAMUS (*to Chalinus, handing him the other marker, icily*) Take this one, please.

CHALINUS (*sulkily*) Hand it over. (*Takes it, examines it for a second, then suddenly looks up*) Wait! I just thought of something. (*To Cleostrata, pointing to the jug*) Just see that there isn't still another one in there under the water.

LYSIDAMUS (*roaring*) You good-for-nothing, you think I'm like you?

CLEOSTRATA (*to Chalinus*) Don't worry, there isn't.

OLYMPIO (*looking upward, fervently*) O lord in heaven, I beg you, today give me—

CHALINUS (*interrupting*) —trouble. Lots of it.

OLYMPIO (*turning on him*) If you want my opinion, that's just what *you're* going to get. I know how much of a saint *you* are. (*Eying the marker Chalinus is holding*) Hey, just a minute. That lot there—is that made of poplar? Or pine?

CHALINUS (*belligerently*) What do you care?

OLYMPIO (*to Lysidamus*) I'm afraid that thing's going to float on top of the water.

LYSIDAMUS Good for you, Olympio. Keep an eye on it. (*Pointing to the jug*) Now both of you drop your lots in here. (*They do so.*) There we are. (*To Cleostrata*) Check them, dear.

OLYMPIO (*to Lysidamus, excitedly*) Don't trust her!

LYSIDAMUS Don't worry.

OLYMPIO (*as before*) I swear, if she touches them she'll put a hex on them.

LYSIDAMUS Quiet, Olympio!

OLYMPIO (*grumbling*) All right. (*Looking upward*) I pray to god—

CHALINUS (*interrupting*) —to get a ball and chain today.

OLYMPIO (*ignoring him*) —that I draw and win—

CHALINUS (*as before*) —a hanging by the heels.

OLYMPIO (*turning on him*) —and you a nose blow that'll send the eyes out of your head right through the nostrils!

CHALINUS (*unruffled*) What are you scared of? By now it must be all ready for you—your noose, I mean.

OLYMPIO (*nervously*) Ah, you don't stand a chance.

LYSIDAMUS (*shouting*) Now pay attention, both of you.

OLYMPIO (*glaring at Chalinus*) I'm quiet.

LYSIDAMUS (*to Cleostrata*) Now, Cleostrata, so you won't have any suspicions or say I tried any tricks on you, I'm going to let you do the drawing yourself.

OLYMPIO (*groaning*) You're ruining me!

CHALINUS (*gleefully*) And helping me!

CLEOSTRATA (*to Lysidamus, icily*) Thank you.

CHALINUS (*to Olympio*) I pray to god your lot jumps out of the jug and runs away.

OLYMPIO Oh yeah? Just because you're a jailbreaker, you want everybody to be like you?

CHALINUS I'd like to see your lot do what they say once happened in Hercules' family: dissolve in the water while we're drawing.

OLYMPIO Pretty soon I'll have your hide so warm from the whip, *you'll* dissolve.

LYSIDAMUS (*to Olympio, shouting*) Come on now! Please!

OLYMPIO (*grumbling*) If this jailbait here lets me.

LYSIDAMUS (*looking upward, fervently*)   O lord in heaven, give me luck today!

OLYMPIO (*following suit*)   Amen. And me too.

CHALINUS   Not you.

OLYMPIO   Yes, me, god damn it!

CHALINUS   No, *me*, god damn it!

CLEOSTRATA (*to Olympio, matter-of-factly, gesturing toward Chalinus*)   He's going to win, and it's going to make you miserable the rest of your days.

LYSIDAMUS (*to Olympio, pointing to Chalinus*)   Sock that so-and-so on the jaw! Come on, what are you waiting for!

CLEOSTRATA (*to Olympio*)   Watch your step! You keep your hands off him!

OLYMPIO (*to Lysidamus*)   Should I slap him or sock him?

LYSIDAMUS (*promptly*)   Take your pick.

OLYMPIO (*throwing a haymaker at Chalinus*)   Take that!

CLEOSTRATA (*to Olympio, hotly*)   How dare you touch that man!

OLYMPIO (*grinning*)   My Jupiter gave me orders.

CLEOSTRATA (*to Chalinus*)   Give it to him right back. Give him a sock on the jaw!

OLYMPIO (*as Chalinus gets to work on him*)   Help, Jupiter! He's punching me to pieces!

LYSIDAMUS (*to Chalinus, hotly*)   How dare you touch this man!

CHALINUS (*grinning*)   My Juno gave me orders.

LYSIDAMUS (*plucking Olympio out of the mêlée, acidly*)   We'll have to put up with it. My wife's giving the orders in the family even before I'm in the grave.

CLEOSTRATA (*to Lysidamus, gesturing toward Chalinus*)   He should have just as much right to speak his mind as (*gesturing contemptuously toward Olympio*) that one!

OLYMPIO (*grumbling*)   Why must he put the curse on my prayers?

LYSIDAMUS   Chalinus, I think you'd better watch your step or you're in for trouble.

CHALINUS   (*nursing his jaw*)   Fine time to tell me! After my face has been pounded to a pulp.

LYSIDAMUS   (*to Cleostrata*)   Now, dear, draw the lots. (*To the servants*) Pay attention, you two. (*Aside*) I'm so scared, I don't know where I'm at! This is awful! The way my heart's been jumping all along, I swear I've got a case of the palpitations. My chest's getting bruised from the pounding!

CLEOSTRATA   (*plunging a hand in the jug*)   I've got one.

LYSIDAMUS   Pull it out.

CHALINUS   (*to Olympio, grinning*)   Aren't you dead yet?

OLYMPIO   (*to Cleostrata, nervously*)   Let me see. (*As she holds it up, at the top of his lungs*) It's mine!

CHALINUS   (*dumb struck*)   Well, I'll be damned!

CLEOSTRATA   (*showing the lot to Chalinus, sadly*)   You lost, Chalinus.

LYSIDAMUS   (*to Olympio, jumping up and down in his excitement*)   God was on our side, Olympio! This is wonderful!

OLYMPIO   (*to Lysidamus, but looking down his nose at Chalinus*)   It's all because I'm so devout. My whole family is.

LYSIDAMUS   (*to Cleostrata, majestically*)   Inside, madam, and start the preparations for the wedding.

CLEOSTRATA   (*impassively*)   Just as you say.

LYSIDAMUS   (*impatiently*)   Don't you realize it's a long trip from here to the farm where he's going to take her?

CLEOSTRATA   (*as before*)   I realize it.

LYSIDAMUS   Inside now. Even though you don't like any part of it, see that you take good care of everything.

CLEOSTRATA   Very well. (*She goes into the house.*)

LYSIDAMUS   (*to Olympio*)   Let's go in too. We'll put the pressure on them to speed things up.

OLYMPIO   Who's holding you back? I'm not anxious for any

more conversation while (*gesturing contemptuously toward Chalinus*) he's around. (*He follows Lysidamus into the house.*)

CHALINUS (*to the audience, utterly deflated*) Why don't I go hang myself? No, I'd just go to a lot of trouble for nothing, and on top of the trouble, I'd be out the cost of a rope. Besides, I'd give joy and comfort to my enemies. (*Mournfully*) Anyway, I don't need to: I'm already a dead man. I lost the draw—Casina's going to marry the foreman.

(*Stomps up and down a few times, shaking his head bitterly. Then, with clenched fists*) Olympio's winning doesn't bother me as much as the way the old man had his heart set on keeping her from me and giving her to him. What a panic the old devil was in! The way he scurried around and then jumped for joy when Olympio won! (*Suddenly turns toward the door.*) Ah—I heard the door open. I'd better go off over here. (*Moves to an unobtrusive spot near the wall of the house.*) My kind and loving friends are coming out. I'll waylay them from ambush here.

(*Lysidamus and Olympio, who is now dressed in his Sunday best, come out of the house.*)

OLYMPIO (*snarling*) Just let him come to the farm. I'll send him back to the city loaded like a longshoreman.

LYSIDAMUS (*nodding approvingly*) That's the way to do it.

OLYMPIO (*as before*) I'll do it. I'll take care of it.

LYSIDAMUS If Chalinus had been around the house, I was going to send him out to do the shopping with you, and add one more misery to our opponent's load of gloom.

CHALINUS (*to the audience*) I'll play crab now and scuttle in reverse up to the wall here. I've got to catch what those two are saying. (*Bitterly*) One of them gets me down and the other one burns me up. (*Backs up to the wall of the house while Lysidamus and Olympio walk downstage.*) Here comes that stinking piece of whipbait, and he's all dressed up. I'm postponing my hanging. I've made up my mind to send him down to hell first!

OLYMPIO (*self-importantly*)   Quite an assistant I turned out to be for you today. I got you what you wanted most in the world. Today you'll have the object of your affections, and your wife won't know a thing.

LYSIDAMUS   Sh! (*Going close to Olympio and fluttering his eyes at him*)   I swear, I can hardly keep my lips from planting a kiss on you for all you've done for me, darling.

CHALINUS (*aside*)   What's this "planting a kiss?" What's up? What's this "darling" business? By god, I think the old boy's out to put the foreskin to the foreman!

OLYMPIO   Hey, are you getting passionate about *me* now?

LYSIDAMUS (*passionately*)   More than about my own soul, so help me. How about my giving you a hug?

CHALINUS (*aside*)   A hug, eh?

OLYMPIO (*shrugging resignedly*)   All right.

LYSIDAMUS (*circling around to get behind Olympio, as before*)   Ah, to touch you is like honey to my lips!

OLYMPIO (*roaring as Lysidamus goes after him from the rear*)   Beat it, lover-boy! Off my back!

CHALINUS (*aside*)   So that's it! So that's why he made him foreman! When I bumped into the old goat the other day he wanted to make me major-domo on the same terms. Right on the doorstep.

OLYMPIO (*plaintively as he warily keeps his distance*)   I did everything you wanted today. I made you blissfully happy.

LYSIDAMUS (*trying to close in*)   And I'll take better care of you than of my own self till the end of my days.

CHALINUS (*aside, making an obscene gesture*)   If you ask me, these two are going to get all tied up with each other before the day is over. That old goat goes after any male beyond the age of puberty!

LYSIDAMUS (*giving up the chase; rapturously*)   I'll cover

Casina with kisses today. What a good time I'll have! And my wife won't know a thing.

CHALINUS (*aside*) Aha! Finally I'm on the right track. *He's* the one who's crazy about Casina! (*Jubilantly*) I've got 'em!

LYSIDAMUS (*as before*) I'm dying to take her in my arms and kiss her this minute.

OLYMPIO (*testily*) Let her get through the wedding first. What the devil's your hurry?

LYSIDAMUS I'm in love!

OLYMPIO (*shaking his head dubiously*) I don't think it can be done by today.

LYSIDAMUS (*sharply*) Yes it can—that is, if you think you can be freed by tomorrow.

CHALINUS (*aside*) I've got to strain my ears for real now. (*Gleefully*) I'm very neatly going to kill two birds with one stone!

LYSIDAMUS (*confidentially, gesturing toward Alcesimus' house*) I've got a place all set next door here, at my friend's house. I let him in on the whole story of my love affair, and he said he'd fix up a place for me.

OLYMPIO What about his wife? Where will she be?

LYSIDAMUS (*chuckling*) I hit on a wonderful plan. My wife will invite her to our house for the wedding, to stand by and give her a hand and then spend the night with her. I gave the orders, and she agreed to do it. So his wife will spend the night (*pointing to his own door*) here, and I'll arrange to get the husband out of the house. You'll take your bride off to the farm—but the farm will be (*pointing to Alcesimus' house*) here, at least until I've spent my bridal night with Casina. Then, at the crack of dawn, you'll carry her away to the country. Clever, eh?

OLYMPIO (*tapping his brow significantly*) Brainy.

CHALINUS (*aside*) Go on, scheme, you two smarties. You'll smart for it, by god!

LYSIDAMUS   You know what I'd like you to do now?

OLYMPIO   Whatever you say.

LYSIDAMUS (*handing him a purse*)   Here's money. Go do the shopping. Hurry! But be on your toes, mind you: get only tender morsels, since (*kissing his fingers*) she's such a tender morsel.

OLYMPIO   Right.

LYSIDAMUS (*rapturously*)   Get squidlets, octopussies, clamkins—

CHALINUS (*aside*)   Where are your brains? Lambkins!

LYSIDAMUS (*as before*)   —sole—

CHALINUS (*aside*)   Sole? Why not a boot—to kick you in the face with, you old goat!

OLYMPIO   How about some snapper?

LYSIDAMUS   What do we need it for? We've got my wife in the house. She's our snapper—she never shuts those jaws of hers.

OLYMPIO (*importantly*)   When I'm on the spot, I can look over the fish display and decide what to buy.

LYSIDAMUS   Good idea. On your way. (*Olympio turns to go but Lysidamus grabs him and hauls him back.*) And don't economize—buy plenty. (*Lets him go.*) And now I've got to hold a meeting with my neighbor here to make sure he does what I asked him to do.

OLYMPIO (*impatiently*)   Can I go now?

LYSIDAMUS   Yes.

(*Olympio races off, stage left, and Lysidamus hurries into Alcesimus' house. Chalinus leaves his hiding place and walks downstage.*)

CHALINUS (*to the audience*)   Offer me my freedom three times over, and that still wouldn't stop me from cooking up trouble for these two today, plenty of it. Or from telling this whole story to the madam right now. I've caught the opposition in the act, red-handed! And if the madam will only do her job, the battle's ours. I'll beat that pair to the punch! Today's our lucky day: now the losers are the winners! I'll go inside and what (*gesturing toward Lysidamus inside the house*) our other cook cooked up, I'll cook over in a different way. The menu he prepared won't be prepared, and I'll have one prepared for which he's unprepared!

(*Chalinus ducks into Lysidamus' house and the stage is now empty.*)

ACT III

(*The door of Alcesimus' house opens, and Lysidamus comes out, tugging after him a respectable looking gentleman of about the same age, whose whole attitude reveals reluctance, harassment, and distaste. It is his neighbor, Alcesimus.*)

LYSIDAMUS (*dramatically*) Now I'm going to find out if I behold friend or foe, Alcesimus. Now I'll have the proof positive, the decision decisive. (*Raising a warning hand as Alcesimus opens his mouth to speak*) And cut out the lectures on my love life. And cut out the (*mimicking the tones of moral outrage*) "A man of your age! With your gray hairs!" And the "You a married man!" routine, you can certainly cut that out!

ALCESIMUS (*eying him distastefully*) I've seen people in love but never a case as bad as yours.

LYSIDAMUS (*ignoring this last remark, warningly*) Get everybody out of the house, now.

ALCESIMUS (*testily*) Damn it all, I decided to send the servants, all of them, male and female, over to your house.

LYSIDAMUS (*nodding approvingly*) Shows you're using your sense with sense. (*Waggling a finger at him*) Just remember, though, the song the birdies sing: (*as if mimicking a bird call*) "With food, with food, with food." Pretend these servants of yours are marching to Sutrium.[3]

ALCESIMUS (*wearily*) I'll remember.

LYSIDAMUS (*all affability again*) That's it. Now you're showing sense—more sense than a censor. Take care of things. I'm going downtown. I'll be back right away.

ALCESIMUS (*acidly*) Have a nice walk.

[3] A historic forced march of the Roman army during which each soldier had to report with his own provisions.

LYSIDAMUS   Have your house learn some letters and numbers.

ALCESIMUS   What do you mean?

LYSIDAMUS   I want it to say M T 4 U when I get back.

ALCESIMUS   Ugh! I could murder you. You and your jokes.

LYSIDAMUS   (*chuckling*)   What's the use of my carrying on a love affair if I can't be cute and crack jokes? (*Raising a warning finger*) Now don't get lost and make me go looking for you.

ALCESIMUS   (*resignedly*)   I won't leave the house.

(*Lysidamus hurries off, stage left, and Alcesimus goes into his house. A minute later Cleostrata emerges from her house.*)

CLEOSTRATA   (*to the audience*)   Well, what do you know! So that's why that husband of mine was begging me so hard to rush out and invite my neighbor over! He wanted everyone out of that house so he could bring Casina there. Well, I'm not issuing any invitations! I'm not giving those nasty old goats any chance to have the place to themselves. (*The door of Alcesimus' house opens.*) Ah! He's coming out, this pillar of society, this bulwark of the nation—this neighbor of mine who's supplying my husband with a place he can have to himself. Buy him for a pound of salt and you'd still be overpaying!

ALCESIMUS   (*grumbling to himself as he comes out*)   I don't understand it: no one's come yet to invite my wife next door. For hours now she's been waiting, all dressed up, to be invited over there. (*Noticing Cleostrata*) There's Cleostrata now. I suppose she's coming to get her. Hello, Cleostrata.

CLEOSTRATA   Hello, Alcesimus. Where's your wife?

ALCESIMUS   Inside. She's been waiting for you to come for her. Your husband begged me to let her go to your house to give you a hand. Shall I call her?

CLEOSTRATA   (*casually*)   Not if she's busy. Let her be.

ALCESIMUS   (*quickly*)   She's not busy.

CLEOSTRATA   Never mind. I don't want to bother her. I'll see her some other time.

ALCESIMUS (*puzzled*)   Aren't you people getting ready for a wedding at your house?

CLEOSTRATA   Yes. I'm making the arrangements.

ALCESIMUS (*as before*)   Well, don't you need help?

CLEOSTRATA (*elaborately casual*)   I have plenty right in the house. I'll drop in on her when the wedding's over. Good-by now. Give her my regards. (*Turns and walks leisurely toward her house.*)

ALCESIMUS (*to the audience, baffled*)   Now what do I do? (*Bitterly*) Damn! That was a dirty trick I played, and all because of that toothless, filthy old goat who got me into this mess. Here I am promising my wife's help as if she was some kitchen maid! That dirty liar tells me his wife is coming to get her—and his wife tells me no, she doesn't want her! By god, I wouldn't be a bit surprised if our lady next door smells a rat. (*After a moment of thought*) On the other hand, come to think of it, if she had any suspicions, she'd have put me through a cross-examination. I'll go in now and (*indicating by a gesture his wife in the house*) put that barge of mine back in her berth.

(*Alcesimus goes in. Cleostrata, having reached her doorway, turns and addresses the audience.*)

CLEOSTRATA   Well, I did a fine job of fooling him, all right. The way those two poor devils are running around! What I'd like, is to see that broken-down, good-for-nothing husband of mine come along so he can take his turn at being fooled, now that I've dealt with this other one. I'd love to stir up some trouble between those two. (*Her attention caught, she looks toward the wings, stage left.*) Well, here he comes. To look at that solemn face, you'd think he was somebody decent!

(*Lysidamus stomps in, obviously in a foul temper.*)

LYSIDAMUS (*to the audience*) If you want my opinion, it's the height of stupidity for a man in love to go downtown on the very day the object of his affections is to be in his arms. That's what I was dumb enough to do. I wasted the whole day, standing around testifying for some relative of mine. (*Grinning maliciously*) As a matter of fact, he lost the case and I'm delighted: at least he got something out of my being a witness for him. I have a theory about witnesses, to wit, that you should first inquire and ascertain whether said witness has his wits about him, and if said witness turns out witless, send him home! (*Suddenly noticing Cleostrata*) There's my wife in front of the house! This is bad. I'm scared: unless she's deaf, she's heard what I said!

CLEOSTRATA (*aside*) I heard, all right, and you'll pay plenty for it!

LYSIDAMUS (*aside*) I'll go up to her. (*To Cleostrata, with a great show of heartiness*) How are you, light of my life?

CLEOSTRATA (*icily*) I've been waiting for you.

LYSIDAMUS (*as before*) Everything in order by now? (*Gesturing toward Alcesimus' house*) Have you had your neighbor brought over yet to give you a hand?

CLEOSTRATA I went to get her as you told me to. But that pal of yours, your best friend, blew up at her over something or other. When I came to get her, he said he wouldn't let her go.

LYSIDAMUS (*snarling*) That's your worst fault: you can't be nice to people.

CLEOSTRATA (*witheringly*) Why, dear, it's the chore of a whore, not a wife, to be nice to another woman's husband. You go get her yourself; there are things to do inside, and I want to take care of them, (*acidly*) dear.

LYSIDAMUS (*promptly*) You hurry along.

CLEOSTRATA All right. (*Aside*) I'll put the fear of god in him, all right. I'll have lover-boy here in a bad way before this day is done!

(She goes into her house. At the same moment Alcesimus comes out of his.)

ALCESIMUS *(to himself, grumbling)*   I'll take a look and see if the fond lover has come back from downtown. The way that old mummy fooled my wife and me! *(Turning and noticing Lysidamus)* There he is, in front of his house. *(Calling)* Damn it all, I was just coming to see you.

LYSIDAMUS   Damn it all, I was just coming to see *you*. Listen, you good-for-nothing, what did I tell you to do? What was it I begged you to do?

ALCESIMUS   What's the matter?

LYSIDAMUS   Fine job you did of getting everyone out of your house! Fine job you did of sending your wife over to my house! All because of you my big chance is gone, and I'm a goner.

ALCESIMUS *(hotly)*   Oh yeah? Well, you can just go hang yourself. Didn't you tell me with your own lips that your wife would come to get my wife?

LYSIDAMUS *(hotly)*   And *she* tells me she did—and that you said you wouldn't let her go.

ALCESIMUS   Oh yeah? Well your wife told me herself that she didn't need her help.

LYSIDAMUS   Oh yeah? Well my wife has just told me herself to go get her!

ALCESIMUS   Oh yeah? Well, that doesn't cut any ice with me.

LYSIDAMUS   Oh yeah? Well, you're just ruining my life!

ALCESIMUS   Oh yeah? Well, that's just fine.

LYSIDAMUS   Oh yeah? Well, I'll just stick around for a while.

ALCESIMUS   Oh yeah? Well, what I'd like—

LYSIDAMUS *(interrupting)*   Oh yeah—

ALCESIMUS *(ignoring the interruption)*   —is to do you dirt.

LYSIDAMUS   Oh yeah? Well, that's what *I'd* like to do. You're not going to have the last "Oh yeah" today.

ALCESIMUS   Oh yeah? Well, *(shouting)* god damn you!

LYSIDAMUS (*between his teeth*) Listen, are you going to send your wife out to me?

ALCESIMUS (*roaring*) Take her and go to hell, all of you! You, she, your wife, *and* that girl friend of yours! (*The two glare at each other for a moment. Alcesimus throws up his hands in surrender.*) Go away and leave it to me. I'll send my wife over to yours right away through the back yard. (*He goes back into his house.*)

LYSIDAMUS (*calling to him, all smiles again*) Now you're a real friend! (*To the audience, exasperated*) Did I start this affair on Friday the thirteenth? Did I commit a sin or something against Lady Venus? Here I am, madly in love, and all I get is delays! (*A piercing shriek suddenly is heard from his house.*) Hey! What's all the noise about in my house?

(*The door flies open, and Pardalisca bursts out, shrieking.*)

SONG

PARDALISCA (*to the audience, burlesquing the style of grand opera*)

> I'm ruined, lost, utterly undone by Fate!
> Horror has my heart, I tremble from head to toe,
> And where to seek and whom to supplicate
> For succor, safety, shelter, I do not know.
> Just now, inside, I saw strange things occur,
> A terrible daring, naked, unparalleled.
> Cleostrata beware! Stay away from her,
> I beg you, before she does you harm. She's held
> In anger's grip. And snatch that sword away
> From her! She's out of her senses, her mind's astray!

LYSIDAMUS (*aside*)

What frightened her to death just now, and made her run out this way?

(*Calling*)

Pardalisca!

PARDALISCA (*without turning around, as before*)
> Lost! Whence comes this sound that caught my
> ears, I pray?

LYSIDAMUS (*impatiently*)
You turn around and look at me!

PARDALISCA (*doing so—and bursting into tears*)
> Dear master!

LYSIDAMUS (*testily*)
> What's wrong with you?
What scared you?

PARDALISCA (*impassioned*)
> Lost!

LYSIDAMUS (*blankly*)
> You're lost? How's that?

PARDALISCA (*as before*)
> Yes, lost. And you are too.

LYSIDAMUS (*as before*)
I'm lost? How come?

PARDALISCA
> Alas for you!

LYSIDAMUS
> Let's make it *you.*

PARDALISCA (*launching into a fainting act*)
> I'm falling!
Please hold me up.

LYSIDAMUS (*holding her with obvious distaste*)
> Now *what's* going on? Speak up and quit the stalling.

PARDALISCA (*as before*)
Please hold me by the waist. Now take your coat and fan
my face.

LYSIDAMUS (*aside, as he obeys orders*)
Now what's this mean? It's got me scared—unless she's been
someplace
Where Bacchus juice was served up straight, and found it
too enthralling!

PARDALISCA *(faintly)*
Now put your hands upon my ears.

LYSIDAMUS *(roaring)*

Oh you go straight to hell!

(Grimly, raising his staff menacingly)
     God damn your ears, waist, head—and you as well.
     Unless I hear from you, and hear it quick,
     What this is all about, with this here stick
     I'll bash in all your brains, you bitch. You'll see—
     By now you've fooled around enough with me.

PARDALISCA *(sobbing)*
Dear master!

LYSIDAMUS *(mimicking her)*
     What now, dear maid?

PARDALISCA *(as before)*

         You're so mad, so upset!

LYSIDAMUS *(between his teeth)*
     You're ahead of yourself—you haven't heard anything
         yet.

(Shouting)
     What's the fuss all about? Talk—and *don't* make it long!
     That ruckus inside just before—what was wrong?

PARDALISCA
Just listen, I'll tell you. Inside there, your maid
Started carrying on just before. I'm afraid
She behaved in the awfullest way that she could.
She did what no well-bred Athenian should.

LYSIDAMUS *(nervously)*
Did what?

PARDALISCA *(dramatically)*
     Fear binds my tongue—no words come out!

LYSIDAMUS *(wearily)*
Can't I *please* find out from you what this is about?

PARDALISCA (*as if making a great effort*)
> That maid you thought your wife should make the
> > bride
> Of your foreman, inside this girl—

LYSIDAMUS (*interrupting anxiously*)
> > > > > Did what inside?
> Tell me what!

PARDALISCA
> > > > > —behaved like a mean and nasty wife.
> She's making threats against her husband's life—

LYSIDAMUS (*interrupting, incredulously*)
> What about his life?

PARDALISCA (*groaning*)
> > > > > Oh god!

LYSIDAMUS (*frantically*)
> > > > > Speak up!

PARDALISCA (*playing the scene to the hilt*)
> > > > > She's got
> A yen to end it. And that sword—

LYSIDAMUS (*interrupting, with a roar*)
> > > > > That *what?*

PARDALISCA (*matter-of-factly*)
> That sword.

LYSIDAMUS
> > > > What about that sword?

PARDALISCA
> It's in her hand.

LYSIDAMUS
> > > > O lord
> In heaven! Why a sword?

PARDALISCA (*rapidly, with trembling voice*)
> She's been chasing us all through the house,
> And she won't let a soul come near.
> We all hide under bureaus and beds
> And don't *dare* say a word for fear!

LYSIDAMUS (*aside, clutching his hair*)
    I'm lost, I'm ruined!
  (*To Pardalisca*)
                            But what could have hit the girl
    So suddenly?

PARDALISCA
              Her mind—it's in a whirl.

LYSIDAMUS (*throwing up his hands helplessly*)
    Who's ever had a fouler role to play?

PARDALISCA
    If you only knew the things she said today!

LYSIDAMUS (*nervously*)
    What was it she said? I'd like to know.

PARDALISCA
                      You may.

  (*Solemnly*)
              She swore an oath by heaven's might
              To murder the man she sleeps with tonight.

LYSIDAMUS (*gulping*)
    What, murder *me*? That can't be true!

PARDALISCA (*all innocence*)
    Just what's this got to do with you?

LYSIDAMUS (*to himself, chagrined*)
    God damn!

PARDALISCA (*as before*)
             Or you to do with her?

LYSIDAMUS (*with a sickly grin*)
    A slip of the tongue. I meant to—er—
    Say Olympio.

PARDALISCA (*aside*)
             How very neat—
    Here's a man who knows how to fall on his feet!

LYSIDAMUS (*with a dismal attempt at casualness*)
    She's not been threatening *me*, has she?

PARDALISCA (*sternly*)
>   Why, you're the very enemy
>   She hates the most!

LYSIDAMUS (*agonized*)
>   But how's that so?

PARDALISCA (*shrugging*)
>   You gave her to Olympio.

>   (*Excitedly*)
>   Neither one of you gets one more day, so she said:
>   By tomorrow you both, plus herself, will be dead.
>   I've been sent here to tell you, to warn you—don't go
>   Anywhere near her.

LYSIDAMUS
>   I'm a goner!

PARDALISCA (*aside*)
>   And rightfully so.

LYSIDAMUS (*lugubriously*)
>   O god, what sugar daddy, present or past,
>   Is as miserable as I?

PARDALISCA (*to the audience, jubilantly*)
>   I'm pulling a fast
>   One on him. It's all a plot cooked up before
>   By Cleostrata and her friend who lives next door.
>   These things I've told him—simply a pack of lies;
>   That's why I'm here, to pull the wool over his eyes!

LYSIDAMUS (*worriedly*)
>   Hey, Pardalisca.

PARDALISCA
>   What?

LYSIDAMUS (*as before*)
>   I want to find out—

PARDALISCA (*not very encouragingly*)
>   Find out what?

LYSIDAMUS *(weakly)*

             There's something I want to ask you about.

PARDALISCA *(with a great show of impatience)*

     Don't make me late.

LYSIDAMUS *(anguished)*

                Don't make me desolate!

   (Nervously)

     That sword—hasn't Casina put that sword down yet?

PARDALISCA *(promptly)*

     No sir! And it's not just one, it's two.

LYSIDAMUS

                       Why two?

PARDALISCA

     She says one to slaughter your man, and the other you.

LYSIDAMUS *(clutching his hair)*

     The deadest man alive, that's what I'll be!

     The thing that's best for me to do, I see,

     Is put on armor—

   (Suddenly getting an idea)

                wait. My wife! I say,

     Didn't she go up and take that sword away?

PARDALISCA

     Oh, no one dares go near the girl.

LYSIDAMUS *(indignantly)*

                  Then she

     Should beg her.

PARDALISCA

           She did. But Casina stubbornly

     Refuses to set it down until she knows

     She's definitely not going to be Olympio's.

LYSIDAMUS *(roaring)*

     God damn it, just because she feels that way,

     Like it or not, she'll marry him today!

     After all, why shouldn't I finish what I began

     And make her marry me—oops, I mean my man.

PARDALISCA (*archly*)
> These slips—they're coming rather frequently.

LYSIDAMUS (*mimicking her tones of a few minutes ago*)
> Fear binds my tongue.

> (*Seriously*)

> > > > > Please give my wife this plea:
> > To plead with the girl to put that sword away,
> > So's I can get back inside my house today.

PARDALISCA
> > I'll tell her that.

LYSIDAMUS
> > You beg her, too.

PARDALISCA (*shrugging disinterestedly*)
> > I'll beg her, too.

LYSIDAMUS
> > > But sweet as pie,
> > > The way that I
> > > Have seen you do.

> (*Confidentially*)

> > Now, listen here. You pull this thing,
> > And your finger gets a golden ring;
> > There's also sandals in it for you,
> > And lots of other goodies, too.

PARDALISCA
> > I'll see what I can do.

LYSIDAMUS
> > And make the girl say yes.

PARDALISCA (*turning toward the door*)
> > > I'm going now, unless
> > > There's something more
> > > You want me for.

LYSIDAMUS
> > > You go ahead.
> > > But do what I said!

(Pardalisca disappears into the house. At the same mo-
ment, enter, stage left, Olympio followed by a cook and a
small army of scullions lugging bundles.)

Look who's here! My associate, back with a stack
Of supplies, plus an army of cooks at his back.

OLYMPIO *(to the cook, gesturing contemptuously at the file of*
assistants)

Don't you dare let these thorns break their ranks now,
you crook.

COOK *(belligerently)*

And just why are they thorns?

OLYMPIO

In a flash they can hook
Whatever they touch. Then just try to get free—
In a flash, there's a slash. Anyplace they're to be,
Anyplace they're to work at, the damage can go
Up to double what's paid them.

COOK

Yah-yah!

OLYMPIO *(catching sight of Lysidamus, draws himself up and,*
unused to such finery, tries to adjust the handsome coat he
is wearing; to himself)

Ho-ho!
Now to wrap this around me in style, *comme il faut*,
And go up to the master just so.

LYSIDAMUS

Well, hello,
My good man.

OLYMPIO *(importantly)*

That I am.

LYSIDAMUS *(jovially)*

Tell me, how do you feel?

OLYMPIO *(eying the bundles longingly)*

You're for love—and I'm hungry and all for a meal.

LYSIDAMUS (*reaching out to caress Olympio's pomaded hair*)
    You've come to me all prettied up—

OLYMPIO (*sternly, ducking and avoiding the hand*)
                                    There I balk!

LYSIDAMUS (*taken aback*)
    Now, wait—not so uppity, you.

OLYMPIO (*starting to walk away toward the door*)
                                    And your talk
    Simply stinks, stinks out loud.

LYSIDAMUS (*reaching out a hand again*)
                            What's the matter with you?

OLYMPIO (*batting the hand away, and continuing to walk*)
    You!

LYSIDAMUS (*trying to keep up but falling behind*)
        Hey, stop!

OLYMPIO (*over his shoulder, disgustedly*)
                    Vous êtes pain in the derrière, vous.

LYSIDAMUS (*snarling*)
                What I'd like to give vous
                Is le whip, entendu?
                And unless you stand still
                I've a hunch that I will!

OLYMPIO (*stopping and throwing up his hands*)
                    Oh, mon dieu!
                    Can't you let me be,
                        And go away?
                    Do you want to see
                        Me puke today?

LYSIDAMUS (*as Olympio sets off again*)
        Wait!

OLYMPIO (*stopping and eying him glassily, with ineffable
    contempt*)
                    What did you say?
    (*To the file of cooks, like a king to his courtiers*)
                Who's this person, anyway?

LYSIDAMUS (*puzzled*)

      I'm the master.

OLYMPIO (*as before*)

                  Of who?

LYSIDAMUS (*as before*)

      Why, of you!

OLYMPIO (*with utter incredulity*)

                    I'm a slave?

LYSIDAMUS

      That's right. Mine.

OLYMPIO (*fixing him with a piercing glance*)

                    But you gave

Me my freedom. It's true.

You remember, don't you?

LYSIDAMUS (*reaching out a hand to stop him as he starts off again*)

      Wait a second.

OLYMPIO (*roaring*)

                Let go!

(*Olympio glares at him. Lysidamus seems to wither up before that scorching glance.*)

LYSIDAMUS (*humbly*)

      I remember. I'm *your* slave.

OLYMPIO (*nodding approvingly*)

                  Bravo.

LYSIDAMUS (*as before*)

      O my master, protector, patron,

Dear Olympio, pray do me one—

OLYMPIO (*interrupting, as before*)

      That's the way. Now you're using your brain.

LYSIDAMUS (*fulsomely*)

      I'm all yours.

OLYMPIO (*the lord of the manor again*)

                Yes, but what do I gain

By having a slave who's a knave?

LYSIDAMUS (*humbly*)
    Well, how soon could you have me remade?

OLYMPIO (*eying the bundles again*)
    Just as soon as the table is laid!

LYSIDAMUS (*pointing to the file of cooks*)
    Then get them all going.

OLYMPIO (*shouting to the cooks*)
                    Get moving! No shirking!
On the double inside, on the double get working!
I'll be here for a while. Now you make me a meal
That a man can get drunk on. But a meal with appeal—
Give me none of that pap that a Roman will eat.

    (*Starts to follow the cooks in, but stops when he notices
that Lysidamus is not budging.*)

    You're going to stay?

LYSIDAMUS (*grimly*)
                    Where I've planted these feet.

OLYMPIO
    What's there left that should keep you out here in the
        street?

LYSIDAMUS (*excitedly*)
                They tell me your bride
                Has a sword there inside
                For dispatching us two
                Without further ado.

OLYMPIO (*with amused contempt*)
                Well, we'll just let her have it. I know
                These damned dames, you see.
                They just do things for fun. You come on
                In the house with me.

LYSIDAMUS
                Damn it all, I'm afraid I'll get hurt.
                    You go in, and hide:
                Look around and check up on just what's
                    Going on inside.

OLYMPIO (*dryly*)
> Your life is no dearer to you
> > Than is mine to me.
> So come on, will you!

LYSIDAMUS
> > > > > Since you insist.
> (*Cautiously falling in in back of Olympio*)
> > I'm behind you, see?

> (*The two enter the house, and the stage is now empty.*)

ACT IV

(Enter Pardalisca from Lysidamus' house.)

PARDALISCA *(to the audience, chuckling)* I'll bet even the Olympic games, or any games anywhere, can't supply as much sport as the sportive events now being held inside for the benefit of our old man and our foreman.

Everybody's madly busy in there, in every corner of the house. In the kitchen there's the old man raising a holler trying to hurry up the cooks: *(mimicking)* "Do something, will you! If you're going to serve anything, start serving! Hurry! Dinner should have been all cooked by now!" Then there's the foreman, who's parading around, scrubbed and polished, all in white and with a garland on his head. In the bedroom there are the two ladies, busy dressing up the orderly to palm him off instead of Casina as our foreman's bride. *(Giggling)* And they're doing a marvelous job of pretending they don't know a thing about what's going to happen. Then there are the cooks who are holding their end up with a marvelous job of seeing to it that the old man gets no dinner. They're tipping over the pots, letting the water put out the fire, doing exactly what the ladies asked them to. And the ladies are dying to get the old man out of the house without his dinner so they can be the only ones to fill their bellies. I know those two: trencherwomen both of them; they can stow the stuff away by the shipload. *(Turning around as a creak catches her attention)* There goes the door!

(Lysidamus comes out. He stops on the threshold to talk to Cleostrata and Myrrhina inside.)

LYSIDAMUS *(through the doorway, doing his best to sound casual)* I'm going to eat at the farm, dear. Why don't you two be smart and go ahead and have dinner anyway, as soon as it's ready? I want to escort the new bride and groom to the farm so there's no chance anyone will run off with her; (*importantly*) I know the dangerous types there are about. You two enjoy yourselves. Now hurry and send both of them out right away so we can get there while it's still light. I'll be back tomorrow, dear. I'll have my share of the banquet then.

PARDALISCA (*to the audience, triumphantly*) There goes what I said would happen: the ladies are getting the old boy out of the house without any dinner in him.

(*Lysidamus turns, walks away from the door, and catches sight of Pardalisca.*)

LYSIDAMUS (*startled*) What are you doing here?

PARDALISCA (*all innocence*) I? On my way where your wife sent me.

LYSIDAMUS (*suspiciously*) Is that so?

PARDALISCA (*as before*) Oh yes, it's so.

LYSIDAMUS (*snarling*) What are you spying here for?

PARDALISCA (*indignantly*) I'm *not* spying!

LYSIDAMUS (*pointing to the door*) Out of here! Inside everyone's rushing around, and you're loitering out here.

PARDALISCA (*scurrying toward the door*) I'm going.

LYSIDAMUS On your way! Out of here, you dirty good-for-nothing! (*To the audience*) Has she gone? (*Hearing the door slam, with a sigh of relief*) Now I can say what I want. (*Rapturously*) When a man's in love, he can be dying of hunger, yet he doesn't feel hungry. (*The door of his house swings open, and Olympio appears in the doorway.*) Ah, here he comes with a garland on his head and a torch in his hand—my ally, my associate, my cohusband, my foreman!

(*Olympio walks downstage. He is resplendent in his full wedding regalia. A flutist follows at his heels.*)

OLYMPIO (*to the flutist, gaily*) Come on, piper, until they bring out my blushing bride, let's have a nice song. Let's flood the whole street with my wedding march!

OLYMPIO and LYSIDAMUS (*who joins in*)
Here comes the bride,
Here comes the bride!

LYSIDAMUS (*heartily*)   How're you doing, savior?

OLYMPIO (*abruptly dropping his gaiety, peevishly*)   I need saving—I'm damned hungry.

LYSIDAMUS   How about me? I'm lovesick!

OLYMPIO (*as before*)   Doesn't mean a damned thing. You can feed on love. Me, my stomach's been growling for hours.

LYSIDAMUS (*grumbling*)   What are those slowpokes being so slow about in there, anyway? The more I rush them, the slower things go. You'd think it was on purpose!

OLYMPIO (*brightly*)   Suppose I hit them with more of the wedding march? Maybe that'll hustle them out here.

LYSIDAMUS   Right. And I'll join you—we're both in this marriage together.

LYSIDAMUS and OLYMPIO (*bellowing*)
Here comes the bride,
Here comes the bride!

LYSIDAMUS (*agonized*)   God, this is killing me! I could sing the wedding march till I split a gut, but I'm not getting the chance (*leering*) to split a gut the way I want to!

OLYMPIO (*eying him distastefully*)   God, if you were a horse, we could never break you in.

LYSIDAMUS   How do you figure that?

OLYMPIO   The way you champ at the bit.

LYSIDAMUS (*leering*)   Ever try to mount me?

OLYMPIO   God forbid! (*Turning around as a creak catches his attention*) There goes the door. They're coming out!

LYSIDAMUS (*fervently*)   The good lord wants me saved!

(*Enter Cleostrata and Pardalisca leading Chalinus, who,*

*heavily veiled and wearing a flowing wedding gown, makes a
convincing enough female figure.)*

CLEOSTRATA (*overhearing, sotto voce to Pardalisca*)   He's already gotten a whiff of Mr. Casina even from this distance!

SONG

PARDALISCA (*tenderly, as she guides the "bride" over the
threshold*)

     Step over the threshold with care, blushing bride.
     Start such steps safe and sound, so you're sure
         To stand over your husband,
         To be stronger and never give in,
         To defeat him and so
         Be his conquering heroine!
     Let your voice, your authority rule everywhere,
     Let him load you with clothes, while *you* strip him bare,
         Pull the wool o'er his eyes night and day—
         Never, never forget this, I pray.

OLYMPIO (*sotto voce, snarling*)

     Let her slip the least bit, and she'll pay for it double!

LYSIDAMUS (*agonized*)

     You be quiet!

OLYMPIO

         I won't!

LYSIDAMUS (*as before*)

             Why not? What's the trouble?

OLYMPIO (*gesturing towards Pardalisca*)

     Why, the bitch there will make her a bitch of a witch!

LYSIDAMUS (*clapping a hand over Olympio's mouth and hiss-
ing into his ear*)

     You'll upset what's all set to go off with no hitch!
     To undo all we've done—how they'd love such a switch!

PARDALISCA (*to Olympio, handing the bride to him and intoning solemnly*)

Now Olympio, since
You wish to be wed,
Please accept from our hands
This bride for your bed.

OLYMPIO (*truculently*)

You plan to give her to me today? Then give!

LYSIDAMUS (*hustling off Pardalisca and Cleostrata*)

Go back inside.

PARDALISCA (*over her shoulder as she is being hustled off*)

You will be sensitive
And spare her virgin innocence, won't you?

OLYMPIO (*taking the bride by the hand, promptly*)

Good-by. Will do.

LYSIDAMUS (*continuing his hustling*)

Now move, you two.

CLEOSTRATA

And now, adieu!

(*Cleostrata and Pardalisca go into the house.*)

LYSIDAMUS

My wife—has she gone?

OLYMPIO

Inside. Relax.

LYSIDAMUS

Yippee!
Finally, once and for all, thank god, I'm free.

(*To the bride, crooning*)

My prettykins, honeykins, spring-blossomkins—

OLYMPIO (*menacingly*)

Hey you!
Be smart and watch out or you'll end up black and
blue.
She's mine!

LYSIDAMUS (*leering*)

> I know. First right of usage, though,
> Belongs to me.

OLYMPIO (*thrusting the torch at him*)

> Here, hold this torch.

LYSIDAMUS (*clamping an arm around the bride*)

> Oh, no.

I'm holding *this*.

(*Raising his eyes to heaven*)

> O Venus all-powerful, who
> By giving this, gives blessings galore, thank you!

(*Embracing the bride passionately*)

> Oh, que belle bodykins!

OLYMPIO (*shoving him away and taking over the embrace*)

> Oh, my sweet wifeykins!

(*Suddenly lets go with a roar and hops about holding one foot.*)

> Hey, what's going on?

LYSIDAMUS

> What happened?

OLYMPIO

> She plants
> A hoof on my foot like an elephant's!

LYSIDAMUS (*taking over the embrace*)

Oh, quiet! Her bosom's soft as any cloud.

OLYMPIO (*again shoving Lysidamus away and taking over*)

This little breast's so cute—

(*Suddenly grabbing his stomach*)

> for crying out loud!

LYSIDAMUS

What's the matter?

OLYMPIO

> Right in the belly I got a slam.
> But not with an elbow—with a battering ram!

LYSIDAMUS (*contemptuously*)

You're handling her too roughly, don't you see?

(*Taking over*)

She's gentle with a gentle gent like me.

(*Suddenly flies backward and barely keeps from toppling over.*)

Ouch!

OLYMPIO

What happened?

LYSIDAMUS

This cutie's strong!

She laid me out—or just about.

OLYMPIO (*leering*)

I'd say she wants to *be* laid out.

LYSIDAMUS (*promptly*)

What's holding us up? Let's move along!

OLYMPIO (*to the bride, crooning*)

On your way, little sweet,

Move those sweet little feet.

(*The three disappear into Alcesimus' house and the stage is now empty.*)

ACT V

(*Cleostrata, Myrrhina, and Pardalisca emerge from Lysidamus' house, all three in high good humor.*)

SONG

MYRRHINA

> Well, having been wined and dined so well inside,
> Let's step out here to watch the fun with the bride.
> I haven't laughed so much since god knows when,
> And I doubt I'll ever laugh as much again.

PARDALISCA (*giggling*)

> I'd love to know what Chalinus does in that room.
> The brand-new husband with his blushing groom!

MYRRHINA (*chuckling*)

> What playwright's ever contrived a trick as smart
> As the one that we've just worked—a work of art!

CLEOSTRATA

> Right now I'd like to see my old buck come out
> With his face bashed in. He is, without a doubt,
> The nastiest codger alive. Or do you presume
> The other's worse, the one who supplied the room?
> Pardalisca, I want you standing guard outside:
> Whoever you see come out, you take for a ride.

PARDALISCA (*giggling*)

> I always do. Delighted to do so now.

[A line has been lost here. This scene was mutilated in the archetype from which are derived the manuscripts we have, and there are frequent gaps where words, sometimes lines, are missing. In these spots I have rendered what is preserved in prose, marking the lacunae with suspension points.]

CLEOSTRATA (*to Pardalisca*)

> Keep an eye from here on all that goes on inside.

[A mutilated line follows in which Cleostrata has Myrrhina
follow her to an unobtrusive spot off to the side.]

MYRRHINA (*nodding approvingly as she follows*)
        And whatever you want to say to her
           From there you're free to speak.

PARDALISCA (*to Myrrhina*)
        Be quiet, will you, please?
           Your door's begun to creak!

(*Cleostrata and Myrrhina take their stand off to the side,
and Pardalisca hers near the door. A second later Olympio
bursts out. He is half-naked and his face is bloody and
swollen.*)

OLYMPIO (*to the audience, panic-stricken*)
        I don't *know* where to flee or to hide, or just how
           To disguise the disgrace I'm so dreading.
        That's how awful a scandal it was that did in
           The old codger and me at our wedding.
        I'm afraid and ashamed, and the both of us are
           In a most ridiculous position.

(*Clapping a hand to his brow*)

        Am I soft in the head? I ashamed? This is strange—
           Never felt up to now the condition!

(*Calming down and speaking more naturally*)

        Take the trouble to listen as I tell you my tale—
           It is well worth your trouble to hear it.
        Both for telling and hearing, the mess I got in
           Is so silly that nothing comes near it.
        As soon as I had the new bride in the house
           Right away to the bedroom I brought her.
        It was darker than pitch. The old gent still en route,
           "You lie down on the bed here," I order.

(*Excitedly*)

I lay her out, put a cushion under her, start the sweet
nothings so that, before the old gent . . . I suddenly slowed
up since . . . I keep looking over my shoulder to make

sure the old gent . . . to put her in the mood for the act,
I start by asking for a kiss . . .

> So I reach, but I miss her—
> Since she won't let me kiss her.
> The more that I hurry, the keener I get
> To break ground in Casina's plot.
> I've a yen to deprive the old gent of the job
> Before he arrives on the spot.
> So I slam the door shut to minimize
> Any chance that he'll take me by surprise.

CLEOSTRATA (*to Pardalisca, sotto voce*)
> All ready? Go up to him now!

PARDALISCA (*to Olympio, archly*)
> Well, Olympio, where's the new frau?

OLYMPIO (*to the world at large, agonized*)
> I'm found out! God, this means my demise!

PARDALISCA (*dropping her archness for a tone of authority*)
> So don't bother to stall,
> Just confess and tell all.

> (*Smirking*)

> How's it going inside?
> How's it go with the bride?
> How does Casina do?
> Being nice to you two?

OLYMPIO (*hanging his head*)
> I'm embarrassed to tell.

PARDALISCA (*dryly*)
> You began very well—
> Just continue from there.

OLYMPIO (*as before*)
> I'm embarrassed, I swear!

PARDALISCA Don't be afraid . . . I want you to start with
what happened after you got into bed . . .

OLYMPIO . . . it's shocking.

PARDALISCA (*grinning*)   It'll be a lesson to our hearers . . .

OLYMPIO (*groaning*)   . . . I'm a goner!

PARDALISCA (*as before*)   Go on!

OLYMPIO   When . . .

PARDALISCA   What?

OLYMPIO   Wow!

PARDALISCA   What!

OLYMPIO   Whew!

PARDALISCA   . . . is it?

OLYMPIO   Oh, it was enormous! I was afraid she had [that sword], so I began to investigate . . .

> And while I'm feeling around to see if she
> Has got a sword, I grab this hilt, you see.

(*Scratching his head in perplexity*)

> But come to think of it, I could have told:
> If that was any sword, it would have felt cold.

PARDALISCA

> Go on.

OLYMPIO (*hanging his head*)

> I'm embarrassed.

PARDALISCA (*as if struck with inspiration*)

> Wait—I think I know:

> A carrot?

OLYMPIO

> No.

PARDALISCA

> Cucumber?

OLYMPIO (*pondering the question*)

> I don't think so.

> I'll swear it wasn't a vegetable. Although,
> If it was, whatever kind it was, the blight
> Never touched the thing, it had grown to such a height.

PARDALISCA

What finally happened?

OLYMPIO

I speak to her and say,
"Please, wifeykins, why spurn your husband this way?
Because I wanted it to be just me and you,
Do I deserve these things you're trying to do?"
Without a word, she pulls her robe to bar
That part that makes you women what you are.
When I see that the promised land has been ruled out,
I ask permission to try the alternate route . . .

I want, in order to turn . . . She doesn't make a sound
. . . I get up . . .

MYRRHINA (*sotto voce to Cleostrata*) Marvelous story he's
telling . . .

OLYMPIO A kiss . . . And a beard like a set of bristles digs
into my lips . . .

The minute I lift myself to my knees, she pokes her feet in
my chest.

Down I go from the bed. She leaps on me and pounds my
face with zest.

So without a word and dressed as you see, I quit and run
outside,

Since I want the old gent to have a taste of the medicine
I've just tried!

PARDALISCA

Very good. But what did you do with your coat?

OLYMPIO

I left it in the room.

PARDALISCA (*gleefully*)

Well, what do you think of the trick we played? Pretty
good?

OLYMPIO (*gloomily*)

We earned our doom.

(*Suddenly raising his head and starting to tremble*)

Hey wait—a creak at the door. Oh, god! Is it *she* coming
    after the groom!

*(Lysidamus comes out of the house, like Olympio in rather
bad shape: he has no coat or stick, his erstwhile pomaded
hair is disheveled, and his whole appearance is evidence that
Chalinus has done his work well.)*

LYSIDAMUS *(to the audience)*

        I'm burning with shame through and through.
        Things are such, I've no clue what to do
        Or how to face up to my wife—
        I'm that near to the end of my life!
        All my sins are now known, so, poor me,
        I'm a goner, I'm done for, fini!

. . . have me by the throat . . . how I can clear myself
with my wife . . . a coatless poor devil, that's what I am
. . . secret marriage . . . I figure . . . the best thing for
me . . .

        I'll go in to my wife, and I'll bare her my back
            To atone for this injury.
        Is there anyone here, any man who would like
            To take over the duty for me?
        I've no clue what to do—except to do like
            A bad slave, and take off through the gate.
        To go back in the house means the end of all hope
            That my back will escape its sad fate.
        You can smile at such talk, but a beating, though earned,
            Is something I'd hardly enjoy.

*(As he heads off, stage right, the door of Alcesimus' house
opens.)*

        So I'll take to my heels and get going this way—

CHALINUS *(calling from the doorway)*

        Hey, stand where you are, lover-boy!

*(Lysidamus stops dead in his tracks. Chalinus, still in cos-
tume except for the veil, and holding Lysidamus' stick and
coat, walks downstage.)*

LYSIDAMUS (*to himself, groaning*) Someone's calling me back—I'm done for! I'll make believe I didn't hear him and keep going.

CHALINUS (*running about the stage as if searching for Lysidamus; shouting*) Where's the man who thinks he can live like a Marseilles degenerate? You can mount me right now if you want, it's a perfect opportunity. Just step back into the bedroom. (*Coming to a stop across his path*) Now you're done for, damn it all! Come on over here; (*brandishing Lysidamus' stick*) no need to go to court—here's an honest judge I can haul you before.

LYSIDAMUS (*to himself*) Oh, my god, he'll crack my shins to splinters with that club! (*Doing an about-face*) I've got to go this way; that other road's a real shincracker!

(*Lysidamus starts heading toward the wings, stage left—and discovers Cleostrata barring his path.*)

CLEOSTRATA (*with amused contempt*) Well, hello, lover-boy.

LYSIDAMUS (*to the audience*) Look at that—now my wife's blocking the road! I'm between the devil and the deep blue sea, I don't know which way to run. On one side the wolves, on the other the bitches baying. And *this* wolf at the door carries a club. I guess I'll be making a change in the old proverb right now—and (*going toward his wife*) I hope I'll do better with a bitch at the door!

CLEOSTRATA Well, how are things, Double-hubby? (*With mock concern*) Why, Lysidamus, where are you going in this get-up? What did you do with your stick and the coat you were wearing?

PARDALISCA (*tartly*) Lost them in lechery while seducing Casina, if you ask me.

LYSIDAMUS (*aside*) I'm done for!

CHALINUS (*in falsetto*) Let's go to bed, you and I. I'm Casina.

LYSIDAMUS (*venomously*) You go to hell!

CHALINUS (*in falsetto, with mock reproach*)   Don't you love me?

CLEOSTRATA (*to Lysidamus, sharply*)   Answer me—what happened to your coat?

LYSIDAMUS (*nervously*)   Why, my dear, Bacchus' lady worshipers—

CLEOSTRATA (*interrupting incredulously*)   Bacchus' lady worshipers?

LYSIDAMUS (*stubbornly starting again*)   Why, my dear, Bacchus' lady worshipers—

MYRRHINA (*to Cleostrata, interrupting contemptuously*)   That's nonsense, and he knows it. There aren't any more worshipers of Bacchus.[4]

LYSIDAMUS (*aside*)   I forgot that! (*Stubbornly*) Well, anyway, these lady worshipers of Bacchus—

CLEOSTRATA (*interrupting, grimly*)   What about them?

LYSIDAMUS (*mumbling*)   Well, if I can't get away with that one—

CLEOSTRATA (*interrupting, amused*)   You certainly are scared.

LYSIDAMUS (*putting on the indignation act*)   Who? Me? That's a lie!

CLEOSTRATA   Well, you're pale as a ghost.

[In the next seven lines, too mutilated to give any consecutive sense, apparently Olympio joins Cleostrata in jumping on the old man.]

OLYMPIO (*self-righteously*)   And he's brought shame and misery on me too, through these crimes of his.

LYSIDAMUS (*sotto voce to Olympio*)   Can't you shut up!

OLYMPIO (*in ringing tones*)   I will *not* shut up! After all, it was you who begged me, and as hard as you could, to ask to marry Casina just to help along your love affair.

---

[4] Probably a topical reference. In 186 B.C. a law had been passed banning the cult from Rome.

LYSIDAMUS (*with histrionic incredulity*)   I did that?

OLYMPIO (*with heavy sarcasm*)   No, it was Hector of Troy.

LYSIDAMUS (*between his teeth*)   Who'd have shut *you* up, all right. (*To Cleostrata and Myrrhina, defiantly*) You mean to say I did all these things you say I did?

CLEOSTRATA (*witheringly*)   What a question!

(*Cleostrata glares at him. Lysidamus tries to glare back but in a few seconds wilts and decides to forgo defense for unconditional surrender.*)

LYSIDAMUS (*abjectly*)   Well, if I did, I did wrong.

CLEOSTRATA (*as before, pointing to the house*)   Just go inside. I'll remind you where your memory's weak.

LYSIDAMUS (*quickly*)   Oh, I think I'd rather rely on what you two say. My dear wife, please forgive me this once. (*Turning to Myrrhina*) Myrrhina, you ask her. (*Turning back to Cleostrata*) If from now on I make love to Casina, or, let alone make love, just even show the symptoms—if I do anything like that from now on, you have my permission, dear, to string me up and flay my hide.

MYRRHINA (*smiling*)   I really think you should forgive him.

CLEOSTRATA (*to Myrrhina*)   If you say so, then I'll do it. (*To Lysidamus*) And there's another reason why I'm forgiving you and not being hard on you: this play is long enough; let's not make it any longer.

LYSIDAMUS (*timidly*)   You're not angry at me?

CLEOSTRATA   No, I'm not.

LYSIDAMUS   Can I believe it? On the level?

CLEOSTRATA   On the level.

LYSIDAMUS (*winking at the audience*)   There's not another man who has as nice a wife as I.

CLEOSTRATA (*to Chalinus*)   Give him back his coat and stick.

CHALINUS (*handing them over*)   Here they are, if you want them. (*In falsetto*) I was done wrong by, today, simply terribly! I was married to two husbands—and neither one gave me what a bride usually gets!

(*All enter Lysidamus' house, and the stage is now empty. A moment later, the speaker of the epilogue enters and addresses the audience.*)

EPILOGUE Ladies and gentlemen, let me tell you what's going to happen inside: they'll find out that Casina is really the next door neighbor's daughter, and she'll marry Euthynicus, the son of the house.

And now it's only proper that you pay us the prize of applause we've properly earned. Anyone who does, is to get the girl he wants without his wife ever hearing of it. Anyone who doesn't clap as loud as he can, is to mount a goat instead of a girl, and one perfumed like a privy at that!

THE MENAECHMUS TWINS

DRAMATIS PERSONAE

SPONGE (PENICULUS), *hanger-on of Menaechmus of Epidamnus, who makes his way by scrounging from him and
other well-to-do people*

MENAECHMUS OF EPIDAMNUS, *a well-to-do young married
man, resident in Epidamnus*

LOVEY (EROTIUM), *a courtesan with whom Menaechmus of
Epidamnus has been having an affair*

ROLL (CYLINDRUS), *her cook (slave)*

MENAECHMUS OF SYRACUSE, *twin brother of Menaechmus of
Epidamnus, resident in Syracuse*

MESSENIO, *his servant (slave)*

MAID OF LOVEY (*slave*)

WIFE OF MENAECHMUS OF EPIDAMNUS

FATHER-IN-LAW OF MENAECHMUS OF EPIDAMNUS

A DOCTOR

[DECIO, *servant of Menaechmus' wife*]

SERVANTS

SCENE

*A street in Epidamnus. Two houses front on it: stage left
Menaechmus', stage right Lovey's. The exit on stage left
leads downtown, that on stage right to the waterfront. The
time is noon or a little after.*

PROLOGUE

(The actor assigned to deliver the prologue enters, walks downstage, and addresses the audience.)

PROLOGUE First and foremost, ladies and gentlemen, health and happiness to all of—me. And to you, too. I have Plautus here for you—not in my hands, on my tongue. Please be kind enough to take him—with your ears. Now, here's the plot. Pay attention, I'll make it as brief as I can.

Every comic playwright invariably tells you that the action of his piece takes place entirely at Athens; this is to give it that Greek touch. Well, I'm telling you the action takes place where the story says it does and nowhere else. The plot, as a matter of fact, *is* Greekish. Not Athensish, though; Sicilyish. But all this is so much preamble. Now I'll pour out your portion of plot for you. Not by the quart, not by the gallon, by the tankload. That's how big-hearted a plot-teller I am.

A certain man, a merchant, lived at Syracuse. His wife presented him with twin sons, two boys so alike that no one could tell them apart, neither the woman who nursed them, nor the mother who bore them. I got this from someone who'd seen them—I don't want you to get the idea I saw them myself; I never did.

Well, when the boys were seven years old, their father filled a fine freighter full of freight and put one twin aboard to take with him on a business trip to Tarentum. The other he left home with the mother. As it turned out, they arrived at Tarentum during a holiday, and—the usual thing during holidays—a lot of people had come to town, and son and sire got separated in the crowd. A merchant from Epidamnus happened to be on the spot; he picked the boy up and carried him off to Epidamnus. At the lad's loss, alas, the love of life left the father; a few days later, there at Tarentum, he died of a broken heart.

A message about all this—that the boy had been carried off and the father had died at Tarentum—was brought back to Syracuse to the grandfather. When he heard the news, he changed the name of the boy who'd been left at home. The old man was so fond of the kidnaped twin that he transferred this one's name to his brother: he called the twin still left Menaechmus, the same name as the other had. (It was the old man's name too—I remember it so well because I heard it so often when his creditors dunned him.) To keep you from getting mixed up later I'm telling you now, in advance, that both twins have the same name.

Now, in order for me to make the whole story crystal clear for you, I have to retrace my steps and get back to Epidamnus. Any of you got some business you want me to take care of for you at Epidamnus? Step up, say the word, give me your orders. But don't forget the wherewithal for taking care of them. Anyone who doesn't give me some cash is wasting his time—and anyone who does is wasting a lot more. But now I'm really going back to where I started, and I'll stay put in one place.

The man from Epidamnus, the one I told you about a few seconds ago who carried off the other twin, had no children of his own—except his moneybags. He adopted the boy he had kidnaped, made him his son, found him a wife with a good dowry, and left him his whole estate when he died. You see, the old fellow happened to be going out to his country place one day after a heavy rain; a short way out of town he began fording a stream that was sweeping along, the sweeping current swept him off his feet the way he had once swept off that boy, and away to hell and gone he went.

So a handsome fortune dropped into his adopted son's lap. He—I mean the twin who was carried off—lives here (*pointing*). Now, the other, the one who lives in Syracuse, will arrive just today, along with a servant; he's searching for his twin brother. This (*gesturing toward the backdrop*) is Epidamnus—but only so long as our play is on the

boards; when some other play goes on, it'll be some other
city. It changes just the way the actors do—one day
they're pimps, next day paupers; next youngsters, next
oldsters; next beggars, kings, scroungers, cheats. . . .

ACT I

(*Enter Sponge* [Peniculus, *literally "brush"*], *stage left, a man in his thirties with a protruding paunch and a general down-at-the-heels look. He is a* parasitus, *"free-loader," the character, standard in ancient comedy, who, to fill his belly, runs errands and acts as general flunky and yes-man to anyone willing to issue an invitation to a meal. He walks downstage and addresses the audience.*)

SPONGE The boys call me Sponge. Because, when I eat, I wipe the table clean.

It's stupid to put chains on prisoners or shackles on runaway slaves, at least to my way of thinking. This misery on top of all their others just makes the poor devils more set than ever on breaking out—and breaking the peace. Prisoners get out of the chains somehow or other, and slaves saw through the shackle or smash the pin with a rock. No, bolts and bars are the bunk. If you really want to keep someone from running away, chain him with dishes and glasses. Belay him by the beak to a groaning board. You give him all he wants to eat and drink daily and, so help me, he'll never run away, not even if he's up for hanging. Holding on to him is a cinch once you chain him with *that* kind of chain. And belly bonds are so firm and flexible—the more you stretch them, the tighter they get.

For example, I'm on my way to Menaechmus' house here (*pointing*). I sentenced myself to his jail years back: I'm going now of my own free will so he can put the irons on me. This Menaechmus is a man who doesn't just feed a man; he bloats the belly for you, he restores you to life—you won't find a finer physician. He's a fellow like this: he's as big an eater as they come himself, so every meal he serves looks like a thanksgiving day banquet: he overloads the tables, he piles up the plates like pyramids; you have to stand on your chair if you want something from on top. But it's been quite a while since my last invitation. I've

had to be homebound with all that's dear to me—you see,
whatever I eat that I pay for is dear, very dear. And there's
this: right now all that's so dear to me has broken ranks
and deserted the table. So (*pointing again to Menaechmus'
house*) I'm paying him a visit. Wait—the door's opening.
There's Menaechmus himself; he's coming out.

(*Sponge moves off to the side. The door opens and Menaechmus of Epidamnus stomps out. He is a good-looking man
in his middle twenties, whose grooming, clothes, and air all
smack of a substantial income. His manifest irascibility is
unusual: normally he is gay, an inveterate jokester, and always out for a good time. He is wearing a coat which he
clutches tightly about him. He turns and addresses his wife
who is visible in the doorway.*)

SONG

MENAECHMUS OF EPIDAMNUS (*angrily*)

    If you weren't so stupid and sour,
    Such a mean-tempered bitch, such a shrew,
    What you see gives your husband a pain,
    You'd make sure would give *you* a pain too.
        From this moment henceforth,
        You just try this once more,
        And, a divorce in your hand,
        You go darken Dad's door.

    Every time that I want to go out
    I get called, I get grabbed, I get grilled:
    "Where are you going to go?"
    "Why are you going outside?"
    "What are you going to do?"
    "What are you going to get?"
    "What have you got in your hand?"
    "What were you doing downtown?"

    Why, the way I declare every act of my life,
    It's a customs official I wed, not a wife!
    Oh, you're spoiled, and I did it myself. Listen, you—
    I'll explain here and now what I'm planning to do.

I've filled your every need:
The clothes you've on your back,
Your servants, food, and cash—
There's nothing that you lack.

If you only had some sense,
You'd watch what you're about.
You'd let your husband be,
And cut the snooping out.

And what's more, so your snooping's not lost
And the time you put in not a waste,
I'll be off to go find me a girl
Who can join me for dinner someplace.

SPONGE (*to the audience, in anguish*)

He pretends to be hard on his wife—
But it's *me* that he's giving the knife!
Eating out! Do you know who he'll hurt?
It's yours truly he'll hurt, not his wife.

MENAECHMUS OF EPIDAMNUS (*to himself, wonderingly, as his
wife disappears inside*)

Well, I finally gave her what for—
And I drove the old bitch from the door!

(*To the audience, triumphantly*)

What's happened to the husbands who've been keeping
mistresses?
What's holding up their plaudits and their cheers for what
I've done?
They *all* owe me a medal for the fight I fought and won!

(*Throws his coat open to reveal a woman's dress he has on
over his clothes*)

I stole this dress from her just now—I'll bring it to my girl.
Now *that's* the way to operate—outfox a foxy guard!
A beautiful piece of work it was, a feat to shout about,
A lovely piece of work it was, superbly carried out.

(*Losing his jubilation suddenly as realization dawns*)

I snitch from the bitch at *my* expense—and my downfall
gets it all.

(*Cheering up again*)

But the enemy's camp's been looted, and we've safely made
our haul!

SPONGE (*calling as Menaechmus starts marching toward Lovey's door*)   Hey, mister, any share in that swag for me?

MENAECHMUS OF EPIDAMNUS (*stopping and closing his coat,
but not turning around; to himself*)   Ambushed! I'm lost!

SPONGE   Saved, you mean. Don't be afraid.

MENAECHMUS OF EPIDAMNUS (*still not turning*)   Who is it?

SPONGE   Me.

MENAECHMUS OF EPIDAMNUS (*turning*)   Hi, friend-in-need
and Johnny-on-the-spot.

SPONGE   Hi.

MENAECHMUS OF EPIDAMNUS   What are you doing these
days?

SPONGE (*grabbing Menaechmus' hand and pumping it*)   I'm
shaking the hand of my guardian angel.

MENAECHMUS OF EPIDAMNUS   You couldn't have timed it
better to meet me.

SPONGE   I'm always like that—I know Johnny-on-the-spotitude
down to the last dotitude.

MENAECHMUS OF EPIDAMNUS   You want to see a brilliant
piece of work?

SPONGE (*smacking his lips*)   Who cooked it? One look at the
leftovers and I can tell in a minute if he slipped up anywhere.

MENAECHMUS OF EPIDAMNUS   Tell me, have you ever seen
those famous pictures they hang on walls? The eagle
carrying off Ganymede or Venus with Adonis?

SPONGE (*testily*)   Lots of times. But what have those pictures got to do with me?

MENAECHMUS OF EPIDAMNUS (*throwing open his coat to reveal the dress*)   See this? Do I look like one?

SPONGE (*staring*)   What have you got on there, anyway?

MENAECHMUS OF EPIDAMNUS (*slyly*)   Tell me I'm the nicest guy you know.

SPONGE (*suspiciously*)   Where do we eat?

MENAECHMUS OF EPIDAMNUS (*pretending to be annoyed*) First tell me what I told you to.

SPONGE   All right, all right. You're the nicest guy I know.

MENAECHMUS OF EPIDAMNUS (*as before*)   How about adding something on your own, please?

SPONGE (*grudgingly*)   And the most fun to be with.

MENAECHMUS OF EPIDAMNUS   Go on.

SPONGE (*exploding*)   God damn it, no going on till I know what for. You're on the outs with your wife, so I'm watching my step with you.

MENAECHMUS OF EPIDAMNUS (*sensing his teasing has gone far enough, gaily and conspiratorially*)   Let's you and I, without letting my wife know a thing, kill off this day—

SPONGE (*interrupting*)   Well, all right! That's something like! How soon shall I start the funeral? The day's already half dead, all the way down to the waist.

MENAECHMUS OF EPIDAMNUS (*with a great show of patience*) Interrupt me, and you just hold things up for yourself.

SPONGE (*hurriedly*)   Menaechmus, poke my eye out if I utter another word. Orders from you excepted, of course.

MENAECHMUS OF EPIDAMNUS (*tiptoeing away from his house with anxious glances over his shoulder at the door*)   Come on over here. Away from that door.

SPONGE (*following*)   Sure.

MENAECHMUS OF EPIDAMNUS (*tiptoeing farther, with more glances*)   Even more.

SPONGE (*following*)   All right.

MENAECHMUS OF EPIDAMNUS (*now far enough away to give up tiptoeing—but still glancing*)   Come on, step along. Farther from that lion's den.

SPONGE   I swear, if you ask me, you'd make a wonderful jockey.

MENAECHMUS OF EPIDAMNUS Why?

SPONGE The way you look behind every second to make sure your wife's not catching up.

MENAECHMUS OF EPIDAMNUS I want to ask you a question.

SPONGE Me? The answer's Yes, if you want yes; No, if you want no.

MENAECHMUS OF EPIDAMNUS If you smelled something, could you tell from the smell—

SPONGE (*with one type of smell in mind, interrupting*) Better than a board of prophets.

MENAECHMUS OF EPIDAMNUS All right, then, try this dress I have. What do you smell? (*He hands Sponge part of the skirt, Sponge sniffs, then jerks his nose away*) What did you do that for?

SPONGE You've got to smell a woman's dress at the top. Down there there's an odor that never washes out, and it's death on the nose.

MENAECHMUS OF EPIDAMNUS (*moving the upper part toward him*) Smell here then. (*Laughing as Sponge sniffs gingerly*) You do a wonderful job of wrinkling up your nose.

SPONGE I had good reason.

MENAECHMUS OF EPIDAMNUS Well? What does it smell from? Tell me.

SPONGE Loot, lechery—and lunch.

MENAECHMUS OF EPIDAMNUS (*clapping him on the back and leading him toward Lovey's door*) Right you are. Now it goes right to my lady friend Lovey here. And I'll have her fix up a lunch for me, you, and her.

SPONGE (*smacking his lips*) Fine!

MENAECHMUS OF EPIDAMNUS (*gaily*) We'll pass the bottle from now till the crack of dawn tomorrow.

SPONGE (*as before*) Fine! Now you're talking. Should I knock on the door?

MENAECHMUS OF EPIDAMNUS Knock away. (*As Sponge races*

up to Lovey's door and raises a fist to deliver a lusty bang)
No, wait!

SPONGE (*bitterly*) You just passed that bottle back a mile.

MENAECHMUS OF EPIDAMNUS Try a tiny tap.

SPONGE What are you scared of? That the door's made of
bone china? (*Turns to knock.*)

MENAECHMUS OF EPIDAMNUS (*excitedly*) Wait! Wait, for
god's sake! See? She's coming out. Look how the sun grows
gray 'gainst the glory of that gorgeous figure!

(*The door opens and Lovey [Erotium, literally "little love"]
comes out, a good-looking girl in a brassy sort of way, flashily
dressed and heavily made up.*)

LOVEY Menaechmus, darling! How nice to see you!

SPONGE How about me?

LOVEY (*witheringly*) You don't count.

SPONGE (*unruffled*) I do so. I'm in this man's army too.
Rear guard.

MENAECHMUS OF EPIDAMNUS (*seeing a chance to tease her,
slyly*) Orders from headquarters, Lovey: invite Sponge
and me to your house today. For a duel.

LOVEY All right. (*Throwing a baleful look at Sponge*) Just
for today.

MENAECHMUS OF EPIDAMNUS (*as before*) A duel of drinks
to the death. Whichever's the better man with the bottle
becomes your bodyguard. You be referee, you decide which
you'll sleep with tonight. (*Abruptly dropping his teasing
as he notices her begin to sulk*) Honey, one look at you
and, oh, do I hate that wife of mine!

LOVEY (*not yet mollified—and catching sight of the dress,
frigidly*) In the meantime, you can't even keep from wearing her clothes. What is this, anyway?

MENAECHMUS OF EPIDAMNUS (*throwing his coat open, gaily*)
Embezzled from her to embellish you, my flower.

LOVEY (*magically thawed out*) You always win out over all

the other men who run after me. You have such winning
ways.

SPONGE (*aside*) That's a mistress for you: nothing but sweet
talk so long as she sees something to get her hands on. If
you really loved him, you'd be kissing his mouth off this
minute.

MENAECHMUS OF EPIDAMNUS (*taking off his coat*) Sponge,
hold this. I want to carry out the dedication ceremony I
scheduled.

SPONGE Hand it over. (*Taking the coat and eying Menaechmus in the dress*) Since you're in costume, how about favoring us with a bit of ballet later?

MENAECHMUS OF EPIDAMNUS Ballet? Me? Are you in your
right mind?

SPONGE You mean are *you* in your right mind. All right, if
no ballet, get out of costume.

MENAECHMUS OF EPIDAMNUS (*taking the dress off and handing it to Lovey*) I took an awful chance stealing this today. Riskier, if you ask me, than when Hercules helped
himself to Hippolyta's girdle. It's all for you—because you're
the only person in the whole world who's really nice to me.

LOVEY What a lovely thought! That's the way all nice lovers
should think.

SPONGE (*aside*) You mean if they're hell-bent to get to the
poorhouse.

MENAECHMUS OF EPIDAMNUS (*to Lovey*) I paid a thousand
dollars last year for that dress you have there. Got it for
my wife.

SPONGE (*aside*) Using your own figures, that works out to a
thousand dollars down the drain.

MENAECHMUS OF EPIDAMNUS (*to Lovey*) You know what
I'd like you to do?

LOVEY I know one thing: I'll do whatever you like.

MENAECHMUS OF EPIDAMNUS Then have your cook prepare
lunch for the three of us. Send him to the market for some

gourmetetitious shopping. Have him bring back the pig family: the Duke of Pork, Lord Bacon, the little Trotters, and any other relatives. Things that, served roasted, reduce me to ravenousness. Right away, eh?

LOVEY But of course!

MENAECHMUS OF EPIDAMNUS Sponge and I are on our way downtown but we'll be back in a few minutes. We can have drinks while the things are on the fire.

LOVEY Come back whenever you like. Everything will be ready.

MENAECHMUS OF EPIDAMNUS Just hurry it up. (*Turning and striding off, stage left; to Sponge*) Follow me.

SPONGE (*running after him*) I'm not only following you, I'm not letting you out of my sight. Today is the one day I wouldn't lose you for all the treasures of heaven!

(*As Menaechmus and Sponge leave, Lovey walks to the door of her house.*)

LOVEY (*calling through the door to her maids inside*) Tell Roll, the cook, to come out here right away. (*A second later, Roll* [Cylindrus], *a roly-poly cook, races out and stands attentively in front of her.*) You'll need a shopping basket and some money. Here's fifteen dollars.

ROLL Yes, ma'am.

LOVEY Go do the marketing. Get just enough for three—not a bit more and not a bit less.

ROLL What people are you having?

LOVEY Menaechmus, his parasite, and myself.

ROLL (*thoughtfully*) That makes ten—a parasite can do for eight. Easily.

LOVEY Now you know who'll be there; you take care of the rest.

ROLL (*importantly*) Right. Consider lunch cooked. Tell your guests to go in and sit down. (*Races off, stage left.*)

LOVEY (*calling after him*)   Come right back!

ROLL (*over his shoulder*)   Be back in a flash.

(*Roll dashes off, Lovey enters her house, and the stage is now empty.*)

ACT II

(*Enter, stage right, Menaechmus of Syracuse and his serv-ant Messenio carrying a satchel; behind them, loaded down with luggage, is a pair of rowers from the skiff that brought them ashore. These two move off to the side of the stage and put their burdens down.*

In appearance Menaechmus of Syracuse is identical with his twin. But there the likeness ends. Menaechmus of Epi-damnus is gay, generous, and fun loving; his brother is shrewd, calculating, and cynical. Messenio, about the same age as his master, is the long-faced type who worries easily and takes himself very seriously.)

MENAECHMUS OF SYRACUSE   Messenio, if you ask me, the greatest joy a sailor can have is to sight land from the open sea.

MESSENIO (*pointedly*)   I'll be honest with you: it's even greater when the land you come near and see is your home-land. Will you please tell me why we're here in Epidamnus? Are we going to do like sea water and go around every island there is?

MENAECHMUS OF SYRACUSE (*grimly*)   We're here to look for my brother. My twin brother.

MESSENIO (*exasperated*)   When are we going to put an end to looking for that man? We've been at it six years! Austria, Spain, France, Jugoslavia, Sicily, every part of Italy near salt water, up and down the Adriatic—we've made the rounds of all of them. Believe me, if you were looking for a needle, and it was anywhere to be found, you'd have found it long ago. We're looking for the dead among the living. Because, if he was alive to be found, you'd have found him long ago.

MENAECHMUS OF SYRACUSE (*as before*)   Then I'm looking for someone who can prove it, someone who'll tell me he knows for certain my brother is dead. Once I hear that,

I'll never look for him again. But until I do, so long as I
live, I'll never stop. *I* know how much he means to me.

MESSENIO (*grumbling*) You're looking for hens' teeth. Why
don't we turn around and go home? Or maybe you and I
are going to write a travel book?

MENAECHMUS OF SYRACUSE (*sharply*) You do what you're
told, eat what you're given, and stay out of trouble! Don't
annoy me now; we're doing things my way, not yours.

MESSENIO (*aside*) Ho-ho! That's telling me who's the slave
around here. Couldn't have put things plainer with fewer
words. But I can't hold this in, I've got to speak up. (*To
Menaechmus*) Listen, Menaechmus. I've been looking over
our finances. So help me, we're traveling with a summer-
weight wallet. If you want my opinion, either you head
for home, or you'll be mourning your long-lost money
while you look for your long-lost brother. Let me tell you
what kind of people live in these parts. The hardest drink-
ers and worst rakes are right here in Epidamnus. Besides,
the town's full of crooks and swindlers. And they say the
prostitutes here have a smoother line of talk than anywhere
else in the world. That's why this place is called Epidamnus:
nobody stays here without a damned lot of damage.

MENAECHMUS OF SYRACUSE (*unperturbed*) I'll keep my eyes
open. You just hand over the wallet.

MESSENIO (*suspiciously*) What do you want with it?

MENAECHMUS OF SYRACUSE After what you've been telling
me, I'm scared to leave it with you.

MESSENIO Scared of what?

MENAECHMUS OF SYRACUSE That you'll do me a damned lot
of damage in Epidamnus. You're a big man with the
women, Messenio, and I'm a man with a big temper, the
explosive type. If I keep the money, I avoid trouble both
ways: you don't lose your head and I don't lose my temper.

MESSENIO (*handing over the wallet*) Here it is. You keep it.
Glad to have you take over.

(*Enter Roll, stage left, lugging a loaded shopping basket.*)

ROLL (*to himself*) No trouble at all with the shopping. I got just what I wanted. I'll serve the diners a delicious dinner. Hey—who's that I see there? Menaechmus! Heaven help my poor back! The guests already at the door before I'm even back from the market! Well, I'll say hello. (*Walking up to Menaechmus*) Good afternoon, Menaechmus.

MENAECHMUS OF SYRACUSE (*surprised but cordial*) Good afternoon to you—whoever you are.

ROLL (*taken aback*) Whoever I am? You don't know who I am?

MENAECHMUS OF SYRACUSE Of course not.

ROLL (*deciding to overlook the exchange as just another of Menaechmus' jokes*) Where are the rest of the guests?

MENAECHMUS OF SYRACUSE Guests? What guests are you looking for?

ROLL That parasite of yours.

MENAECHMUS OF SYRACUSE (*blankly*) Parasite of mine? (*To Messenio, sotto voce*) The man's daft.

MESSENIO (*sotto voce to Menaechmus*) Didn't I tell you the place was full of swindlers?

MENAECHMUS OF SYRACUSE Now, mister, who is this parasite you're looking for?

ROLL Sponge.

MESSENIO (*digging into the satchel he is carrying*) Got it safe right here in the satchel. See?

ROLL (*apologetically*) Menaechmus, you're too early. Lunch isn't ready. I just got back from the shopping.

MENAECHMUS OF SYRACUSE (*with exaggerated concern*) Tell me, mister, what were fresh fish selling for today?

ROLL Dollar apiece.

MENAECHMUS OF SYRACUSE Here's a dollar. Buy some for yourself; it's on me. The food'll do your brains good. Because there's one thing I'm dead sure of: you're out of your senses, whoever you are. Otherwise why would you make such a nuisance of yourself to a total stranger?

ROLL (*smiling indulgently*) You don't know *me?* You don't know Roll?

MENAECHMUS OF SYRACUSE (*testily*) I don't care if you're roll or loaf. Go to the devil! I don't know you, and, what's more, I don't want to!

ROLL (*with an I'll-play-along-with-your-little-joke smile*) Your name's Menaechmus, isn't it?

MENAECHMUS OF SYRACUSE (*anger giving way to curiosity*) To the best of my knowledge. And when you call me "Menaechmus" you talk sense. Where do you know me from, anyway?

ROLL (*chuckling*) You're carrying on an affair with my owner Lovey (*gesturing toward the house*), and you have to ask *me* where I know you from?

MENAECHMUS (*tartly*) I'm not carrying on any affairs, and I haven't the slightest idea who you are.

ROLL (*as before*) You don't know who *I* am? Me? Your glass-filler all the times you come over to our house for drinks?

MESSENIO (*to the world at large*) Damn! Here I am without a thing to split that skull of his in half!

MENAECHMUS OF SYRACUSE You my glass-filler? When I've never set foot in Epidamnus, never set eyes on the place in my life till today?

ROLL You mean you deny it?

MENAECHMUS OF SYRACUSE I certainly do deny it!

ROLL (*pointing to the house of Menaechmus of Epidamnus*) You mean to say you don't live in that house there?

MENAECHMUS OF SYRACUSE (*roaring*) To hell with any and everyone who lives in that house there!

ROLL (*to the audience, smiling*) Swearing at himself. *He's* the one who's daft. (*To Menaechmus*) Listen, Menaechmus.

MENAECHMUS OF SYRACUSE (*sourly*) What do you want?

ROLL   You know that dollar you offered to give me a minute ago? Take my advice and use it to buy fish for your own brains. You swore at your own self just now, you certainly can't be in your right mind.

MENAECHMUS OF SYRACUSE   God! Talk, talk, talk! He's getting on my nerves!

ROLL   (*to the audience*) He always kids around with me like this. He's a real card—when his wife's not around. (*To Menaechmus*) I say, Menaechmus. (*As Menaechmus stubbornly stands with his back to him*) I say there, Menaechmus! (*Menaechmus throws up his hands in despair and turns around. Roll holds out the basket.*) Take a look. You think I bought enough for you, your parasite, and your lady? Or should I go back for more?

MENAECHMUS OF SYRACUSE   (*wearily*) What lady? What parasite are you talking about?

MESSENIO   (*to Roll, truculently*) What's the matter? Something on your conscience that's driving you out of your mind? Is that why you're making a nuisance of yourself to this man?

ROLL   (*resentfully*) What are *you* butting in for? I don't know you. I'm talking to this man here. Him I know.

MESSENIO   There's one thing I know: you're stark-raving mad, you are.

ROLL   (*pointedly ignoring Messenio; to Menaechmus, reassuringly*) I'll have everything cooked in a minute. You won't have to wait. So please don't go too far from the house. (*Turning to go*) Anything I can do for you before I go in?

MENAECHMUS OF SYRACUSE   (*stalking away*) Yes. Go to hell.

ROLL   (*muttering*) No, damn it, you go—(*as Menaechmus whirls around*) and have a seat while I (*importantly*) expose all this to the flame's fiery fury. I'll go and tell my mistress you're here so she can invite you in and not leave you standing around outside. (*Goes into the house.*)

MENAECHMUS OF SYRACUSE   (*to Messenio*) Has he gone?

(*Hearing the door slam*) He's gone. So help me, now I know that what you said was no lie.

MESSENIO (*importantly*) You just watch your step. It's my theory that one of those prostitutes lives here. That's what that lunatic who just left said.

MENAECHMUS OF SYRACUSE (*puzzled*) What amazes me is how he knew my name.

MESSENIO (*with the air of an expert*) Nothing amazing about that. These girls have a system. They send their tricky little maids and houseboys down to the docks. Whenever a foreigner heads for a berth, they start asking the name and the home port. The next minute the girls are hanging around his neck and sticking to him like glue. And, if he once takes the bait, he goes home a goner. (*Pointing to Lovey's house*) Now, there's a privateer moored in this berth right here. My advice is, let's steer clear of her.

MENAECHMUS OF SYRACUSE Good advice. Messenio, you're on your toes.

MESSENIO I'll know I'm on my toes when I see you on your guard, not before.

MENAECHMUS OF SYRACUSE Sh! Quiet a minute. I hear the door opening. Let's see who's coming out.

MESSENIO I'll get rid of this in the meantime. (*Handing the satchel to one of the rower-porters*) Hey, oar-power, keep an eye on this, will you please?

(*Lovey appears in the doorway. She turns and addresses a maid who was about to close the door behind her.*)

SONG

LOVEY (*adjusting the door*)
          No, not closed. Just like this, open wide.
          Now go in and get going inside.
          See that everything's set in the room.
          Spread some cushions. And lots of perfume.

(*Turns and addresses the audience*)

> Sophistication—that's the way
> To bring a lover-boy to bay.
> Plus saying Yes—to men a curse,
> To girls a way to fill a purse.

(*Looks around and, at first, doesn't see Menaechmus*)

> Now, where's he gone? My cook reports
>   He's standing by the door.
> Oh, there he is—my useful and
>   Most profitable amour.

> He's lord and master in my house.
>   He's earned the right to be,
> And so I let him. Now I'll go
>   And let him talk to me.

(*Walks up to Menaechmus*)

> Sweetie-pie! You surprise me, you do,
> With this standing around outside here.
> Why, my door's open wider to you
> Than your own. This is *your* house, my dear.

> Not a thing that you asked to be done
> Have my servants forgotten, not one.
> They're all ready inside, honeybunch,
> They've made *just* what you ordered for lunch.
> So, whenever you'd like to come in,
> We can all take our seats and begin.

MENAECHMUS OF SYRACUSE (*to Messenio*) Who's this woman talking to?

LOVEY (*with a dazzling smile*) You, of course.

MENAECHMUS OF SYRACUSE And just what have you, in the present or past, ever had to do with me?

LOVEY (*meltingly*) So much! And just because Cupid told me to pick you out of all the men in the world and make you the most important man in my life. And it's no more than you deserve. I can't tell you how happy you've made

me, just you alone, by all the nice things you've done for
me.

MENAECHMUS OF SYRACUSE (*sotto voce to Messenio*) Messenio, this woman's either drunk or daft. She treats a total
stranger like a bosom friend.

MESSENIO (*sotto voce*) Didn't I tell you? That's the kind of
thing that goes on around here. But this is just the leaves
falling. Stay three days longer and see what you get then:
a tree trunk on your head. That's what prostitutes here are
like—gold diggers, every one of them. (*Tapping himself importantly on the chest*) You just let *me* talk to her. Hey,
lady! (*As Lovey looks at him blankly*) Yes, you.

LOVEY What is it?

MESSENIO Where do you know this man from?

LOVEY (*with a that's-a-silly-question air*) Same place he's
known me from, all these years. Epidamnus.

MESSENIO Epidamnus? When he never set foot in the place
till today?

LOVEY Tee-hee! You make such funny jokes. (*Taking
Menaechmus by the arm*) Menaechmus dear, why don't
you come inside? It's much nicer in here.

MENAECHMUS OF SYRACUSE (*extricating himself; sotto voce to
Messenio*) What the devil! This woman's called me by my
right name. I don't get it. What's going on here?

MESSENIO (*sotto voce*) She got a whiff of that wallet you're
carrying.

MENAECHMUS OF SYRACUSE (*sotto voce*) Darned good thing
you warned me. (*Handing over the wallet*) Here, you take
it. Now I'll find out whether it's me or my money she's so
passionate about.

LOVEY Let's go in and have lunch.

MENAECHMUS OF SYRACUSE It's awfully nice of you, but,
thank you, I really can't.

LOVEY (*staring at him in amazement*) Then why did you
tell me to make lunch for you a little while ago?

MENAECHMUS OF SYRACUSE   *I* told you to make lunch?

LOVEY   You certainly did. For you and that parasite of yours.

MENAECHMUS OF SYRACUSE (*peevishly*)   Damn it all, what parasite? (*Sotto voce to Messenio*) This woman must be out of her mind.

LOVEY   Sponge.

MENAECHMUS OF SYRACUSE   Sponge? What sponge? For cleaning shoes?

LOVEY (*accustomed to Menaechmus' jokes, patiently*)   The one who was here with you a little while ago, of course. When you brought me the dress you stole from your wife.

MENAECHMUS OF SYRACUSE (*clutching his head*)   What's this? I brought you a dress I stole from my wife? Are you crazy? (*Sotto voce to Messenio*) She's dreaming; she sure goes to sleep like a horse—standing up.

LOVEY (*starting to sulk*)   You always get such pleasure out of teasing me. Why do you say you didn't do what you definitely did do?

MENAECHMUS OF SYRACUSE (*slowly, emphasizing each word*)   Now, will you kindly tell me just what I did do that I say I didn't do?

LOVEY   Give me one of your wife's dresses today.

MENAECHMUS OF SYRACUSE (*helplessly*)   And I *still* say I didn't! Listen: I never had a wife, I don't have one now, and never, since the day I was born, have I set foot inside this city till this minute. I had lunch aboard ship, I came from there here, and I ran into you.

LOVEY (*tearfully*)   Well! Oh, this is terrible, this will be the end of me! What ship are you talking about?

MENAECHMUS OF SYRACUSE (*glibly*)   A wooden one. Been scraped, calked, and repaired time and again. More pine plugs patching the planks than pegs holding pelts at a furrier's.

LOVEY (*pleading*)   Please, dear, no more games. Come inside with me now.

MENAECHMUS OF SYRACUSE   Lady, it's not me you want. It's some other man, I haven't the slightest idea who.

LOVEY (*with a let's-be-serious-now air*)   I know perfectly well who you are. You're Menaechmus, your father's name was Moschus, and I've heard say you were born in Syracuse in Sicily. (*Like a schoolgirl reciting—and getting most of her lesson wrong*) The king of Syracuse was Agathocles, then Phint-something, then Etna, and now Hiero. Etna gave it to Hiero when he died.

MENAECHMUS OF SYRACUSE (*amazed—and amused; dryly*) Absolutely right, lady, every word.

MESSENIO (*sotto voce to Menaechmus*)   By god, I bet she comes from there, and that's how she knows all about you.

MENAECHMUS OF SYRACUSE (*sotto voce*)   Then I really don't think I can turn down her invitation.

MESSENIO (*sotto voce*)   You do nothing of the sort! You go through that door, and you're through.

MENAECHMUS OF SYRACUSE (*sotto voce, peevishly*)   Shut up, will you? Everything's going fine. I'm going to say yes to whatever she says: maybe I can get myself some free entertainment. (*To Lovey*) My dear girl, I knew what I was doing when I kept saying no to you up to now. I was afraid that fellow (*gesturing toward Messenio*) would tell my wife about the dress and our date. Since you'd like to go in now, let's.

LOVEY   You're not going to wait for your parasite?

MENAECHMUS OF SYRACUSE (*exploding*)   No, I am *not* going to wait for my parasite, I don't give a damn about my parasite, and, if he shows up, I want him kept out.

LOVEY   It'll be a pleasure, believe me. (*Going up to him and stroking his cheek*) Menaechmus, do you know what I'd like you to do for me?

MENAECHMUS OF SYRACUSE   Just say the word.

LOVEY   I'd like you to take that dress you just gave me to the dressmaker and have her make some alterations and add some touches I want.

MENAECHMUS OF SYRACUSE (*enthusiastically*)   By god, you're

right! That way nobody'll recognize it, and my wife won't
know you have it on if she sees you in the street.

LOVEY Then remember to take it with you when you leave.

MENAECHMUS OF SYRACUSE I sure will!

LOVEY Let's go in.

MENAECHMUS OF SYRACUSE I'll be right with you; I want to
have a last word with this fellow here. (*Lovey goes into
the house; he turns to Messenio.*) Hey, Messenio, come over
here.

MESSENIO (*angrily*) What's going on? What do you have to
do *this* for?

MENAECHMUS OF SYRACUSE I have to. (*As Messenio opens
his mouth*) I know all about it, you can save your breath.

MESSENIO (*bitterly*) That makes it even worse.

MENAECHMUS OF SYRACUSE (*triumphantly*) Initial operation
proceeding according to plan. I'm practically looting the
enemy camp. Now, get going as fast as you can and take
these fellows (*gesturing toward the rower-porters*) to the
hotel this minute. Be sure you come back for me before
sundown.

MESSENIO (*pleading*) Menaechmus, listen, you don't know
these girls.

MENAECHMUS OF SYRACUSE (*sharply*) Enough talk. If I do
anything stupid it'll be my neck, not yours. The stupid
one's this woman. She doesn't have a brain in her head.
From what I saw just now, there's rich pickings in here
for us. (*Goes into the house.*)

MESSENIO (*calling after him*) Good lord, are you really going in? (*Shaking his head, to himself*) He's a dead duck.
The privateer has our rowboat in tow and is hauling it
straight to hell and gone. But I'm the one without a brain
in my head for thinking I can run my master. He bought
me to listen to what he says, not order him around. (*To
the rower-porters*) Follow me. I have orders to get back
here in time, and I don't want to be late.

(*Messenio and his men file out, stage right. The stage is
now empty.*)

ACT III

(*Enter Sponge, stage left, in a mad hurry. The sight of Lovey's closed door brings him to an abrupt halt. He claps a hand to his brow, then turns and walks downstage to address the audience.*)

SPONGE I'm over thirty now, and never have I ever in all those years pulled a more damned fool stunt than the one I pulled today: there was this town meeting, and *I* had to dive in and come up right in the middle of it. While I'm standing there with my mouth open, Menaechmus sneaks off on me. I'll bet he's gone to his girl friend. Perfectly willing to leave me behind, too!

(*Paces up and down a few times, shaking his head bitterly. Then, in a rage*) Damn, damn, damn the fellow who first figured out town meetings! All they do is keep a busy man away from his business. Why don't people pick a panel of men of leisure for this kind of thing? Hold a roll call at each meeting and whoever doesn't answer gets fined on the spot. There are plenty of persons around who need only one meal a day; they don't have business hours to keep because they don't go after dinner invitations or give them out. They're the ones to fuss with town meetings and town elections. If that's how things were run, I wouldn't have lost my lunch today. He sure wanted me along, didn't he? I'll go in, anyway. There's still hope of leftovers to soothe my soul. (*He is about to go up to the door when it suddenly swings open and Menaechmus of Syracuse appears, standing on the threshold with a garland, a little askew, on his head; he is holding the dress and listening to Lovey who is chattering at him from inside. Sponge quickly backs off into a corner.*) What's this I see? Menaechmus—and he's leaving, garland and all! The table's been cleared! I sure came in time—in time to walk him home. Well, I'll watch what his game is, and then I'll go and have a word with him.

MENAECHMUS OF SYRACUSE (*to Lovey inside*) Take it easy,
will you! I'll have it back to you today in plenty of time,
altered and trimmed to perfection. (*Slyly*) Believe me,
you'll say it's not your dress; you won't know it any more.

SPONGE (*to the audience*) He's bringing the dress to the
dressmaker. The dining's done, the drinks are down—and
Sponge spent the lunch hour outside. God damn it, I'm
not the man I think I am if I don't get even with him for
this, but really even. You just watch. I'll give it to him, I
will.

MENAECHMUS OF SYRACUSE (*closing the door and walking
downstage; to the audience, jubilantly*) Good god, no
one ever expected less—and got more blessings from heaven
in one day than me. I dined, I wined, I wenched, and
(*holding up the dress*) made off with this to which, from
this moment on, she hereby forfeits all right, title, and
interest.

SPONGE (*straining his ears, to the audience*) I can't make
out what he's saying from back here. Is that full-belly talking about me and my right title and interest?

MENAECHMUS OF SYRACUSE (*to the audience*) She said I
stole it from my wife and gave it to her. I saw she was
mistaking me for someone else, so I promptly played it as
if she and I were having a hot and heavy affair and began
to yes her; I agreed right down the line to everything she
said. Well, to make a long story short, I never had it so
good for so little.

SPONGE (*clenching his fists, to the audience*) I'm going up
to him. I'm itching to give him the works. (*Leaves his corner and strides belligerently toward Menaechmus.*)

MENAECHMUS OF SYRACUSE (*to the audience*) Someone
coming up to me. Wonder who it is?

SPONGE (*roaring*) Well! You featherweight, you filth, you
slime, you disgrace to the human race, you double-crossing
good-for-nothing! What did I ever do to you that you had
to ruin my life? You sure gave me the slip downtown a

little while ago! You killed off the day all right—and held the funeral feast without me. Me who was coheir under the will! Where do you come off to do a thing like that!

MENAECHMUS OF SYRACUSE (*too pleased with life to lose his temper*)   Mister, will you please tell me what business you and I have that gives you the right to use language like that to a stranger here, someone you never saw in your life? You hand me that talk and I'll hand you something you won't like.

SPONGE (*dancing with rage*)   God damn it, you already have! I know god damned well you have!

MENAECHMUS OF SYRACUSE (*amused and curious*)   What's your name, mister?

SPONGE (*as before*)   Still making jokes, eh? As if you don't know my name!

MENAECHMUS OF SYRACUSE   So help me, so far as I know, I never heard of you or saw you till this minute. But I know one thing for sure: whoever you are, you'd better behave yourself and stop bothering me.

SPONGE (*taken aback for a minute*)   Menaechmus! Wake up!

MENAECHMUS OF SYRACUSE (*genially*)   Believe me, to the best of my knowledge, I am awake.

SPONGE   You don't know me?

MENAECHMUS OF SYRACUSE (*as before*)   If I did, I wouldn't say I didn't.

SPONGE (*incredulously*)   You don't know your own parasite?

MENAECHMUS OF SYRACUSE   Mister, it looks to me as if you've got bats in your belfry.

SPONGE (*shaken, but not convinced*)   Tell me this: didn't you steal that dress there from your wife today and give it to Lovey?

MENAECHMUS OF SYRACUSE   Good god, no! I don't have a wife, I never gave anything to any Lovey, and I never stole any dress. Are you in your right mind?

SPONGE (*aside, groaning*) A dead loss, the whole affair. (*To Menaechmus*) But you came out of your house wearing the dress! I saw you myself!

MENAECHMUS OF SYRACUSE (*exploding*) Damn you! You think everybody's a pervert just because you are? I was wearing this dress? Is that what you're telling me?

SPONGE I most certainly am.

MENAECHMUS OF SYRACUSE Now you go straight to the one place fit for you! No—get yourself to the lunatic asylum; you're stark-raving mad.

SPONGE (*venomously*) God damn it, there's one thing nobody in the world is going to stop me from doing: I'm telling the whole story, exactly what happened, to your wife this minute. All these insults are going to boomerang back on your own head. Believe you me, you'll pay for eating that whole lunch yourself. (*Dashes into the house of Menaechmus of Epidamnus.*)

MENAECHMUS OF SYRACUSE (*throwing his arms wide, to the audience*) What's going on here? Must everyone I lay eyes on play games with me this way? Wait—I hear the door.

(*The door of Lovey's house opens, and one of her maids comes out holding a bracelet. She walks over to Menaechmus and, as he looks on blankly, hands it to him.*)

MAID Menaechmus, Lovey says would you please do her a big favor and drop this at the jeweler's on your way? She wants you to give him an ounce of gold and have him make the whole bracelet over.

MENAECHMUS OF SYRACUSE (*with alacrity*) Tell her I'll not only take care of this but anything else she wants taken care of. Anything at all. (*He takes the piece and examines it absorbedly.*)

MAID (*watching him curiously, in surprise*) Don't you know what bracelet it is?

MENAECHMUS OF SYRACUSE Frankly no—except that it's gold.

MAID   It's the one you told us you stole from your wife's jewel box when nobody was looking.

MENAECHMUS OF SYRACUSE (*forgetting himself, in high dudgeon*)   I never did anything of the kind!

MAID   You mean you don't remember it? Well, if that's the case, you give it right back!

MENAECHMUS OF SYRACUSE (*after a few seconds of highly histrionic deep thought*)   Wait a second. No, I *do* remember it. Of course—this is the one I gave her. Oh, and there's something else: where are the armlets I gave her at the same time?

MAID (*puzzled*)   You never gave her any armlets.

MENAECHMUS OF SYRACUSE (*quickly*)   Right you are. This was all I gave her.

MAID   Shall I tell her you'll take care of it?

MENAECHMUS OF SYRACUSE   By all means, tell her. I'll take care of it, all right. I'll see she gets it back the same time she gets the dress back.

MAID (*going up to him and stroking his cheek*)   Menaechmus dear, will you do me a favor too? Will you have some earrings made for me? Drop earrings, please; ten grams of gold in each. (*Meaningfully*) It'll make me *so* glad to see you every time you come to the house.

MENAECHMUS OF SYRACUSE   Sure. (*With elaborate carelessness*) Just give me the gold. I'll pay for the labor myself.

MAID   Please, you pay for the gold too. I'll make it up to you afterward.

MENAECHMUS OF SYRACUSE   No, you pay for the gold. I'll make it up to *you* afterward. Double.

MAID   I don't have the money.

MENAECHMUS OF SYRACUSE (*with a great air of magnanimity*)   Well, any time you get it, you just let me have it.

MAID (*turning to go*)   I'm going in now. Anything I can do for you?

MENAECHMUS OF SYRACUSE   Yes. Tell her I'll see to both

things—(*sotto voce, to the audience*) that they get sold as quickly as possible for whatever they'll bring. (*As the maid starts walking toward the door*) Has she gone in yet? (*Hearing a slam*) Ah, she's in, the door's closed. (*Jubilantly*) The lord loves me! I've had a helping hand from heaven! (*Suddenly looks about warily*) But why hang around when I have the time and chance to get away from this (*jerking his thumb at Lovey's house*) pimping parlor here? Menaechmus! Get a move on, hit the road, forward march! I'll take off this garland and toss it to the left here (*doing so*). Then, if anyone tries to follow me, he'll think I went that way. Now I'll go and see if I can find my servant. I want to let him know all the blessings from heaven I've had.

(*He races off, stage right. The stage is now empty.*)

ACT IV

(*The door of Menaechmus' house flies open and his wife bursts out, shrieking, with Sponge at her heels.*)

WIFE Am I supposed to put up with a marriage like this? Look the other way while that husband of mine sneaks off everything in the house and hands it all over to his lady friend?

SPONGE (*looking around uneasily*) Not so loud, please! I'll see to it you catch him red-handed right now. Just follow me. (*Starting to walk off, stage left*) He was on his way to the dressmaker with that dress he stole from you today. Had a garland on his head and was dead drunk. (*Noticing the garland Menaechmus of Syracuse had thrown down*) Hey, look! The garland he had on! I wasn't lying to you, was I? There you are. That's the way he went if you want to follow his trail. (*Looking toward the wings, stage left*) Well, look at that! He's coming back. Perfect! (*Peering hard*) But he doesn't have the dress!

WIFE (*grimly*) What should I do to him this time?

SPONGE Same as usual: lace into him. That's what I'd vote for. (*Pulling her off to the side*) Let's go over here. Then jump on him from ambush.

(*Enter Menaechmus of Epidamnus, hot, tired, and in a foul temper. He walks downstage and addresses the audience.*)

SONG

MENAECHMUS OF EPIDAMNUS

> What a custom we have! Bothersome, bad,
> Stupid, silly, senseless, mad!
> And practiced most by our leading lights:
> They all adore,
> They're passionate for
> A flock of fawning satellites.

Whether good or bad never bothers them:
The fawner's funds they're bothered about.
How people regard his character—
    They leave that out.

Is he good as gold but rather poor?
    He's a bum.
Is he worthless but has lots of gold?
    The best they come!

A patron goes wild with worry and care
    Because of his charges' acts.
They know no truth or law or justice;
    They deny undeniable facts;

They're vicious, avaricious crooks
    Forever up for trial—
Through usury and perjury
    They've made their pile.

In summary, civil, or criminal court,
Whenever a case of theirs comes up,
    We patrons come up too—
Of course: we have to take the stand
    And defend what the dastards do.

(*Pauses, shakes his head despondently, then continues bitterly.*)

That's what *I* had to do just today.
One of mine simply held me at bay.
I couldn't do what I wished, nor with whom,
For he hung and he clung; it was doom.
I went up on the stand and I entered a plea
On behalf of this creature's chicanery.

I proposed the most twisted and tortuous terms;
    Here I'd skim, there go on for a while.
I was arguing to settle the case out of court;
    What does *he* do? Insist on a trial!

There were three solid citizens who'd witnessed each crime—
Most open-and-shut case since the beginning of time!

He ruined this day for me.
God damn that stupid clown!
And god damn me as well!
For setting foot downtown.

I told her to make me lunch;
She's expecting me, I know.
A perfect day set up—
And I had to ruin it so!

I left as soon as I could
And hurried back uptown.
She'll be sore at me, I'm sure—
But that dress will calm her down,
The one I sneaked today from my wife
And handed to Lovey, the light of my life!

SPONGE (*sotto voce to the wife, triumphantly*)   Well, what do you say?

WIFE (*sotto voce*)   That I'm the miserable wife of a miserable husband.

SPONGE (*sotto voce*)   You can hear what he's saying, can't you?

WIFE (*sotto voce, grimly*)   I can hear, all right.

MENAECHMUS OF EPIDAMNUS (*to the audience, gesturing toward Lovey's door*)   Now why don't I be smart and go right inside here where I can have myself a good time?

SPONGE (*springing out of his corner, shouting*)   Wait! You're going to have a bad one, instead.

WIFE (*following him, shrieking*)   You'll pay me and with interest, you burglar.

SPONGE (*gleefully*)   That's giving it to him!

WIFE   So you thought you could commit all these crimes and get away with it, eh?

MENAECHMUS OF EPIDAMNUS (*all innocence*)   My dear wife, what are you talking about?

WIFE (*witheringly*)   You ask *me?*

MENAECHMUS OF EPIDAMNUS (*acting puzzled, and gesturing*

toward Sponge) Should I ask him? (*Walks toward her as if to put an arm about her.*)

WIFE   Don't you dare touch me!

SPONGE (*to the wife*) Keep at him!

MENAECHMUS OF EPIDAMNUS (*switching from puzzlement back to innocence*) What are you so mad at me for?

WIFE (*grimly*) You ought to know.

SPONGE   He knows, all right, but he's pretending he doesn't, the dirty rat!

MENAECHMUS OF EPIDAMNUS (*to his wife, as before*) What *is* this all about?

WIFE   That dress—

MENAECHMUS OF EPIDAMNUS (*quickly*) Dress?

WIFE   Yes, dress. Which a certain person— (*Menaechmus begins to shake. She observes him with grim satisfaction.*) What are you so scared about?

MENAECHMUS OF EPIDAMNUS (*with a sickly attempt at non-chalance*) Me? Nothing. Nothing at all.

SPONGE (*to Menaechmus, sneering*) With one exception— dress distress. (*As Menaechmus looks at him startled and then begins to pass frantic nods and winks*) So you *would* eat lunch behind my back, would you? (*To the wife*) Keep at him!

MENAECHMUS OF EPIDAMNUS (*sotto voce to Sponge*) Shut up, will you!

SPONGE (*answering Menaechmus' stage whisper in ringing tones*) I most certainly will *not* shut up. (*To the wife*) He's making signs to me not to speak.

MENAECHMUS OF EPIDAMNUS   Me? I most certainly am not! I'm not winking, I'm not nodding, I'm not doing anything of the kind.

SPONGE (*to the wife, shaking his head incredulously*) Of all the nerve! He actually denies what you can see with your own eyes!

MENAECHMUS OF EPIDAMNUS (*to the wife, solemnly*) My

dear wife, I swear to you by all that's holy, I did *not* make any signs to (*jerking his head contemptuously in Sponge's direction*) that there. Now are you satisfied?

SPONGE   All right, she believes you about that there; now get back to the point.

MENAECHMUS OF EPIDAMNUS (*with angelic innocence*)   Get back where?

SPONGE   Get back to that dressmaker, *I* say. Go ahead. And bring back the dress.

MENAECHMUS OF EPIDAMNUS (*as before*)   What dress are you talking about?

SPONGE   It's time for me to stop doing the talking. This lady is forgetting her duty.

WIFE (*responding promptly to the cue*)   Oh, I'm a poor, unhappy woman!

MENAECHMUS OF EPIDAMNUS (*going over to her, solicitously*)   Why are you so unhappy, dear? Please tell me. Has one of the servants done something wrong? Are the maids or the houseboys answering you back? (*Switching from solicitousness to righteous indignation*) You just let me know about it. They'll pay for it, they will!

WIFE (*witheringly*)   Nonsense!

MENAECHMUS OF EPIDAMNUS (*tenderly, to himself—but aloud*)   She's so out of sorts. This distresses me.

WIFE (*as before*)   Nonsense!

MENAECHMUS OF EPIDAMNUS (*nodding with sympathetic understanding*)   Yes, you must be angry at one of the servants.

WIFE (*as before*)   Nonsense!

MENAECHMUS OF EPIDAMNUS (*chuckling, as if what he's going to say is a great joke*)   You can't be angry at *me*, at any rate.

WIFE (*grimly*)   Now you're making sense.

MENAECHMUS OF EPIDAMNUS   I certainly haven't done anything wrong.

WIFE Hah! Back to nonsense again.

MENAECHMUS OF EPIDAMNUS (*going up and putting his arm about her*) My dear, *please* tell me what's troubling you so much.

SPONGE (*to the wife, sneering*) Your little bunny's buttering you up.

MENAECHMUS OF EPIDAMNUS (*over his shoulder to Sponge, exasperated*) Can't you lay off me? Who's talking to you?

WIFE (*suddenly screaming*) Take your hands off me! (*Menaechmus leaps back as if stunned.*)

SPONGE (*to the wife*) That's giving it to him! (*To Menaechmus*) So you'll hurry off to eat lunch without me, will you? And then get drunk and walk out the door with a garland on your head and make fun of me, eh?

(*Menaechmus grabs Sponge and yanks him over to the side.*)

MENAECHMUS OF EPIDAMNUS (*sotto voce*) So help me, I not only haven't eaten lunch, I haven't set foot inside that house today!

SPONGE (*sotto voce*) You mean you deny it?

MENAECHMUS OF EPIDAMNUS (*sotto voce*) Of course I deny it.

SPONGE (*sotto voce*) What a nerve! You mean to say I didn't see you a little while ago standing in front of the door there with a garland on your head? When you said I had bats in the belfry and that you didn't know me and that you were a stranger here?

MENAECHMUS OF EPIDAMNUS (*sotto voce, blankly*) How could I? I just this minute came back home after you and I got separated.

SPONGE (*sotto voce, sneering*) Oh, I know your type. Didn't think I could get even with you, did you? I told the whole story to your wife, that's what I did!

MENAECHMUS OF EPIDAMNUS (*sotto voce, anxiously*)   What did you tell her?

SPONGE (*sotto voce, blandly*)   I don't know. Ask the lady herself.

(*Menaechmus turns on his heel and hurries to where his wife is standing.*)

MENAECHMUS OF EPIDAMNUS (*nervously*)   My dear wife, what's going on here? What sort of story did this fellow hand you? What is it? Why don't you answer me? Why don't you tell me what's the matter?

WIFE (*witheringly*)   As if you don't know! (*Slowly, emphasizing each word*) A dress was stolen from me.

MENAECHMUS OF EPIDAMNUS (*with wide-eyed innocence*)   A dress was stolen from you?

WIFE (*as before*)   Do you have to ask?

MENAECHMUS OF EPIDAMNUS (*as before*)   If I knew, I certainly wouldn't ask.

SPONGE   Damn you! What a faker! But you can't cover up any longer—she knows the whole story; I told it to her myself down to the last detail.

MENAECHMUS OF EPIDAMNUS (*as before*)   What story?

WIFE (*grimly*)   Since you have such an unmitigated gall and refuse to confess of your own free will, listen and listen hard. Believe you me, you'll find out what I'm mad about and what this fellow told me. (*Looking him straight in the eye*) A dress was stolen from me.

MENAECHMUS OF EPIDAMNUS (*with histrionic astonishment*)   A dress was stolen from me?

SPONGE (*to the wife*)   Look at that! The dirty rat's trying to fool you! (*To Menaechmus*) Stolen from *her*, not you. Damn it all, if it had been stolen from *you*, then it really would be lost.

MENAECHMUS OF EPIDAMNUS (*to Sponge, savagely*)   You keep out of this. (*To his wife*) Now, what were you saying, dear?

WIFE (*tight-lipped*) I was saying that one of my dresses disappeared from the house.

MENAECHMUS OF EPIDAMNUS Who could have stolen it?

WIFE (*meaningfully*) I should think the man who made off with it knows the answer to that one.

MENAECHMUS OF EPIDAMNUS Who is he?

WIFE Some one named Menaechmus.

MENAECHMUS OF EPIDAMNUS (*thundering*) God in heaven, the man's a criminal! Who is this Menaechmus?

WIFE I'll tell you: *you*.

MENAECHMUS OF EPIDAMNUS Me?

WIFE You.

(*They stand in silence for a few seconds, eying one another.*)

MENAECHMUS OF EPIDAMNUS (*blustering*) Who says so?

WIFE I do.

SPONGE So do I. And I also say you gave it to your lady friend Lovey here.

MENAECHMUS OF EPIDAMNUS *I* gave it?

WIFE Yes, you. You yourself.

SPONGE What do you want us to do? Bring an owl here to keep saying "yoo yoo" to you? We're getting hoarse, the both of us.

MENAECHMUS OF EPIDAMNUS (*solemnly, one hand on heart, the other raised*) My dear wife, I swear to you by all that's holy, I didn't give it. Does that satisfy you?

SPONGE And, damn it all, we take the same oath that you're lying!

(*Menaechmus looks from one to the other. They glower back. He quails visibly.*)

MENAECHMUS OF EPIDAMNUS (*feebly*) Well, you see, I didn't *give* it away, I sort of lent it out.

WIFE (*exploding*) Good god in heaven! *I* don't lend out your coats or suits, do I? If there's any lending to do, the wife will see to her things and the husband to his. Now you get that dress back into this house, do you hear?

MENAECHMUS OF EPIDAMNUS (*meekly*)   I'll see you get it back.

WIFE (*grimly*)   And my opinion is, you'd better. Because you don't enter this house unless that dress is with you. I'm going in now. (*Turns her back on him and stalks off toward the door.*)

SPONGE (*calling after her, alarmed*)   Don't I get anything for all I've done for you?

WIFE (*pausing at the threshhold, contemptuously*)   I'll do the same for you when something's stolen from your house. (*Slams the door behind her.*)

SPONGE (*to the audience, horror-stricken*)   My god! That means never—I don't have anything to steal! Husband, wife—to hell with the both of you! I'm off downtown in a hurry—one thing I know for sure: I've worn out my welcome with this household! (*Scuttles off, stage left.*)

MENAECHMUS OF EPIDAMNUS (*to the audience, gaily*)   My wife thinks she's giving me a bad time by shutting me out. As if I don't have another place to go into, lots better. (*Addressing the closed door*) You don't like me, eh? (*With a mock sigh*) I'll just have to put up with it. But Lovey here likes me. She's not going to shut me out, she's going to shut me *in*. (*Turning back to the audience*) I'll go see her and ask her to return the dress I just gave her. I'll buy her another one, even better. (*Walking up to Lovey's door and knocking*) Hey! Anybody minding this door? Open up, someone, and call Lovey out here!

LOVEY (*from inside*)   Who wants me?

MENAECHMUS OF EPIDAMNUS   Someone who'd sooner see his own self hurt than hurt you.

LOVEY (*opening the door*)   Menaechmus! Darling! What are you standing outside for? Come on in. (*Turns to go inside.*)

MENAECHMUS OF EPIDAMNUS (*seriously*)　No, wait. You don't know what I've come for.

LOVEY (*walking up to him and stroking his cheek*)　Sure I do. So you can have your fun with me.

MENAECHMUS OF EPIDAMNUS (*as before*)　Damn it all, it's not that. Would you please do me a big favor and give me back that dress I just gave you? My wife's found out everything, she knows exactly what happened. I'll buy you another that costs twice as much, anyone you like.

LOVEY (*staring at him blankly*)　But I just gave it to you a few minutes ago to take to the dressmaker! Along with that bracelet you were to take to the jeweler so he could make it over.

MENAECHMUS OF EPIDAMNUS (*staring at her blankly*)　What's that? You gave *me* the dress and a bracelet? Oh, no. You never did. Figure it out. Right after I gave it to you, I went downtown, I came back from there just a few minutes ago, and this is the first I've seen of you since.

LOVEY (*stepping back and eying him frigidly*)　I see what your game is. I trusted you with the dress, and now you're looking for a way to do me out of it.

MENAECHMUS OF EPIDAMNUS (*earnestly*)　I swear I'm not asking for it to do you out of it. I tell you my wife knows everything!

LOVEY (*building up a head of feminine steam*)　I didn't ask you to give it to me. *You* brought it to me of your own free will. You gave it as a gift, and now you want it back. Well, I don't mind. Take it. Keep it. Let your wife wear it, wear it yourself, lock it up in a closet, for all I care. But don't you fool yourself: you're not setting foot inside this door from now on. After all I've done for you, you'll treat me like dirt under your feet, will you? Unless you come with cash in your hands, you're wasting your time, you'll get nothing out of me. Find some other girl to treat like—like a fool under your feet!

MENAECHMUS OF EPIDAMNUS　Don't carry on so, please! (*As

she turns her back on him and flounces inside) Hey, wait,
I tell you! Come on back! Stop, won't you? Please, do me
a favor, and come back! (*She slams the door behind her.
Menaechmus turns despondently to the audience*) She's
gone in and shut the door. I'm the shuttest-out man there
is: my wife, my mistress—nobody believes a thing I say.
Well, I'll go and talk things over with my friends and see
what they think I ought to do.

(*Menaechmus leaves, stage left. The stage is now empty.*)

ACT V

(*Menaechmus of Syracuse enters, stage right, back from his search for Messenio along the waterfront. At the same moment, the door of Menaechmus of Epidamnus' house opens, and the wife comes out.*)

MENAECHMUS OF SYRACUSE (*to himself, disgustedly*) That was a stupid stunt I pulled a little while ago, to trust the wallet with all our money to Messenio. If you ask me, he's made himself at home in some dive somewhere.

WIFE (*to herself*) I'll keep an eye out for that husband of mine. See how soon he comes back. (*Noticing Menaechmus of Syracuse*) Well! There he is! And the day's saved—he's bringing back my dress.

MENAECHMUS OF SYRACUSE (*to himself, testily*) I wonder where that Messenio would be wandering about now?

WIFE (*to herself*) I'll go up to him and give him the welcome he deserves. (*Striding up to Menaechmus*) Aren't you ashamed to show yourself in front of me with that dress, you criminal!

MENAECHMUS OF SYRACUSE (*startled*) What's the matter, madam? What's all the agitation about?

WIFE (*shrieking*) The nerve of him! How dare you talk to me! How dare you utter a single solitary word in my presence!

MENAECHMUS OF SYRACUSE (*in astonishment*) Will you please tell me what I did that I'm not allowed to utter a word?

WIFE (*as before*) What a question! The unmitigated gall of this man!

MENAECHMUS OF SYRACUSE (*tartly*) Madam, do you happen to know why the Greeks called Hecuba a bitch?

WIFE (*huffily*) No, I don't.

MENAECHMUS OF SYRACUSE (*as before*) Because she used

to do exactly what you're doing now. Everyone she laid eyes on, she loaded with insults. And so they began to call her The Bitch—and she deserved it.

WIFE (*after staring at him blankly for a few seconds, unable to believe her ears*) I *will* not put up with this criminal behavior! I'd sooner spend the rest of my days a divorcée than put up with this absolutely criminal behavior of yours!

MENAECHMUS OF SYRACUSE (*shrugging*) What difference does it make to me whether you put up with your marriage or walk out on your husband? Is it the custom around here for people to talk nonsense to every stranger who comes to town?

WIFE (*as before*) Talk nonsense? Well! I tell you I can't stand this one second longer. I'll die a divorcée rather than put up with the likes of you.

MENAECHMUS OF SYRACUSE (*as before*) Die a divorcée or live till doomsday. Believe me, it makes no difference to me.

WIFE A minute ago you were insisting you hadn't stolen it and now you're holding it right in front of my eyes. Aren't you ashamed of yourself?

MENAECHMUS OF SYRACUSE (*finally needled into an angry retort*) Good god, woman, you certainly have a nerve! You're a bad one, you are! How dare you say I stole from you what another woman gave me to have trimmed and altered for her?

WIFE (*throwing up her hands*) So help me, you know what I'm going to do? I'm going to call my father right here and now and tell him about every one of your crimes. (*Calling*) Decio! (*A scared houseboy scurries out and listens breathlessly.*) Go get my father and bring him right here; tell him he must come. (*Decio dashes off, stage left.*) In a few minutes the whole world will know all about these crimes of yours.

MENAECHMUS OF SYRACUSE Are you in your right mind? What crimes of mine?

WIFE   That you stole dresses and jewelry from your own wife and carried them off to your lady friend. Is it the truth or isn't it?

MENAECHMUS OF SYRACUSE (*helplessly*)   Please, lady, if you know of any tranquilizer I can take to help me put up with your tantrums, for god's sake, lead me to it! I haven't the vaguest idea of who you think I am. I know you about as well as I know the man in the moon.

WIFE (*pointing toward the wings, stage left*)   You can make fun of me, all right, but, believe me, you're not going to make fun of *him*. There's my father coming this way. Turn around and look. I suppose you don't know him.

MENAECHMUS OF SYRACUSE (*his gaze following her finger*)   About as well as I know the old man of the mountain. You know when I saw him before? The same day I saw you.

WIFE   You deny that you know me? You deny that you know my father?

MENAECHMUS OF SYRACUSE (*airily*)   And the same goes for your grandfather, if you want to add him.

WIFE (*disgustedly*)   Ugh! Just what I'd expect from you!

(*Menaechmus moves away, stage right, and stands moodily, looking off into the wings trying to catch the first glimpse of Messenio. A wizened graybeard emerges from the wings, stage left, leaning heavily on a stick; he makes his way at a snail's pace across the stage.*)

SONG

FATHER (*stopping to address the audience*)
> As fast as these old legs can go—
> When duty calls I can't say no—
> I'll step, I'll stride, I'll speed, I'll run.
> I'm well aware this is no fun:
> The spryness has gone out of me,
> I'm buried deep in senility,
> My body's hard to haul along,
> I've lost the strength I had when young.

> In getting old you don't do well;
> It's bad stuff, age. Do well? It's hell!
> Its coming brings a load of grief—
> But, to tell it all, I can't be brief.

(*Totters on a few more steps, then stops abruptly and shakes his head worriedly*)

> Now here's the thing that's on my mind
>   And worries me to the core:
> What brought my daughter so suddenly
>   To call me to her door?
> What does she want? She doesn't say!
>   What is it she's called me for?

(*Goes on for a few more steps, then halts again*)

> I'm sure I know what it's all about:
> A fight with her husband has broken out.
> It's bound to happen to every shrew
> Who feels her dowry entitles her to
> A husband whose sole aim in life
> Is to fetch and carry for his wife.

(*A few more steps, then another stop and more worried headshakings*)

> Yet the men are not exactly pure.
> And there's just so much a wife can endure.
> A daughter doesn't call her dad
> Unless the insult's pretty bad,
> Or else the squabbling got too rough.
> Whatever it is, I'll know soon enough.

(*Turns and catches sight, finally, of his daughter and Menaechmus*)

> There she is before the door.
> There's her husband, looking sore.
> Just what I thought—a brawl once more.

FATHER (*to himself*)   I'll have a word with her.

WIFE (*to herself*)   I'll go up to him. (*Walking up to her father*) Papa! I'm *so* glad to see you!

FATHER Glad to see you too. Well, here I am; any glad tidings? Were things glad around here when you sent for me? What are you looking so black for? (*Pointing to Menaechmus still watching out moodily for Messenio*) And what's he standing off over there in a huff for? You two have had a skirmish about something, all right. Well, speak up. Who's to blame? And make it short—no long lectures.

WIFE *I* haven't done a thing wrong. Let me put your mind at ease about that first, Papa. It's simply that I can't go on living here, it's impossible, I can't stand it. So please take me away from here.

FATHER (*wearily*) What's the trouble this time?

WIFE Papa, he's making a fool of me.

FATHER Who is?

WIFE That man you trusted me to. That husband of mine.

FATHER (*throwing up his hands*) I knew it! Another squabble. (*Peevishly*) How many times have I expressly warned you to watch out about coming to me with your complaints. Both of you.

WIFE (*plaintively*) Watch out about *that*? How can I, Papa!

FATHER (*snappishly*) What a question! You can if you want to. How many times have I pointed out to you that you *must* give in to your husband and not keep checking on what he does and where he goes and how he spends his time.

WIFE (*expostulating*) But, Papa, he's passionately in love with that prostitute who lives next door!

FATHER Very sensible of him. And, believe me, all this effort of yours will simply make him more passionate.

WIFE (*sulking*) He goes there for drinks too.

FATHER (*angrily*) If he likes to have a drink there—or anywhere—what's he supposed to do? Not go just to please you? You do have a devil of a nerve! By the same token

you ought to stop him from accepting invitations to eat out
or from bringing dinner guests to the house. If you think
husbands are such slaves, why don't you hand him some
wool, sit him down with the maids, and have him do a
daily stint of spinning.

WIFE (*with heavy sarcasm*) Naturally, it wasn't *me* I
brought you here to defend, but my husband. You take
the stand for *me*—and plead *his* case!

FATHER (*sharply*) If he's done anything wrong, I'll go after
him lots harder than I've gone after you. Since he keeps
you in money and clothes, gives you maids, and pays for
the household, the best thing you can do, my lady, is to
start getting some sense.

WIFE (*in desperation*) But he steals my jewelry and dresses
right out of my closets, he robs me, he carries off my things
behind my back and brings them to those whores of his!

FATHER If he does that, he's to be blamed. But if he doesn't,
you're to be blamed for blaming a blameless man.

WIFE Papa, he's got the dress and bracelet that he gave her
with him right now. I found out all about it, so he's bringing them back.

FATHER (*shaking his head perplexedly, to himself*) I'll find
out all about this right now. I'll go up and have a word
with him. (*Tottering over to Menaechmus, who is still
looking impatiently, stage right, for Messenio*) Tell me,
Menaechmus, what have you two been—er—discussing?
What are you looking so black about? What are you
standing off here in a huff for?

MENAECHMUS OF SYRACUSE My dear sir, I don't know who
you are or what your name is, but I swear to you by god
almighty and—

FATHER (*interrupting in astonishment*) Swear? What in the
world about?

MENAECHMUS OF SYRACUSE (*holding up the dress*) This
woman claims I stole this out of her house and made off
with it. She's crazy. I swear I never did a thing wrong to

her. (*Solemnly*) So help me, may I become more miserable than the most miserable specimen of humanity alive if I ever set foot in the house where she lives.

FATHER   Listen, you madman, if you take an oath like that, if you say you never set foot in your own house, you're stark-raving mad.

MENAECHMUS OF SYRACUSE (*pointing to Menaechmus of Epidamnus' house*)   My dear sir, are you telling me that I live in that house?

FATHER   Do you deny it?

MENAECHMUS OF SYRACUSE   I most certainly do deny it.

FATHER   No, you most certainly can't deny it. (*Suddenly struck by a thought*) Unless you moved out last night. (*Turning to the wife*) Daughter, come over here. What's this? You two haven't moved out of here?

WIFE   Now, just where or why would we be moving?

FATHER   Good god, *I* don't know.

WIFE (*disgustedly*)   It's so obvious. He's pulling your leg. Don't you get it?

FATHER (*turning back to Menaechmus, sharply*)   All right, Menaechmus, enough jokes. Now get to the point.

MENAECHMUS OF SYRACUSE (*finally losing his patience*) Please, what do you want with me? Where do you come from? Who are you? What have I got to do with you or this woman here who's pestering the life out of me?

WIFE (*fearfully, to her father*)   Look! His eyes are green! He's turning green around his temples and his forehead! Look at the glitter in his eyes!

MENAECHMUS OF SYRACUSE (*to the audience*)   They say I'm insane. Well, in that case, the best thing for me to do is act the part and scare them away.

(*Menaechmus proceeds forthwith to put on a garish performance.*)

WIFE (*as before*)   Look at the way he's throwing his arms

around! Look at the faces he's making! Papa! What should
I do!

FATHER (*taking her by the arm and tottering off with her*)
Come over here, daughter. As far away from him as we
can get.

MENAECHMUS OF SYRACUSE (*pretending to be calling to the
God of Wine*) Yoho! Yoho! Bacchus! Where away in
what wood do you call me for the hunt? I hear you—but
I can't leave these parts. They've got their eyes on me—on
my left that mad bitch and, behind, that old stink-goat
who's perjured himself plenty of times in his day to the
ruination of innocent men.

FATHER   You go to hell!

MENAECHMUS OF SYRACUSE (*listening attentively as if to an
unseen voice, and nodding briskly*) Ah! Orders from the
Oracle of Apollo for me to burn her eyes out with blazing
brands.

WIFE   Papa! This will be the end of me! He says he's going
to burn my eyes out!

MENAECHMUS OF SYRACUSE (*aside, chuckling*) They say *I'm*
crazy. Damn it all, they're the ones who're crazy.

FATHER   Psst! Daughter!

WIFE   What is it? What are we going to do?

FATHER   Why don't I call the servants out here? I'll go get
some to carry him in the house and tie him up before he
causes any more commotion.

MENAECHMUS OF SYRACUSE (*aside*) Stuck! If I don't come
up with some scheme first, they're going to haul me into
the house. (*Resumes his elaborate listening and nodding
to celestial commands.*) Yes, Apollo: I'm not to spare the
socks on the jaw unless she gets the hell out of my sight.
I will carry out your orders, Apollo. (*Advances menacingly toward the wife.*)

FATHER (*frantically*) Run home as fast as you can or he'll
beat you to a pulp!

WIFE (*making for the door*)   I am! Papa dear, please, please keep an eye on him and don't let him get away. (*To herself*) Oh, this is terrible! The things I have to listen to! (*Rushes into the house and slams the door behind her.*)

MENAECHMUS OF SYRACUSE (*aside*)   Not bad at all, the way I got rid of her. Now for this Titan here—a Titan with the shakes, a bearded, benighted one begat by the Holy Swan. (*Starts listening and nodding again.*) So your orders are to grab that stick he's holding and make pulp of his arms, legs, bones, and joints?

FATHER (*raising his stick*)   You lay a hand on me or come any closer, and you're in for trouble!

MENAECHMUS OF SYRACUSE (*as before*)   I will carry out your orders, Apollo: I'm to take an ax and chip off every scrap of flesh this old boy has until I'm down to the bone.

FATHER (*aside*)   I've got to watch out and take care of myself now. These threats of his have me worried: he might hurt me.

(*Menaechmus advances, brandishing an imaginary ax, but the old man, instead of running, whirls his stick menacingly, and Menaechmus stops short before that formidable instrument. Forced to take another tack, he resumes his listening and nodding act.*)

MENAECHMUS OF SYRACUSE   That's a big order, Apollo. Now I'm to get a team of fierce wild horses, harness them to a chariot, and mount it so I can trample down this stinking, toothless, broken-down lion, eh? (*Launches into an elaborate dumb show.*) Now I'm in the chariot, I'm holding the reins, the whip's in my hand. (*Mimicking the manner of grand opera*) Come, my steeds! Let the clatter of your hoofs ring out! Bend the nimble knee in headlong haste!

FATHER (*grimly*)   Threatening me with a team of horses, eh?

(*Menaechmus gallops madly about, then, full tilt, makes for the old man, who holds his ground gamely, swinging his stick. Just before getting within range, Menaechmus pru-*

dently swerves aside, pulls up, and readies himself for another try.)

MENAECHMUS OF SYRACUSE   Ah, Apollo, the orders are to make a second charge and wipe out this one who insists on standing his ground, eh? (*Charges down on the old man but the stick, whistling through the air, brings Menaechmus to an abrupt halt. He throws his head back and staggers backward as if irresistibly dragged against his will.*) What's this? Someone has me by the hair and is hauling me from my car! Who is it? Apollo! He's changing your direct orders!

FATHER (*shaking his head dolefully, to the audience*)   Dear, oh dear! These fits are such terrible things! Heaven help us! This fellow, for instance, was perfectly sane a minute ago and now he's completely out of his mind. And it came on him so suddenly and with such force! I'll go get a doctor as quick as I can. (*Rushes out, stage left.*)

MENAECHMUS OF SYRACUSE (*to himself, in surprise*)   Have they really gone? That pair who made a sane man insane? What am I waiting for? I should be off for the ship while the coast is clear. (*Walking downstage and addressing the audience*) Please, all of you, if the old fellow comes back, don't show him which street I took to get out of here.

(*Menaechmus of Syracuse dashes off, stage right. A second later the father re-enters, stage left, followed by a self-important little man who struts along majestically.*)

FATHER (*to the audience, grumbling*)   My seat hurts from sitting and my eyes from watching while I waited for the doctor to finish his rounds. Finally the pain-in-the-neck tore himself away from his patients and came back. "Aesculapius fractured a leg and Apollo an arm, and I was mending the breaks," he tells me. I wonder what I'm bringing, a doctor or a repairman? Look at that walk! (*Under his breath*) Shake a leg, you ant!

DOCTOR (*in his professional manner*)   What did you say his trouble is? Please describe it to me. Is it hallucinations or delirium? I'd like to know. Is he in a coma? Does he have water on the brain?

FATHER (*testily*) Listen, that's just the reason I brought you here. To give *me* the answers—and to cure him.

DOCTOR (*airily*) Nothing easier. He'll be a well man, I give you my word.

FATHER I want you to be careful to take good care of him.

DOCTOR Listen, I'll heave sixty sighs an hour for him. That's how careful I'll be to take good care of him.

FATHER (*pointing toward the wings, stage left*) Look, there's your patient. Let's watch what he does.

(*The two back off to an unobtrusive spot. As they do, Menaechmus of Epidamnus trudges in despondently. Without noticing them, he walks downstage and addresses the audience.*)

MENAECHMUS OF EPIDAMNUS God! What a day this one's been! Everything's gone against me. I thought I had kept what I did a secret—and my parasite spills the whole story, leaving me scared to death and in disgrace. That Ulysses of mine! The trouble he stirred up for his lord and master! (*Shaking his fist so hard his mantle slips from his shoulder*) As sure as I'm alive, I'll see to it he and his life part company. (*Snorting*) Now that's stupid of me, to call it *his* life. It's *mine*: he's stayed alive eating my food and at my expense. All right then, I'll make him part company with his soul. And that whore was every bit as bad. What else can you expect from a whore? Because I ask for the dress, so I can bring it back to my wife, she tells me she's already given it to me! Lord, oh lord, what a miserable life I lead!

FATHER (*sotto voce to the doctor*) You hear what he's saying?

DOCTOR (*sotto voce, with a knowing air*) Claims he's miserable.

FATHER (*sotto voce*) I wish you'd talk with him.

DOCTOR (*walking up to Menaechmus*) Good afternoon, Menaechmus. Will you please tell me why you have to leave your arm bare? Don't you realize the harm this can do to a man in your condition?

MENAECHMUS OF EPIDAMNUS (*glaring*) Oh, go hang yourself.

FATHER (*sotto voce to the doctor, anxiously*) Notice anything?

DOCTOR (*sotto voce to the father*) Lord, yes! (*Shaking his head*) Even an acre of hellebore[1] couldn't cure this case. (*Turning back to Menaechmus*) I say, Menaechmus—

MENAECHMUS OF EPIDAMNUS (*impatiently*) What do you want?

DOCTOR (*assuming his professional manner*) Answer my questions, please. Do you drink white or red wine?

MENAECHMUS OF EPIDAMNUS Why don't you go straight to hell?

DOCTOR (*sotto voce to the father, clucking mournfully*) Beginning to show the initial symptoms of a seizure.

MENAECHMUS OF EPIDAMNUS (*disgustedly*) Why don't you ask me whether my diet includes purple or red or yellow bread? Or birds with scales? Or fish with feathers?

FATHER (*sotto voce to the doctor, urgently*) Good god! You hear him talk? He's delirious! What are you waiting for? Quick, give him some medicine before he goes completely insane!

DOCTOR (*sotto voce, pontifically*) Not yet. I still have some questions to ask.

FATHER (*to himself, between his teeth*) Your nonsense will be the death of me!

DOCTOR (*to Menaechmus*) Tell me this: do your eyes at times become fixed and staring?

MENAECHMUS OF EPIDAMNUS What's that? You damned fool! What do you think I am, a lobster?

---

[1] The standard ancient remedy for insanity.

DOCTOR (*ignoring the outburst and nodding knowingly*) Now tell me this: does your stomach ever growl, so far as you've noticed?

MENAECHMUS OF EPIDAMNUS After meals, no; when I'm hungry, yes.

DOCTOR (*sotto voce to the father, puzzled*) So help me, there's nothing insane about that answer! (*Turning back to Menaechmus*) Do you sleep through the night? Do you have trouble falling asleep when you go to bed?

MENAECHMUS OF EPIDAMNUS When my bills are paid, I sleep through. (*Suddenly losing his patience*) You and your questions! God damn you to hell!

DOCTOR (*sotto voce to the father, nodding knowingly*) The start of a fit of insanity. Did you hear what he said? Watch out for him!

FATHER (*sotto voce to the doctor*) Oh no. To hear him talk now, he's Nestor himself compared with what he was before. After all, just a few minutes ago he was calling his wife a mad bitch.

MENAECHMUS OF EPIDAMNUS (*overhearing this, roaring*) *What* did I call her?

FATHER I was saying that, in a fit of insanity—

MENAECHMUS OF EPIDAMNUS (*interrupting, as before*) Insanity? Me?

FATHER (*angrily*) Yes, you. And you threatened to trample me down with a four-horse chariot. I saw you do it with my own eyes. I can prove you did it.

MENAECHMUS OF EPIDAMNUS (*snorting*) Oh sure. And I can prove you stole the holy halo from god almighty. And that you were packed off to prison for it. And that after they let you out, you were tarred and feathered. And what's more, I can prove you killed your father and sold your mother. What do you say? Don't I swap insult for insult just like some one who's sane?

FATHER (*to the doctor, pleading*) For god's sake, please, doctor, hurry and do whatever you're going to do! Don't you see the man's losing his mind?

DOCTOR Do you know the best thing to do? Have him brought to my clinic.

FATHER (*doubtfully*) You really think so?

DOCTOR (*heartily*) Of course. I'll be able to treat him there just the way I want.

FATHER Well, as you wish.

DOCTOR (*to Menaechmus, cheerily*) I'll dose you with hellebore for about three weeks.

MENAECHMUS OF EPIDAMNUS And I'll string you up and dose you with a whip for four. (*Stomps away angrily out of earshot.*)

DOCTOR (*to the father*) Go get some men to carry him.

FATHER How many will we need?

DOCTOR Considering the symptoms I've observed, four would be the minimum.

FATHER I'll have them here right away. Doctor, you keep an eye on him.

DOCTOR (*hastily*) Oh no. I've got to get back to make ready whatever—er—has to be made ready. (*Airily, as he prudently hustles off, stage left*) You just have your servants bring him to me.

FATHER I'll see to it. He'll be there.

DOCTOR (*as he disappears into the wings*) I'm off now.

FATHER (*as he limps off resignedly at his top speed after the doctor*) Good-by.

MENAECHMUS OF EPIDAMNUS (*to the audience*) My father-in-law's left; the doctor's left; I'm alone. God almighty, what's going on? What are these men saying I'm crazy for? Why, I haven't had a sick day since the day I was born. Me insane? I don't even start fights or get into arguments! And I'm sane enough to think everyone else is sane and to recognize people and talk with them. If they can make the mistake of saying I'm crazy, maybe they're the ones who are crazy!

(*Paces up and down a moment in silence. Then, shaking his head despondently*) Now what do I do? I want to go home but my wife won't let me. (*Gesturing toward Lovey's house*) And no one's going to let me in *there*. Oh, the whole thing's a mess! I'll stay right where I am. I suppose when it gets dark I'll be allowed to go inside. (*Sits down gloomily in front of the door of his house.*)

(*Enter Messenio, stage right. He walks downstage and addresses the audience.*)

SONG

You know what marks the servant who's good,
The kind that'll watch, take care, arrange,
And plan for a master's livelihood?
It's taking as good—or better—care
When the master is out as when he's there.

If a slave's more concerned for his belly than back,
And his gullet than shins, then his brain's out of whack.

He must not forget that masters pay
The good-for-nothings in just one way:
With shackles, whip, and mill,
Hunger, fatigue, and chill;
The wage of no work and all play.

So to hell with bad acting, I'll be good, I've decided,
Since I hellishly hate to get hurt or get hided.
I can stomach the curses and cries—
It's the beatings and blows I despise.
And I'm many times happier having for lunch
The bread that's been browned
From what others have ground
Than grinding myself for all others to munch.

So I see that orders get obeyed
With speed and skill and no fuss made.
The system works out well for me:
>Others are free to test
>What seems for them the best,
But *I'll* be as I have to be.

Be a Johnny-on-the-spot when the master commands—
If I only can keep this one worry in mind,
Not a fault will he ever be able to find.

But the day's soon to come when my worrying's done,
When he'll pay me the freedom I've worked for and won.
>So till then I'll behave
>Like a dutiful slave,
>And I'll practice my knack
>Of being kind to my back!

(*He turns and walks briskly toward Lovey's door.*)

Well, I settled the bags and the servants in the hotel as he ordered, and now I've come to get him. I'll knock on the door so he knows I'm here. Let's see if I can spring him safe and sound from this sink of iniquity. I'm afraid, though, I may be too late; the battle may be all over.

(*Enter, stage left, the father with four husky slaves at his heels.*)

FATHER (*to the slaves*)   I'm warning you: in the name of all that's holy, make sure you use your head when you carry out my orders, the ones I gave you before and am giving you now. Unless you don't give a damn for your shins and ribs, you'll pick up that man there (*pointing to Menaechmus of Epidamnus*) and carry him to the clinic. And none of you are to pay the slightest attention to any threats he makes. Well, why are you standing there? What are you waiting for? You should have had him up on your shoulders and on his way by now! I'm off to the doctor's; I'll be waiting when you get there.

(The old man hurries off, stage left. The four huskies make for Menaechmus, who looks up as they gallop toward him.)

MENAECHMUS OF EPIDAMNUS *(to himself)*   This looks bad! What's going on here? God knows why, but these men are running toward me! *(To the men as they draw near)* What do you want? What are you after? *(Frantically)* Why are you surrounding me? *(With a rush they grab him and swing him on to their shoulders.)* Where are you taking me? Where am I going? Help! Murder! Save me, citizens of Epidamnus! *(To his abductors)* Let go of me!

MESSENIO *(whirling about at the commotion)*   Good god in heaven, what's this I see? Some strangers carrying off my master! This is an outrage!

MENAECHMUS OF EPIDAMNUS *(despairingly)*   Doesn't anyone have the heart to help me?

MESSENIO *(calling)*   I do, master, the heart of a hero! *(Orating at the top of his lungs, as he races to the rescue)* People of Epidamnus! This is a foul, a criminal act! In a city street, in broad daylight, in peacetime, to kidnap my poor master, a gentleman on a visit to your town! *(Tearing into the abductors)* Let go of him!

MENAECHMUS OF EPIDAMNUS   Whoever you are, for god's sake, stand by me! Don't let them get away with this flagrant miscarriage of justice!

MESSENIO *(shouting, as he flails away)*   They won't. I'll stand by you. I'll help you. I'll defend you to the death. I won't let them kill you—better I get killed myself! Master, for god's sake, the one there that's got you by the shoulder —gouge his eye out! These three here, why I'll plow their jaws and plant my fists there. *(To his opponents)* Kidnap him, will you? You'll pay for it and pay plenty! Let go of him!

MENAECHMUS OF EPIDAMNUS *(triumphantly)*   I got him by the eye!

MESSENIO   Tear it out of the socket! (*To his adversaries*)
Criminals! Kidnapers! Bandits!

THE SLAVES (*shouting*)   Don't kill us! Please!

MESSENIO (*snarling*)   Then let go!

MENAECHMUS OF EPIDAMNUS (*to his abductors*)   What do
you mean by laying hands on me! (*To Messenio*) Sock 'em
on the jaw!

MESSENIO (*as his three opponents break and run*)   On your
way! Go to hell, the bunch of you! (*Rushes over and lands
a haymaker on Menaechmus' opponent*) And here's this
from me! A bonus for being the last one out of here. (*To
Menaechmus, smugly, as the four scamper off, stage left*)
Well, I rearranged the geography of their faces to suit my
taste. Believe me, master, I came to the rescue just in time.

MENAECHMUS OF EPIDAMNUS (*fervently*)   I don't know who
you are, mister, but god's blessings on you forever. If it
hadn't been for you, I wouldn't have lived to see the sun
go down today.

MESSENIO (*promptly*)   Then if you want to do right by me,
damn it all, you'll set me free.

MENAECHMUS OF EPIDAMNUS   Set you free? Me?

MESSENIO   Sure, master. I just saved your life, didn't I?

MENAECHMUS OF EPIDAMNUS   What are you talking about?
Mister, you're making a mistake.

MESSENIO   Me making a mistake? What do you mean?

MENAECHMUS OF EPIDAMNUS   I give you my solemn oath, I'm
not your master.

MESSENIO (*taking this as a cruel joke, bitterly*)   Don't give
me that!

MENAECHMUS OF EPIDAMNUS (*earnestly*)   I'm not lying to
you. (*Ruefully*) No servant of mine ever did as much for
me as you have.

MESSENIO (*as before*)   All right. If you say I'm not your
slave, why don't you let me go free?

MENAECHMUS OF EPIDAMNUS (*smiling*) If it's up to me, by all means. Be a free man. Go where you like.

MESSENIO (*unable to believe his ears*) You mean it? It's official?

MENAECHMUS OF EPIDAMNUS (*as before*) If I have any official rights over you, it certainly is.

MESSENIO (*ecstatically*) Hail, my patron! (*Menaechmus winces at the title, remembering the experience in that capacity that cost him his lunch. Messenio launches into an imaginary dialogue with his fellow slaves*) "Well, well, Messenio, so you're a free man. Congratulations!" "Thank you, thank you all." (*Turning back to Menaechmus, earnestly*) Patron, I want you to keep ordering me around the same as when I was your servant. I'll live with you, and, when you go back home, I'll go with you.

MENAECHMUS OF EPIDAMNUS (*aside, wincing again*) Not a chance!

MESSENIO I'll go back to the hotel now and get the bags and the money for you. The wallet with our cash is safe under lock and key in my satchel. I'll bring it to you right now.

MENAECHMUS OF EPIDAMNUS (*promptly*) You do that. And hurry.

MESSENIO (*over his shoulder as he rushes off, stage right*) You'll get it back just as it was when you gave it to me. Wait for me here.

MENAECHMUS OF EPIDAMNUS (*to the audience, shaking his head in bewilderment*) Amazing, the amazing things that have happened to me! People tell me I'm not me and lock me out of the house. Then this fellow, (*grinning*) the one I just now emancipated, comes along, claims he's my slave, and tells me he's going to bring me a wallet full of cash. If he actually does, I'll tell him he's a free man and he's to leave me and go wherever he likes; I don't want him asking for the money back when he gets his sanity back. My father-in-law and the doctor say *I'm* mad. It's all a mystery to me. I must be dreaming the whole business.

Well, I'll pay a call on this whore here, even if she is sore at me. Maybe I can get her to give back the dress so I can bring it home.

(*He enters Lovey's house. A second later Menaechmus of Syracuse and Messenio enter, stage right, deep in conversation.*)

MENAECHMUS OF SYRACUSE (*angrily*)   I sent you off with orders to come back here for me. Where do you get the nerve to tell me I saw you anywhere since?

MESSENIO (*frantically*)   Just a minute ago I rescued you, right in front of this house, from four men who were carrying you off on their shoulders. You were hollering to heaven and earth for help, and I ran up and by fighting hard made them let you go. And, because I saved your life that way, you set me free. (*Bitterly*) And then, when I said I was going for the money and the bags, you ran ahead and got there first just so you could deny everything you did!

MENAECHMUS OF SYRACUSE (*incredulously*)   I set you free?

MESSENIO   You certainly did.

MENAECHMUS OF SYRACUSE (*grimly*)   I'll tell you what I certainly did: made up my mind to be a slave myself before I ever set you free. (*Starts stalking off, stage right.*)

(*The door of Lovey's house opens, and Menaechmus of Epidamnus stomps out. He turns and talks to Lovey and her maid inside.*)

MENAECHMUS OF EPIDAMNUS (*through the doorway, excittedly*)   Listen, you bitches, you can cross your heart and swear all you want but, damn it all, that's not going to change things: I did *not* walk off with that bracelet and dress.

(*Messenio glances over his shoulder at the sound of the voice—and does a double take.*)

MESSENIO   Good god in heaven! What's this I see?

MENAECHMUS OF SYRACUSE (*sourly, and without stopping*) What?

MESSENIO   Your reflection!

MENAECHMUS OF SYRACUSE (*stopping*)   What are you talking about?

MESSENIO (*excitedly*)   He's your image! He couldn't be more like you.

MENAECHMUS OF SYRACUSE (*following Messenio's gaze*)   By god, you know, when I think about what I look like, he *does* resemble me.

MENAECHMUS OF EPIDAMNUS (*turning from the door and noticing Messenio*)   Hello there, my savior, whoever you are.

MESSENIO (*to Menaechmus of Epidamnus, tensely*)   Mister, would you please do me a favor and tell me your name, if you don't mind?

MENAECHMUS OF EPIDAMNUS (*earnestly*)   I mind any favors you ask for? I should say not. That isn't the treatment you deserve from me! The name's Menaechmus—

MENAECHMUS OF SYRACUSE (*interrupting*)   Hell, no! That's my name!

MENAECHMUS OF EPIDAMNUS (*ignoring him*)   —and I was born at Syracuse in Sicily.

MENAECHMUS OF SYRACUSE (*resentfully*)   That's *my* city and country.

MENAECHMUS OF EPIDAMNUS (*looking at him for the first time*)   What's that you say?

MENAECHMUS OF SYRACUSE (*glowering*)   Nothing but the truth.

MESSENIO (*stares at the two in utter puzzlement. Then, to himself, uncertainly, pointing to Menaechmus of Epidamnus*)   This must be the one I know; *he's* my master. I thought I was (*pointing to Menaechmus of Syracuse*) his servant, but I'm really (*pointing to Menaechmus of Epidamnus*) his. (*Addressing Menaechmus of Epidamnus*) I thought he was you; (*guiltily*) matter of fact, I gave him quite a bit of trouble. (*To Menaechmus of Syracuse*) Please forgive me if I said anything to you that sounded stupid. I didn't mean to.

MENAECHMUS OF SYRACUSE (*in astonishment*) Are you crazy? You sound it. You and I came off the ship together today. Don't you remember?

MESSENIO (*astonished in his turn*) You're absolutely right. *You're* my master. (*To Menaechmus of Epidamnus, apologetically*) You'd better find yourself another servant. (*To Menaechmus of Syracuse*) Hello. (*To Menaechmus of Epidamnus*) Good-by. Take my word— (*pointing to Menaechmus of Syracuse*) this man is Menaechmus.

MENAECHMUS OF EPIDAMNUS No. *I* am.

MENAECHMUS OF SYRACUSE (*to Menaechmus of Epidamnus*) What sort of nonsense is this? You're Menaechmus?

MENAECHMUS OF EPIDAMNUS That's what I said. Son of Moschus.

MENAECHMUS OF SYRACUSE (*bewildered*) The son of my father? You?

MENAECHMUS OF EPIDAMNUS (*smiling*) No, mister, of *mine*. I have no intention of adopting your father or stealing him from you.

MESSENIO (*to the audience, in great excitement*) Something just dawned on me! A hope that no one could have hoped for! God in heaven, make it come true! I tell you, unless my mind is going back on me, these two are the twin brothers! After all, they both give the same names for father and fatherland. I've got to have a word with my master in private. (*Calling out*) Menaechmus!

MENAECHMUS OF EPIDAMNUS ⎱
MENAECHMUS OF SYRACUSE ⎰ What do you want?

MESSENIO I don't want you both! Which one of you was on the ship with me?

MENAECHMUS OF EPIDAMNUS Not I.

MENAECHMUS OF SYRACUSE I.

MESSENIO   Then you're the one I want. Step over here, will you?

(Messenio walks a few steps off to the side, and Menaechmus of Syracuse joins him.)

MENAECHMUS OF SYRACUSE   Here I am. What's up?

MESSENIO *(sotto voce, excitedly)*   That man there is either a swindler or your twin brother! I've never seen two people more alike. Believe me, you two are more like each other than one drop of water or one drop of milk to another. Besides, he gives the same names as you for father and fatherland. We'd better go up to him and ask him some questions.

MENAECHMUS OF SYRACUSE *(catching Messenio's excitement)* That's a darned good idea! Thanks very much. But, please, do me a favor: you do it. *(As they walk back toward Menaechmus of Epidamnus)* Messenio, you're a free man if you can find out he's my brother.

MESSENIO *(fervently)*   I hope I can.

MENAECHMUS OF SYRACUSE   I hope so too.

MESSENIO *(to Menaechmus of Epidamnus, drawing himself up self-importantly, like a judge questioning a party to a case)* Harrumph! *(As Menaechmus of Epidamnus looks at him inquiringly)* You stated, as I remember, that your name was Menaechmus.

MENAECHMUS OF EPIDAMNUS   That's right.

MESSENIO *(gesturing toward Menaechmus of Syracuse)* This man's name is Menaechmus too. You stated you were born at Syracuse in Sicily; he was born there. You stated your father's name was Moschus; so was his. Now you can both help me—and yourselves at the same time.

MENAECHMUS OF EPIDAMNUS   Anything you want from me, the answer's yes; you've earned it. I'm a free man, but I'm at your service just as if you'd bought and paid for me.

MESSENIO *(solemnly)*   My hope is that the two of you will discover you are twin brothers, born the same day to the same mother and the same father.

MENAECHMUS OF EPIDAMNUS (*wistfully*) What you're talking about is a miracle. Ah, if you could only do what you hope to!

MESSENIO (*determinedly*) I can. But now let's start. Answer my questions, both of you.

MENAECHMUS OF EPIDAMNUS (*promptly*) Ask away. I'll tell you everything I know.

MESSENIO Is your name Menaechmus?

MENAECHMUS OF EPIDAMNUS It is.

MESSENIO (*to Menaechmus of Syracuse*) And yours too?

MENAECHMUS OF SYRACUSE Yes.

MESSENIO (*to Menaechmus of Epidamnus*) And you say your father's name was Moschus?

MENAECHMUS OF EPIDAMNUS I do.

MENAECHMUS OF SYRACUSE So do I. (*Receives a lordly look of disapproval from Messenio for anticipating the question.*)

MESSENIO (*to Menaechmus of Epidamnus*) And you were born at Syracuse?

MENAECHMUS OF EPIDAMNUS Absolutely.

MESSENIO (*to Menaechmus of Syracuse*) What about you?

MENAECHMUS OF SYRACUSE You know I was.

MESSENIO So far everything agrees perfectly. We'll go on; your attention please. (*To Menaechmus of Epidamnus*) Tell me, what is your earliest recollection of your homeland?

MENAECHMUS OF EPIDAMNUS (*holding his forehead and closing his eyes as he struggles to remember*) Going off to Tarentum with my father on a business trip. Then wandering off in the crowd and being carried away.

MENAECHMUS OF SYRACUSE (*exclaiming involuntarily*) God in heaven! Help me now!

MESSENIO (*with the voice of authority*) What's the meaning of this shouting? Can't you keep quiet! (*To Menaech-*

mus of Epidamnus) How old were you when your father took you from your fatherland?

MENAECHMUS OF EPIDAMNUS Seven. I remember because I was just beginning to lose my baby teeth. (*Sadly*) I never saw my father again.

MESSENIO Answer this: how many sons were there in your family?

MENAECHMUS OF EPIDAMNUS As best as I can remember, two.

MESSENIO Which was the older, you or your brother?

MENAECHMUS OF EPIDAMNUS We were the same age.

MESSENIO How is that possible?

MENAECHMUS OF EPIDAMNUS We were twins.

MENAECHMUS OF SYRACUSE (*exclaiming fervently*) Heaven has come to my rescue!

MESSENIO (*icily*) If you're going to interrupt, I'm not going to say another word!

MENAECHMUS OF SYRACUSE (*meekly*) No, no—I won't say another word.

MESSENIO (*to Menaechmus of Epidamnus*) Tell me: did you both have the same name?

MENAECHMUS OF EPIDAMNUS Oh, no. You see, I was called Menaechmus, as now, but his name was Sosicles.

MENAECHMUS OF SYRACUSE (*to himself, wildly excited*) For me the case is proved. I can't hold back, I've got to take him in my arms. (*Taking his hands*) Welcome, my brother, my twin brother! I'm Sosicles!

MENAECHMUS OF EPIDAMNUS (*gently disengaging his hands; uncertainly*) If that's so, how come you got the name Menaechmus?

MENAECHMUS OF SYRACUSE When the news came about you and about father's death, grandfather changed it: he gave me yours instead.

MENAECHMUS OF EPIDAMNUS I guess it could have happened that way. But answer this question.

MENAECHMUS OF SYRACUSE (*eagerly*)   What is it?

MENAECHMUS OF EPIDAMNUS (*intently*)   What was our mother's name?

MENAECHMUS OF SYRACUSE   Teuximarcha.

MENAECHMUS OF EPIDAMNUS (*rushing to embrace him*) Right! Welcome to you, my brother! I never expected to see you again, and now, after so many years, I have you before me.

MENAECHMUS OF SYRACUSE   And welcome to you, my brother. I searched and searched for you right up to this moment, and now, after so many trials and tribulations, I have the joy of having found you.

MESSENIO (*to Menaechmus of Syracuse, a light dawning*) That explains it! That girl called you by your brother's name. I'm sure she thought it was he she was inviting in to lunch, not you.

MENAECHMUS OF EPIDAMNUS (*smiling broadly*)   As a matter of fact, I had told her to prepare lunch for me today. My wife wasn't to know a thing about it. I sneaked a dress of hers out of the house and gave it to the girl.

MENAECHMUS OF SYRACUSE (*holding up the dress*)   You mean the one I have here?

MENAECHMUS OF EPIDAMNUS (*astonished*)   That's it! How did it ever get to you?

MENAECHMUS OF SYRACUSE (*laughing*)   That girl who carried me off to give me lunch insisted I had given it to her. The wench wined me and dined me in style and then went to bed with me. I made off with the dress and this bracelet (*holding it up*).

MENAECHMUS OF EPIDAMNUS   Believe me, I'm delighted to hear something nice happened to you because of me. When she invited you in, she thought it was me, you know.

MESSENIO (*breaking in, anxiously*)   There's nothing to stop you now, is there, from giving me my freedom the way you promised?

MENAECHMUS OF EPIDAMNUS A perfectly proper and fair request, my brother. Do it for my sake.

MENAECHMUS OF SYRACUSE Messenio, you're a free man.

MENAECHMUS OF EPIDAMNUS (*his eyes twinkling, mimicking the exact tone of voice Messenio had used a few moments ago*) Well, well, Messenio, so you're a free man. Congratulations!

MESSENIO (*meaningfully, holding out his hand, palm upward*) But I could use a better beginning to make sure I stay free.

MENAECHMUS OF SYRACUSE (*pointedly ignoring the hand and the remark*) Now that things have turned out just the way we wanted, my brother, let's both of us go back to our homeland.

MENAECHMUS OF EPIDAMNUS Brother, I'll do whatever you wish. I can hold an auction and sell whatever I own around here. (*Leading him toward the door of his house*) But let's go inside for now.

MENAECHMUS OF SYRACUSE Yes, let's.

MESSENIO (*who had been listening avidly to the last exchange*) Do you know what favor I'd like to ask?

MENAECHMUS OF EPIDAMNUS What?

MESSENIO (*eagerly*) Let me run the auction.

MENAECHMUS OF EPIDAMNUS It's all yours.

MESSENIO (*rubbing his hands delightedly*) Then how about my announcing right now that an auction will take place?

MENAECHMUS OF EPIDAMNUS All right. Make it a week from today. (*The two brothers enter the house.*)

MESSENIO (*to the audience, in an auctioneer's chant*): Hear ye, hear ye! Selling at auction, one week from today, rain or shine, the property of Menaechmus. For sale: slaves, household effects, farm land, and buildings. All items to go for whatever they'll bring, and all payments strictly cash. Sale includes one wife—if anyone will bid. (*Leaning for-*

ward, in a confidential tone) If you ask me, the whole auction won't net fifty cents.

(*Straightening up, in ringing tones*) And now, ladies and gentlemen, good-by. Your loudest applause, please!

PSEUDOLUS

DRAMATIS PERSONAE

PSEUDOLUS, *servant of Simo* (*slave*)

CALIDORUS, *a young man about town, son of Simo*

BALLIO, *a pimp*

SIMO, *an elderly gentleman, father of Calidorus*

CALLIPHO, *an elderly gentleman, neighbor of Simo*

HARPAX, *orderly of an officer in the Macedonian army* (*slave*)

CHARINUS, *friend of Calidorus*

A SLAVE BOY OF BALLIO

A COOK

MONKEY (SIMIA), *servant belonging to Charinus' family* (*slave*)

SERVANTS AND COURTESANS

SCENE

A street in Athens. Three houses front on it: stage left Simo's, center Callipho's, right Ballio's. The exit on stage left leads downtown, that on stage right to the country.

PROLOGUE

You'd better get up and stretch your legs. There's a play by Plautus coming on, and it's a long one.[1]

ACT I

(*The door of Calidorus' house opens, and Calidorus and Pseudolus walk out.*

Calidorus, "beauty's gift," is ancient comedy's traditional rich man's son: handsome, well-dressed, empty-headed, and unemployable. At the moment he is in a ludicrously blank state of despair, staring wordlessly at a set of waxed wooden tablets bound with cord (the ancient equivalent of folded sheets of paper) which he clutches with both hands.

If Calidorus has no brains, Pseudolus, "tricky," the family servant, has enough for both. These are encased in an enormous head, which, along with a bulging belly and a pair of oversize feet, give Pseudolus a most deceptively clownlike appearance.)

PSEUDOLUS If I could figure out from this silence of yours what's the misery that's making you miserable, I'd have the pleasure of saving two men trouble: me of asking you questions and you of answering them. But I can't, so I've got to put the question. Tell me, what's the matter? For days now you've been going around more dead than alive, holding that letter in your hands, washing it down with tears, and not confiding in anyone. Talk, will you! I'm in the dark; share the light with me.

CALIDORUS (*dully*) I'm miserable. Miserably miserable.

PSEUDOLUS God forbid!

[1] The original prologue has been lost.

CALIDORUS   God has no jurisdiction in my case. I'm serving a sentence from Love, not God.

PSEUDOLUS   Am I allowed to know what it's all about? After all, up to now I was Accessory-in-Chief to all your projects.

CALIDORUS   I haven't changed.

PSEUDOLUS   Then let me in on what's ailing you. (*Importantly*) Resources, services, or good advice at your disposal.

CALIDORUS   (*handing him the tablets*)   Take this letter. Then you can recite yourself the story of the worry and woe that's wasting me away.

PSEUDOLUS   (*taking the tablets*)   Anything to make you happy. (*Turning them every which way and holding them at various distances from his eyes*) Hey, what's this?

CALIDORUS   What's what?

PSEUDOLUS   If you ask me, the letters here want to have babies: each one's mounting the other.

CALIDORUS   (*bitterly*)   Got to have your joke, don't you?

PSEUDOLUS   (*still turning and twisting the tablets*)   Maybe our Lady of the Riddles can read them, but I swear nobody else can.

CALIDORUS   (*choking up*)   Why are you so cruel to the lovely letters of this lovely letter written in such a lovely hand?

PSEUDOLUS   Damn it all, I ask you now: do hens have hands? Because, believe me, some hen scribbled these letters.

CALIDORUS   (*exasperated*)   You make me sick! (*Reaching for the tablets*) Either read it or hand it back.

PSEUDOLUS   (*holding them out of reach*)   Oh no. I'll read it to the bitter end. Listen, and keep your mind on what I say.

CALIDORUS   (*dumbly*)   I can't—it left me.

PSEUDOLUS   Call it back.

CALIDORUS   No, I'll keep quiet. *You* call it back. From that letter there. Because that's where my mind is now; it's not inside me.

PSEUDOLUS (*slyly*) I see your girl friend, Calidorus.

CALIDORUS (*coming out of his apathy with a start*) Pseudolus, please, I beg you! Tell me where she is!

PSEUDOLUS (*holding up the tablets and pointing to the signature*) Here. Stretched out in this letter here. Lying on the lines.

CALIDORUS (*throwing a punch at him*) I swear by all that's holy, I hope you go straight—

PSEUDOLUS (*ducking nimbly and grinning*) —to heaven.

CALIDORUS (*tragically*) I was like grass in summer, a minute ago: suddenly sprang up, and just as suddenly died down.

PSEUDOLUS Quiet now while I read the letter. (*Clears his throat, adjusts the tablets, and makes other elaborate preparations.*)

CALIDORUS (*impatiently*) Get going, will you!

PSEUDOLUS (*reading aloud*) "Dear sweetheart Calidorus. With tears in my eyes and tremors in my mind and heart and soul, through these waxed boards and piece of line and lines of communication, I send you my best wishes for *your* well-being—and my prayers for your help with *mine*."

CALIDORUS (*frenzied*) Pseudolus! I'm lost! I'll never get what I need to help with hers!

PSEUDOLUS What do you need?

CALIDORUS (*dolefully*) Gold.

PSEUDOLUS (*sticking the tablets in front of Calidorus' nose*) She sends best wishes in wood, and you want to answer in gold? Watch what you're doing, will you!

CALIDORUS (*dully*) Just go on reading. You'll find out soon enough how urgent it is that I get my hands on some gold.

PSEUDOLUS (*resuming his reading*) "The pimp has sold me for five thousand dollars to a foreigner, a major from Macedon. He's already left for home, after putting up a deposit of four thousand; all that's holding matters up is a mere one thousand dollars. To arrange payment of this, the major left behind as means of identification his own picture stamped by his seal ring on a wax seal; the pimp is to hand me over to whoever arrives with an identical seal. And the date fixed for my departure is this coming Dionysus Day."

CALIDORUS (*miserably*) That's tomorrow. My end is practically upon me—unless you can help.

PSEUDOLUS (*impatiently*) Let me finish reading.

CALIDORUS Go ahead. (*Starry-eyed*) It makes me feel I'm talking with her. Read on; now you'll mix in some sweet for me along with the bitter.

PSEUDOLUS (*reading*) "Now our love, our life, the things we shared, our jokes and play and talks and soft-sweet kisses, the tight embrace of impassioned bodies in love, the soft pressure of parted lips meeting tenderly, the burgeoning of my breasts under the sweet caress of your hand —all these joys will be taken away, torn away, trampled away—for you as well as for me—if you do not come to my rescue and I to yours. I have done my share: now you know all that I know. I shall soon find out whether your love is real or pretended. Your loving Rosy."

CALIDORUS (*sobbing*) A piece of writing to make a man miserable, Pseudolus.

PSEUDOLUS (*glancing at the handwriting again*) Oh yes. Absolutely miserable.

CALIDORUS (*reproachfully*) Then why aren't you crying?

PSEUDOLUS My eyes are made out of sand. I can't get them to squirt a single tear.

CALIDORUS How come?

PSEUDOLUS (*dryly*) Chronic dryness of the eyes. Runs through the whole family.

CALIDORUS (*dismayed*) You don't have the heart to help me?

PSEUDOLUS (*shrugging disinterestedly*) What do you expect from me?

CALIDORUS (*groaning*) Ai!

PSEUDOLUS Ai's? Good god, don't spare *them*. I'll be your supplier.

CALIDORUS (*dolefully*)   I'm in a bad way. I can't borrow a sou from a soul—

PSEUDOLUS (*grinning*)   Ai!

CALIDORUS   —and I don't have a cent of my own—

PSEUDOLUS (*as before*)   Ai!

CALIDORUS   —and tomorrow that man's going to take my girl away.

PSEUDOLUS   Ai!

CALIDORUS (*bitterly*)   Is this the way you help me?

PSEUDOLUS   I'm giving you what I've got to give. (*Shaking his head ruefully*) It's the one item I have a vast accumulation of in our house.

CALIDORUS (*resigned*)   Then it's all over with me today. Could you please lend me two dollars? I'll pay you back tomorrow.

PSEUDOLUS   I couldn't raise that much even if I put my own self in hock. What are you going to do with two dollars, anyway?

CALIDORUS   Buy myself a rope.

PSEUDOLUS   What for?

CALIDORUS   To turn myself into a pendulum. I've decided to darken my eyes before dark today.

PSEUDOLUS   Then who'll pay me back my two dollars if I lend it to you? (*Suspiciously*) Are you deliberately planning to hang yourself just to do me out of two dollars if I lend it to you?

CALIDORUS (*starting to sob again*)   I simply can't go on living if she's taken away from me and carried far, far away.

PSEUDOLUS   Stop crying, you dumb cluck! You'll live.

CALIDORUS   Why shouldn't I cry? I don't have a penny in my pocket and not the slightest prospect of borrowing anything from anybody.

PSEUDOLUS (*impatiently*)   As I gather from this letter, unless you can cry some cash for her, all this shedding of tears to demonstrate your affections does about as much good as using a sieve for a cistern. (*As Calidorus starts wailing louder than ever*) But stop worrying, fond lover: I won't desert you. I'm a good operator; I have high hopes of finding salvation for you somewhere—financial salvation. Where am I going to get it? I can't tell you where; I don't know where. But I'll get it all right: I have a hunch today's my lucky day.

CALIDORUS (*hopelessly*)   You say you can do it—if only you can do what you say!

PSEUDOLUS (*hurt*)   Why, you know darn well the kind of ruckus I can raise once I start my hocus-pocus.

CALIDORUS (*desperately*)   My life depends on you! You're my only hope!

PSEUDOLUS (*airily*)   I'll arrange either to get you the girl or the five thousand. Will that satisfy you?

CALIDORUS (*doubtfully*)   Yes—if you'll do it.

PSEUDOLUS (*in the best lawyerlike fashion*)   Now put in a formal request for five thousand so I can prove I perform what I promise. (*Calidorus stares at him blankly*) For god's sake, ask, will you! I'm dying to make you a promise.

CALIDORUS (*his heart not in it*)   Do you hereby agree to give me five thousand in cash today?

PSEUDOLUS   I hereby agree. And now stop bothering me. And, just so you won't tell me later that I didn't tell you, I'm telling you in advance: if I can't get it from anyone else, I'll hit your father up for it.

CALIDORUS (*fervently*)   God bless you! (*Becoming very grave*) But I want to be a dutiful son, so, if possible, put the touch on my mother too.

PSEUDOLUS (*confidently*)   You're all set. Go to bed. Close your little ears.

CALIDORUS   Ears? Don't you mean eyes?

PSEUDOLUS   Less hackneyed the way I said it. (*Turning to the audience; in the tones of a town crier*) And now, so no one will say I didn't warn him, I hereby give public notice

to everybody, voters, citizens, all my friends and acquaint-
ances: watch out for me all day long! Don't trust me!

CALIDORUS Shh! Keep quiet! Please!

PSEUDOLUS (*surprised*) What's up?

CALIDORUS The pimp's door handle just twisted.

PSEUDOLUS I wish to god it was his neck.

CALIDORUS And there he is, the dirty double-crosser. He's
coming out.

(*The two move to an unobtrusive spot off to the side. The
door swings open, and Ballio, "tosser around," the pimp, steps
out, hefting a mean-looking whip.*

*Ballio is a businessman in a thoroughly unpleasant business:
he owns a bevy of slave girls whom he supplies to those with
the wherewithal to hire them or buy them outright. A strag-
gly beard on his chin, a permanent snarl on his lips, an
avaricious glint in his eye, and a filthy miserly get-up make
him as unappetizing in appearance as in métier.*)

SONG

BALLIO (*turning and shouting through the open door*)
    Come out of the house, good-for-nothings, come out!
    What a mistake to have bought you and kept you about!

(*Six terrified slave boys—miserable, underfed specimens in
rags—scamper out of the door and huddle in front of it; one
holds a shopping basket and a purse, another a jug, another
an ax. Ballio eyes them distastefully, then turns to the audience.*)

    Not a one in the lot ever got the idea
    To do anything good.
    (*Brandishing the whip*)
                        Without using this here,
    They're all useless. To put them to use takes abuse.
    And I've never seen hides more like donkeys', I swear:
    They've been drubbed so, they've even grown calluses
        there;

Why, to thrash them takes less out of them than of you.
To be wear-the-whip-outers comes natural to
    The whole breed. The one thought in their heads
        Is to snatch, steal,
        Grab, make hay,
        Gorge, swill,
        And run away.
It's their one, single purpose in life. Why, I say
I'd as soon let a wolf guard my sheep any day,
As let these watch my house any time I'm away.

(*Ballio glares at them. They summon up sickly smiles. He turns back to the audience.*)

    Oh, their faces look fine; you can't go by their looks.
    It's at work that they pull every trick in the books.

(*He swings around abruptly and starts flailing with the whip.*)

    Get the sleep from your eyes! Get the sloth from your
      brain!

(*Lowers the whip. Importantly*)

    Pay attention. I'll shortly begin to explain
        The orders of the day.
    Listen hard or I'll batter your butts till they turn
        Every color, as gay
    As a highly embroidered Neapolitan shawl
    Or a Persian brocade with its beasties and all.

(*Shifts to a deadly menacing tone*)

I issued orders yesterday assigning each of you
A station and official list of things he had to do.
You're such a bunch of loafers, though, such inborn stink-
    ers that

(*Shaking the whip*)

You've forced me to remind you of your duties with this
    cat!

(*Wearily lowering the whip*)

My whip and I admit defeat; the victory's yours instead.
And it's all because of the way you're made—so hard in
    hide and head!

(*As the slaves visibly relax, he suddenly flails about madly
with the whip, and they all make a wild scramble for safety.
He addresses the audience with mock exasperation, gesturing
toward the cowering slaves who are paying far more attention
to the arc described by the whip than to him.*)

Now look at that, if you please! You see the way their
    minds will stray?

(*Turning back to the slaves*)

You mind me now, you hear! You tune those ears to what
    I say.

You stinkers, born and bred with special whip-proof back
    and side,

Remember that my rawhide's always harder than your hide.

(*Lunges suddenly and lands a blow on the nearest one,
who lets out a howl.*)

What's up? It hurts? It's what I give a slave who's snotty
    to

His master. Now come here; face me, and hear what you're
    to do.

(*The slaves line up, keeping a wary eye on the whip. Ballio
addresses the one who is carrying a jug.*)

First you who's got the jug. Get water and fill the cooking
    pot.

(*He turns to the one carrying an ax.*)

And you with the ax I appoint my Chief of Fuel Supply.

SLAVE (*timidly showing the ax*)

                                        But it's not

Got an edge, it's too dull to use!

BALLIO (*grinning like a hyena*)

                    So what?

(*Gesturing toward the whole cowering group*)

                    The whip's dulled your edge too.

Doesn't make the slightest difference to me—I keep using
   all of you.

(*Ballio turns to the third.*)

You make that whole house shine. You've got your job, now
   hop, you lout!

(*To the fourth*)

And you're Official Chair-Man.

(*To the fifth*)

                              And you clean silver and lay it out.

(*To all of them*)

Once I'm back from shopping, mind I find that everything's
   done—

Sweeping, setting, cleaning, shining—no chore undone, not
   one!

(*Switching to a tone of bloodcurdling enthusiasm*)

   It's my birthday today. You must help celebrate.
   Put the pig in the pot, from the trotters to pate.
   Is that clear? I'm inviting big names; a big splash
   Is the thing—make them think that I squander the cash.
   Now go in and get going so there'll be no delay
   When the chef makes it here. Because *I'm* on my way
   To the market; I'm off on a fish-buying jag.

(*To the slave carrying a basket under one arm and a purse
over one shoulder*)

   Go in front. I'm back here to keep thieves from that bag.

(*They start walking off, while the others race inside. Ballio
suddenly stops short.*)

   Wait a second. I almost forgot. I'm not through.

(*Goes to the doorway and calls through it*)

   Can you hear me, you girls? I've an announcement for
      you.

(*Four flashily dressed, heavily made-up girls step out and
line up sullenly in front of him. He gives them his hyena grin,
and then addresses them.*)

You're all living in clover, my sweet little sprites.
You're all girls with a name, and the town's leading
    lights
Are your clients. Today I'll find out what you're at.
Do you work to get free? Or to gorge and get fat?
To acquire a nest egg? Or sleep until three?
Yes, today I'll work out who I think will get free
Or I think will wind up being sold for a whore.

(*Rubbing his hands, his eyes gleaming*)

Have your clients bring in birthday presents galore!
For today we lay in one year's bread, drink, and meat,
Or tomorrow I'll have you out walking the street.
Now, you know it's my birthday. Well, have them kick
    in,
All the boy friends for whom you've been "Doll," "Bunny-
    kin,"
"Cutie-pie," "Honeybunch," "Sweetheart," and "Pet,"
"Snookle-puss," "Babykins," "Ducky," et cet.
Make their slaves, bearing gifties, come by in brigades!

(*Glaring at them*)

All the jewelry, money, the clothes and brocades
That I've had to provide—what's it got me, I say?
Not a dime, only woe, from you bitches today!
All your passion's for drink, to tank up, whereas I
Have to live my whole life with a gullet bone dry!

(*He paces up and down a few seconds in a rage. Then, in
calmer tones*)

And now I'll call you up by name and give you each the
    word.
This plan's the best since no one then can claim she hadn't
    heard.
               So, all of you,
               Here's what you do.
I'll start with Sweetsie, darling of the men who market
    grain.

Since each one stocks a good-sized hill, you're please to make them rain

Enough on me to give our house a year's supply to eat,

A flood so big my name will change from "Pimp" to "King of Wheat."

PSEUDOLUS (*sotto voce, to Calidorus*)

Do you hear the rat talk? Like a pretty big dealer, Don't you think?

CALIDORUS (*sotto voce, to Pseudolus*)

Good god, yes! And a pretty big stealer.

Now shut up. Pay attention to what he says next.

BALLIO (*turning to the second girl*)

Now listen, Golddig. You're the girl the butchers all adore.

(They're like us pimps: they take their cut—their pound of flesh and more!)

You bring me in three meathooks loaded down with beef today

Or tomorrow you play Dirce—and her story goes this way:

Her stepsons squared accounts with her by hitching her to a bull.

Well, you I'll stretch on a meathook, see—and *that's* a bull with pull!

PSEUDOLUS (*aside, raging*)

You hear him talk? I'm burning up—he's got me hopping mad!

How *can* you, Youth of Athens, patronize a man this bad?

Come out here, all you youngsters who've been buying love from pimps,

Let's gather altogether, boys, and everyone take part

To rid the citizen body of this canker at its heart!

(*Shakes his head gloomily, all his excitement suddenly drained from him.*)

Pseudolus, you've got to learn,

Pseudolus, you've got no brains.

> Why, sex makes youngsters all behave
> Toward any pimp just like his slave
> And rush to do his every whim.
> And *you* want them to be so brave
> They'll up and do away with *him!*

CALIDORUS (*sotto voce, wildly*)

Oh, shut your trap! You give me a pain—you're drowning out what he's saying!

PSEUDOLUS (*meekly, deflated by his horrendous discovery*)

All right, I will.

CALIDORUS (*sotto voce, urgently*)

> Well, don't just say so. Do it! Stop your braying.

BALLIO (*turning to the third girl*)

Your turn. Now listen, Olive, sweetheart of the oil-trade crew.

When it comes to ready stock on hand, your lovers keep beaucoup.

I want a load of jugs of oil, and you'll produce tout' suite,

Or tomorrow *you'll* get boiled in oil and dumped out on the street;

I'll set a bed for you out there, where *you* won't get much rest

Though you'll be plenty tired—why say more? By now you've guessed.

You've got a mob of boy friends who just roll in oil, but you

Couldn't give your fellow slaves today a drop for their shampoo

Or give your lord and master some for juicing up his stew.

> I know the reason too:
> You don't have very much use for oil—
> Your anointing's done with alcohol!

(*Glaring at all of them*)

All right! You carry out the orders that I've given you today,

(*Shaking the whip*)

Or, gad, I'll let you have it, all at once and in one way!

*(He turns to the last girl, by far the best looking of the four.
It is* Phoenicium, *"Rosy," Calidorus' inamorata.)*

And now the girl always just about to buy her freedom
   and dash.

You're good at promising payment—but no good at raising
   cash.

Now, heartthrob of the upper crust, to you I've this to say.

Your boy friends, Rosy, own big farms; so you produce
   today

A load of all the stuff they raise or tomorrow *you* will pay:
>   I'll have you walking streets, my dame,
>   Your hide tanned brighter than your name.

*(Ballio and his marketing attendant remain where they are.
The girls, shuffling despondently, start filing into the house
under Ballio's baleful gaze. He does not hear the following
conversation which Calidorus and Pseudolus hold sotto voce.)*

CALIDORUS *(agonized)*

   Pseudolus! Hear what he says?

PSEUDOLUS *(mimicking his tone)*

>   Calidorus! I heard.

(Thoughtfully)

   And I'm thinking it out.

CALIDORUS *(as before)*

>   What ideas have you got
>   Of a gift I can send so he'll weaken and not
>   Make a whore of my girl.

PSEUDOLUS *(patting his back encouragingly)*

>   Don't you worry. Don't be blue.

(Tapping his breast importantly)

   Because *I'll* do the worrying for me and for you.

(Smiling cannily)

   We've been swapping good wishes for years, he and I;
   We're old friends. Since today is his birthday, let's try

To prepare as a gift, which we'll send very soon,
A whole potful of trouble, one big as the moon!

CALIDORUS (*hopelessly*)

What's the use?

PSEUDOLUS (*taking him by the arm and starting to haul him off*)

Won't you please run along? You just go
And get thinking about something else.

CALIDORUS (*stubbornly resisting the pulling*)

Whoa there, whoa!

PSEUDOLUS (*tugging harder*)

No there, no!

CALIDORUS (*almost in tears*)

But I'm heartbroken!

PSEUDOLUS (*still hauling, though without much effect*)

Harden your heart.

CALIDORUS (*piteously*)

No, impossible.

PSEUDOLUS (*as before*)

Do the impossible. Start.

CALIDORUS (*dumbly*)

I'm to start the impossible? How?

PSEUDOLUS (*as before*)

Fight your heart.
Turn your mind to what's good. Heart's in tears? Close
your ears!

CALIDORUS (*sadly and thoughtfully*)

Oh, that's nonsense. A lover must act like a fool.
Otherwise it's no fun.

PSEUDOLUS (*giving up the hauling and throwing up his hands in disgust*)

Since you won't stop this drool—

CALIDORUS (*taking him by the arm, piteously*)

My dear Pseudolus, please! Let me stay just a fool!

PSEUDOLUS (*pulling himself free, icily*)
Will you *please* let me go?

CALIDORUS (*dumbly*)

                    Let me be, let me be—

PSEUDOLUS (*ostentatiously turning on his heel and stalking off*)
All right, *I'll* let you be. In return you let *me*
Go on home.

CALIDORUS (*frantically*)

            No, no, wait!

(*As Pseudolus stops, unenthusiastically*)

                  I'll be just as you wish.

PSEUDOLUS (*swiveling about and clapping him on the back*)
Now you're using your head!

(*At this moment the last of the girls shuffles inside, and Ballio turns around.*)

BALLIO (*to his marketing attendant*)

                We should go for that fish.
Time's awasting. Lead on.

CALIDORUS (*catching sight of them going off, frantically*)

                Hey, he's off! Call him back!

(*He wheels about to go after Ballio. Pseudolus grabs him.*)

PSEUDOLUS (*calmly*)
Easy, boy! What's the hurry?

CALIDORUS (*frantically*)

              Because, if we're slack
He'll be gone!

BALLIO (*to his slave boy, kicking him brutally*)

           So you're taking it easy, boy, eh?

PSEUDOLUS (*calling in dulcet tones*)
May I speak with you, birthday boy? Birthday boy! Hey!
Turn around and look back, will you please? Yes, we know
That you're rushed but we *must* hold you up, even so.

(*As Ballio keeps walking*)

Hey there, stop, will you! Look, there's some people here
who

Are most anxious to talk over matters with you.

BALLIO (*stopping—but not turning; exasperated*)

It's just when I'm rushed that these goddam yahoos

Hold me up! What's the matter? Who is it?

PSEUDOLUS (*dramatically*)

One who's

Spent his life making sure that you prosper and thrive!

BALLIO (*as if to himself, muttering*)

Spent his life? Then he's dead. I prefer one who's alive.

PSEUDOLUS

Don't be snooty, there, you!

BALLIO

Don't annoy me, there, you!

(*Ballio, still without turning around, starts walking again.*)

CALIDORUS (*to Pseudolus, frantically*)

Hurry up! Hold him back!

BALLIO (*over his shoulder to his slave who is standing goggle-eyed*)

Get a move on, you, too!

PSEUDOLUS (*to Calidorus*)

Hey, come this way! Don't let him through!

(*The two race around and stand blocking Ballio's way.*)

BALLIO (*to Pseudolus*)

Whoever you are, I'll see you in hell!

PSEUDOLUS (*his voice carefully maintaining the ambiguity*)

I'd like to see you.

BALLIO (*to Calidorus*)

And you as well.

(*Over his shoulder to his slave as he charges off on a different tack.*)

This way!

PSEUDOLUS (*nimbly barring the way again*)

There's some things I'd like to clear.

BALLIO

But *I* wouldn't.

PSEUDOLUS (*wheedling*)

Things you'll like to hear.

BALLIO (*beginning to lose his temper*)

Will you let me go or not?

PSEUDOLUS (*grabbing his arm*)

At ease!

BALLIO (*thundering*)

Hands off!

CALIDORUS (*grabbing the other arm, desperately*)

But, Ballio, listen, please!

BALLIO (*contemptuously*)

I'm deaf to boys who talk hot air.

CALIDORUS (*humbly*)

I gave while I had.

BALLIO (*grinning evilly*)

And I took. That's fair.

CALIDORUS (*as before*)

When I get, I'll give.

BALLIO (*as before*)

When you do, I'll give too.

CALIDORUS (*tearing his hair*)

Oh my god! All the money and gifts that I gave!
And to think how I lost it! All gone to the grave!

BALLIO (*airily*)

With your cash dead and buried, you're just talking for
    fun.
You're a fool if you try to go over what's done.

PSEUDOLUS (*to Ballio, trying bluster and pointing importantly
to Calidorus*)

Let me tell you, at least, who he happens to be—

BALLIO (*contemptuously*)

Oh, I've known all along who he was. And now he
Can just know who he is by himself, without me.

(*He wheels about and starts to stomp off, calling over his shoulder to his slave.*)

    Shake a leg, will you!

PSEUDOLUS (*slyly*)

                Ballio, turn around, please;
    Turn around just this once, and you'll pocket some fees!

(*Ballio stops in his tracks and swivels about.*)

BALLIO (*to the audience*) For that price I'll turn around. I could be praying to god almighty, I could have the holy offerings in my hand ready to give to him, and if a chance to make a buck came along, I'd forget all about religion. No matter what, the almighty dollar's one religion there's no resisting.

PSEUDOLUS (*to the audience*) We bend the knees to heaven —and he snaps his finger at it.

BALLIO (*to the audience, rubbing his hands*) I'll have a talk with them. (*To Pseudolus*) Greetings, stinkingest slave in Athens!

PSEUDOLUS (*with radiant benevolence*) Heaven put its blessing upon you and give you what (*winking to Calidorus*) this boy and I wish for you. (*Switching to moral sternness*) But, if you deserve otherwise, may it put its curse upon you!

BALLIO (*blandly*) How're you doing, Calidorus?

CALIDORUS I'm dying. Perishing for love—and dead broke.

BALLIO I'd have some pity—if I could feed my household on pity.

PSEUDOLUS (*breaking in impatiently*) Look, we know what you're like, so you can skip the speeches. Do you know what we're here for?

BALLIO (*grinning*) Just about. To see me in hell.

PSEUDOLUS That plus what we just called you back for. Now listen carefully.

BALLIO (*brusquely*) I'm listening. But whatever it is you're after, make it short. I'm busy now.

PSEUDOLUS (*gravely*) This boy here promised you five thousand for his girl, he promised it for a certain day, he hasn't
paid it yet, and he feels terribly sorry about it all.

BALLIO (*snarling*) Feeling sorry is a lot easier for a fellow
than feeling sore. He feels sorry because he didn't pay; I
feel sore because I didn't get paid.

PSEUDOLUS (*earnestly*) He'll pay; he'll find a way. Just hold
everything these next few days. You see, he's afraid you'll
sell his girl because you have it in for him.

BALLIO (*sullenly*) He had the chance to give me my money
a long time ago—*if* he had really wanted to.

CALIDORUS (*helplessly*) What if I didn't have it?

BALLIO (*to Calidorus, contemptuously*) If you were really in
love you'd have negotiated a loan—gone to a moneylender,
given him his few pennies interest, and then stolen it all
back from your father.

PSEUDOLUS (*with histrionic rage*) He steal from his father?
You have a nerve! No chance of *your* ever giving lessons in
honesty.

BALLIO (*grinning*) I'm a pimp. That's not my job.

CALIDORUS (*bitterly*) How could I steal anything from my
father? He's always so careful! (*Suddenly remembering
himself, in ringing tones*) What's more, even if I could, I
wouldn't. Filial duty, you know.

BALLIO (*disgustedly*) I hear you. Then snuggle up to that
filial duty of yours at night instead of Rosy. So filial duty
is more important to you than your love life, is it? All right,
then: is every man in the world your father? Isn't there
anyone you can hit up for a loan?

CALIDORUS (*miserably*) Loan? There's no such word any
more.

PSEUDOLUS (*to Ballio, confidentially*) Listen, ever since that
gang of fakers finished tanking up at the till—the ones who
always guard their own pockets but take from others' and
never pay back—all the moneylenders have been playing it
safe, they're not trusting anyone.

CALIDORUS (*to Ballio, nodding dumbly*) I'm in a bad way.
I can't scrape up a cent anywhere. I'm so bad off I'm dying
twice, from love and insufficient funds.

BALLIO (*helpfully*) Why don't you buy olive oil on credit
and sell for cash? Believe me, you could end up fifty thousand to the good in no time.

CALIDORUS (*brightening visibly—then wilting again*) Damn!
I'm damned by that damned law against minors. Everyone's scared to give me credit.

BALLIO (*grinning*) I come under the same law, you know.
I'm scared to give you credit too.

PSEUDOLUS (*exploding*) Scared to give him credit? After all
you've taken him for? Are you still not satisfied?

BALLIO (*loftily*) All decent, upright lovers never let their
largess lapse. Clients should give and keep on giving. When
there's nothing left to give, they should quit being in love.

CALIDORUS (*dumbly*) So you won't take pity on me?

BALLIO Money talks—and you're here with empty pockets.
(*Assuming a funereal expression and shaking his head
mournfully*) Yet I'd have liked to see you alive and well.

PSEUDOLUS Hey! He's not dead yet!

BALLIO Whatever he is, when he talks the way he's been
talking, believe me, to me he's dead. The minute a lover
begins to plead with a pimp, life's over for him. (*To Calidorus*) When you come running to me, come with tears
that clink. For example, this sob story of yours about not
having any money. You're weeping on a stepmother's shoulder, boy!

PSEUDOLUS Well! And just when did *you* marry his father?

BALLIO (*irascibly*) God forbid!

PSEUDOLUS (*earnestly, in a last stab at persuasion*) Do what
we're asking, Ballio, please! If you're afraid to give *him*
credit, trust me. Somewhere, on land or sea, I'll excavate
the cash for you.

BALLIO (*in astonishment*) I trust *you*?

PSEUDOLUS (*stoutly*)   Why not?

BALLIO   Good god, I'd sooner tie up a runaway dog with a string of sausages than trust you.

CALIDORUS (*bitterly*)   Is this the thanks I deserve from you? I act nice and you act nasty?

BALLIO (*savagely*)   What do you want now, anyway?

CALIDORUS   Just hold everything for the next six days or so. Don't sell her. (*Tragically*) Don't destroy the man who loves her!

BALLIO (*suddenly effusively affable*)   Don't worry. I'll even hold off for the next six months.

CALIDORUS (*in a transport of delight*)   That's wonderful! Ballio, you're terrific!

BALLIO (*expansively*)   Now that you're so happy, would you like me to make you even happier?

CALIDORUS   What do you mean?

BALLIO (*beaming*)   Rosy's not even for sale now.

CALIDORUS (*his jaw dropping*)   She's not?

BALLIO   Nosirree!

CALIDORUS (*deliriously*)   Pseudolus! Quick! Get fatted calves and lambs! Get slaughterers! I want to make an offering to God Almighty. (*Pointing to Ballio*) Because this god here is lots more almighty in my book than God Almighty.

BALLIO (*haughtily*)   No fatted calves. I want the sacramental meats of the sacrificial lamb!

CALIDORUS (*to Pseudolus, as before*)   Hurry! What are you standing there for? Go get lambs! Didn't you hear what God Almighty said?

PSEUDOLUS (*to Calidorus*)   Be back in a flash. (*Gesturing in the direction of the city gate, beyond which lie the public execution grounds*) But first I'll have to run down past the city gate.

CALIDORUS   Why there?

PSEUDOLUS (*to Calidorus—but eying Ballio*)   To bring back slaughterers from *there*. Two of them. With bells for the victim—the kind that clank. And I'll drive back two whole herds—of birch rods. (*Grimly*) Then we'll have plenty for a successful sacrifice today to God Almighty here.

BALLIO (*to Pseudolus*) You go to hell.

PSEUDOLUS (*genially*) That's where our Patron God of Pimps is going.

BALLIO (*gravely*) Do you know it's to your advantage if I die?

PSEUDOLUS How's that?

BALLIO I'll tell you. Because you'll never be an honest man as long as I live. (*Roars at his joke, recovers, and resumes his gravity.*) Do you know it's to your advantage if I stay alive?

PSEUDOLUS How's that?

BALLIO Because, if *I* die, *you'll* be the worst stinker in Athens. (*Second roar.*)

CALIDORUS (*to Ballio, deadly serious*) Listen, I've got a question to ask you, and I want a serious answer. Do I understand that Rosy is not for sale?

BALLIO She most certainly is not. (*Flashing his hyena grin*) You see, I've already sold her.

CALIDORUS (*stunned*) How?

BALLIO (*deadpan*) Garments excluded; just the carcass, guts and all.

CALIDORUS (*as before*) You sold *my* girl?

BALLIO (*cheerfully*) That's right. For five thousand dollars.

CALIDORUS (*gulping*) Five thousand?

BALLIO (*as before*) Let's say five times one thousand, if you prefer. To a major from Macedon. And I've already collected four thousand.

CALIDORUS (*still unable to believe his ears*) What's this you're telling me?

BALLIO That your girl friend's had a transformation. Into cash.

CALIDORUS (*as before*)   And you dared do a thing like that?

BALLIO (*shrugging*)   I felt like it. She was my property.

CALIDORUS (*to Pseudolus, roaring*)   Pseudolus! Get my sword!

PSEUDOLUS   What do you need a sword for?

CALIDORUS   To kill him. (*Tragically*) And myself.

PSEUDOLUS (*brightly*)   Why don't you just kill yourself? After all, starvation's going to take care of him before long.

CALIDORUS (*to Ballio*)   Listen here, you dirtiest double-crosser that ever walked the face of the earth, didn't you give me your solemn word you'd sell her to nobody but me?

BALLIO (*blandly*)   I admit it.

CALIDORUS   Didn't you even cross your heart?

BALLIO (*as before*)   I crossed my fingers *too*.

CALIDORUS (*thundering*)   You filthy liar, you went back on your word!

BALLIO (*as before*)   But I came into my money. (*Contemptuously*) I'm a filthy liar, but now I've got money to burn tucked away. You're a model son, you come from the right family—and you don't have a dime.

CALIDORUS   Pseudolus! Stand on the other side of him and cuss him out!

PSEUDOLUS (*racing around*)   Right! I'm covering ground faster than I would en route to City Hall for my emancipation proclamation.

(*The two take up positions on either side of Ballio. Calidorus, breathing fire, and Pseudolus, champing at the bit, face each other; Ballio, standing unconcerned between them, faces the audience.*)

CALIDORUS (*to Pseudolus*)   Give it to him! Pile it on!

PSEUDOLUS (*to Ballio*)   Now I'm going to tear you to tatters. With my tongue. (*At the top of his lungs*) Good-for-nothing!

BALLIO (*nodding agreeably*)   That's right.

PSEUDOLUS (*as before*) Dirty rat!

BALLIO (*as before*) It's the truth.

PSEUDOLUS Jailbait!

BALLIO Naturally.

PSEUDOLUS Grave robber!

BALLIO Of course.

PSEUDOLUS Skunk!

BALLIO (*admiringly*) Very good!

PSEUDOLUS You'd rob your best friend!

BALLIO Yes, I'd do that.

PSEUDOLUS And kill your father!

BALLIO (*to Calidorus, enthusiastically*) Now you take a turn.

CALIDORUS Church-robber!

BALLIO I admit it.

CALIDORUS Dirty double-crosser!

BALLIO (*reproachfully*) Old hat. You sang that song before.

CALIDORUS Criminal!

BALLIO Absolutely.

PSEUDOLUS Corrupter of the young!

BALLIO That's the stuff!

CALIDORUS Housebreaker!

BALLIO Voilà!

PSEUDOLUS Jailbreaker!

BALLIO Voici!

CALIDORUS Lawbreaker!

BALLIO Obviously.

PSEUDOLUS Crook!

CALIDORUS Lousy—

PSEUDOLUS —pimp!

CALIDORUS Scum!

BALLIO (*bursting into a round of applause*) In fine voice, both of you!

CALIDORUS (*losing steam*) You beat your father and mother.

BALLIO (*imperturbably*) What's more, I killed them sooner than pay for their upkeep. Nothing wrong in that, was there?

PSEUDOLUS (*to Calidorus, disgusted*) We're pouring into a punctured pot. We're wasting our breath.

BALLIO (*making preparations to move on*) Any further comments you two would like to make?

CALIDORUS (*weakly*) Aren't you ashamed of anything?

BALLIO (*angrily*) Aren't *you* ashamed of turning out to be a lover as broke as a nutshell? (*Starts to leave, then suddenly turns around.*) In spite of all the nasty names you've called me, I'll do this for you. Today's the last day for payment; if before tonight that major hasn't handed over the thousand he owes, I think I'll be in a position to do my duty.

CALIDORUS What's that?

BALLIO If you pay me first, I'll break my promise to him. (*With his hyena grin*) That's doing my duty. Well, if there was anything in it for me, I'd go on with this chat, but, without any cash, you're just kidding yourself if you think I'll have any pity on you. That's my considered opinion, so you can start figuring out what you're going to do next.

(*Ballio turns and stalks off, stage left, his attendant at his heels.*)

CALIDORUS (*in alarm*) Leaving already?

BALLIO (*over his shoulder*) I'm busy every minute right now.

PSEUDOLUS (*shaking his fist at the retreating back*) You'll be even busier a little later! (*To himself*) That fellow's my meat, unless god and man both desert me. I'll fillet him just the way a cook fillets an eel. (*To Calidorus*) Calidorus, I want your help now.

CALIDORUS (*promptly*) At your orders, sir!

PSEUDOLUS (*gesturing toward Ballio's house, thoughtfully*)
I want this town besieged and taken by storm before tonight. For this we need a cagey, clever, careful, competent
man capable of carrying out orders, who won't go to sleep
on his feet.

CALIDORUS Tell me—what are you up to?

PSEUDOLUS I'll let you know when the time comes. I don't
want to go over it twice. (*Grinning at the audience*) Plays
are long enough as is.

CALIDORUS (*nodding vigorously*) Absolutely and perfectly
right.

PSEUDOLUS Get going! Bring your man back here fast.

CALIDORUS (*doubtfully*) Out of a whole group of friends,
there are very few you can really rely on.

PSEUDOLUS I know that. So do it in two steps: first make a
rough selection; then pick the one man you're sure of.

CALIDORUS (*enthusiastically*) I'll have him here right away.

PSEUDOLUS (*pushing him off*) Can't you get going? All this
talk is holding you up.

(*Calidorus dashes off, stage left. Pseudolus stands where
he is, meditating.*)

PSEUDOLUS (*to himself, despondently*) Well, Pseudolus, he's
gone off, and you're here on your own. What are you going
to do now after all the big talk you handed him? What's
going to happen to those promises of yours? You haven't
even the shred of a plot in mind. You'd like to weave one,
but you don't have a beginning to start from or an end to
finish at. It's like being a playwright: once he's picked up
his pen, he's on the hunt for something that exists nowhere
on the face of the earth; yet he finds it anyway, he makes
fiction sound like fact. I'll play playwright: that five thousand exists nowhere on the face of the earth, yet I'll find it
anyway. I told the boy a long time ago that I'd come up
with the money for him. I wanted to get it out of the old

man but somehow or other he always caught wise first. (*Looking toward the wings, stage left*) But I've got to turn off the talk and shut up! Look who I see coming—our Simo and his neighbor, Callipho. (*Gesturing derisively toward Simo*) This is the grave I'm going to rob today for the five thousand I need for his son. (*Going over to an unobtrusive spot off to one side*) I'll just move over here where I can listen in on what they say.

(*Two graybeards, deep in conversation, totter in, leaning heavily on their sticks.*

Simo, Calidorus' father and Pseudolus' owner, has the face you would expect on a man who all his life has been a canny, tightfisted businessman; a card shark would look benevolent in comparison. Callipho is the exact opposite; his round, innocent countenance exudes goodness and implicit faith in his fellow man.

From the waggling of the head and other gesticulating, it is clear that Simo is in a foul mood.)

SIMO (*angrily*)   If we decided to pick a spendthrift or a rake for Governor of Athens, no one, I swear, would be any competition for that son of mine. He's the one topic of conversation in the whole town, how he's got his heart set on freeing his girl friend and is hunting for the money to do it. I've been getting reports from all sides. But I had smelled something fishy and knew all about it a long time ago; I just pretended I didn't.

PSEUDOLUS (*aside, dismayed*)   So his son smelled fishy! The campaign's collapsed, the offensive's stuck in a rut. There's a tight roadblock across the route I wanted to take to the cash depot. He found out! No looting any loot there.

CALLIPHO (*indignantly*)   If I had my way, people who babble gossip or listen to it would all hang—babblers by the tongue and listeners by the ears. Why, these reports that you're getting, that your son has a love affair and wants to steal from you, may be all just talk, a pack of lies. But even if every word is true, the way people behave these

days, what's he done that's so out of the ordinary? What's
so odd about a young fellow falling in love and setting his
girl friend free?

PSEUDOLUS (*aside*)   What a nice old man!

SIMO (*snarling*)   Well, I'm an old fellow, and I don't want
it!

CALLIPHO (*smiling indulgently*)   It won't do you the slightest
good not to want it. It *might* have, if you hadn't behaved
the same way when you were young. Only a parent who
was a paragon can expect his son to be better than he was.
And you—the money you threw away and the affairs you
had could have taken care of every single solitary male in
the city, barring none! Is it any wonder that the son takes
after the father?

PSEUDOLUS (*to himself—but good and loud*)   *Mon dieu!* How
few of you decent people there are in this world. Now,
there's the kind of father a father should be to a son!

SIMO (*whirling around*)   Who's that talking? (*To Callipho,
disgusted*)   It's my servant Pseudolus. He's the archcriminal
who's corrupted my son; he's his guide and mentor. I'd
like to see him at the end of a rope!

CALLIPHO (*sotto voce*)   Now that's very silly of you, to
show how angry you are. You'll get much further by being
nice to him and finding out whether those reports you're
getting are true. (*Wagging his head sagely*)   "Trouble's
double for the hasty heart."

SIMO (*sotto voce*)   All right. I'll take your advice.

(*The two oldsters start walking toward Pseudolus.*)

PSEUDOLUS (*to himself*)   The offensive's under way, Pseudolus! Have some fast talk ready for the old man. (*As they
draw near, beaming*)   Greetings to you first, master, as is
only right and proper. And, if any are left over, (*with a
respectful bow to Callipho*)   greetings to the neighbors.

SIMO   Greetings. (*All affability*)   Well, now, how are we
doing?

PSEUDOLUS (*leaning back negligently and grinning*) Oh, we're just standing here this way.

SIMO (*reverting immediately to type, to Callipho*) Look at that pose, will you? His lordship!

CALLIPHO I think his pose is very nice. (*Nodding approvingly*) Self-confident.

PSEUDOLUS (*virtuously*) If a servant is honest and his conscience is clear, he *should* hold his head high, especially in front of his master.

CALLIPHO (*beaming on Pseudolus*) We have a few things we'd like to ask you about. Some rumors we've been hearing that we're a bit vague about.

SIMO (*to Callipho, disgusted*) He'll talk you to death. You'll think it's Socrates and not Pseudolus you're talking to.

PSEUDOLUS (*to Simo, pathetically*) Yes, you haven't thought very well of me for quite some time now, I can see it. I know—you don't have very much faith in me. (*Squaring his jaw*) You'd like to see me bad and wicked, but, in spite of you, I'm going to be honest and decent!

SIMO (*resignedly*) Pseudolus, will you kindly vacate the rooms in your ears so some things I have to say can move in?

PSEUDOLUS (*gravely*) Even though I'm very annoyed with you, you go right ahead, say whatever you like.

SIMO (*staring at him*) You annoyed with me? The servant annoyed with the master?

PSEUDOLUS (*haughtily*) And does that seem so strange to you?

SIMO My god, the way you talk, I'd better watch out you don't get angry with me. (*Eying him narrowly*) You're thinking of giving me a beating, aren't you? And *not* the kind I'm accustomed to give you! (*To Callipho*) What's your idea?

CALLIPHO (*vehemently*)   I really think he has every right to be angry. After all, you *don't* have much faith in him.

SIMO (*sneering*)   Well, let him be angry. I'll see to it he does me no damage. (*To Pseudolus, brusquely*) Listen, you. What about the things I want to find out?

PSEUDOLUS (*all co-operation*)   Anything you want to know, just ask. And consider whatever you hear from me an oracle from heaven.

SIMO (*curtly*)   Then pay attention and don't forget your promise. Listen, are you aware that my son is having an affair with a certain chorus girl?

PSEUDOLUS (*like an oracle from heaven*)   Yea, verily.

SIMO   And that he wants to set her free?

PSEUDOLUS   Yea, verily to that too.

SIMO   And that you're getting your stunts and smart schemes set to steal a certain five thousand dollars from me?

PSEUDOLUS (*wide-eyed*)   *I* steal from *you*?

SIMO (*grimly*)   That's right. To give to my son so he can set the girl free. (*Impatiently, as Pseudolus hesitates*) Admit it, just say "Yea, verily to that too."

PSEUDOLUS (*meekly*)   Yea, verily to that too.

CALLIPHO (*in shocked surprise*)   He admits it!

SIMO (*to Callipho, smugly*)   I told you so, all along.

CALLIPHO (*sadly*)   Yes, I remember.

SIMO (*to Pseudolus, angrily*)   Why didn't you tell me the minute you heard instead of hiding it from me? Why didn't *I* hear about it?

PSEUDOLUS (*readily*)   I'll tell you why. I didn't want to be the one to start a bad precedent—this business of a servant carrying tales about one master to another.

SIMO (*to Callipho, snarling*)   He should have been hauled off by the heels to the mill wheel!

CALLIPHO (*anxiously*)   He didn't do anything wrong, did he?

SIMO   Anything? Everything!

PSEUDOLUS (*to Callipho*) Don't, Callipho. I know how to handle my own affairs. I deserve the blame. (*To Simo*) Now listen carefully. Why did I keep you in the dark about your son's love affair? Because he had the mill wheel all set for me if I talked.

SIMO And you didn't know *I'd* have it all set for you if you kept quiet?

PSEUDOLUS I knew that.

SIMO (*menacingly*) Then why wasn't I told?

PSEUDOLUS (*glibly*) Because one evil was in front of me and the other a little farther on. His was right there; with yours I had a teensy breathing spell.

(*Simo glares at him. Pseudolus looks him in the eye serenely.*)

SIMO (*deciding to accept the explanation*) What are you two going to do now? After all, you can't get any money out of me; I know everything. And I'm going to pass the word right now to everyone in town not to lend you a dime.

PSEUDOLUS (*blandly*) Believe me, I'm not going to go begging. Not as long as *you're* alive. Because, by god, *you're* going to give me the money. I'm going to get it from you.

SIMO (*superciliously*) So you're going to get it from me, eh?

PSEUDOLUS And how!

SIMO Well, by god, you can poke my eyes out if I ever give you that money!

PSEUDOLUS (*airily*) You will. I'm telling you about it right now so you'll be on your guard.

SIMO One thing I'm sure of: if you do pull it off, you deserve a citation for the sensation of the century.

PSEUDOLUS (*casually*) I will.

SIMO (*ghoulishly*) Suppose you don't?

PSEUDOLUS (*promptly*) Whip me to shreds. But suppose I do?

SIMO (*promptly*) As god's my witness, I won't lay a finger on you and you can keep the money all your life.

PSEUDOLUS (*pointing a warning finger at him*)   Don't you
forget that.

SIMO (*taken aback by Pseudolus' cocksureness, uneasily*)
How can you possibly catch me off guard, now that I've
been forewarned?

PSEUDOLUS   I gave you fair warning to be on your guard.
And I'm telling you now, in so many words: be on your
guard. BE ON YOUR GUARD! (*Pointing to Simo's hands*)
Watch out—today, with those two hands, you're going to
give me the money.

CALLIPHO (*goggle-eyed*)   The man's a virtuoso, a maestro,
if he keeps his word!

PSEUDOLUS (*to Callipho, in ringing tones*)   Carry me off and
make me your slave if I don't!

SIMO   Very nice and friendly of you—but don't you happen
to be *my* slave at the moment?

PSEUDOLUS (*ignoring the last remark*)   Would you like to
hear something that'll amaze the both of you even more?

CALLIPHO (*enthusiastically*)   Oh yes! I'm dying to hear it. I
love listening to you.

PSEUDOLUS (*turning to Simo*)   Before I conduct my campaign against you, I'm going to fight still another glorious
and memorable campaign.

SIMO   What campaign?

PSEUDOLUS (*gesturing toward Ballio's house*)   Against the
pimp who lives next door. You watch—with my stunts and
smart schemes I'm going to pluck that chorus girl your
son's pining for plunk from under his pimpish nose.

SIMO   What's that you say?

PSEUDOLUS (*triumphantly*)   And I'll have both jobs done by
tonight!

SIMO (*dubiously*)   Well, if you make good on all this big
talk, you're a better man than Alexander the Great.
(*Sternly*) But, if you don't, is there any reason why I
shouldn't have you shut up in the mill, pronto?

PSEUDOLUS (*promptly*) And not just for one day. For every day of my life as long as I live. But, if I do, will you, of your own free will, give me money for the pimp, pronto?

CALLIPHO (*as Simo hesitates*) That's a fair proposition. Tell him you will.

SIMO (*clutching Callipho's arm*) You know what I just thought of? Supposing those two have a deal on! Suppose they're in cahoots and have a scheme cooked up to do me out of the money?

PSEUDOLUS (*laughing off the suggestion*) Even I wouldn't have the nerve to pull a stunt like that! No, Simo, it's not that way at all. (*Earnestly*) If he and I have any deal on, or if we ever had a single meeting or discussion about any deal, you can take a rawhide pen and scribble over my whole hide just as if you were filling up a page with writing.

SIMO (*shrugging in acquiescence*) You can announce your act now, whenever you want.

PSEUDOLUS (*to Callipho*) Callipho, would you please help me and not get tied up in any other business? It's just for today.

CALLIPHO (*hesitating*) But I've had everything set up since yesterday to go off to the country . . .

PSEUDOLUS Well, please dismantle the set-up, will you?

CALLIPHO (*suddenly making up his mind*) All right, I've decided to stay, for your sake. (*His eyes glistening*) I'm dying to watch your act, Pseudolus. And, if I hear that (*gesturing toward Simo*) he won't pay you the money he promised, I'll pay it myself rather than see you lose out.

SIMO (*muttering*) I won't go back on my word.

PSEUDOLUS (*to Simo, promptly*) Darned right—because, if you don't come across, I'll dun you, and the din will be long and loud. Now out of here, both of you; get inside and leave the field clear for my hocus-pocus.

CALLIPHO (*moving off toward his house*) Right. Anything you say.

PSEUDOLUS (*calling to him*)   Now I don't want you to leave the house, you hear?

CALLIPHO   Of course. Glad to oblige.

SIMO (*to Pseudolus*)   But I have to go downtown. I'll be back right away.

PSEUDOLUS (*warningly*)   Then hurry.

(*Callipho goes into his house, and Simo leaves, stage left. Pseudolus walks downstage and addresses the audience.*)

PSEUDOLUS   I suspect that you suspect that I've made all these big promises just to keep you entertained until I get through this play, and that I'm not going to do the things I said I'd do. (*Mimicking Simo's tones*) "I won't go back on my word." (*Gaily*) So far as I can see, I can't see how I'm going to do it—but, if there's one thing I *can* see, it's that I *will* do it. After all, when a character comes on stage, he ought to bring something fresh and new in a fresh and new way. And, if he can't, let him make way for someone who can. (*Moving off toward Simo's house*) And now I'd like to step inside here for a minute while I carry out a mental mobilization of my underhand forces. I won't keep you long; I'm coming right out. Our flutist will entertain you with a selection in the meantime.

(*Pseudolus races into Simo's house, leaving the stage empty. A second later the flutist comes on to play an entr'-acte.*)

ACT II

(The door of Simo's house flies open. Pseudolus bursts out and races downstage to address the audience.)

SONG

PSEUDOLUS *(excitedly)*

Holy mackerel! It's marvelous! Everything I try
  Works out just like a charm.

(Tapping his brow)

Up in here is a scheme I can certify
  Is guaranteed free of harm.

(Importantly)

When your eye's on the big things, it's madness, I say,
To proceed in a timid or half-hearted way.

  The way that things work out
  Is completely up to you.
  You want to do big things?
  Then think and act big too!

  You take *me*. Why, up here in this head,
   Standing by for the fray,
  Are my armies—plus ambush, intrigue,
   Dirty deals, and foul play.

With the courage inherited from a long line of heroes,
  With the double-cross serving as shining shield,
The enemy's mine wherever I'll meet him—
  I'll phony my foemen from the field!

  Just watch me now. I'm set to go,
  To fight the man who's our common foe,
  To rally-oh,
  And sally-oh
   'Gainst Ballio!

(*Pointing to Ballio's house*)

Here's the fortress I want to lay siege to today.
So I'll draw up my forces in battle array,
And I'll take it by storm—to the joy of the nation—
And then quickly re-form for the next operation,

(*Pointing to Simo's house*)

To lay siege to the doddering fort over here.
Here I'll load my allies and myself with such plunder
I'll be hailed as the scourge of my foes, as a wonder.

(*Puffing out his chest*)

> I was born to be great;
> It's a family trait—
> To fight battles victorious,
> Memorable, glorious.

(*Suddenly looking toward the wings, stage right*)

Someone's coming this way. Who's this man that I spy?
Who's this stranger so suddenly in the way of my eye?
What's he want with that cutlass there, I'd like to know.
What's his business here? Pseudolus! Ambush the foe!

(*Pseudolus moves to an unobtrusive spot off to the side,
and, a second later, Harpax, "snatcher," enters. Harpax has a
sort of primitive cunning and suspicion in his make-up but,
aside from that, is not very bright. He is an officer's orderly;
he wears a uniform and carries a sword. In one hand he
clutches a purse, obviously well-filled.*

*The hesitant way in which he walks along, stopping to peer
at the doorways, reveals immediately that he is a stranger in
town.*)

HARPAX (*to himself*)

The report of my eyes confirms, I can see,
The report my commander imparted to me,
     Here's the district and quarter he meant.
Seven blocks from the entrance to town I should spot
The pimp's house, where the master said leave the whole
     lot,
     Both this cash and the seal that he sent.

But I'd like to see someone come by who'd make clear
If a pimp, name of Ballio, lives around here.

PSEUDOLUS (*to himself*)

Not a sound! Not a word! Unless heaven and men
    All desert me, this man is my meat!
But I need a new gambit since all of a sudden
    A new path has appeared at my feet.
All the plans I worked out must be jettisoned now;
    In my new start I'll concentrate here (*pointing to
    Harpax*).
So you've come as an errand boy, *mon général?*
    Watch me soon stand you up on your ear!

(*Harpax walks up to Ballio's house and raises his hand to
knock.*)

HARPAX (*to himself*) I'll knock on the door and get someone
to come out.

PSEUDOLUS (*calling*) Hey, whoever you are, I wish you'd
cut out that knocking. You see, I'm patron protecter of
portals. Popped out here for a precautionary peep.

HARPAX (*dubiously*) Are you Ballio?

PSEUDOLUS (*importantly*) Not exactly. I'm Vice-Ballio.

HARPAX What's that mean?

PSEUDOLUS (*as before*) Chief layer-outer and layer-inner.
Lord of the larder.

HARPAX (*impressed*) You mean to say you're the major-
domo?

PSEUDOLUS Me? I give orders to the major-domo!

HARPAX (*puzzled, unable to square Pseudolus' tones with his
slave's get-up*) Are you a slave or aren't you?

PSEUDOLUS (*deflated*) Well, for the moment, still a slave.

HARPAX (*inflated*) You look it. You don't look the type to be
anything but.

PSEUDOLUS (*promptly*) Ever take a look at yourself before
making cracks about others?

HARPAX (*to the audience, gesturing toward Pseudolus*) Must be a bad egg, this one here.

PSEUDOLUS (*to the audience, gesturing toward Harpax*) Well, look what heaven sent me! A nest all my own—I'll hatch plenty of schemes in it today!

HARPAX (*to himself, suspiciously*) What's he talking to himself about?

PSEUDOLUS (*calling*) Hey, mister!

HARPAX What?

PSEUDOLUS Are you from that Macedonian major? Servant of the fellow who bought a girl from us and paid my master four thousand and still owes him a thousand?

HARPAX (*surprised*) That's right. But where in the world do you know me from? Where did you ever see me or talk to me, anyway? I never set foot in Athens before and never laid eyes on you till this minute.

PSEUDOLUS (*studiedly offhand*) You looked as if you came from him. After all, when he left he agreed on today as the last day for payment, and he hasn't yet made good.

HARPAX (*hefting the purse*) Oh, no. It's here.

PSEUDOLUS (*affecting surprise*) You brought it?

HARPAX (*importantly*) I certainly did.

PSEUDOLUS (*reaching for the purse, as if in a considerable hurry*) What are you waiting for? Hand it over.

HARPAX (*jerking the purse out of his reach*) Hand it over to who? You?

PSEUDOLUS Certainly to me. I'm in charge of Ballio's books. I handle the cash—receive all receivables, pay all payables.

HARPAX (*grimly*) Certainly *not* to you. You could be cashier for god almighty and all the treasures of heaven, but I'm not trusting you with a cent.

PSEUDOLUS (*ignoring the last remark, all business*) Why, in two shakes of a lamb's tail, we could have the whole thing done.

HARPAX (*as before, showing the tightly bound purse*) I'd rather keep it *undone*.

PSEUDOLUS You go to the devil! So you've come here to blacken my good name, eh? As if people don't trust me personally with a thousand times that much money!

HARPAX (*stubbornly*) Others can think that way. Doesn't mean *I* have to trust you.

PSEUDOLUS (*working himself up*) You mean to say I'm trying to do you out of your money?

HARPAX Oh, no. *You* mean to say it. I mean to say I have my suspicions. What's your name, anyway?

PSEUDOLUS (*to the audience*) The pimp has a servant named Syrus. That's who I'll say I am. (*To Harpax*) Syrus.

HARPAX Syrus, eh?

PSEUDOLUS That's my name.

HARPAX (*impatiently*) Enough talk. Listen, whatever your name is, if your master's home, call him out so I can do what I was sent here to do.

PSEUDOLUS (*apologetically*) If he *were* here, I'd call him out. (*Earnestly*) But don't you want to give it to me? (*Innocently*) You'll be relieved of the whole business— more so than if you gave it to him in person.

HARPAX (*contemptuously*) You don't get the point. The commander gave it to me to pay with, not play with. Oh, I can see you're practically running a fever because you can't dig your claws into it. I don't hand over a cent to a soul except to Ballio in person.

PSEUDOLUS He's tied up right now. In court on a case.

HARPAX Well, I hope he wins. I'll come back when I figure he'll be at home. (*Pulling out a letter and handing it to Pseudolus*) Here, take this letter and give it to him. It's got the identification seal my master agreed on with yours in this deal for the girl.

PSEUDOLUS (*taking it, studiedly casual*) Yes, I know. The major told us what he wanted: we're to send the girl off with a fellow who'd bring the money and a seal with his picture. He left a duplicate with us, you know.

HARPAX (*impressed in spite of himself*) You know everything, don't you?

PSEUDOLUS (*with a shrug, carelessly*) Why shouldn't I?

HARPAX (*pointing to the letter*) So you give him that identification.

PSEUDOLUS Right. What's your name, anyway?

HARPAX Snatcher.

PSEUDOLUS (*pretending fright*) On your way, Snatcher boy, I don't like you. You're not coming inside this house, believe me; I want none of your snatching there.

HARPAX (*puffing out his chest*) I take my enemies alive, right out of the front line. That's how I got the name.

PSEUDOLUS If you ask me, you take the silverware right out of the front rooms.

HARPAX (*loftily*) No, sir! (*Struck by a thought*) Say, Syrus, you know what I'd like to ask you to do?

PSEUDOLUS Tell me and I'll know.

HARPAX I'm staying at the third inn outside the city gate. The one run by that old buttertub, Chrysis, the lame dame.

PSEUDOLUS What do you want?

HARPAX Come and pick me up there when your master gets back.

PSEUDOLUS Sure. Anything you say.

HARPAX I'm tired from the trip. Want to get some rest.

PSEUDOLUS (*nodding vigorously*) Very smart. Good idea. But don't make me go looking all over the place when I come to get you.

HARPAX Oh, no. After a bite to eat, a nap is all I'm interested in.

PSEUDOLUS (*as before*) I'll bet.

HARPAX (*preparing to leave*) Well, anything I can do for you?

PSEUDOLUS   You go take that nap.

HARPAX   I'm going. (*Starts walking off, stage right.*)

PSEUDOLUS (*calling after him, solicitously*)   Snatcher! Listen! Use plenty of blankets. You get a good sweat up, and you'll feel tiptop.

(*Harpax leaves. The minute he is out of earshot, Pseudolus races downstage and addresses the audience.*)

PSEUDOLUS (*exultantly*)

Ye gods! That fellow saved my life by turning up, I swear!

I was heading wrong, he set me right—and *he's* to pay the fare!

Lady Luck herself could never have come at a luckier time, you see,

Than when I had this lucky letter luckily left with me.

(*Brandishing the letter*)

He's handed me a horn of plenty, in here's what I want and more:

Embezzlement, swindle, double-cross, dirty tricks, shady deals galore,

The cash we're after plus that girl the boy is crazy for.

And now I'll show my generous soul; my name and fame shall soar!

(*Shaking his head wonderingly*)

My army of plans had been mobilized, was at stations, was all set—

The way I'd go about the job, approach the pimp and get

The girl away from him. It all was in my head, but it seems

Lady Luck by herself can overturn a hundred wise men's schemes.

The fact is that, when we're doing well, and people say we're smart,

We owe it all to just how much Lady Luck has taken our part.

We hear that someone's plans have worked out; "He's a genius!" all of us chime.

We hear that someone's plans went wrong; "What a fool!" we chime this time.

Why, we're the fools—we're unaware how wasted is our whole

Benighted, greedy struggle toward any particular goal,

As if the right path's ever known to any human soul!

The bird in hand we always leave to go for those in the bush;

And then 'mid all our sweat and strain, enter Death to give his push!

(*Suddenly snapping his fingers*) But enough of this philosophizing. I've been talking too much and too long. (*Gleefully*) Ye gods! That brain storm I suddenly got a little while ago, to bluff and say I belonged to the pimp, is worth a fortune! Now, with this letter, I'll double-cross the three of them, master, pimp, and letter giver. (*His attention suddenly caught, looks toward the wings, stage left.*) Well, look at that! Something else I wanted is happening, just as good as this. Here comes Calidorus, and he's got somebody with him.

(*Calidorus and his friend Charinus [pronounced ka-RYE-nus], "charitable," enter, so deep in conversation they don't notice Pseudolus.*)

CALIDORUS So I've told you everything, the sweet and the bitter. You know my toils, my troubles, my financial tribulations.

CHARINUS (*nodding*) I have everything in mind. Now just tell me what you want me to do.

CALIDORUS Pseudolus gave me orders to bring someone who can get things done and who'd be willing to do me a good turn.

CHARINUS You carry out orders to the letter: you're bringing a good friend ready to do you a good turn. But who's this Pseudolus? He's new to me.

CALIDORUS (*enthusiastically*) The greatest virtuoso alive,

my maestro of miracles. He's the one who told me he was
going to do all the things I told you about.

PSEUDOLUS (*to himself, importantly*)   I'll go up and greet
him in the grand manner.

CALIDORUS (*his attention caught*)   Whose voice is that?

PSEUDOLUS (*adopting the tones and gestures of a character in
grand opera*)

'Tis thee I seek, Your Majesty, yea thee
Whom thy servant Pseudolus serves. 'Tis thee I seek
To give thee thrice, in triplewise, in form
Threefold, three thrice-deserved delights derived
From dumbbells three and by devices three:
Deceit, deception, and double-cross.

(*Waving the letter*)

Delights that I bring thee signed and sealed
In this here paltry piece of paper.

CALIDORUS (*to Charinus, excitedly*)   That's the fellow!

CHARINUS (*admiringly*)   The devil's better than an opera
star!

PSEUDOLUS (*walking toward them, as before*)

Advance thy step as I do mine and boldly
Extend to me thy hand and welcome words.

CALIDORUS

To welcome rescue true—or welcome *words?*

PSEUDOLUS (*dropping the act and grinning*)   Both!

CALIDORUS (*with great relief*)   Welcome, words and rescue!
(*Tensely*) What happened?

PSEUDOLUS (*amused*)   What are you so nervous about?

CALIDORUS (*pointing to Charinus, proudly*)   I've produced
your man.

PSEUDOLUS   What's this "produced" business?

CALIDORUS (*meekly*)   I mean I've brought him here.

PSEUDOLUS (*looking Charinus over*)   Who is he?

CALIDORUS   Charinus.

PSEUDOLUS   Bravo!
>   No man named Charinus
>   Will ever malign us.

CHARINUS (*energetically*)   What do you need done? Step up and give me my orders.

PSEUDOLUS (*playing disinterested to test his man's interest*) Thanks just the same and all the best to you, Charinus, but we really don't want to put you to any trouble.

CHARINUS (*promptly*)   You won't put me to any trouble. Not a bit.

PSEUDOLUS (*promptly*)   Then stick around. (*Ostentatiously examines the letter.*)

CALIDORUS   What's that?

PSEUDOLUS (*triumphantly*)   I've just intercepted this letter and this identification!

CALIDORUS   Identification? What identification?

PSEUDOLUS   The one the major just sent. His servant, the fellow who came to take your girl away, brought it along with the one thousand dollars—(*grinning*) and did I make a monkey out of him just now!

CALIDORUS   How?

PSEUDOLUS (*gesturing toward the audience*)   Look, this play's being given for the benefit of these people. And they were here, they know all about it. I'll tell you two later.

CALIDORUS   What do we do now?

PSEUDOLUS (*in ringing tones*)   By tonight you'll have your girl friend in your arms—and she'll be a free woman!

CALIDORUS (*dumfounded*)   I?

PSEUDOLUS   Yes, you, I say—if I manage to stay alive. Provided, however, you two find me a man in a hurry.

CHARINUS   What kind of man?

PSEUDOLUS   A good-for-nothing. But one who's slick and smart enough, once he's been given a start, to figure out what to do next on his own. And it mustn't be anyone too well known around here.

CHARINUS Does it matter if he's a slave?

PSEUDOLUS (*in a what-a-silly-question tone of voice*) On the contrary, I prefer a slave.

CHARINUS I think I have the man for you. He's a good-for-nothing, he's smart, and my father just sent him here from overseas. He came to Athens only yesterday, and he hasn't been out of the house yet.

PSEUDOLUS (*to Charinus, nodding*) That'll be a great help. (*Frowning in thought*) Now I've got to borrow a thousand dollars which I'll need just till tonight. (*Gesturing toward Calidorus, grinning*) His father owes me money.

CHARINUS (*expansively*) Oh, I'll give it to you. Don't bother going to anyone else.

PSEUDOLUS My lifesaver! (*Thoughtful again*) But I also need a uniform and a sword.

CHARINUS I've got some to spare.

PSEUDOLUS (*exultantly*) Ye gods! This Charinus is all plus and no minus! Now, about that servant of yours who's just arrived—is he strong in the head?

CHARINUS No, just under the armpits.

PSEUDOLUS He ought to wear long sleeves. Is he tough? Does he have the old vinegar in the veins?

CHARINUS As sour as it comes.

PSEUDOLUS Suppose he has to give out with the old sweetness, instead? Has he got it in him?

CHARINUS Has he! Honey, sugar, syrup—he once tried to run a grocery in his guts.

PSEUDOLUS (*grinning*) Touché, Charinus: beat me at my own game. But what's this servant of yours called?

CHARINUS Monkey.

PSEUDOLUS Can he do a good turn?

CHARINUS Like a top.

PSEUDOLUS Does he grasp things easily?

CHARINUS   All the time—other people's things.

PSEUDOLUS   Suppose he's caught in the act?

CHARINUS   He slips out. He's an eel.

PSEUDOLUS   Has he got any sense?

CHARINUS   More sense than the Board of Censors.

PSEUDOLUS   Well, from what you say he sounds like a good man.

CHARINUS   You have no idea how good! Why, the minute he sees you he'll tell *you* what you want him for. What have you got in mind, anyway?

PSEUDOLUS   I'll tell you. When I'm done dressing your man up, I want him to impersonate the major's orderly. He'll take this identification along with a thousand dollars to the pimp and make off with the girl. There, now you know the whole plot. The mechanics of how to do it I'll save for our impersonator.

CALIDORUS   (*impatiently*) Well, what are we standing around for?

PSEUDOLUS   I'm off to the Aeschinus Loan Company. You two dress your man in dress uniform and bring him to me there. But hurry!

CHARINUS   We'll be there before you will.

PSEUDOLUS   Then you'd better shake a leg! (*As Calidorus and Charinus dash off, stage left, he turns and addresses the audience.*)

It's left my mind, it's gone away, the last shred of doubt and fear
I'd had before. My mind's been scoured, the road ahead is clear.
With flying flags I'm leading out the troops in my command;
The sky is blue, all dark clouds gone, and everything goes as planned;
Morale is high: I can—I know it!—wipe out the enemy band.
But first downtown to hand a load of sage advice to Monk:

Tell him what to do so he plays it smart and doesn't go
kerplunk.

And then to storm Castle Pimp itself—and the enemy's cause
is sunk!

*(Pseudolus dashes off triumphantly, stage left, and the
stage is empty.)*

ACT III

(*The door of Ballio's house opens, and Ballio's catamite steps out, a repulsive little boy with an ugly face as heavily made up as any whore's. He minces downstage and addresses the audience.*)

BOY   When Fate makes a boy a slave in a pimp's home and, on top of that, makes him homely, believe me, as I can tell from my feelings right now, she's made him plenty of toil and trouble. Take me—that's the kind of slavery that came my way; I'm the sole support of all sorts of sorrows, small and large. (*Whimpering*) And I can't find any lover boy to love me and care for me so that for once in my life things would be a teeny bit brighter.

(*Whimpers a second or so longer, then continues worriedly*) Today is this pimp's birthday, and he's laid down the law to everyone in the house from the lowest to the highest: whoever doesn't get him a gift today gets the life tortured out of him tomorrow. In the position I'm in, what in heaven's name can I do? I can't give what people who can give usually give. And, if I don't give the pimp a gift today, tomorrow he'll empty the chamber pots down my throat. (*Blubbering*) I'm still too small for things like that!

(*Getting his blubbering under control*) Golly, poor me, I'm so scared of swilling slops, (*leering*) if someone slipped something into my palm to give it a little weight, (*archly*) I think I could somehow grit my teeth and bear it even though it makes a person cry hard—(*innocently*) so they tell me.

(*His attention caught, looks toward the wings, stage left*)   But right now I have to shut my mouth and bear it —there's Ballio coming back bringing a cook with him.

(*The boy hurries into the house. A second later Ballio enters, at his heels his slave boy, and at his side an enormously fat cook behind whom trails a long line of young assistants.*)

BALLIO (*to the world at large*) And people, the damn fools, say the market is where you hire cooks! It's where you hire crooks, not cooks! I tell you, if I had actually taken an oath to find a worse cook than the one I've got here, I couldn't have done it. Useless, brainless, a blowhard and a blabbermouth! I know why he never died and went below: so he could be on hand here to cater funeral feasts: he's the only one who can cook what a corpse would eat.

COOK (*unabashed*) If you really think I'm the type you tell me I am, why did you hire me?

BALLIO Shortage. There was no one else. If you're such a great cook, why were all the others already gone from the square and you were still sitting there all by yourself?

COOK (*with a great air of candor*) I'll tell you. I'm considered a poorer cook. Not through any fault of my own, mind you. Through human greed.

BALLIO How's that?

COOK (*as before*) I'll tell you. It's because, when people come to hire a cook, they never go after the best who'll cost the most; they'd rather hire the cook who costs the least. That's why I was sitting in sole possession of the square today. (*Contemptuously*) Let those other poor devils cook their five-buck feeds. (*Pounding his chest*) Nobody gets me off my seat for less than ten. I don't do a dinner like other cooks. They pile up plates with potted pasture, that's what they do. They make cattle out of the guests—feed 'em fodder! And even the fodder they season with still more fodder. Inside they put coriander, fennel, garlic, celery. Outside they put cabbage, beets, sorrel, spinach. On top of it all, they throw in a pound of asafetida. Then they'll grate in that damned mustard, which has the graters' eyes going at a great rate before they're done grating. When these cooks cook a meal and it comes to the seasoning, they don't season with seasonings, they season with vultures—gives 'em a chance to get at the easy livers around the table while still alive. That's why people hereabouts don't live very long: they bloat their bellies with all this fodder that's horrible to mention let alone eat. Fodder a cow wouldn't eat, a person will.

BALLIO (*snarling*) What about yourself? If you sneer at these seasonings, what do you use? Seasonings from heaven to make people live longer?

COOK (*promptly*) You can say that again. If people ate regularly the meals I prepare, they could live to even two hundred. Once I drop some clovidoopus in a pan, or some dillipoopus, or a dash of fathead or cutathroat, right away the pan starts sizzling on its own. (*Becoming the maître d'hôtel*) Now, these seasonings are for your dishes made from the finny tribe. For your dishes made from the earthy tribes I season with nutmegoopus. Or tenus tenerus or even muvius fluvius.

BALLIO (*exploding*) You and your seasoning can go plumb to hell! And take all your damned lies with you!

COOK (*unruffled*) Will you kindly allow me to continue?

BALLIO Continue—and then go to hell!

COOK When every pot is hot, I uncover every one, and (*closing his eyes in rapture*) the aroma flies to heaven with feet outspread.

BALLIO The aroma with feet outspread, eh?

COOK (*apologetically*) Made a slip. Didn't realize it.

BALLIO How's that?

COOK (*straight-faced*) With arms outspread, I meant to say. (*Resuming his rapture*) The lord in heaven sups nightly on this aroma.

BALLIO (*sarcastically*) And if you don't happen to be cooking anywhere, what in the world does the lord in heaven sup on?

COOK (*promptly*) He goes to bed unsupped.

BALLIO (*roaring*) And you go to hell! (*Indicating by a contempestuous wave of the hand all the cook's big talk*) So for all this I'm supposed to pay you ten dollars today, am I?

COOK (*smugly*) Oh, I admit I'm a very expensive cook. But I make sure the people get their money's worth in any house I go to cook in.

BALLIO To rob in, you mean.

COOK (*shrugging*) You think you can find a cook who doesn't have a pair of claws like a vulture?

BALLIO And you think you can go just anywhere to cook and not pull those claws in while you're cooking? (*Turning to his slave boy*) Now listen, you, you're on my side, so I'm giving you orders right now to get everything that belongs to us out of sight in a hurry. And after that you keep your eyes on (*gesturing toward the cook*) his. Wherever he looks, you look too. If he takes a step in any direction, you take a step in the same direction. If he reaches a hand in any direction, you reach a hand in the same direction. If he takes hold of anything that's his, you let him. If he takes hold of anything that's ours, you take hold of the other end. If he moves, you move. If he stands, you stand. If he squats, you squat. (*Looking down the line of the cook's assistants*) And I'm appointing personal watchmen for these assistants of his too.

COOK (*soothingly*) Now you just stop worrying.

BALLIO I ask you, just show me how I can stop worrying when I'm bringing *you* into my house?

COOK (*heartily*) Because I'll make a concoction for you today that'll do for you what Medea did for Pelias when she cooked the old fellow up. They say that by using her poisonous potions she turned the old fellow back into a young one. Well, I'll do the same for you.

BALLIO So you poison people, do you?

COOK No sir. On the contrary, I cure them.

BALLIO Look here, how much will you charge to teach me that one recipe?

COOK Which?

BALLIO The one that'll cure me from your stealing.

COOK (*promptly*) If you trust me, ten dollars; if you don't, even five hundred's not enough. (*Thinking for a moment*) This dinner you're giving, is it for friends or enemies?

BALLIO My god! For my friends, of course.

COOK (*enthusiastically*) Why don't you invite your enemies instead? I'll do your diners such a dinner, make such deliciously delicious dishes, that, as soon as they pick up something and taste it, they'll chomp off their fingers in the process.

BALLIO Please do me a favor, will you? Before you serve anything to any of my guests, you first take a taste and let your assistants taste too—so all of you can chomp off those thieving hands of yours.

COOK (*innocently*) Maybe you don't believe what I'm telling you?

BALLIO (*impatiently*) Now don't be a nuisance, please! I've had enough of your cackling. Shut up! (*Gesturing toward his house*) Look, there's where I live. Go on in and cook dinner. And get a move on!

(*The cook stalks in, Ballio's slave boy scampers in in his wake, and the line of assistants follows. The last boy in line turns and calls out to Ballio.*)

ASSISTANT (*like a butler making an announcement*) Kindly take your place at the table and call your guests. Dinner's now being—spoiled! (*Disappears into the house.*)

BALLIO (*to the audience*) Look at that, will you! What a breed! (*Gesturing toward the boy who has just gone in*) That Chief Dishlicker there is already a full-fledged good-for-nothing. (*Shaking his head*) I honestly don't know which to keep an eye on first: I've got thieves inside my house and (*gesturing toward Pseudolus' house*) a bandit next door. You see, just a few minutes ago while downtown, my neighbor here, Calidorus' father, warned me over and over to watch out for his servant Pseudolus, not to trust him. Says Pseudolus is out to pull a fast one and get the girl away from me if he can. Claims Pseudolus swore up and down that he was going to sneak Rosy away from me. I'll go in now and warn the household that none of them is to trust that Pseudolus one bit.

(Ballio enters his house, and the stage is now empty.)

ACT IV

(Enter Pseudolus, stage left, walking on air.)

SONG

PSEUDOLUS *(as if to Monkey who he assumes is at his heels)*
If Fate has ever felt an urge to help a mortal out,
She feels it now for the boy and me, of that I have no doubt:
If she's produced an assistant like you, with brains and education,
Then she wants to see the saving of us, and the pimp's extermination.

(Turns to face Monkey—and discovers there is no Monkey to face.)

Where is he? I'm talking to myself
  Like someone not all there!
By god, he's put one over on me
  And left me flat, I'll swear.
For one crook dealing with another,
  I've been caught off guard for fair.

If Monk's made off, my goose is cooked. The job I wanted done
I'll never be able to do today. But wait, I see someone—
There he is. He's coming now, our answer to a hangman's prayer.
And look at the way he steps along. Quite a strut our boy has there!

(Enter Monkey, resplendent in a uniform somewhat like Harpax's, and swaggering along as magnificently as a major general.)

PSEUDOLUS *(calling to him, petulantly)*
  Hey, I've been looking all over for you,
    Damned scared you'd run out on me.

MONKEY (*haughtily*)

> And if I'd been acting the way that I should
> I damned well would, I agree.

PSEUDOLUS (*as before*)

> Well, where did you stop?

MONKEY (*coolly*)

> Where I wanted to be.

PSEUDOLUS (*peevishly*)

> I know that.

MONKEY (*shrugging*)

> You do? Then why ask me?

PSEUDOLUS (*hastily changing the subject*)

> I wanted to give you this warning to—

MONKEY (*interrupting*)

> Don't you warn me, I'm warning *you!*

PSEUDOLUS (*resentfully*)

> Now you look here. You're treating me
> Like dirt, and I don't like it, see?

MONKEY (*ostentatiously adjusting his hat and sword, distastefully*)

> A holder of the *croix de guerre*
> Be nice to you? I wouldn't dare!

PSEUDOLUS (*throwing a worried look at Ballio's door*)

> We've started something, and now I'd like
> To do the job.

MONKEY (*drawing his sword and trying a few practice thrusts*)

> For the love of Mike,
> Just what do you think I'm doing, eh?

PSEUDOLUS (*as before*)

> Then shake a leg. Don't take all day!

MONKEY (*ambling along with maddening slowness*)

> I do things in a leisurely way.

PSEUDOLUS (*urgently, gesturing toward Ballio's house*)

> Here's our chance! While our soldier boy snores,
> I want *you* to be first through those doors.

MONKEY (*lazily*)

> What's your hurry?
> Take it easy, don't worry.
> The good lord can let
> That soldier be set
> On *this* same spot, right here with me.
> Whatever's the name
> Of this fellow who came,
> I'll make a better Snatcher than he!
> So don't worry, I'll see
> That it's done, one two three.
> I'll bamboozle him so,
> With my lying, I'll throw
> Such a scare in our foe
> He'll deny that he really is he
> And declare that he really is me!

PSEUDOLUS (*doubtfully*)

> Yes, but how?

MONKEY (*working himself up*)

> All these questions I get!
> Oh, you *will* be the death of me yet!

PSEUDOLUS (*sweetly*)

> You're so gracious and charming, my pet.

MONKEY (*snarling*)

> Now there's something I'd like you to know:
> I admit you're my boss in this show,
> But in cheating and double-cross you
> Can't come close to the things I can do.

PSEUDOLUS (*all innocent gratitude*)

> Oh, god bless you! For my sake.

MONKEY (*with gracious condescension*)

> No, *mine.*

(*Squaring his shoulders and straightening his uniform*)

> Look me over now, please. Does the line
> Of this uniform suit me this way?

PSEUDOLUS (*enthusiastically*)

> Oh, it's perfect, it's great!

MONKEY (*condescendingly*)

> > Then okay.

PSEUDOLUS (*humbly*)

> May god in heaven hear your prayers and grant them all, my hero—
>
> For if he listens to mine instead, he'll grant your worth, and that's zero.

(*To the audience, gesturing toward Monkey*)

> The lowest, sneakiest good-for-nothing I ever laid eyes upon.

MONKEY (*menacingly*)

> You'd say a thing like that to me?

PSEUDOLUS (*swiftly switching back to humility*)

> > My lips are sealed from now on.

(*Clamps his lips shut—and manages to stay that way for five full seconds at least; then, bursting out—*)

> You do a careful job for me and what gifts you'll get!

MONKEY (*snarling*)

> > Shut up!
>
> Remind a man who remembers things, and you'll make the man forget
>
> The things he has to remember. I've got it all by heart, it's set

(*Tapping his head*)

> In here. My tricks are all worked out—and worked out trickily.

PSEUDOLUS (*to the audience, admiringly*)

> This man is good.

MONKEY (*to the audience, gesturing toward Pseudolus*)

> > And this one's not—and the same is true for me.

PSEUDOLUS (*worriedly*)

> Now watch your step.

MONKEY

            Oh, shut your mouth.

PSEUDOLUS

                        I swear, so help me god—

MONKEY (*interrupting witheringly*)

  Help you? Not he! You're set to spout the lies and spout
    them hard!

PSEUDOLUS (*unruffled*)

  —by my love and fear and vast respect for your consum-
    mate treachery—

MONKEY (*as before*)

  I teach that sort of thing to others. *You* can't soft-soap *me*.

PSEUDOLUS (*as before*)

  —you pull this job successfully, and I'll see you have things
    nice—

MONKEY

  Some joke!

PSEUDOLUS (*gathering momentum*)

  —nice wine, hors d'oeuvres and food, a regular paradise,
  Plus a nice little girl to make things nice with kiss upon
    kiss upon kiss.

MONKEY (*acidly*)

  You're too nice to me.

PSEUDOLUS (*rising to a climax*)

            You pull this job, and the word you'll use is bliss!

(*Monkey stares at him for a full ten seconds, deadpan and
without batting an eyelash. Suddenly he breaks into a broad
grin and slaps him resoundingly on the back.*)

MONKEY (*enthusiastically*)

            If *I* don't do
            This job for you,
            Tell the torturer to
            Give me rack and screw!

(*Monkey sets his hat firmly on his head, adjusts his sword
and, girded for action, turns to Pseudolus.*)

MONKEY (*all business*) All right, hurry and show me where I enter the jaws of the pimp's house.

PSEUDOLUS (*pointing*) The third this way.

(*The "jaws" suddenly open, and Ballio appears on the threshold.*)

MONKEY Shh! They've opened wide.

PSEUDOLUS If you ask me, the house has a bellyache.

MONKEY Why?

PSEUDOLUS It's throwing up the pimp.

MONKEY Is that the fellow?

PSEUDOLUS That's the fellow.

MONKEY (*distastefully*) Rotten piece of merchandise, that.

PSEUDOLUS (*as Ballio sidles out the door*) Look, will you? He walks sideways, not frontwards. Like a crab!

(*Pseudolus and Monkey move off to the side where they can overhear without being seen. Ballio sidles downstage and addresses the audience.*)

BALLIO He wasn't as bad as I thought, that cook I hired. All he's made off with so far is a cup and a jug.

PSEUDOLUS (*to Monkey, sotto voce*) Hey! Now's our chance!

MONKEY (*to Pseudolus, sotto voce*) My feelings exactly.

PSEUDOLUS (*to Monkey, sotto voce*) On your way and play it smart. I'll stay here in ambush.

(*Monkey steps into the street while Ballio's back is turned, and walks slowly along, acting as if he is looking for some house.*)

MONKEY (*to himself—but good and loud*) I kept count carefully: this is the sixth street from the town gate, and this is where he told me to turn in. But how many houses he said, I can't for the life of me remember.

BALLIO (*swiveling about at the sound of a voice, to himself*) Who's this fellow in uniform? Where does he come from?

Who's he looking for? Looks like a stranger; I don't recognize the face.

MONKEY (*turning and assuming an expression of pleased surprise at seeing Ballio; to the world at large*)   Well, here's someone who certainly can relieve my uncertainty.

BALLIO (*to himself*)   He's heading straight for me. Now where in the world could he be from?

MONKEY (*like a top sergeant*)   Hey, you standing there, you with the beard like a billy goat, I have a question for you.

BALLIO (*snappishly*)   Just like that, eh, without even a "Good afternoon"?

MONKEY   Anything good I don't give away.

BALLIO (*snarling*)   Then, damn it all, the same goes for me!

PSEUDOLUS (*aside, shaking his head despairingly*)   Doing just great, right from the start!

MONKEY   Know anybody who lives in this street? (*As Ballio remains stubbornly silent*) How about it, you?

BALLIO (*sullenly*)   Me? Sure, myself.

MONKEY   Aren't many who can say that. Downtown there isn't one in ten who really knows himself.

PSEUDOLUS (*aside, sarcastically*)   I'm safe—now he's become a philosopher!

MONKEY   I'm looking for someone around here—a nasty, filthy, low-down, lawbreaking liar.

BALLIO (*aside, promptly*)   He's looking for me. Those are all my titles. Now, if he'd only mention the name—(*To Monkey*) What's the fellow's name?

MONKEY   Ballio. A pimp.

BALLIO (*aside*)   I knew it! (*To Monkey, tapping himself on the chest*) Mister, the man you're looking for is right here.

MONKEY (*incredulously*)   You're Ballio?

BALLIO   Sure I'm Ballio.

MONKEY (*eying the unappetizing get-up*)   From the clothes I'd say you're a pickpocket.

BALLIO (*promptly*) So when *you* hold me up some dark night, you won't bother to put your thieving hands on them.

MONKEY (*getting down to business*) My master wants me to give you his best regards. (*Taking out the letter*) Here, take this letter; I have orders to give it to you.

BALLIO Orders from whom?

PSEUDOLUS (*aside, clutching his hair*) I'm a goner! My man's in a jam—he doesn't know the name! We're stuck!

BALLIO (*noticing Monkey hesitate, sharply*) Who do you say sent this to me?

MONKEY (*in his best top sergeant's manner, pointing to the seal*) Identify that picture, and then *you* tell me his name. I want to make sure you're really Ballio.

BALLIO Give me the letter.

MONKEY (*handing it over*) Here. Now identify the seal.

BALLIO (*taking a quick look, to himself*) Major I. Kutall Hedzoff to the life. I recognize him. (*To Monkey*) Hey, his name is I. Kutall Hedzoff.

MONKEY (*dryly*) Well, now that you've told me his name is I. Kutall Hedzoff, I know I gave the letter to the right man.

BALLIO What's he doing these days, anyway?

MONKEY (*striking a military pose*) What any brave, honest soldier does, by god! (*Relaxing*) Now get a move on and read the letter through—that's first on the docket—then take the money and deliver the girl, and make it snappy. Because if I'm not in Sicyon by today, I'm in my coffin by tomorrow. That's the way the major operates.

BALLIO (*nodding understandingly*) Don't I know! You're talking to someone who knows him.

MONKEY (*curtly*) Then get a move on and read the letter.

BALLIO Just keep quiet and I will. (*Opens the letter and starts reading*) "Letter of Major I. Kutall Hedzoff to Pimp Ballio sealed with picture as provided by previous mutual agreement."

MONKEY (*pointing*)   It's the seal on the letter.

BALLIO   I see it, I recognize it. But does he always write letters this way? With no salutation?

MONKEY (*sternly*)   Standard military procedure, Ballio. They send greetings to friends (*saluting*) with the hand—and (*going through the motions of a saber cut*) destruction to enemies with ditto. But keep on with the reading. Go ahead, find out what the letter says.

BALLIO   Then listen. (*Reading*) "This is my orderly Harpax who has come to you—" (*Looking up*) Are you Harpax?

MONKEY   That's me—the Snatcher in the flesh.

BALLIO (*resuming his reading*)   "—and who is delivering this letter. I want you to accept payment of the money from him and at the same time send the girl off with him. Deserving people deserve a letter with a salutation. If I thought you were deserving, I'd have sent one."

MONKEY (*as Ballio looks up*)   What do we do now?

BALLIO (*promptly*)   You hand over the money and take the girl.

MONKEY (*impatiently*)   Well, who's holding up who?

BALLIO (*going toward his door*)   Follow me in, then.

MONKEY   I'm following.

(*The two go into Ballio's house. The minute the door closes behind them, Pseudolus bursts out of his hiding place.*)

PSEUDOLUS (*to the audience, excitedly*)   I swear to god, never in all my life have I seen a dirty rat as fiendishly clever as that fellow! I'm afraid of him. I'm really scared of him. He might pull the same sort of dirty trick on me he pulled (*gesturing toward Ballio's house*) on him. With things going so well, he might lower his horns and charge *me*, if he ever gets the chance to do me dirt. And that's something I would not like—because (*smiling*) I like the guy!

(*Shaking his head despairingly*) Right now I've got three good reasons to be scared stiff. First of all, I'm scared that

that colleague of mine will desert me and defect to the enemy. Next, I'm scared that Simo will be back any minute from downtown: we'll capture the loot, and *he'll* capture the looters. And, along with all these scares, I'm scared (*gesturing in the direction of the town gate*) that *that* Harpax will get here before *this* Harpax gets out of here with the girl.

(*Staring intently at the door*) This is killing me! They're taking so long to come out! My heart's all ready with its bags packed: if he doesn't come out of there with the girl, it's saying good-by to my chest and taking off for good. (*The door opens and Monkey and Rosy step out.*) I win! My guards were all on their guard, and I beat them all!

(*Monkey walks from the door dragging a reluctant Rosy who is dissolved in tears.*)

MONKEY (*earnestly*) Please don't cry, Rosy. You don't understand what's happening. I promise you, you'll find out very soon, at the party. I'm not taking you to that snaggle-toothed monster of a major from Macedon, who's making you cry this way. I'm taking you to the one man you want to belong to most of all. I promise you, in a little while you'll be giving Calidorus a big hug.

PSEUDOLUS (*frantically*) What were you hanging around inside there for? My heart's been pounding in my chest so long, it's all bruised!

MONKEY (*angrily*) Damn you, a fine time you pick to cross-examine me, in the middle of an enemy ambush! Out of here on the double!

PSEUDOLUS (*swiveling about*) You're a good-for-nothing but, so help me, you have good ideas. (*Shouting*) Hip, hip, hooray! Forward march! Straight for that jug, men!

(*They dash off, stage left, dragging the bewildered Rosy after them. A second later the door of Ballio's house opens, and Ballio sidles out. He looks positively gay for a change.*)

BALLIO (*to the audience*)   Whew! My mind's finally at rest, now that that fellow's gone and taken the girl away. Now let that dirty rat of a Pseudolus come and try to sneak her away from me! There's one thing I know for sure: I'd sooner commit perjury under oath a thousand times than have him pull a fast one and get the laugh on me. Now I'll have the laugh on him, if I ever meet him. You ask me, though, the only thing he'll be meeting is his deserts—on a mill wheel. I wish Simo would come along so he could enjoy some of my joy.

(*At this point Simo conveniently enters, stage left.*)

SIMO (*to himself*)   I've come to see what that Ulysses of mine has accomplished. Whether he's stolen the statue from Fort Ballio yet.[2]

BALLIO (*heartily*)   Hey, lucky fellow, let me shake that lucky hand.

SIMO (*taken aback by the strange phenomenon of a genial Ballio*)   What's the matter?

BALLIO (*deliberately*)   There is no longer—

SIMO (*impatiently*)   No longer what?

BALLIO   —anything for you to be afraid of.

SIMO   What's happened? Has he been to your house?

BALLIO (*smiling beatifically*)   Nope.

SIMO (*sourly*)   Then what's happened that's so good?

BALLIO (*as before*)   That five thousand Pseudolus solemnly swore he'd get out of you today is safe and sound.

SIMO (*fervently*)   God, do I wish it!

BALLIO (*cockily*)   If he gets his hands on that girl today or gives her to your son today, the way he said he would, you get the five thousand from *me*. Do me a favor: let's make it official. I'm dying to do it that way just to prove that

[2] Ulysses in the *Iliad* stole the sacred statue of Athena from the citadel of Troy.

there's absolutely no chance for a slip-up anywhere. I'll even throw in the girl as a gift, too.

SIMO (*shrugging*) I can't see a thing I've got to lose by taking you up. All right—do you hereby agree to give me five thousand dollars on those terms?

BALLIO (*airily*) I hereby agree.

SIMO (*finally convinced, rubbing his hands delightedly*) Well, this isn't a bad turn of affairs at all. Did you run into him?

BALLIO Into the both of them, as a matter of fact.

SIMO (*eagerly*) What did he say? What did he tell you? What kind of story did he give you?

BALLIO (*shrugging*) The nonsense you hear on the stage. The stuff they always say about pimps in comedies, stuff any schoolboy knows by heart. He told me I was a dirty, filthy double-crosser.

SIMO Believe me, he wasn't lying.

BALLIO (*grinning*) I wasn't the least bit sore. What difference do insults make to a fellow who doesn't give a damn or bother to deny them?

SIMO But why don't I have to be afraid of him? That's what I want to hear.

BALLIO (*gleefully*) Because he'll never get the girl away from me. He can't! Remember I told you a little while ago that I had sold her to a major from Macedon?

SIMO Yes.

BALLIO (*deliberately drawing his story out*) Well, his orderly brought me the money plus a sealed letter with identification—

SIMO (*impatiently*) Yes, yes.

BALLIO (*not to be hurried*) —which he and I had agreed on between us. (*Triumphantly*) Well, just a few minutes ago, the orderly took the girl away with him!

SIMO (*excitedly*) Is this the truth you're telling me? On your honor?

BALLIO (*grinning*)   Where would *I* get any honor?

SIMO (*doubtfully*)   Just watch out that he hasn't pulled some fancy stunt on you.

BALLIO (*cockily*)   The letter and the picture make me absolutely certain. I tell you, he just left the city with her. He's headed for Sicyon.

SIMO (*jubilantly*)   Well done, by god! Why don't I have Pseudolus put his name down for immigration to Treadmill Town this minute? (*His attention caught, looks toward the wings, stage right.*) Who's this fellow in uniform?

BALLIO (*following Simo's gaze*)   I don't know. Let's watch where he goes and what he does.

(*Enter Harpax looking a bit worried. He walks downstage and addresses the audience.*)

SONG

HARPAX

The servant who doesn't give a damn for the orders a master's issued
>   Is a dirty good-for-nothing, that's a fact.
And *I* don't give a damn for the kind whose memory's so short
>   They need a second warning before they'll act.

>>   And those who think they're emancipated
>>   The minute they find themselves located
>>   Out of the master's sight, and drink and whore
>>   And go through every cent they've saved and more,
>>   Will bear the name of slave
>>   To the grave.
>>   There's nothing good in them—unless you add
>>   The knack to stay alive by being bad.

Now *I* won't mix or be seen with this ilk; I cut them dead on the spot.
When *I* get orders, and the master's away, I act as if he's not.

It's when he's gone I start to fear—
In order not to when he's near.

(*Holds up the purse and continues more agitatedly.*)

Here's a job that I'd better begin.
Up till now I've been out at the inn,
Where that Syrus—the fellow that I
Gave the documents to—let me lie.
There I stayed, since he told me to stay:
He'd come back and he'd fetch me away,
So he said, when the pimp had come home.
When he didn't show up, on my own
I came here to find out what the matter could be,
And not give him a chance to get funny with me!

(*Walking up to the pimp's door*)

The best I can do is knock right here and find someone
who's free;
I want the pimp to take this cash, and send the girl with me.

BALLIO (*to Simo sotto voce, his eyes glistening*)

Hey, Simo!

SIMO (*sotto voce*)
                        What?

BALLIO (*as before*)
                                He's mine!

SIMO
                                        How's that?

BALLIO (*smacking his lips*)
                                        Because this man's my meat.
He wants a wench, he's got the cash—I'm dying to start to
eat!

SIMO (*incredulously*)

You'll eat him up this minute?

BALLIO (*as before*)
                                Fresh and hot and nicely brown
And served you on a platter thus, that's the time to gulp
them down.

(*Flashing his hyena grin*)

All decent people let me starve, but the sinners don't, you
see;

The solid citizen slaves for the state—and the sinner slaves
for me!

SIMO (*disgusted*)

You're such a rat, when the good lord acts, what tortures
he'll decree!

HARPAX (*to himself*)   I'm wasting time. I'll knock on the
door this minute and find out whether Ballio's in or not.

BALLIO (*to Simo, sotto voce, gleefully*)   These blessings come
to me from Lady Love. She brings them here, these people
who run away from profit to chase after loss by spending
their lives having a good time. They eat, they drink, they
whore, (*eying Simo distastefully*) they have different ideas
from the likes of you, who won't let yourself have a good
time and begrudge those who do.

HARPAX (*banging on the door and shouting*)   Hey, where is
everybody?

BALLIO (*to Simo, sotto voce, rubbing his hands*)   The fellow's coming straight at me by the straightest route.

HARPAX (*shouting even louder*)   Hey, where are you people?

BALLIO (*calling to Harpax*)   Hey, mister, someone in there
owe you money? (*To Simo, sotto voce*) I'll get a good haul
out of him. I can tell: this is my lucky day.

HARPAX (*not hearing, despairingly*)   Isn't anyone going to
open this door?

BALLIO (*calling louder*)   Hey, soldier, someone in there owe
you money?

HARPAX (*finally looking up and seeing the two of them*)   I'm
looking for the master of the house. Ballio, the pimp.

BALLIO   Mister, you can cut your looking short, whoever you
are.

HARPAX   Why?

BALLIO Because you are personally in the flesh looking at him personally in the flesh.

HARPAX *(pointing to Simo)*   You're Ballio?

SIMO *(visibly shuddering and shaking his stick)* Soldier, you watch your step or you'll be in trouble from this stick. Point that finger at *him;* he's your pimp.

BALLIO *(to Harpax, with a contemptuous gesture in Simo's direction)* Oh yes, *he's* an honest man. *(To Simo, sneering)* And you, my honest man, every time you go downtown you get plenty of dunning from your creditors since you don't have a cent outside of what said pimp helps you out with.

HARPAX *(impatiently)*   Would you mind talking to *me?*

BALLIO *(leaving Simo's side and walking up to Harpax)*   I am. What's on your mind?

HARPAX *(holding out the purse)*   Take this money.

BALLIO *(whipping his hand out)*   I've had my hand out for hours ready for you to hand over.

HARPAX *(handing it over)*   Take it: exactly one thousand dollars, every coin full weight. Major I. Kutall Hedzoff, my master, gave me orders to deliver it—it's the balance he owes—and take Rosy away with me.

BALLIO *(studying him closely)*   Your master?

HARPAX   That's right.

BALLIO   A major?

HARPAX   That's correct.

BALLIO   From Macedon maybe?

HARPAX   Exactly.

BALLIO   I. Kutall Hedzoff sent you to me, eh?

HARPAX   Precisely.

BALLIO   To give me this money?

HARPAX   If you're Ballio the pimp.

BALLIO   And to take the girl away with you?

HARPAX   Right.

BALLIO   Rosy he said her name was?

HARPAX   You've got a good memory.

BALLIO   Wait a second. I'll be right back. (*Turns and rushes over to Simo.*)

HARPAX   (*calling after him*)   But hurry, because *I'm* in a hurry. You can see for yourself how late it is.

BALLIO   (*calling back*)   I see, all right. I want to consult with this man here. You just wait there. I'll be right with you. (*To Simo, sotto voce, gleefully*) What's next, Simo? What do we do now? This fellow who's brought the money—I've caught him in the act!

SIMO   (*sotto voce, blankly*)   What do you mean?

BALLIO   (*sotto voce, chuckling*)   Don't you know what this is all about?

SIMO   (*as before*)   I haven't the slightest idea.

BALLIO   (*sotto voce, triumphantly*)   That Pseudolus of yours has sent this fellow to make believe he's from the major!

(*Ballio grins delightedly. An answering grin gradually spreads over Simo's face as the import sinks in. They continue talking, sotto voce.*)

SIMO   (*his eyes gleaming*)   Did you get the money from him?

BALLIO   (*hefting the purse*)   Do you have to ask? Can't you see?

SIMO   (*quickly*)   Just remember to hand over half of that loot to me. It's only right we share it.

BALLIO   (*his grin widening*)   Why the hell not? It all comes from you!

HARPAX   (*calling impatiently*)   When are you going to take care of me?

BALLIO   (*calling back, meaningfully*)   I am right now! (*To Simo*) What do you suggest I do now?

SIMO   (*excitedly*)   Let's have some fun with our spy, the faker! And let's keep it up till he catches on we're making fun of him.

BALLIO Let's go. (*The two walk up together to Harpax.*) So you're the major's orderly, eh?

HARPAX Of course.

BALLIO (*sneering*) How much did you cost him?

HARPAX (*drawing himself up*) Every ounce of strength he had, to win me in battle. I'll have you know I was commander in chief of the armed forces back in my homeland.

BALLIO (*as before*) Your homeland? When did the major ever capture a jail?

HARPAX (*sharply*) You pass any nasty cracks and you'll hear some yourself.

BALLIO How long did it take you to get here from Sicyon?

HARPAX Day and a half.

BALLIO Pretty fast traveling, that.

SIMO (*To Ballio*) Oh this fellow's quick, all right. One look at those legs and you can see they're just the kind for— carrying shackles, extra-heavy shackles.

BALLIO (*to Harpax*) Tell me, when you were a boy, did you used to (*leering*) play around with girls?

SIMO (*to Ballio, eying Harpax distastefully*) Of course he did.

BALLIO (*to Harpax*) And did you used to—(*leering*) you know what I'm going to say?

SIMO (*to Ballio, with alacrity*) Of course he did.

HARPAX (*looking from one to the other blankly*) Are you two in your right mind?

BALLIO Answer me this. When the major stood watch at night and you used to go along with him, (*making an obscene gesture*) did his sword fit in your scabbard?

HARPAX (*losing his temper*) You go to the devil!

BALLIO (*unruffled*) You can go there yourself. Today. Very soon today.

HARPAX (*grimly*) Are you going to give me the girl? If not, hand back the money. (*Reaches for the purse.*)

BALLIO (*quickly putting it behind his back*)   Wait a second.

HARPAX   Why should I?

BALLIO (*mockingly*)   Tell me, how much did it cost to hire that uniform?

HARPAX   What are you talking about?

SIMO (*to Harpax*)   And how much for the sword?

HARPAX (*to himself*)   These fellows need a dose of helle-bore![3]

BALLIO (*to Harpax, reaching for his cap*)   Hey—

HARPAX (*pulling back*)   Hands off!

BALLIO (*to Harpax*)   —how much is that headpiece earning for its owner?

HARPAX (*bewildered*)   What do you mean, owner? What are you two dreaming about? Everything I'm wearing belongs to me, bought with my own money.

BALLIO (*leering*)   Sure—earned by the sweat of your thighs.

HARPAX (*to himself, grimly, as he girds for action*)   This pair has had the steam bath. Now what they're asking for is a good old-fashioned massage.

BALLIO (*promptly backing away, and changing his tune*)   In all seriousness now, I ask you: how much are you getting out of this? What's the pittance Pseudolus is paying you?

HARPAX (*blankly*)   Pseudolus? Who's Pseudolus?

BALLIO   Your trainer, the fellow who coached you in this swindle so you could swindle the girl away from me.

HARPAX (*as before*)   What Pseudolus? What's this swindle you're talking about? I don't know the man, never saw hide nor hair of him.

BALLIO (*wearily*)   Why don't you just be on your way. There's no pickings for any crooks around here today. You tell Pseudolus that someone else made off with the loot, that Harpax beat him to it.

HARPAX (*angrily*)   God damn it, *I'm* Harpax!

---

[3] The standard ancient remedy for mental illness.

BALLIO (*sneering*) God damn it, you mean you wish you were! (*To Simo*) This man's a crook, plain as the nose on your face.

HARPAX (*heatedly*) Listen, I just now gave you the money and a little while ago, the minute I arrived, right in front of this door I handed your servant the identification, the letter sealed with the major's picture.

BALLIO (*taken aback*) You handed a letter to my servant? What servant?

HARPAX Syrus.

BALLIO (*to Simo, nervously*) He lacks confidence. Not very good at being a crook, this fellow here: hasn't even thought up a good story. Damn that good-for-nothing Pseudolus! He sure figured out a smart stunt: he gave this fellow the exact amount of money the major owed and dressed him all up so he could do me out of the girl. (*With great assurance—as if to convince himself*) As a matter of fact, this letter he's talking about was delivered to me by the real Harpax himself.

HARPAX (*frantically*) *I'm* Harpax! *I'm* the major's orderly! I'm not trying any tricks or pulling any swindles! I haven't the faintest idea who that Pseudolus of yours is, I never heard of him in my life!

(*There is a dead silence as Ballio and Simo stare at each other.*)

SIMO (*slowly and emphatically*) Pimp, unless I am very much mistaken, you are out one girl.

BALLIO (*nodding gloomily*) Damn it all, the more I hear, the more I'm afraid of just that. Damn it all, I got cold shivers a second ago from that there Syrus who took this fellow's identification. I wouldn't be at all surprised if it was Pseudolus. (*To Harpax*) Listen, that fellow you gave the identification to before, what did he look like?

HARPAX Red hair, pot belly, piano legs, big head, pointy eyes, darkish skin, red face, and whopping big feet.

BALLIO (*groaning*) The minute you mentioned those feet,

you did for me! It was Pseudolus, all right. (*To Simo*)
Simo, it's all over with me. I'm a dead man!

HARPAX (*promptly*)   I'm not letting you do any dying until
I get my money back—five thousand dollars.

SIMO (*blandly*)   And another five thousand for me.

BALLIO (*reproachfully*)   You mean you'd actually take a
bonus like that from me when I promised it just for a joke?

SIMO (*archly*)   It's a man's duty to take bonuses—or booty—
from crooks.

BALLIO (*between his teeth*)   At least hand Pseudolus over
to me.

SIMO (*shrugging*)   I hand Pseudolus over to you? What
crime did he commit? Didn't I tell you a thousand times to
watch out for him?

BALLIO (*desperately*)   He's killed me!

SIMO   And hit me for a forfeit of a measly five thousand.

BALLIO (*as before*)   What do I do now?

HARPAX   Pay me back my money, and you can go hang
yourself.

BALLIO (*to Harpax*)   Damn your hide! (*Turns and starts
walking off, stage left.*) All right, follow me downtown and
I'll settle up.

HARPAX (*falling in behind with alacrity*)   I'm following.

SIMO (*calling after him*)   What about me?

BALLIO (*stopping*)   Aliens today, citizens tomorrow. (*To the
audience*) Pseudolus practically held a session of the Supreme Court and got a death sentence against me when he
sent that fellow today to sneak off my girl. (*To Harpax*)
Follow me, you. (*To the audience, gesturing toward the
street*) Don't think I'm coming back by this street here.
The way things have worked out, I've decided to use the
back alleys.

HARPAX (*impatiently*)   If you did as much walking as talking, you'd be downtown by now.

BALLIO (*starting to trudge off, forlornly*)   I've decided to change today from my birthday to my deathday. (*He exits, stage left, with Harpax at his heels.*)

SIMO (*to the audience*) I made a monkey out of him for fair—and my servant made a monkey out of his worst enemy for fair.

(*After a moment's thought*) I've decided not to spring on Pseudolus what they always do in comedies. No whips, no canes. I'm going in now to get the five thousand I promised him if he pulled off this stunt. I'll hand it over to him without waiting to be dunned. (*Shaking his head admiringly*) There's a fellow who's really smart, really tricky, a real scoundrel. He did better than Ulysses and the Trojan Horse, that Pseudolus. I'll go in now, bring out the money, and spring my surprise on him.

(*Simo enters his house, and the stage is now empty.*)

ACT V

(*Enter Pseudolus, stage left. He has just left a wild party at Charinus' house—and looks it: he has a chaplet askew on his head, is grinning drunkenly from ear to ear, and is staggering along, combating, with not too much success, a certain rubberiness in shanks and feet.*)

SONG

PSEUDOLUS

> What's goin' on? What a way to act!
> Hey, feet, will *you* stand up or not?
> You want to leave me lying here
> Till someone heaves me from the spot?
> If *I* go into a somersault,
> Believe you me, it's all your fault!

(*Makes a wild lurch*)

> Insist on keeping at it, eh?
> I'll have to tell you off today!

(*Finally makes the center of the stage and stands there weaving*)

> 'At's the trouble with wine. Always wrestles unfair;
> First thing in the ring, has your feet in the air.

(*Grins blissfully*)

> I'm as drunk as a lord, I'm loaded, I'm high!
> What with elegance fit for the gods in the sky,
>   And the choicest of foods for us all,
> And a spot just as gala as a room for a ball,
>   Boy, oh boy, did *we* have a ball!

(*With drunken gravity*)

> Now, why should I beat about the bush?
>   This is why we stay alive,
>   This is where all pleasure lies,
>   This is where all joys derive—
>   And *my* view is—it's paradise!

(*Rapturously*)

When a man takes a girl in his arms,
When he presses his mouth against hers,
When the two, without trying to hide,
Hold on fast, tongue on tongue—neither stirs,
When her bosom is pressed to his breast,
Or their bodies, if they choose, become one—
Ah, that's when the time is the best
To take from a dainty white hand
A full glass, and to drink—it's just grand!
It's the time when we're all out for fun,
And the feelings are good all around,
And the talk isn't just empty sound . . .

(*Working himself up*)

Let's not spare the bouquets or perfume!
Or the stuff for the looks of the room!
And the cooking and all of the rest—
No need asking: only the best!

(*Breaks off and smiles blissfully. Then continues a little more matter-of-factly.*)

That's how we spent the rest of the day,
The boy and I; we were *gai, très gai*,
When once I'd done my job as planned
And driven off the enemy band.

(*Gesturing drunkenly toward the wings, stage left*)

I left them gorging, guzzling, whoring,
(Left my own girl too), all getting roaring
Drunk and happy. When I stood up,
They asked me please to do a dance.

(*Lumbering through a few weird steps*)

I gave them this, performed, of course,
With all my usual elegance.
The steps I did were the very best kinds—
I've had lessons, you know, in bumps and grinds.

(*More lumbering*)

> Then I put on my coat and gave them one
> That goes like this—but just for fun.
> They stamped, they clapped, they yelled "en-
>   core,"
> And called me back to give them more.

(*Still lumbering*)

> I start again and give them this,
> (Didn't want to do the same thing twice)
> I play it up to the girl I'm with,
> (Make sure that later she'd treat me nice)
> I whirl, I skid—and down I go,
> And that was the swan song for my show.
>
> So then I try to get on my feet,
>   And—whoops—all over my coat!
> I hand them a laugh with that—and get
>   The jug as antidote.
> I take a drink, I change my coat,
>   I leave the old one there,
> I come out here to clear my head
>   By getting a breath of air.

(*Lurching up to Simo's door*)

I've left the son to see the father, and put a word in his ear
About our deal.

(*Shouting*)

> Open up! Tell Simo, Pseudolus is here!

(*He pounds like a madman, then lurches a few feet away. A second later the door opens, and Simo appears clutching a purse.*)

SIMO (*as he comes out*)

It's the voice of that scoundrel that's brought me out here.

(*Catching sight of Pseudolus advancing boozily*)

But what's *this* that I see? And how come? Very queer!

PSEUDOLUS (*affably*)

    It's your Pseudolus, fresh from a party—and tight.

SIMO

    From loose living, by god. Look at that! What a sight!
    That your master's right here doesn't scare you one bit.

    (*To himself*)

    What's this call for? Sweet reason or throwing a fit?

    (*Caressing the purse, ruefully*)

    Ah, but *this* which I'm holding rules out being rough,

    (*Gesturing contemptuously toward Pseudolus*)

    If I have any hopes out of *that* for this stuff.

PSEUDOLUS (*in the grand manner*)

    Common sinner comes calling on saint nonpareil.

SIMO (*grimly managing a smile and going up to him*)

    Hearty greetings, dear Pseudolus—

    (*As Pseudolus belches resoundingly*)

                    you go to hell!

PSEUDOLUS (*trying hard to keep his balance, as Simo gives him a shove.*)

    Hey, what's that for?

SIMO (*snarling*)

                Just what do you mean, you disgrace,
    By belching your drunken breath in my face?

PSEUDOLUS (*grabbing him for support, reproachfully*)

    Take it easy! Hey, hold me and spare me more spills—
    Can't you see that I'm tight? I'm soused to the gills!

SIMO (*holding him up, grimly*)

    You sure have a nerve going around in this way—
    As drunk as a lord in the broad light of day!

PSEUDOLUS (*grinning fatuously*)

    I just felt I'd like doing it.

SIMO (*as before*)

               Felt like it, eh?

(*As Pseudolus drags up another roaring belch*)

What again? What's all this? You still belching at me?

PSEUDOLUS

Aw, my belches smell sweet, so you *just* let me be.

SIMO (*disgustedly*)

I swear, you could swill in an hour
All the alcohol Italy's manpower,
Using bumper crops only, could press
In four years.

PSEUDOLUS (*grinning*)

Not an hour. Much less.

SIMO (*nodding tight-lipped*)

Guess you're right. Here's a point I've ignored:
At what dock was this load put aboard?

PSEUDOLUS (*carelessly*)

With your son. We've been boozing away.

(*Gleefully*)

I sure gave it to Ballio, eh?
I did what I told you I would!

SIMO (*unhappily*)

You're a model of stinkerhood.

PSEUDOLUS

It's the girl's fault, you know. She's been freed,
And she's there with your son at the feed.

SIMO (*wearily*)

Oh, I've heard a complete résumé.

PSEUDOLUS (*stoutly*)

Then what's holding things up? Where's my pay?

SIMO (*summoning up a ghastly smile, holding out the purse*)

It's your right. I agree. Here you are.

PSEUDOLUS (*unable to believe his eyes*)

You said you'd never come across—and here I get my pay!

(*He grins from ear to ear. Then, like a master ordering his slave, he points to his shoulder.*)

Well, load it on this shoulder, boy, and follow me this way.

SIMO (*shocked*)

You're asking *me* to put this there?

PSEUDOLUS (*grinning*)

                        You will, and I know why.

SIMO (*to the world at large*)

He takes my money and then gets funny—what can I do
   with this guy?

PSEUDOLUS (*as before*)

           The victor gets the spoils, they say.

SIMO (*grimly*)

           Then bend that shoulder down.

PSEUDOLUS

                            Okay.

SIMO (*between his teeth*)

          I'd never thought I'd see the day
          That I'd be on my knees to *you*.
          Oh my god, my god!

PSEUDOLUS (*sharply*)

                 Now that's taboo!

SIMO (*whimpering*)

          It hurts!

PSEUDOLUS (*shaking his head feelingly*)

          If *you* didn't hurt right now,
          Then *I* would have the hurt—and how!

SIMO (*managing to work up an ingratiating smile*)

Now my boy, would you rob your old master of this
   treasure?

PSEUDOLUS (*promptly*)

You're darned right. There's nothing would give me more
   pleasure.

SIMO (*wheedling*)

Won't you please, as a favor, leave me *some* little part?

PSEUDOLUS

> I will not! Go on, call me a miser at heart,
> But you'll never be richer by a penny from me.
> Had my plans not worked out so successfully, I'd
> Have got damned little pity out of *you* for my hide.

SIMO (*losing control and shaking his stick*)

> Just as sure as I live, I'll get even, you'll see!

PSEUDOLUS (*shrugging*)

> With the hide that I've got, do you think you scare me?

SIMO (*turning away and walking off baffled*)

> All right, then. Good-*by!*

PSEUDOLUS (*calling*)

> > > > > Hey, come back!

SIMO (*in high dudgeon*)

> I come back? And what for?

PSEUDOLUS

> > > > > Just come back.
> I won't fool you.

SIMO (*walking back, suspiciously*)

> > > > I'm back.

PSEUDOLUS (*taking his arm and starting to pull him, gaily*)

> > > > > Well, just think—
> Here's the two of us off for a drink!

SIMO (*trying to hold back as Pseudolus tugs energetically*)

> For a drink?

PSEUDOLUS (*holding up the purse enticingly*)

> > > > You just do as I say
> And I promise you half of this pay—
> Maybe more.

SIMO (*suddenly giving up all resistance*)

> > > > Show the way and I'll go
> Any place that you want.

PSEUDOLUS (*innocently*)

> > > > > Is that so?
> You're not angry at me or your son
> On account of these things that I've done?

SIMO (*eying the purse hungrily*)
>   Not at all.

PSEUDOLUS (*starting to walk off, stage left*)
>   Come this way.

SIMO (*following him*)
>   I'm behind.
> (*Stopping and pointing to the audience*)
>   Let's invite the whole crowd. Do you mind?

PSEUDOLUS (*stopping and eying the audience*)
>   Lord, they and I have never exchanged
>   A single invitation.
> (*To the audience*)
>   But if you're willing to give a hand,
>   A loud and warm ovation,
>   To all our actors and their play—
>   I invite you all—but not today!

THE ROPE

DRAMATIS PERSONAE

SCEPARNIO, *Daemones' servant (slave)*

PLESIDIPPUS, *a wealthy young Athenian residing in Cyrene*

DAEMONES, *an elderly Athenian living in straitened circumstances near Cyrene*

PALAESTRA, *a beautiful young courtesan, the property of Labrax*

AMPELISCA, *an attractive young courtesan, also the property of Labrax*

PTOLEMOCRATIA, *priestess of the shrine of Venus*

FISHERMEN

TRACHALIO, *Plesidippus' valet (slave)*

LABRAX, *a slave dealer*

CHARMIDES, *an elderly vagabond who has recently struck up an acquaintance with Labrax*

ROUGHNECK (TURBALIO) ⎫ *slaves of Daemones*
CUTTHROAT (SPARAX) ⎭

GRIPUS, *a fisherman, slave of Daemones*

[DAEDALIS, *wife of Daemones*]

SCENE

A barren shore near Cyrene. In the background are, stage right, Daemones' simple cottage, and, stage left, a shrine of Venus consisting chiefly of a modest temple with an altar in front. The exit near the temple (stage left) leads to Cyrene. That near the cottage (stage right) leads to the beach; sand and rocks and a patch of reeds are visible near it.

PROLOGUE

(The Prologue, dressed in a spangled costume and wearing a glittering star on his forehead, steps forward. He represents Arcturus, the star that, rising in September and setting in November, marks the period of the equinoctial storms.)

ARCTURUS I am from the city of the celestials, fellow citizen of him who holds sway over all peoples, all seas, and all lands. My appearance is as you see: a bright star that glitters and gleams, that rises and sets in heaven and on earth, forever and ever, in its season. My name is Arcturus.

At night I shine among the gods in the sky; by day I walk among men on earth. Other stars, too, come down here from heaven: great Jove, lord of gods and men, assigns us stations, one here and another there, all over the world. We find out for him what men are doing, how they are behaving, particularly which are reverent and honest so that he can show them his favor. If we find people trying to win cases by bearing false witness, or forswearing themselves to deny a debt, we note their names and report them to Jove. From day to day he knows precisely who here on earth is out to do wrong. When rascals go into a trial ready to perjure themselves and trick a judge into awarding them the verdict, *he* reopens the case, reviews it, and passes a sentence so stiff it far outweighs whatever they may have won.

In another set of records he keeps a list of the good. And if the wicked have the idea that they can get on it by winning him over with gifts and offerings, they're wasting their time and money. Why? Because he has no mercy for men who are two-faced. The appeal of the honest man finds favor far more easily than that of the wicked despite all their gifts. And so I advise those of you who are good, who live your lives in reverence and honesty, to go on in this way so that you may reap your reward in time to come.

But now I want to tell you about the play; after all, that's what I'm here for.

(*Gesturing toward the scene behind him*) To begin with, this city is Cyrene; that's the way Diphilus[1] wanted it. This cottage on the seashore and the farm alongside it belong to Daemones. He's an old man who came here as an exile from Athens. He's not a bad man; he didn't leave his homeland because of any wrong he had done. It's simply that, in helping others, he got himself involved and, through his generosity, dissipated a hard-earned fortune. He once had a daughter, and he lost her, too, when she was a little child: she was kidnaped. The kidnaper sold her to a dealer in courtesans, one of the worst men alive.

Now the pimp who bought her brought the girl here to Cyrene. A certain young fellow, an Athenian—which makes him the girl's fellow citizen—happened to see her one day as she was coming home from her music lesson. He fell in love with her, went straight to the pimp, and arranged to buy her for seventy-five hundred dollars. He paid a deposit and had a contract drawn up. But the pimp, true to type, didn't care the least bit either about keeping his word or about the contract he had signed. He happened to have staying with him an old fellow from Agrigentum in Sicily, someone just like himself, a scoundrel who'd sell his own mother. This fellow began to rave about how beautiful the girl was, as well as all the others the pimp owned. And he began to talk the pimp into going to Sicily with him: he kept telling him there were lots of fast livers in Sicily, that courtesans made big money there, and that he could become a rich man there. He convinced him. And so the pimp secretly chartered a vessel and, one night, moved everything out of his house and put it on board. He told the boy who had bought the girl that he was going to the shrine of Venus to make a sacrifice and pay off an obligation—(*pointing*) this is the shrine right here—and even invited the young fellow to share the remains of the animal and have

[1]See pp. xiv and xvii.

lunch with him there. Then he went straight to the ship and sailed off with his girls. Word reached the boy of what had happened, that the pimp had left town, but by the time the young fellow made it down to the waterfront the ship was already far out at sea.

When I saw that the pimp was carrying the girl off, I stepped in to help her and hurt him. I raised a storm and stirred up the waves. You all know that I, Arcturus, am the fiercest star of all; things get stormy when I rise and worse when I set. Right now both the pimp and his cohort are castaways, sitting on a rock; their ship's been shattered. The girl and one other from the troupe got frightened and jumped out of the vessel into the ship's boat; at this moment the waves are carrying them to shore near where old Daemones lives in exile. As a matter of fact, the storm ripped off his roof with all its tiles. (*As the door of the cottage opens and a figure comes out*) That's his servant there, coming out. In a minute you'll see the young fellow who arranged to buy the girl from the pimp. Good-by and good luck!

ACT I

(*Daemones' servant, Sceparnio, "the wood chopper," comes out of the cottage carrying a spade. Sceparnio, a young fellow in his twenties, is the sort whose face feels more comfortable wearing a scowl than a smile, and his disposition has not been improved by years of work for a penniless master. His expression is even more sour than usual as he looks over the damage done to the cottage during the night.*)

SCEPARNIO (*to the audience*)   God in heaven, what a storm we had here last night! The wind took the roof right off the cottage. Wind? That was no wind; that was a hurricane right out of a play by Euripides! Look how it ripped all the tiles off the roof! It's made the cottage a lot brighter—put in some new skylights for us.

(*Unnoticed by Sceparnio, Plesidippus enters, stage left, followed by three friends; all are wearing coats and carrying swords. Plesidippus is a good-looking young fellow, well and expensively dressed. His face at the moment shows signs of worry and strain. He and his friends are deep in conversation as they come on stage.*)

PLESIDIPPUS (*apologetically*)   And so I rushed you away from your own affairs and all for nothing; I wasn't able to get my hands on that pimp down at the dock. But I didn't want to let up for one minute, I didn't want to give up hope; that's why I've kept you with me all this time. I've come out here to take a look around this shrine of Venus; he told me he was going to make a sacrifice here.

SCEPARNIO (*to himself, eying the spade distastefully*)   If I've got any brains, I'd better start getting some of this blasted clay ready.

PLESIDIPPUS (*overhearing, to his friends*)   Wait—I hear someone talking.

(*The door of the cottage opens and Daemones comes out. Daemones is middle-aged. Though he is dressed in worn work clothes, there is something about his manner and carriage that indicates he was not born a peasant.*)

DAEMONES (*calling*)   Hey, Sceparnio!

SCEPARNIO (*as he turns around*)   Who wants me?

DAEMONES   The man who paid good money for you.

SCEPARNIO (*sourly*)   Why don't you come right out with it and call me your slave?

DAEMONES   We're going to need lots of clay, so there's lots of digging for you to do. It looks as if we'll have to reroof the whole cottage. Daylight's coming through everywhere; there are more holes up there than in a sieve.

PLESIDIPPUS (*to Daemones*)   Good morning, Dad. (*Noticing Sceparnio*) Good morning to you both.

DAEMONES   Good morning.

SCEPARNIO   What do you mean by calling him "Dad"? You his— (*Eying his rather dandified dress distastefully*) What are you anyway, male or female?

PLESIDIPPUS (*astonished*)   I? I'm a man.

SCEPARNIO   Well, my man, go find your father farther on.

DAEMONES (*sorrowfully*)   I once did have a little daughter, but I lost her. She was the only child I had; I never had a son.

PLESIDIPPUS (*politely*)   God will give you one.

SCEPARNIO (*snarling*)   And he'll give you, whoever you are, what you won't want. Bothering busy people with your blabbering!

PLESIDIPPUS (*pointedly ignoring him, to Daemones; gesturing toward the cottage*)   Do you live here?

SCEPARNIO   What do you want to know for? What are you doing, casing the place? Looking for someone to rob?

PLESIDIPPUS (*turning on him*)   You must be one important and trusted slave to be able to answer for your master when he's present—and insult a gentleman.

SCEPARNIO And you must be one nervy boor to be able to come up to the house of a total stranger who doesn't owe you the time of day and make a nuisance of yourself.

DAEMONES Keep quiet, Sceparnio. (*To Plesidippus*) What would you like, my boy?

PLESIDIPPUS (*testily*) I'd like to see that slave of yours get what's coming to him for taking it on himself to do the talking when his master's around. (*Politely*) If you don't mind, there are a few questions I'd like to ask you.

DAEMONES Well, I'm busy right now, but I'll be glad to help even so.

SCEPARNIO (*to Daemones, quickly*) Why don't you go down to the swamp and cut some canes for the roof while the weather's still clear?

DAEMONES (*curtly*) Quiet! (*To Plesidippus*) Now, what can I do for you?

PLESIDIPPUS (*eagerly*) Tell me, have you seen a fellow around here with curly gray hair? A sneaking, wheedling, lying—

DAEMONES (*interrupting, grimly*) Lots of them. It's because of men like that that I live the way I do.

PLESIDIPPUS I mean right here, at the shrine. Fellow with two girls with him, coming to make a sacrifice? Yesterday or maybe this morning?

DAEMONES (*shaking his head*) No, my boy, I haven't seen anyone come here to make a sacrifice for a good many days now. And when they do, I see them all right—they always drop in to get water or fire or borrow dishes or a knife or a spit or a cooking pot or something. You'd think I kept a kitchen and a well for Venus and not myself. But they've left me alone for quite a while now.

PLESIDIPPUS (*in anguish*) You know what you've just done? Pronounced my death sentence!

DAEMONES Believe me, if I had my way, you'd be alive and healthy.

SCEPARNIO (*to Plesidippus*) Listen you, if you're hanging around this shrine to beg some scraps to fill your belly, you'll do a lot better having lunch at home.

DAEMONES (*to Plesidippus*) What happened? Someone invite you to lunch and not show up?

PLESIDIPPUS Exactly.

SCEPARNIO It's all right; *we* don't mind if you go home from here with your belly empty. Why don't you try Ceres' shrine instead? She handles the commissary; Venus only deals with love.

PLESIDIPPUS (*half to himself, bitterly*) The way that man put one over on me is a crying shame!

DAEMONES (*happening to look off, stage right*) Good god! Sceparnio, what are those men doing there in the surf?

SCEPARNIO If you ask me, they're going to a fancy breakfast.

DAEMONES Why?

SCEPARNIO Because they took a bath last night.

DAEMONES (*gazing intently*) They've been wrecked at sea!

SCEPARNIO Sure. Take a look at the roof of our cottage—we've been wrecked on land.

DAEMONES Poor fellows! Tossed overboard and having to swim for it.

PLESIDIPPUS (*trying to follow the direction of his gaze*) Where do you see these men, anyway?

DAEMONES (*pointing*) There, toward the right. See? Near the beach.

PLESIDIPPUS I see them now. (*To his friends*) Follow me. I only hope one of them is that blasted crook I'm after. (*To Daemones and Sceparnio*) Well, take care of yourselves. (*They rush off, stage right.*)

SCEPARNIO (*calling after him*) We've got it in mind; we don't need any reminders from you. (*Watches them go off, then suddenly gives a start*) Oh, my god in heaven, what's that I see?

DAEMONES What is it?

SCEPARNIO (*excitedly*) Two girls in a boat, all by themselves. Look at the way the poor things are being tossed about! (*Gazes intently in silence for a moment.*) Good, good! The waves just carried the boat away from the rocks and toward the shore; there isn't a helmsman alive who could have done better. I don't think I've ever seen the surf this bad in my life! If they can only get clear of those breakers they'll be all right. Now's the moment they have to watch out for—oh, a wave just hit them and one fell overboard—wait, it's shallow there—she can swim out easily. Good work! She's on her feet—she's coming this way—she's safe! (*Turning his head as if looking in a slightly different direction*) The other's just jumped out of the boat to get on shore—oh, she lost her nerve, she's fallen in the water, she's on her knees—no, she's safe! She's wading out—now she's on the beach—oh, oh, she turned to the right, she's going off in that direction. Damn! That poor girl's going to do a lot of hiking today!

DAEMONES What do you care?

SCEPARNIO (*still gazing intently*) If she falls off that cliff she's heading toward, she'll finish her hike in a hurry.

DAEMONES (*with some asperity*) If you were going to eat at their expense tonight, Sceparnio, I think you should worry about them. But if you're going to eat at mine, you'd better pay attention to me.

SCEPARNIO True. You're absolutely right.

DAEMONES Follow me.

SCEPARNIO I'm right behind.

(*The two enter the cottage. A moment later Palaestra, "the struggler," enters, stage right. Her face is haggard, her hair dripping, her clothing drenched, and she barely has the energy to drag herself along. Despite all this, we can see that she is a remarkably fine-looking young girl. She makes her way downstage and addresses the audience.*)

SONG

PALAESTRA

> The tales they tell of men's mishaps are mild,
> Compared to actual experience.
> It seems that Heaven's pleased to leave me thus—
> A frightened castaway in lands unknown.
> Oh, god, what can I say? That I was born
> For this? Have I received this as reward
> For all my honest and devoted prayer?
> For me to undergo such hardships would
> Be understandable if I had sinned
> Against my parents or, perhaps, my god.
> But when I've striven so to lead a life
> That's free of all such blame, this treatment is,
> O god, unfair, unjust, and undeserved.
> What mark hereafter will you place on guilt
> If such is the reward for innocence?
> If I were conscious that I'd done you wrong,
> Or that my parents had, then I would be
> More reconciled to all this misery.

(*Pauses a moment, then resumes with bitterness and passion.*)

> But the crimes of my owner are the cause of my grief.
> It is *his* sins I suffer for—his, and not mine!
> All he owned has gone down with his ship in the sea;
> I am all that is left of his worldly possessions.
> And that girl who escaped in the boat at my side,
> Even she has been lost; I'm alone, all alone.
> If she'd only been saved! Then at least, with her help,
> This sad blow would have been a bit lighter to bear.
> For what hope have I now or whose help can I seek?
> I'm deserted, alone in a desolate spot
> Where there's nothing but rocks and the sound of the sea,
> Where there isn't a chance of my meeting a soul.
> All I own in this world are the clothes on my back,
> And I've no idea where to find shelter or food.

Oh, it's hopeless! Why try to go on with my life?
I don't know where I am; it's a place strange to me.
How I wish that some person would come and point out
Where a road or a path is! I'm so at a loss
I can't make up my mind to go right or go left;
It's all wild—not a sign of a field can I see.
All the horrors of cold and distraction and fear
Have me now in their grasp. Poor dear parents of mine,
You can have no idea of your daughter's despair!
I was born a free girl, but my birth was in vain—
At this moment how more of a slave could I be
Had I been one from birth? Oh, what good have I been
All these years to the parents who cherished me so!

(*She staggers back to the rocks on stage right, sinks down
on them, and buries her face in her arms. The next moment
there enters, stage right, the companion she thought had been
lost. Ampelisca, "tender grape," is a pretty girl with an attractive, gay, vivacious manner. Right now she is as bedraggled and forlorn as Palaestra. She makes her way downstage
and addresses the audience.*)

AMPELISCA

Oh, what act could be better or more suitable now
    Than to sever my soul from my body?
For my life is a torment and my breast is beset
    By an army of cares that destroy me!
In the face of all this I've no stomach for life,
    All the hope that once buoyed me is ended:
For I've roamed everywhere, used my voice, eyes, and
        ears,
    Crept through thorns, to track down my companion;
She's been lost without trace, and I have no idea
    Where to turn, in what place to go searching.
And I haven't been able to meet anyone
    I could speak to and ask for directions.
Why, this region's a desert—in all of the world
    There's just no place so lonely and barren.

Yet as long as I live—granted she's alive too—
I'll persist in the search till I find her.

PALAESTRA (*to herself, raising her head in alarm*)
Whose voice is that I hear?
Was that a sound nearby?
Oh, god, I'm so afraid!

AMPELISCA (*to herself*)
Did I hear someone speak?

PALAESTRA (*in desperation*)
O god of hope! Please help!

AMPELISCA (*to herself, hopefully*)
Does this mean my release
From misery and fear?

PALAESTRA (*to herself, listening intently*)
I'm absolutely sure
I heard a woman's voice.

AMPELISCA (*to herself, listening intently*)
A woman's somewhere here—
I heard a woman's voice.

PALAESTRA (*dubiously*)
It can't be Ampelisca!

AMPELISCA (*calling uncertainly*)
Palaestra! Is that you?

PALAESTRA (*jumping to her feet, excitedly*)
Oh, I *must* make her hear me—I'll call out her name!
Ampelisca!

AMPELISCA (*calling*)
Who's there?

PALAESTRA
It's Palaestra! It's me!

AMPELISCA (*looking about without seeing her*)
I can't see where you are.

PALAESTRA
I'm in all sorts of trouble.

AMPELISCA

    I've a share in it too—one as big as your own.
    But I'm dying to see you.

PALAESTRA

                        And I to see you.

AMPELISCA

    Let's both talk and we'll follow the sounds. Where are
    you?

PALAESTRA

    Over here. Come this way. Now walk up to me. Come!

AMPELISCA (*walking slowly and hesitantly toward her*)
    This is the best I can do.

PALAESTRA (*as she comes near*)
                  All right, give me your hand.

AMPELISCA (*doing so*)
    Here it is.

PALAESTRA (*grabbing it, pulling her near, and embracing her*)
           Ampelisca! You're safe! You're alive!

AMPELISCA (*tearfully*)
    Yes—and now that I'm able to touch you, Palaestra,
    You've restored the desire to go on with my life.
    But I scarcely believe that you're here in my arms!
    Oh, my dear! Hold me tight! How you make me forget
    All my troubles!

PALAESTRA

            You've taken the words from my mouth!
    But we ought to get out of this place.

AMPELISCA

                     And go where?

PALAESTRA

    Shall we follow the beach?

AMPELISCA

                  Go wherever you like;
    I'll be right at your heels. But we're both sopping wet—
    Are we going to tramp up and down in these clothes?

PALAESTRA

Yes, we must. We just have to take things as they come.

(*Starts trudging off with Ampelisca close behind and then suddenly stops and points.*)

What is that, do you think?

AMPELISCA

What is what?

PALAESTRA

Don't you see?

There's a shrine over there.

AMPELISCA

Over where?

PALAESTRA

On the right.

AMPELISCA (*following the direction of her hand*)
I can make out a spot that would serve for a shrine.

PALAESTRA

It's so pleasant a place that I'm sure we shall find
There are people about. Now let's pray that the god
Dwelling here will have pity on us in our plight,
And will come to the rescue and bring to a close
All these torments and terrors, these worries and woes!

(*As the two girls slowly make their way toward the little temple that marks the shrine, the door opens and Ptolemocratia, the priestess, comes out. She is an elderly woman dressed in flowing white robes that, although spotlessly clean, have obviously seen better days. Her face is kindly and serene.*)

PTOLEMOCRATIA (*to herself*)
The sound of prayer just roused me now
To step outside. But who has come
To ask my mistress for a favor?
The goddess they implore is quick
To yield, and loath to hide, her grace,
A patroness both kind and good.

PALAESTRA (*timidly*)
>   Good morning, Mother.

PTOLEMOCRATIA (*responding perfunctorily*)
>   Morning, girls.

(*Suddenly aware of their appearance*)
>   Tell me, where have you come from, my dears?
>   You're in rags! And you're both sopping wet!

PALAESTRA
>   Well, right now from a place that's nearby.
>   But our homeland is far, far away.

PTOLEMOCRATIA (*in mock-tragic style*)
>   Then you came o'er the blue of the sea
>   On a charger of canvas and wood?

PALAESTRA
>   Yes, we did.

PTOLEMOCRATIA (*reproachfully*)
>   But you should have come here
>   Dressed in white and prepared to give gifts.
>   This is simply unheard of, my dears—
>   Coming into this shrine in this way.

PALAESTRA (*taken aback*)
>   From two castaways fresh from the sea?
>   Tell me, where would you have us find gifts?

(*The two girls drop to the ground and embrace Ptolemocratia's knees.*)
>   Here we are on our knees at your feet.
>   We need help! We don't know where we are,
>   We don't know what's in store for us next.
>   Oh, I beg you, please pity our plight.
>   Give us shelter and save us, please do!
>   We are homeless and hopeless, and all
>   That we own you can see on our backs!

PTOLEMOCRATIA (*gently*)
>   Now I want you to give me your hands
>   And get up from your knees, both of you.

There's no woman alive with a heart
That's as tender as mine, I am sure.
But this shrine's very humble, my girls.
I can barely keep living myself.
And the offerings for Venus come from me.

AMPELISCA

Then is this one of Venus' shrines?

PTOLEMOCRATIA

Yes, it is, dear. And I am in charge.
We'll make do. You will both be put up
Just as well as my means will permit.
Come with me.

PALAESTRA

We're most grateful to you
For a welcome so friendly and kind.

PTOLEMOCRATIA

It's a duty I've always in mind.

(*Ptolemocratia and the girls enter the temple, and the stage
is now empty.*)

ACT II

(A group of fishermen, dressed in rags and carrying tackle, enters, stage left.)

FISHERMEN *(to the audience)*

> The poor in every single way
> > Find life a sad progression
> Of miseries, especially men
> > Without a trade or profession.
> Their living's strictly limited
> > To things in their possession.
> What *our* financial status is,
> > You see by this here get-up.
> These hooks and rods we have are our
> > Sole economic set-up.
> Each day we hike from town to beach
> > To forage for our rations.
> (It's our substitute for wrestling, gym,
> > And other sporting passions.)
> We grub for limpets, oysters, clams,
> > Sea urchins, scallops, mussels.
> And then to try our luck with fish,
> > With rod to rock each hustles.
> We fill our bellies from the sea;
> > But when the sea's defaulted,
> We take a swim—if not the fish,
> > The fishers get cleaned and salted—
> Then sneak back home and climb in bed
> > Without a thing for dinner.
> With seas as rough as they are right now,
> > Our hopes are getting thinner;
> Unless we find a clam or two,
> > We've had today's collation.
> To get some help, let's proffer to
> > Kind Venus veneration.

(Trachalio, "bull-necked," Plesidippus' servant, enters, stage left. He's a burly young fellow, honest and good-natured at heart, and gay in temperament. He rather fancies himself as a man of importance, and with—or without—provocation often begins orating instead of talking.)

TRACHALIO *(to himself, worriedly)* And I watched so carefully all the way so's not to miss that master of mine on the road! When he left the house he said he was going to go to the waterfront, and gave me orders to meet him here at the shrine of Venus. *(Catching sight of the fishermen)* Now, that's convenient: there are some fellows over there I can ask. *(Calling)* Hail, heroes of the hook and half shell, despoilers of the deeps, members of the Honorable Order of the Empty Belly, how're you doing? How're you dying?

FISHERMAN The way fishermen always do—of optimism followed by starvation.

TRACHALIO Did you happen to see a young fellow come along while you've been standing here? Husky, red-faced fellow looking as if he meant business? He had three others with him; they were all wearing cloaks and daggers.

FISHERMAN Nobody answering to that description's come along, so far as we know.

TRACHALIO How about an old guy, pretty big, with a bald forehead like an old satyr, a fat belly, bushy eyebrows, and a dirty look? A low-down, filthy, lying, thieving, swindling crook? Had two good-looking girls with him?

FISHERMAN Anyone with those sterling virtues ought to be headed for a town jail, not a temple of Venus.

TRACHALIO But did you see him?

FISHERMAN No. He hasn't been here. So long. *(They leave, stage right.)*

TRACHALIO *(calling after them)* So long. *(To himself)* I thought so; I had a suspicion this would happen. They've put one over on that master of mine: that damned pimp skipped town. Took passage on a ship and took the girls away. I'm a prophet, that's what I am. The lousy liar! He even invited Plesidippus for lunch out here. Well, the best thing I can do is wait around here until Plesidippus shows up. And while I'm at it, if I see the priestess, I'll quiz her and find out if she knows anything more about all this. She'll tell me.

(*The door of the temple opens and Ampelisca comes out, carrying a pitcher. Her first words are addressed to the priestess inside.*)

AMPELISCA (*through the doorway*) Yes, I understand. I'm to go to the cottage right next door to the shrine, knock, and ask for water.

TRACHALIO (*pricking up his ears, to himself*) Now whose voice is that the wind has wafted to mine ears?

AMPELISCA (*turning at the sound*) Who's that talking out there, please? (*Seeing him*) Look who's here!

TRACHALIO (*turning, to himself*) Isn't that Ampelisca coming out of the temple?

AMPELISCA (*to herself*) Isn't that Trachalio, Plesidippus' valet, I see?

TRACHALIO (*to himself*) That's who it is, all right.

AMPELISCA (*to herself*) That's who it is, all right. (*Calling*) Trachalio! Hello there!

TRACHALIO (*going up to her*) Hello, Ampelisca. What have you been doing with yourself?

AMPELISCA (*bitterly*) Spending the best years of my life in the worst possible way.

TRACHALIO Don't say things like that!

AMPELISCA (*as before*) Sensible people should tell the truth —and listen to it. But where's Plesidippus?

TRACHALIO (*looking at her blankly*) What a question! He's inside with you people, isn't he?

AMPELISCA (*emphatically*) He is not. He hasn't been here today.

TRACHALIO Hasn't been here?

AMPELISCA You never said a truer word.

TRACHALIO (*grinning*) Rather unusual for me. Well, when will lunch be ready?

AMPELISCA (*taking her turn at looking blank*) What lunch are you talking about?

TRACHALIO You people are making a sacrifice here, aren't you?

AMPELISCA My dear boy, will you please wake up?

TRACHALIO But I know for certain our masters were getting together for lunch here. Labrax invited Plesidippus.

AMPELISCA (*bitterly*) I'm not at all surprised. Exactly what you'd expect of a pimp—as ready to cheat a goddess as a man.

TRACHALIO You mean you people and Plesidippus *aren't* making a sacrifice here?

AMPELISCA (*scornfully*) You're a prophet.

TRACHALIO What are you doing around here, then?

AMPELISCA (*breathlessly*) We were in terrible trouble, scared to death, in danger of losing our lives, with not a thing to our name and not a soul to help us. And the priestess here took us in. The two of us—me and Palaestra.

TRACHALIO (*excitedly*) You mean Palaestra's here? His sweetheart's here?

AMPELISCA Of course.

TRACHALIO (*as before*) Ampelisca, that's the best possible news you could have brought me. But what was this danger you were in? I'm dying to hear about it.

AMPELISCA Trachalio, last night our ship was wrecked!

TRACHALIO What ship? What are you talking about?

AMPELISCA Didn't you hear what happened? The pimp wanted to move all of us to Sicily without anybody knowing about it. So he loaded all his belongings on board a ship. And now he's lost everything!

TRACHALIO (*exulting*) Good work, Father Neptune! Congratulations! Nobody can play the game better than you:

you hit the jackpot; you gave that liar his lumps. But where is our pimping friend Labrax now?

AMPELISCA   Probably died of drink. Neptune was serving in the big glasses last night.

TRACHALIO (*chuckling*)   And he probably insisted on bottoms up, every round. Ampelisca, I love you! You're so sweet! What honeyed words you have for me! (*Suddenly becoming serious*) But how were you and Palaestra rescued?

AMPELISCA   I'll tell you just how it happened. We saw that the ship was being carried toward the rocks, and we both got so scared we jumped into the ship's boat. Then, while everybody on board was busy having the shakes, I hurried and cast off the rope. The storm carried us away from them, to the right. And then we were tossed about by the wind and waves in the worst way imaginable, all night long. Finally, just this morning, the wind drove us up on the beach. We were half dead!

TRACHALIO   I know. That's what Neptune always does. (*Grinning*) Most meticulous purser in the business: any bad merchandise around, and he heaves it right overboard.

AMPELISCA   Oh, go to the devil!

TRACHALIO   You almost did, Ampelisca, my girl. (*Becoming serious*) I knew that pimp would do something like that; I said so all along. You know what I really ought to do? Grow a beard and be a prophet.

AMPELISCA (*tartly*)   Considering that you knew all about it, you and that master of yours certainly took good care not to let him get away.

TRACHALIO (*defensively*)   What should he have done?

AMPELISCA (*angrily*)   If he really loved her, you wouldn't have to ask such a question! He should have kept his eyes open night and day, been on his guard every minute. My god! That Plesidippus of yours certainly took fine care of her! Shows how much she mattered to him!

TRACHALIO (*reproachfully*)   Why do you say that?

AMPELISCA (*severely*) It's plain as day, isn't it?

TRACHALIO Can't you understand? Why, you take a fellow who goes to a public bath: he watches his clothes like a hawk and still he gets robbed. There are so many people around, he doesn't know which one to keep an eye on. It's easy enough for the crook to spot the man *he* wants to keep his eye on, but it's tough for the fellow who's on guard to spot the crook. (*Quickly changing the subject*) But how about taking me to Palaestra?

AMPELISCA Just go inside the temple here. You'll find her sitting there crying her eyes out.

TRACHALIO Crying? That I'm sorry to hear. What's she crying about?

AMPELISCA I'll tell you what she's crying about: she's all broken up because the pimp took away a little jewel box she had in which she kept some things that were her only means of identifying her parents. She's afraid it's lost.

TRACHALIO Where was this box?

AMPELISCA On board with us. He kept it locked up in a satchel. He wanted to make sure she'd never be able to find her parents.

TRACHALIO What a criminal thing to do! A girl who ought to be free and he wants to keep her a slave!

AMPELISCA It must have gone down to the bottom with the ship. The pimp had all his money in the same satchel.

TRACHALIO (*comfortingly*) Oh, someone's probably dived down and rescued it.

AMPELISCA The poor girl is simply miserable at the thought of having lost those things.

TRACHALIO All the more reason for me to go in and cheer her up. I don't want her to go on tormenting herself that way. I know for a fact there are lots of people whose affairs turned out much better than they ever expected.

AMPELISCA And I know for a fact there are lots who expected their affairs to turn out well and they never did.

TRACHALIO When you come down to it, the best medicine for trouble is a level head. Well, if there's nothing more I can do for you, I'll run along inside. (*Enters the temple.*)

AMPELISCA Go ahead. (*To herself*) And I'll do that errand for the priestess and ask them next door for some water. She told me they'd give it to me right away if I said it was for her. (*Walking toward the cottage*) I don't think I've ever met anyone nicer than that old lady. I think she deserves every kindness god or man can do for her. There we were, castaways, frightened to death, drenched to the skin, helpless, half alive, and she took us in and was so sweet and generous and open and unbegrudging—just as if we were her own daughters! She even tucked up her robe and heated the water herself so that we could take a bath. Well, I don't want her to be held up on my account, so I'll go where she told me right now and get some more water. (*Knocking on the door of the cottage*) Hello there! Anyone inside? Anyone there to open this door? Will someone please come out?

SCEPARNIO (*throwing the door open and looking past her as he does*) Who's the wild animal trying to break this door down?

AMPELISCA Here I am.

SCEPARNIO (*breaking into a pleased smile as he sees her, to himself*) Hey, here's a piece of luck. Damn it all, that's one good-looking girl there!

AMPELISCA Good morning, mister.

SCEPARNIO Good morning to *you*, miss.

AMPELISCA I've come here to—

SCEPARNIO (*interrupting with a leer*) It's a little too early in the morning for me to entertain you, my girl. Come back later this evening and I'll really take care of you. (*Putting his arm around her*) Well, how about it, baby?

AMPELISCA (*deftly fending him off*) Hey, don't you get so familiar with those hands!

SCEPARNIO (*aside*) Lord in heaven, this is Lady Venus herself! Look at those eyes—this girl's the lively type. And those cheeks! Like silt—silk, I mean. And those breasts! And that mouth calls for a kiss. (*Makes another pass at her.*)

AMPELISCA (*as before*) Can't you keep your hands off me? I'm for your betters, boy!

SCEPARNIO Come on, little one, just one little hug, nice and gentle, like this. (*Tries to get an arm around her again.*)

AMPELISCA Later on, when I'm not busy, you and I'll have time to play around, but right now I have a favor to ask and please just tell me yes or no.

SCEPARNIO All right, what do you want?

AMPELISCA (*holding up the pitcher*) If you had any brains, this would show you what I want.

SCEPARNIO (*making an obscene gesture*) And if you had any, this would show you what *I* want.

AMPELISCA (*remembering her instructions, importantly*) The priestess of the shrine of Venus sent me to ask you for some water for her.

SCEPARNIO (*tapping his chest*) *I'm* lord and master around here. Unless you ask me for it, you don't get a drop. We risked our own necks to dig this well, and we did it with our own tools. (*Leering*) And no one gets a drop without asking me nicely.

AMPELISCA What's the matter? You won't give me some water? What any stranger would give to another?

SCEPARNIO What's the matter? You won't give me what any friend would give to another?

AMPELISCA (*enticingly*) I? Of course I will. I'll do anything you want, honey.

SCEPARNIO (*aside*) Congratulations, old boy, you're in; she just called you "honey." (*To Ampelisca*) Sure I'll give you the water. I don't want you to fall in love with me and get nothing for it. Give me the pitcher.

AMPELISCA Here it is. And please hurry.

SCEPARNIO (*taking the pitcher*)   You wait here. I'll be right back—honey. (*Enters the cottage.*)

AMPELISCA (*worriedly*)   What should I tell the priestess took me so long? (*Gazes about abstractedly, and her eye falls on the sea.*) Ugh! When I look at that water, I get frightened even now. (*Starting*) Oh, my god, what's that I see on the beach? It's the pimp and his friend from Sicily! And I, like a poor fool, thought the two of them had drowned! That means more trouble in store for us than we had thought. But what am I waiting for? I've got to hurry into the temple and tell Palaestra so that we can throw ourselves on the altar before that filthy pimp comes here and catches us. I'd better run—every minute counts!

(*She hurries into the temple. A second later Sceparnio comes out carrying the pitcher.*)

SCEPARNIO (*smiling fatuously, to himself*)   Lord, oh, lord, I never thought water had so much happiness to offer. It was a sheer pleasure to draw it—the well never seemed that shallow before. Practically no work at all to haul it up. Sceparnio, knock on wood, you're quite a guy. Got yourself a love affair going today, eh, boy? (*Calling*) Where's my pretty girl? Here's your water. (*Putting the bucket on his head and mincing about*) See? This is the way I want you to carry it, like a lady. Want me to like you? Then do it just like this. (*Calling*) Sweetie-pie, where are you? Come on and get your water. Where are you? (*Grinning even more fatuously*) Well, what do you know—the little devil's playing hide-and-go-seek. Boy, did she fall for me! (*Calling*) Where are you? (*After waiting a moment in silence*) Hey, are you going to come and get this pitcher? Where are you? Come on, no more games, I'm serious. How about taking this here pitcher? (*Removes the pitcher from his head and starts searching in earnest.*) Where the devil are you? Good god, I don't see her anywhere. Is she playing a trick on me? (*Slamming the pitcher down, angrily*) I'll just leave the blasted pitcher right in the road. (*Starts walking away, then stops abruptly.*) Wait a second—what if someone walks off with it? That's no ordinary pitcher; it belongs to the shrine. I'll get into trouble. (*Excitedly*) I think that girl framed me—wanted me to get caught with a holy pitcher on me. If anyone sees me with this thing, the judge'll have every right to throw the book at me. Look—it's even got its name on it—it practically shouts to high heaven whose it is. Holy god, I'm going to call the priestess out here right now to get her pitcher. I'm heading right for her door! (*Rushes up to the door and starts shouting frantically.*) Hey! Ptolemocratia! Come on out and get your pitcher! Some blamed girl brought it to me. (*Waits a moment; then, getting no reply, disgustedly*) I'll have to carry it in. Fine business if, on top of everything else, I've got to deliver the water right to the house!

(*Sceparnio goes into the temple. A second later Labrax, "the shark," enters, stage right. He is wet, bedraggled, and shivering.*)

LABRAX (*to himself*)   If anyone wants to become a beggar, just let him trust himself, body and soul, to Father Neptune. Believe me, whenever you do business with him, this (*indicating his appearance*) is the way he sends you home. I remember a story about a girl who always refused to set foot on a ship with Hercules—she was a smart one, all right. But where's that guest of mine who's been my ruination? Oh, there he is. Look at him taking his time!

(*Charmides enters, stage right, in the same condition as Labrax.*)

CHARMIDES (*sourly*)   What the devil's the hurry, Labrax? I can't keep up when you go that fast.

LABRAX (*bitterly*)   I wish to god you had gone to the gallows in Sicily before I ever set eyes on you. You're to blame for getting me into this!

CHARMIDES   And I wish to god I had spent the night in the town jail rather than let you take me home with you that day. There's only one favor I want from heaven—that from now on till the end of your days, your guests be the same breed as yourself, every one of them.

LABRAX The day I took you in I let Bad Luck walk right in the front door. Why did I ever listen to a good-for-nothing like you? Why did I ever leave here? Why did I get aboard that ship? (*Thinking of the money he took from Plesidippus*) I've lost even more than I owned!

CHARMIDES I'm not surprised that ship went down—not when it was carrying a crook like you and all that crooked stuff you had.

LABRAX You ruined me, you and that slick talk of yours.

CHARMIDES How about that filthy meal you served me? Believe me, Thyestes and Tereus[2] didn't get worse.

LABRAX (*holding his stomach*) Oh, god, I feel sick. Hold my head, will you?

CHARMIDES Damn you, I hope you puke up your lungs while you're at it.

LABRAX Poor Palaestra and Ampelisca. I wonder where they are now.

CHARMIDES Probably feeding the fish down in the drink.

LABRAX It's all your doing that I'm a beggar now. I had to listen to that big talk of yours!

CHARMIDES (*grinning maliciously*) You ought to be grateful to me. You never knew how to get along before. I taught you how to get along swimmingly.

LABRAX Why don't you go straight to hell and leave me alone?

CHARMIDES That's just what I was going to invite you to do.

LABRAX God, there isn't a man alive worse off than I am.

CHARMIDES Oh, yes there is. One lots worse off—me.

LABRAX How so?

CHARMIDES Because you deserved what you got. I didn't.

---

[2] Mythological characters who had been served their own sons.

LABRAX Look at those bulrushes. I envy them. Always nice and dry.

CHARMIDES I'm practicing to be a Spanish dancer. I'm shivering so much, every time I speak I clack like a castanet.

LABRAX That Neptune sure runs a cold bathing establishment. I leave the place, have all my clothes on, and I'm still freezing. And he doesn't even have a hot-drink counter. Only drinks he serves are cold and salty.

CHARMIDES The fellows I envy are the blacksmiths. Around a fire all day. Always nice and warm.

LABRAX What I'd like to be right now is a duck. Come straight out of the water and still be dry.

CHARMIDES I think I'll get me a job playing a ghost in a theatrical troupe.

LABRAX Why?

CHARMIDES Listen to the terrific clatter I can make with my teeth. (*Shaking his head ruefully*) If you ask me, being cleaned out of everything I owned was just what was coming to me.

LABRAX Why?

CHARMIDES How could I have had the nerve to get aboard a ship with someone like you? I'll bet you made all those waves yourself, just to spite me.

LABRAX I listened to you, that's what I did. You kept telling me girls made big money where you came from. You promised I'd rake in the cash there.

CHARMIDES And you expected to swallow up the whole island of Sicily in one gulp, like a damned vulture.

LABRAX Talk about swallowing, I wonder what whale got my satchel. I had all my money in it.

CHARMIDES Probably the same one that got my wallet. The inside pocket was full of cash.

LABRAX Do you know that all I've got left to my name is this shirt and this rag of a coat? I'm done for!

CHARMIDES You and I could set up a perfect partnership. We'd hold identical shares.

LABRAX If only my girls were still alive, there'd be some hope. If that young fellow Plesidippus sees me now, the one I took a down payment from for Palaestra, he's going to make real trouble for me—and soon.

CHARMIDES What are you crying about, stupid? So long as that tongue of yours is alive, you've got what it takes to get you out of any debts you owe.

(*The door of the temple opens, and Sceparnio comes out, looking puzzled.*)

SCEPARNIO (*to himself*) What's going on here, anyway? Two girls inside the temple, holding on to the altar and crying their eyes out. The poor things are scared to death of someone but I don't know who. They said they'd been shipwrecked last night and tossed up on the beach this morning.

LABRAX (*to Sceparnio, eagerly*) Say there, mister, where are these girls you're talking about?

SCEPARNIO Here, in the temple.

LABRAX How many of them are there?

SCEPARNIO Two.

LABRAX (*half to himself*) I'll swear they're mine.

SCEPARNIO And I'll swear I don't know about that.

LABRAX What do they look like?

SCEPARNIO Not bad. I could go for either one of them—if I was good and drunk.

LABRAX They're pretty young, aren't they?

SCEPARNIO You're pretty much of a nuisance, aren't you? Go on in and take a look if you want.

LABRAX (*to Charmides, excitedly*) Charmides! Those girls in there must be mine!

CHARMIDES Whether they are or they aren't, you can go to hell for all I care.

LABRAX I'm going into that temple this minute. (*Rushes into the temple.*)

CHARMIDES (*calling after him*) I wish you were going straight to hell this minute. (*To Sceparnio*) Say, how about playing host and giving me a place where I can stretch out and get some sleep?

SCEPARNIO Stretch out wherever you want. No one's stopping you. It's a free country.

CHARMIDES But look at me—these clothes I'm wearing are wringing wet. How about putting me up in your house and giving me some dry clothes until these get dry? I'll make it up to you sometime.

SCEPARNIO (*pointing to a homely coverall of rushes hanging up alongside the cottage*) See that mat there? That's all I've got. It's dry, and if you want it you're welcome to it. It's my coat, and it doubles as umbrella when there's rain. Here, give me your things and I'll dry them out.

CHARMIDES (*backing away suspiciously*) Oh, no. Isn't the cleaning out I got at sea enough for you? Do you have to put me through it all again on land?

SCEPARNIO I don't give a damn whether you get cleaned out or rubbed out. I'm not trusting you with anything of mine without security. Go ahead—freeze to death or sweat to death, get sick or get well. Who cares? I don't want any foreigners around the house, anyway. And that's that. (*Stomps into the cottage.*)

CHARMIDES (*calling after him*) Hey, where are you going? (*To himself*) Whoever he is, the man must be a slave dealer—doesn't know what it is to feel pity. But what am I standing around here in these wet clothes for? Why don't I go into this temple here and sleep off last night's party? Drank too much; lots more than I wanted. You'd think we were cheap wine, the way Neptune watered us. Maybe he was figuring on giving us a salt-water laxative. When you come right down to it, if he had kept on serving drinks much longer we'd have gone to sleep then and there; this way he let us go home—half alive, but alive. Well, I'll see what my fellow drunk is doing inside here now.

(*Enters the temple, and the stage is now empty.*)

ACT III

(*Daemones comes out of the cottage shaking his head wonderingly.*)

DAEMONES (*to the audience*) It's amazing the way heaven plays tricks on us mortals. The amazing dreams heaven sends you when you're asleep! A person's not left in peace and quiet even in bed. Last night, for example, I had an incredible dream, something unheard of. I dreamed that an ape was trying to climb up to a swallow's nest and get his hands on the swallows, but couldn't quite make it. After a while it came to me to ask for the loan of a ladder. I refused, pointing out that swallows were descended from Philomela[3] and Procne, and I pleaded with it not to do any harm to what were, in effect, my fellow countrymen. That just made it more belligerent than ever, and it threatened to beat me. It hauled me into court. There I lost my temper and, somehow or other, managed to grab the filthy creature around the middle and chain it up. (*Scratching his head perplexedly*) Now, what does it all mean? I've thought all morning but I just can't figure it out. (*A clamor is heard in the temple.*) What's that? Noise in the shrine next door? That's queer.

(*The door of the temple flies open and Trachalio bursts out.*)

TRACHALIO (*at the top of his lungs—and at his oratorical best*) Citizens of Cyrene! Farmers! Anyone who lives in the area! In god's name, help for the helpless! Harm for the harmful! Are the merciless to be mightier than the meek who shrink at the very name of crime? Then help right a wrong, give the righteous their reward and the dastards their deserts. Fight the good fight to let us live by law and order and not by fists and force. Everyone here, everyone who hears my

[3] A mythological princess of Athens.

voice, in god's name, into this shrine of Venus as fast as you can! Help the poor souls who have entrusted life and limb to the protection of Venus and her priestess in accordance with our ancient custom! Wring the neck of wrong before it reaches *you!*

DAEMONES (*impatiently*) What's this all about?

TRACHALIO (*throwing himself on the ground and embracing Daemones' knees*) My dear sir, by these knees, I call upon you, whoever you are—

DAEMONES (*interrupting, as before*) Let go of my knees and tell me what this yelling's about. And make it short!

TRACHALIO (*not budging*) I beg you, I implore you! Do you want a good crop on your farm this year? Do you want to see it arrive at an overseas market safe and sound? Do you want to get rid of what ails you? Do you—

DAEMONES (*interrupting*) Are you in your right mind?

TRACHALIO (*unabashed*) Do you want an ample supply of seed for sowing? Then, my dear sir, please don't refuse to do what I'm asking you to.

DAEMONES (*testily*) And I call upon *you* by that back of yours and those legs and heels. Do you want a good harvest of birch-rod welts? Do you want a bumper crop of trouble this year? Then you'd better tell me what's going on here and what this shouting's all about.

TRACHALIO (*getting up, reproachfully*) You're not fair: I asked only for nice things for you.

DAEMONES (*promptly*) I am so fair: I asked only for what you deserve.

TRACHALIO Please! Listen to me!

DAEMONES What is it?

TRACHALIO There are two innocent girls in there. They need your help. The treatment they've had—and are getting this minute—is a blot on the escutcheon of justice and law. Right in the temple of Venus, too! Even the priestess is being manhandled.

DAEMONES (*finally aroused*)   Who would have the gall to lay hands on a priestess? Who are these girls? How are they being mistreated?

TRACHALIO   If you'll listen to me for a minute, I'll tell you. (*Breathlessly*) They ran to Venus' altar for safety. Now this fellow has the colossal nerve to want to pull them away. And both of them by rights ought to be free.

DAEMONES   Who's the man who's so free and easy with priestesses and temples? And no speeches!

TRACHALIO   A swindler, a crook, a murderer, a liar, a law-breaker; a foul, filthy, unprincipled—in a word, a pimp. Need I say more?

DAEMONES   You've said enough. Perfect material for a flogging.

TRACHALIO   He even tried to strangle the priestess.

DAEMONES   By god, he's going to pay for that, and pay plenty. (*Shouting to his servants inside*) Hey! Roughneck and Cutthroat! Come on out here! Where are you, anyway?

TRACHALIO   Please, I beg you. Go in the temple and rescue them.

(*Two husky slaves rush out of the house and stand at attention before Daemones.*)

DAEMONES (*to Trachalio, reassuringly*)   One word from me will be enough. (*To the slaves*) Follow me! (*They charge toward the temple.*)

TRACHALIO (*remaining prudently behind and calling to Daemones*)   Give it to him! Tell those boys to make believe they're cooks scaling fish and have them scratch his eyes out!

DAEMONES (*to the slaves*)   Drag him out here by the feet, like a stuck pig.

(*The three enter the temple. Trachalio stands near the door, listening intently.*)

TRACHALIO (*to the audience*) I hear a racket: the pimp's getting a going-over. I hope they knock every tooth out of the rascal's mouth. (*Stepping back as the door opens*) Here come the girls. They look scared to death.

(*Palaestra and Ampelisca come out and rush past Trachalio without noticing him.*)

SONG

PALAESTRA (*to the audience*)

    The dread moment's at hand; now we're utterly helpless.
    There's just no one to come to our aid or defense,
    No release from our danger, no way to find safety.
    And we're both so afraid we can't think where to run.
    Oh, the vicious and brutal ordeal that that pimp
    Put us through just a moment ago in the shrine!
    Why, the monster attacked the old priestess, poor thing,
    Shoved her this way and that—it was dreadful to see—
    And then dragged us by force from the innermost altar.
    In the state that we're in, we'd be better off dead.
    In the depths of despair what is dearer than death?

TRACHALIO (*to himself*)

    Hey, what's this? What a way for a young girl to talk!
    I must swing into action—they need cheering up.
    (*Calling*)
    Hey, Palaestra!

PALAESTRA (*too frightened to turn around*)

                 Who's there?

TRACHALIO (*calling*)

                     Ampelisca!

AMPELISCA (*clutching Palaestra*)

                       Who wants me?

PALAESTRA (*as before*)

    Who's that calling our names?

TRACHALIO

                   Turn around and you'll see.

PALAESTRA (*turning and seeing him, fervently*)
Oh, some hope for our safety at last!

TRACHALIO (*walking over to them, importantly*)
                                    Now be calm.
Take it easy. Trust me.

PALAESTRA
                        Yes—if you'll give your word
We need fear no more violence and force. Otherwise
I'll be brought to a violent act on myself!

TRACHALIO (*as before*)
Now you're just being silly. No more of this talk.

PALAESTRA (*dully*) Don't try to console me in my misery
with mere words. If you don't have some real help to offer,
Trachalio, it's all over with us.

AMPELISCA (*wildly*) I've made up my mind to die rather
than suffer at the hands of that pimp any longer. (*Hesitatingly*) But I'm just a woman, after all; every time I even
think of death I get paralyzed with fright. Oh, what a nightmare this day is!

TRACHALIO (*heartily*) Courage, girls!

PALAESTRA (*dully*) Courage? Where am I going to find it?

TRACHALIO (*as before*) Take my word for it, there's no reason to be afraid. (*Pointing to the altar outside the shrine*)
Come, sit down on this altar.

AMPELISCA Why should this one do us any more good than
the one in the shrine? We were clutching it just now when
they pulled us away by brute force.

TRACHALIO (*leading them to the altar and seating them on it*)
You just sit down. I'll stand guard over here. See? The altar's your fort, here are the walls, and I'm the garrison.
With Venus at my side I'm ready to counter the pimp's
sneak attacks.

AMPELISCA All right, we'll do whatever you say. (*Falling on
her knees and praying*) Dear Venus, here we are, both of
us, on our knees, in tears, before your altar. We beg of you:

guard us, watch over us. Give us our revenge on those criminals who had so little respect for your shrine. Be gracious and let us find safety by this altar. Thanks to Neptune we had a bath last night; please don't be offended or hold it against us if you feel such a washing isn't all that your ritual requires.

TRACHALIO (*looking up toward heaven, importantly*) Venus, if you ask me, that's a perfectly valid request and they deserve to have it granted. You should make allowances for them: the scare they had forced them into this informality. They tell me that you were born from a sea shell; don't leave these poor shells abandoned on the beach! (*As the door of the temple opens*) Look! Here's your savior and mine—the old man's coming out. He couldn't have picked a better time.

(*Daemones comes out followed by the two slaves, who are unceremoniously shoving Labrax ahead of them.*)

DAEMONES (*to Labrax*) Get out of that shrine, you scum of the earth! (*Turning to address the girls*) And you two sit down on the altar—where are they?

TRACHALIO Over here.

DAEMONES Perfect. Exactly what I wanted. Just let him try to get near them now. (*To Labrax*) So you thought you could get away with your lawbreaking inside a temple while we were around, eh? (*To one of the slaves*) Give him a sock on the jaw.

LABRAX (*blustering*) This is an outrage—and you'll pay for it!

DAEMONES What's that? You've got the nerve to make threats?

LABRAX (*as before*) You're depriving me of my rights. These are my girls and you took them from me without my consent.

TRACHALIO You go right down to City Hall here at Cyrene and pick yourself a judge—anyone you want, the most influential you can find. Let *him* decide whether these girls should be yours or should go free—and whether you shouldn't be clapped into jail and stay there until you wear the place out.

LABRAX (*turning on him*)   I'm in no mood today for conversation with a blasted slave. (*To Daemones*) It's you I want to talk to.

DAEMONES (*gesturing toward Trachalio*)   First you'll have it out with this fellow here. He knows you.

LABRAX (*curtly*)   My business is with you.

TRACHALIO   But you're going to take it up with me whether you like it or not. So these girls are yours, eh?

LABRAX   That's right.

TRACHALIO   Well, you just try touching either one of them with the tip of your little finger.

LABRAX (*belligerently*)   And what'll happen if I do?

TRACHALIO (*very brave with the odds four to one in his favor*) So help me, I'll make a punching bag out of you, that's what'll happen. I'll tie you up and knock the stuffings out of you, you damned liar.

LABRAX (*to Daemones*)   You mean I can't take my own girls away from that altar?

DAEMONES   That's what I mean. That's the law around here.

LABRAX (*scornfully*)   Your laws have nothing to do with me. I'm taking both those girls out of here right now. (*Leering*) If you're so much in love with them, you old goat, you're going to have to come across with hard cash. And if they're such favorites with Venus, she's welcome to them—if she pays me.

DAEMONES   Pay you! There's something you'd better get straight: if you try the least bit of rough stuff, even as a joke, on these girls, I'll send you away from here in such a state you won't recognize yourself. (*To the slaves*) Listen, you two. The minute I give the signal, knock the eyes out of his head. If you don't, I'll wrap a whip around you like twine on a spool.

LABRAX So you're going to use force on me, eh?

TRACHALIO (*exploding*) Look who's talking about force! You stinking hypocrite!

LABRAX (*shouting*) No blasted slave can talk to me like that!

TRACHALIO Sure, I'm a blasted slave and you're a saint—but that doesn't change the fact that these girls should be free.

LABRAX What do you mean, free?

TRACHALIO What's more, damn it, you ought to be their slave. They come from the heart of Greece. (*Pointing to Palaestra*) This one was born in Athens. Her parents were respectable Athenians.

DAEMONES (*eagerly*) What's that you say?

TRACHALIO I said this girl is an Athenian and was no slave when she was born.

DAEMONES You mean she's from my own city?

TRACHALIO (*surprised*) You weren't born here in Cyrene?

DAEMONES Oh, no. I'm a native Athenian, born and raised in Athens.

TRACHALIO Then I implore you to defend your fellow citizens.

DAEMONES (*sighing*) How I'm reminded of my own daughter when I look at this girl! The very thought stirs up old sorrows. Three years old she was, when I lost her, and if she's alive she'd be just that tall, I'm sure of it.

LABRAX I paid their owner good money for both of them. What do I care whether they come from Athens or Thebes so long as I'm satisfied with the way they slave for me.

TRACHALIO (*confident enough now to assume his orator's manner*) So, you sneaking cradle snatcher, you think you're going to get away with snatching infants from their mother's breast and grinding them to nothingness in your foul trade? I admit I don't know where this other girl comes from. But I know one thing: she's far above scum like you.

LABRAX (*sneering*) I suppose they belong to you?

TRACHALIO All right. Let's you and I take a back test to see which of us tells the truth. First I'll inspect you. And if that back of yours hasn't more welts from the whip than a ship's hull has nails, *I'm* the world's worst liar. Then you look at me. And if my hide isn't so smooth and unblemished that any leatherworker would classify it as absolutely top grade, give me one good reason why I shouldn't tan yours until I get tired of it. (*As Labrax glances toward the altar*) What are you staring at those girls for? You lay a hand on them and I'll gouge your eyes out!

LABRAX (*belligerently*)   You know what? Just because you say I can't do it, I'm going to take them both away with me right now.

DAEMONES (*scornfully*)   And just how do you propose to do that?

LABRAX   You've got Venus on your side? I'll use Vulcan. (*Rushing toward the door of the cottage*) I'm going for fire.

TRACHALIO (*alarmed*)   Where's he going?

LABRAX (*as he nears the door*)   Hey! Anybody inside? Hey, there!

DAEMONES (*calling*)   You touch that door and I'll fill that face of yours with fists for you. (*Nods to the two slaves, who run over and haul Labrax back.*)

SLAVE (*to Labrax, grinning*)   We don't use fire. All we eat is dried figs.

TRACHALIO   I'll give you fire all right—I'll light one on your head.

LABRAX   Damn it, I'll get fire from somewhere else then.

DAEMONES   And just what are you going to do with it when you get it?

LABRAX (*gesturing toward the altar*)   I'll start a bonfire right here.

DAEMONES   Funeral pyre for yourself, eh?

LABRAX   No, sir. I'm going to burn the both of them alive right here on the altar, that's what I'm going to do.

TRACHALIO   The minute you try it, I'll heave you in the fire by that beard of yours, haul you out just as you begin to brown, and feed you to the vultures.

DAEMONES (*to himself*)   Now it comes to me! This is the ape I saw in my dream, the one I wanted to keep from pulling the swallows out of their nest.

TRACHALIO (*to Daemones*)   Would you please do me a favor? Would you keep an eye on these girls and see that no harm comes to them while I go get my master?

DAEMONES   Go ahead. Find him and bring him here.

TRACHALIO (*gesturing toward Labrax*)   But don't let him—

DAEMONES (*interrupting*)   If he lays a hand on them, or even tries to, he'll be sorry.

TRACHALIO   Be careful now.

DAEMONES   I'm being careful. You go along.

TRACHALIO   But keep an eye on him too, so's he doesn't get away. We agreed to forfeit fifteen thousand dollars to the hangman if we didn't produce him today.

DAEMONES   Just run along. I'll take care of everything until you get back.

TRACHALIO   I'll be back right away. (*Exits, stage right.*)

DAEMONES (*to Labrax*)   Hey, pimp! I'll give you your choice: you prefer a beating to keep you quiet or will you stay still without one?

LABRAX   I don't give a damn what you say. These girls are mine, and I'm going to drag them off this altar by the hair whether you or Venus or god almighty himself likes it or not.

DAEMONES   Just try to touch them.

LABRAX   Sure I'll touch them.

DAEMONES (*with elaborate cordiality*)   Go right ahead. Step right this way. (*Points toward the altar.*)

LABRAX   You just tell those boys of yours to step back that way. (*Points away from the altar.*)

DAEMONES   Oh, no. Any stepping they do will be toward you.

LABRAX (*belligerently*) Oh, yeah? I don't think so.

DAEMONES What'll you do if they step closer? (*Nods to the slaves, who advance on Labrax.*)

LABRAX (*taking a hasty step backward*) I'll move back. Listen, you old goat, if I ever catch you back in town, believe me, I'll have my fun out of you before I let you go, or I'm no pimp.

DAEMONES (*grimly*) You do that. But, in the meantime, if you lay a hand on these girls I'll let you have it—and hard.

LABRAX Yeah? How hard?

DAEMONES Hard enough for a pimp.

LABRAX I don't give a damn for your threats. I'm dragging those girls out of here right now whether you like it or not.

DAEMONES Just try to touch them.

LABRAX Sure I'll touch them.

DAEMONES So you'll touch them, will you? And do you know what's going to happen? (*To one of the slaves*) Roughneck! Hurry into the house and bring out two clubs.

LABRAX (*taken aback*) Clubs?

DAEMONES (*to the slave*) Be sure they're thick ones. Quick! On the double! (*The slave dashes off. He turns back to Labrax.*) I'll see that you get the reception you deserve.

LABRAX (*to himself*) And I had to lose my helmet in the wreck! If I still had it, now's the time I could use it. (*To Daemones*) Look, can't I at least talk to them?

DAEMONES No, you can't. (*As the slave hurries back carrying two hefty clubs, jovially*) Look who's here—my clubman. Couldn't have come at a better time.

LABRAX (*to himself*) Look what's here—an earache. Couldn't have come at a worse time.

DAEMONES (*to the slaves*) Cutthroat, take one of those clubs. (*Pointing to either side of the altar*) Now one of you stand there, and one here. Take your positions. (*Nodding with satisfaction as they do*) That's the way. Now listen to me. If he lays a finger on them and you don't lay those clubs on him until he doesn't know which way is up, so help me, I'll murder you both. If he tries to talk to either one of them, stay just where you are and answer instead. And the minute he tries to get away from here, wrap those clubs around his shins as fast as you can.

LABRAX You mean they're not even going to let me leave here?

DAEMONES (*distastefully*) I've got no more to say to you. (*To the slaves*) And when that servant who went for his master gets back here with him, you come right home. Mind you—do exactly what I told you. (*Goes into the cottage.*)

LABRAX (*to himself*) Amazing how quickly shrines change around here. A minute ago this one belonged to Venus; now it's Hercules'—that's what it looks like with these two statues, clubs and all, that the old man just set up. God almighty, I don't know where I can run to now. Storms everywhere: first on sea, and now on land. (*Calling*) Palaestra!

SLAVE What do you want?

LABRAX Hey, must be some mistake; this Palaestra isn't the one I know. (*Calling*) Ampelisca!

SLAVE Watch yourself or I'll let you have it.

LABRAX (*to himself*) Not bad advice, even though it comes from a pair of clods like this. (*To the slaves*) Hey, you two, I'm talking to you. No harm in my going a little closer to them, is there?

SLAVE Not at all—for us.

LABRAX How about for me?

SLAVE None for you either—if you can keep your eyes open.

LABRAX Keep my eyes open for what?

SLAVE (*brandishing the club*) See this? For a good hard wallop.

LABRAX For god's sake, please just let me get out of here! (*Takes a tentative step away.*)

SLAVE   Go right ahead, if you want. (*The two take a step toward him.*)

LABRAX (*backing away in a hurry*)   Very kind of you; thanks very much. No, I think I'll stick around—and you fellows can stand right where you are. (*To himself*) God damn it, I'm not doing well at all. (*Settling himself for a long wait*) Well, I'll get those girls yet. I'll stay put and starve them out.

(*Plesidippus and Trachalio enter, stage right, deep in conversation.*)

PLESIDIPPUS (*shocked*)   You mean that pimp wanted to drag my girl away from Venus' altar by brute force?

TRACHALIO   Exactly.

PLESIDIPPUS   Why didn't you kill him on the spot?

TRACHALIO (*glibly*)   I didn't have a sword.

PLESIDIPPUS   You should have picked up a stick or a rock.

TRACHALIO (*as if appalled at the suggestion*)   What? Chase a man with stones like a dog?

PLESIDIPPUS   That scum? Of course!

LABRAX (*catching sight of them, to himself*)   Oh, lord, now I'm in for it! Here comes Plesidippus. By the time he gets done, there won't be a speck of me left.

PLESIDIPPUS   Were the girls still sitting on the altar when you left to get me?

TRACHALIO (*looking toward the altar*)   They're there right now.

PLESIDIPPUS   Who's minding them?

TRACHALIO   Some old fellow who lives next door to the shrine. He gave us all the help you could ask for. He and his servants are standing guard. (*Importantly*) I ordered him to.

PLESIDIPPUS   Take me right to that pimp. Where is he?

LABRAX (*ingratiatingly*)   Good morning, Plesidippus.

PLESIDIPPUS   Don't you good-morning me! You're getting a

1

rope around your neck: do you prefer to be carried or dragged? Make up your mind while you still have the chance.

LABRAX (*gulping*)   Neither, thanks.

PLESIDIPPUS (*to Trachalio*)   Trachalio, get down to the beach on the double. You know those fellows I brought out here with me to help me hand this creature over to the hangman? Tell them to go back to town and meet me down at the docks. Then come back here and stand guard. I'm hauling this godforsaken good-for-nothing into court. (*As Trachalio dashes off, stage right, Plesidippus goes up to Labrax and ties a rope around his neck.*) Come on, get moving. We're heading for the courthouse.

LABRAX (*with injured innocence*)   What did I do?

PLESIDIPPUS (*exploding*)   What did you do? I suppose you didn't take a deposit from me for the girl and then carry her off?

LABRAX   I did *not* carry her off.

PLESIDIPPUS   How can you say a thing like that?

LABRAX   I only carried her on board. It was my damned luck that I wasn't able to carry her off. Look—I told you I'd meet you at the shrine of Venus. Didn't I do just what I said? I'm here, ain't I?

PLESIDIPPUS (*grimly*)   Tell it to the judge. There's been enough talk around here. Follow me. (*Starts walking off, jerking Labrax after him at the end of the rope.*)

LABRAX (*shouting*)   Charmides! Help! They've tied a rope around my neck and they're hauling me off!

CHARMIDES (*appearing in the doorway of the temple*)   Who's calling me?

LABRAX (*frantically*)   See the way they're hauling me off?

CHARMIDES (*coolly*)   I sure do. And I'm delighted to see it.

LABRAX (*unbelievingly*)   You mean to say you're not going to help me?

CHARMIDES (*disinterestedly*)   Who's hauling you off?

LABRAX   That young fellow Plesidippus.

CHARMIDES   (*grinning*)   You were out to get him, now keep him. You ought to creep into jail happy as a lark. You've just had happen to you what most people in the world wish for.

LABRAX   What's that?

CHARMIDES   (*as before*)   Getting what they've been looking for.

LABRAX   (*desperately*)   Please, Charmides, stick with me! (*Grabs hold of him.*)

CHARMIDES   (*disgustedly*)   Just like you to ask a thing like that. You're being hauled off to jail, so you want me to go along too. Come on, let go of me! (*Brushes Labrax's arm away.*)

LABRAX   I'm sunk!

PLESIDIPPUS   I hope to god you're right. (*Turning to the girls*) Palaestra, dear, and you, Ampelisca, stay right here until I get back.

SLAVE   I think they'd be better off in our house until you come back for them.

PLESIDIPPUS   Good idea; thanks very much. (*The two slaves lead the girls into the cottage.*)

LABRAX   (*shouting at them*)   You're a bunch of robbers!

SLAVE   What's that? Robbers? (*To Plesidippus*) Haul him out of here.

LABRAX   (*calling*)   Palaestra, please, I beg you—

PLESIDIPPUS   (*jerking the rope*)   Damn you, follow me!

LABRAX   (*to Charmides*)   My friend—

CHARMIDES   (*distastefully*)   I'm no friend of yours. You and I are quits.

LABRAX   So you're throwing me over, eh?

CHARMIDES   That's exactly what I'm doing. One drinking session with you was enough.

LABRAX (*as Plesidippus hauls him off, stage left*)　God damn you to hell!

CHARMIDES (*calling after him*)　Same to you! (*To the audience*) I'm a believer in the theory that men get turned into different kinds of animals. If you ask me, that pimp is being turned into a bird—a jailbird. He's going to build a nest in the town lockup right now. But I'm going to stand by him in court. Maybe I can help convince the judge to let him go—to jail.

(*Exits, stage left, and the stage is now empty.*)

ACT IV

(*Daemones comes out of the cottage.*)

DAEMONES (*to the audience*) That was a good turn I did today, helping those girls, and a very pleasant one to do. Now I have a pair of devoted followers—young ones, too, and not bad looking. But that shrew of a wife of mine is watching me like a hawk to make sure I don't start anything with either one of them. (*Looking off, stage right, toward the sea*) I wonder how my servant Gripus is doing? He took the boat out last night for some fishing. Believe me, he'd have shown more sense if he had stayed in bed. With the weather we had last night, and are having right now, he's wasting his time, his energy, and his nets. Look how rough that water is! I'll be able to fry what he catches on my fingers. (*A call is heard from inside.*) There's my wife calling me for lunch. (*Heaving a sigh*) I'd better go in; it's time for my earful of her gabble.

(*Daemones goes into the cottage. A second later Gripus, "the fisherman," enters, stage right. He is hauling mightily at his net, dragging along in it a satchel that, to judge by the effort it takes to move it, is no light weight; a rope, tied to the satchel, trails loosely behind. Gripus is by nature sour and uncommunicative, very much like his fellow slave Sceparnio; at the moment, however, his face is wearing an expression that is almost beatific.*)

SONG

GRIPUS (*to the audience*)
        I'm sending many thanks down to
        My benefactor Neptune, who
        Resides where salt and fish abound.
        When I left his bailiwick, you see,
        He sent me off decked royally:
        A load of loot and my boat still sound.

Through heavy seas it had carried me
To a rich, new type of fishing ground.

(*Breathlessly*)

It's a marvel, a freak, to have made such a haul!
Best fishing I've ever done yet.
Though I didn't pull in one more ounce of fresh fish
Than what I've got here in my net.

(*Pauses, then resumes less excitedly*)

At 1:00 A.M. I jumped from bed—
I felt a chance to get ahead
Was better than a good night's sleep.
I had in mind, though the seas were steep,
To see if I could somehow ease
This hard-up family's miseries.
(And help myself as well, I'll add.)
I gave the project all I had.

(*Vehemently*)

Any man who is lazy is not worth a damn;
The whole bunch of them makes me see red.
If a man wants to finish his work in good time,
He should know when to get out of bed
And not wait for his master to call him to work.
If a man likes to sleep or to sun, he
Will get plenty of rest, but he'll find there's a quirk:
It pays off—but in trouble, not money.

(*Rapturously*)

I, who've never lazed a day,
Now have found the means for a
Life of lazing, if I like.
On the sea this lucky strike
Came my way. Who knows just what
This contains—but it weighs a lot!

(*Excitedly*)

Do you know what I think? That there's gold inside here!

Not a soul knows about it but I.
Now's your chance, Gripus boy, to be free as a bird.
Here's my plan, here's the scheme that I'll try.
I'll go up to the master, and, playing it smart,
Make a very low bid for my head.
I'll keep upping the price till he lets me go free.
Once I'm free of this life that I've led,
I'll go buy me a farm and a house and some slaves.
I'll invest next in shipping, that's what.
I'll be rolling in money and known far and wide.
Then I'll build me a luxury yacht,

(*Working himself up*)

And I'll do what the millionaires do,
Take a round-the-world cruise, maybe two.
When I get enough fame and renown,
I'll erect a big fortified town,

(*Reaching his climax*)

A metropolis named Gripopolis,
A memorial to Gripus, the hero renowned,
The capital of a nation, one that I'll found!

(*Pauses for a moment transfixed, then comes to*)

I'm standing here with big ideas
        Of the things I'll do some day,
When I'd better take this satchel here
        And hide it right away.
And then, King Gripus, soon you'll munch
        The bread and beans you'll get for lunch!

(*As he starts walking toward the cottage, Trachalio enters, stage left, sees him and his catch—and immediately becomes extremely interested.*)

TRACHALIO (*calling*)
        Hey, wait.
GRIPUS (*suspiciously*)
                What for?

TRACHALIO (*casually reaching down to pick up the trailing rope, cheerily*)

>   Your rope is dragging, see?
> I'll coil it up for you.

GRIPUS (*curtly*)

>   Just let it be.

TRACHALIO (*holding on, brightly*)

> Please let me help. No matter what the cost,
> To do good folks good turns is never lost.

GRIPUS (*uneasily*)

> That windstorm yesterday just wouldn't end.
> Don't get ideas—I've got no fish, my friend.
> Why, can't you see I'm dragging back a net
> With nothing scaly in it, only wet?

TRACHALIO (*heartily*)

> It's not your fish I want, oh no indeed.
> Your charming conversation's what I need.

GRIPUS (*pulling on the net and trying to walk away*)

> You bore me to tears, whoever you are. Let go!

TRACHALIO (*pulling in the opposite direction and bringing him to a halt*)

> Now, *I'm* not letting you leave this place. So, whoa!

GRIPUS

> Hey, what's the big idea of holding me back?
> You watch your step or that jaw will get a smack.

TRACHALIO

> Now, listen here—

GRIPUS (*interrupting*)

>   I won't.

TRACHALIO (*grimly*)

>   You won't right now,
> But later on you'll listen, boy, and how!

GRIPUS (*trying, without much success, to sound indifferent*)

> Oh, speak your piece.

TRACHALIO

                What I want to tell to you,
You'll find well worth your while to listen to.

GRIPUS (*as before*)

    All right, start talking, you. What's on your mind?

TRACHALIO (*looking around warily*)

    First look and see if anyone's behind.

GRIPUS (*looks around and turns back; nervously*)

    Is it something to do, say, with me?

TRACHALIO

    Well, of course! What I'm after, you see,
Is your view on a matter in doubt.

GRIPUS

    You just tell me what this is about.

TRACHALIO

    Just keep quiet. You'll hear. But I must have fair play—
Do you give me your word you won't give me away?

GRIPUS (*anxiously*)

    Whoever you are, here's my word. It's okay.

TRACHALIO (*confidentially*)

    Now then, listen. I happened to see
A thief rob a man known to me.
So I later go up to the crook,
And I give him this deal, I say, "Look,
As it happens, I know whom you robbed.
He'll hear nothing about it at all
If you'll hand over half of the haul."
Now, I've not heard a word from him yet.
Well, how much of a share should I get?
I expect you'll say half. Am I right?

GRIPUS (*blurting*)

    God, I'd ask even more! You're all set:
If he won't come across, don't think twice,
Turn him in to his victim on sight!

TRACHALIO (*promptly*)

    Now I'm ready to use your advice.

(*Pointing a finger at him*)
>   Listen carefully now. It's all true—
>   And the crook it applies to is *you!*

GRIPUS (*startled*) What do you mean?

TRACHALIO That satchel there—I've known all along whose it is—

GRIPUS (*interrupting, defensively*) What are you talking about?

TRACHALIO —and how it was lost.

GRIPUS (*heatedly*) But *I* know how it was found and *I* know who found it and *I* know who owns it now. What you know is none of my business, any more than what I know is yours. You know whose it used to be. I know whose it is now. (*Grimly*) There isn't a man alive who can take it away from me, so don't get your hopes up that you can.

TRACHALIO You mean you won't give it up if the owner comes for it?

GRIPUS The owner? Make no mistake about it, my friend, there's only one man in this world who owns this thing— me. I caught it when I was fishing.

TRACHALIO You did, eh?

GRIPUS (*argumentatively*) You won't deny my right to the fish in the sea, will you? If, as, and when I catch any, they're mine. I keep them; they're my property. No one else lays a hand on them or puts in any claims for any share. They're my goods and I sell them as such in the fish market. The sea is absolutely public domain; everybody shares it in common.

TRACHALIO (*promptly*) Agreed. So then, my friend, why shouldn't I share this satchel in common? It came from the sea—public domain, you know.

GRIPUS Don't be a wise guy. If the law was the way you put it, fishermen would be finished. The minute any fish went up for sale in the market, everyone would start claiming a share; no one would buy a thing. Everyone'd say they were caught in the public domain.

TRACHALIO   Who's the wise guy now? Compare a satchel to a fish? What a nerve! Are you trying to tell me you think they're the same?

GRIPUS   (*shrugging*)   That's no problem of mine. When I throw over a net or a line, whatever gets caught there I pull up. And what my nets or lines catch is mine, absolutely and positively mine.

TRACHALIO   Oh, no, it isn't. Not if you pulled up some pot, say.

GRIPUS   (*scornfully*)   What are you, a lawyer?

TRACHALIO   Listen, you stinker, did you ever in your life see a fisherman catch a satchel-fish or peddle one in the market? You can't take over just any trade you want, not by a long shot. Damn you, you want to be a fisherman and a satchel-maker all in one. Either you show me exactly how a satchel is a fish or you don't walk off with something that doesn't have scales and certainly wasn't born in salt water.

GRIPUS   (*affecting incredulity*)   What? You never heard of a satchel-fish before?

TRACHALIO   Cut it out. There's no such thing.

GRIPUS   (*assuming the air of an expert*)   Oh, yes there is. I'm a fisherman, I know. But you don't often catch them. Isn't a fish around landed less often.

TRACHALIO   You're wasting your time. You can't kid me, you crook. All right, what color is it?

GRIPUS   (*as before, pointing to the satchel*)   Very few are like this one here. Some of them have a dark red skin. Then there are some that are big and black.

TRACHALIO   Oh, sure. (*Savagely*) If you want my opinion, you better watch out or you'll turn into a satchel-fish yourself: that skin of yours is going to get dark red, and then wind up black—and blue.

GRIPUS (*half to himself*)   The god-damned trouble I had to run into today!

TRACHALIO (*impatiently*)   This argument's getting us nowhere. We're wasting time. Come on, my friend, who do you want to pick as judge to settle this for us?

GRIPUS (*eying him balefully*)   Judge? The satchel.

TRACHALIO   Oh, yeah?

GRIPUS   Yeah.

TRACHALIO (*exasperated*)   God, you're stupid!

GRIPUS (*scornfully*)   Well, listen to the professor!

TRACHALIO (*getting a firm grip on the rope*)   You're not moving an inch with this thing today—not unless you agree to a third party to hold it or a judge to judge the matter.

GRIPUS   Look here, are you in your right mind?

TRACHALIO (*scornfully*)   I'm as mad as a hatter.

GRIPUS (*tightening his grip on the net*)   Then I'm as crazy as a loon—but I'm not letting go.

TRACHALIO   You say one more word and I'll sink my fists in your skull. You know what they do to a new sponge? If you don't let go, that's the way I'll squeeze the juice out of you.

GRIPUS   You know how I slam the ink out of an octopus? You lay a finger on me and that's what I'll do to you. (*Sticking his chin in Trachalio's face*) So you want to fight, eh?

TRACHALIO (*abruptly losing his belligerence*)   Why do we have to fight? Why don't you and I just split the swag?

GRIPUS   Don't get any ideas: the only thing you'll be able to get for yourself out of all this is a sock on the jaw. (*Starts pulling the net toward the cottage*) I'm getting out of here.

TRACHALIO (*running ahead and yanking the rope so that the net—and Gripus—are spun about*)   No, you're not getting out of here—I'm putting this ship about. You stay where you are.

GRIPUS (*between his teeth*)   If you're going to play deck

hand on this ship, I'll be skipper. (*Roaring*) Damn you, let go that rope!

TRACHALIO   Sure I'll let go. You let go that satchel.

GRIPUS   By god, you're not going to get one single solitary square inch of this satchel.

TRACHALIO (*standing his ground*)   You can't get around me just by saying no. Either you cut me in, or you put up security, or you let a judge decide.

GRIPUS   What do you mean? Something I caught in the sea—

TRACHALIO (*interrupting*)   But I saw it from the shore.

GRIPUS (*disregarding him*)   —with my own hands, my own net, and my own boat?

TRACHALIO   I saw you get it from the shore, right? So, if the owner should come along, then I'm in this thing just as deep as you are, I'm an accomplice, right?

GRIPUS   Right.

TRACHALIO   All right, you stinker, you just prove to me how I can be an accomplice and not be entitled to a cut. Come on, show me how!

GRIPUS (*baffled and confused*)   I don't know. I don't know anything about that legal stuff you city boys do. All I say is that this satchel is mine.

TRACHALIO   And I say it's mine.

GRIPUS (*switching suddenly to affability*)   Wait a second. I just figured out how you don't have to be an accomplice—or get a cut.

TRACHALIO   Yeah? How?

GRIPUS   First you let me leave here. Then you go your own way—and keep your mouth shut. You don't say a word about me to anybody—and I don't give you anything. You stay mum, and I keep my trap shut. That's the fairest and squarest way to do it.

TRACHALIO   You mean you're not going to offer me a deal?

GRIPUS (*promptly*)   I already did: that you let go that rope, go away, and stop bothering me.

TRACHALIO   Wait a second. I've got a counteroffer to make.

GRIPUS   Yeah? Well offer to get the hell out of here.

TRACHALIO   (*disregarding the last remark, with elaborate casualness*)   Do you know anybody hereabouts?

GRIPUS   (*evasively*)   My own neighbors, naturally.

TRACHALIO   (*as before*)   Whereabouts do you live?

GRIPUS   (*waving vaguely*)   Farther on. Lots farther on. 'Way off at the end of those fields out there.

TRACHALIO   (*concealing his satisfaction at the answer, even more casually than before*)   How'd you like the fellow who lives in this cottage to be judge?

GRIPUS   (*concealing his satisfaction at the suggestion*)   Suppose you give me a little slack on that rope so I can step off to the side and think it over?

TRACHALIO   Sure. (*Slacks off the rope, letting Gripus lug the net a few feet off to the side.*)

GRIPUS   (*to the audience, jubilantly*)   Hooray! I'm in! The swag's mine for keeps. He's inviting me to call in my own master as judge, right here on my own home grounds. Good old Daemones wouldn't judge anyone in his household out of a penny. This fellow here has no idea what kind of deal he's offering me. Sure I'll take a judge!

TRACHALIO   Well, what do you say?

GRIPUS   (*as if grudgingly*)   Even though I know for sure that by rights this thing is mine, rather than have a fight with you, I'll do it your way.

TRACHALIO   (*heartily*)   That's what I like to hear.

GRIPUS   (*as before*)   And even though you're bringing me up before a judge I don't know, if he turns out honest, I may not know him but I want to; if he doesn't, I may know him but he's the last man in the world I want to. (*The door of the cottage opens and Daemones and the two girls come out.*)

DAEMONES   (*to the girls*)   Much as I want to do what you want me to, girls, I'm afraid that wife of mine will kick me out of the house on account of you. She'll say I'm bringing in a pair of mistresses right under her nose. I'd rather have you two running to that altar for help than me.

PALAESTRA Oh, my god! This is the end!

DAEMONES (*reassuringly*) Don't be afraid. I'll make sure you're safe. (*Noticing that the two slaves with the clubs are tagging along after the girls*) What are you following them outside for? No one's going to hurt them with me around. All right, guards, off guard and into the house, both of you. (*They go back into the cottage.*)

GRIPUS Hello, master.

DAEMONES Why, Gripus! Hello! How did things go?

TRACHALIO (*startled, to Daemones*) Is he your servant?

GRIPUS (*grinning*) His servant, and proud of it.

TRACHALIO (*glaring at him*) I've got nothing to say to you.

GRIPUS Yeah? Then get out of here.

TRACHALIO (*to Daemones*) Please, mister, tell me: is he your servant?

DAEMONES Yes, he is.

TRACHALIO (*jubilantly*) Oh, boy! If he's yours, that's the best thing that could have happened! I'll say it for the second time today: I'm mighty glad to meet you.

DAEMONES (*cordially*) Glad to meet you too. Aren't you the one who left here to get your master a little while ago?

TRACHALIO I'm the one.

DAEMONES Well, what can we do for you?

TRACHALIO So he's yours, eh?

DAEMONES Yes, he is.

TRACHALIO (*grinning broadly*) If he's yours, that's the best thing that could have happened.

DAEMONES What's this all about?

TRACHALIO (*pointing to Gripus, vehemently*) That devil there is a damned crook!

DAEMONES (*patiently*) And just what has the "damned crook" done to you?

TRACHALIO I want him drawn and quartered!

DAEMONES Now what is this you two are making such a case about?

TRACHALIO I'll tell you.

GRIPUS (*quickly*) Oh, no you don't. I'll tell him.

TRACHALIO (*with elaborate formality*) If I'm not mistaken, I have the right to open this action.

GRIPUS If you had any decency, you'd get into action and get out of here.

DAEMONES (*sharply*) Gripus! Shut up and listen.

GRIPUS (*unbelievingly*) You mean he's going to speak first?

DAEMONES (*nodding curtly*) You listen. (*To Trachalio*) And you start talking.

GRIPUS (*as before*) You're going to let an outsider talk ahead of one of your own household?

TRACHALIO (*eying him balefully*) Isn't there any way to handle this fellow? (*Turning to Daemones*) What I started to tell you was this. Remember that pimp you kicked out of the temple? Well, this fellow has his satchel. (*Pointing*) See? There it is.

GRIPUS (*trying to edge in front of the net*) I haven't got it.

TRACHALIO What do you mean you haven't got it? I'm not blind.

GRIPUS (*aside*) I only wish you were! (*To Trachalio*) I have it, I don't have it—what are you sticking your nose into my affairs for?

TRACHALIO (*doggedly*) What's more important is how you got it, whether legally or illegally.

GRIPUS (*to Daemones, heatedly*) You can string me up by the neck this minute if I didn't find this satchel while I was fishing. (*To Trachalio*) And if I fished it up from the sea with my own net, how do you figure it's yours instead of mine?

TRACHALIO (*to Daemones*) He's trying to pull the wool over your eyes. What I just told you are the facts.

GRIPUS (*menacingly*) What did I hear you say?

TRACHALIO (*to Daemones*) He's yours, isn't he? Can't you handle him somehow? Get him to shut up until his betters finish speaking?

GRIPUS (*leering and making an obscene gesture*) So you want me to get what your master gives you, eh? Well, yours may "handle" you, all right, but ours doesn't pull that stuff with us.

DAEMONES (*to Trachalio, smiling*) He got the better of you there, my boy. Now, what is it you want? Speak up.

TRACHALIO For myself, nothing. I don't want any part of that satchel there, and I never once said it was mine. But there's a little jewel box in it that belongs to this girl here (*gesturing toward Palaestra*). She's the one I was telling you earlier was no slave.

DAEMONES (*nodding*) You mean the one you said came from the same city I did?

TRACHALIO Exactly. Well, the birth tokens she wore when she was a child are there in that box, and the box is there in that satchel. (*Nodding scornfully in Gripus' direction*) It's no earthly use to him, but he'll be doing this poor girl a real service if he gives her the only means she has for finding her parents.

DAEMONES Say no more. I'll have him hand it over.

GRIPUS So help me, I'm not giving him a thing!

TRACHALIO (*to Daemones*) All I'm asking for is the jewel box and birth tokens.

GRIPUS Oh, yeah? What if they're gold?

TRACHALIO What difference should that make to you? (*Loftily*) Any gold or silver will be bought and paid for in cash.

GRIPUS All right, my friend, you let me see that cash and I'll let you see the box.

DAEMONES   Gripus, shut up or you'll be sorry. (*To Tracha-lio*) Finish what you started to say.

TRACHALIO (*earnestly*)   I have just one favor to ask of you: have pity on this girl—I mean, if the satchel really is that pimp's, as I suspect it is. (*Pointedly*) You see, at this moment I can't say anything for sure, I can only guess.

GRIPUS (*to Daemones, excitedly*)   Don't you see? That good-for-nothing's trying to lay a trap for us!

TRACHALIO (*to Gripus*)   Will you let me finish talking? (*To Daemones*) I say the satchel belongs to that filthy pimp. Now, if it does, the girls will be able to recognize it. So will you please make him show it to them?

GRIPUS (*spluttering*)   What's that? Show it to them?

DAEMONES (*mildly*)   There's nothing wrong with his suggestion, is there, Gripus? Just to show it to them?

GRIPUS (*roaring*)   I should say there is! A hell of a lot wrong!

DAEMONES   How so?

GRIPUS   Because the minute I show it to them, naturally they'll say they recognize it.

TRACHALIO (*heatedly*)   Damn you, you think everybody's as big a liar as you are!

GRIPUS (*gesturing toward Daemones*)   So long as he's on my side, you can say anything you like; it won't bother me in the least.

TRACHALIO   He may be standing on your side, but he's going to take his testimony from this side (*pointing to the girls*).

DAEMONES (*sharply*)   Gripus, you listen. (*To Trachalio*) And you explain what you want—and make it short.

TRACHALIO (*patiently*)   I already did. But if you didn't follow me, I'll do it again. As I've already told you, neither of these girls should be slaves. (*Gesturing toward Palaestra*) This one here was kidnaped from Athens when she was a child.

GRIPUS   Suppose you explain to me just what their being slaves or not has to do with this satchel?

TRACHALIO (*angrily*) Damn you, you want me to tell the story all over again just to waste the whole day.

DAEMONES (*to Trachalio, sharply*) Cut out the cursing and do what I asked you.

TRACHALIO It's just as I told you before. There should be a little jewel box in that satchel. It contains the birth tokens she can use to identify her parents. She was wearing them when she was snatched from Athens as a child.

GRIPUS (*savagely*) I wish to god someone'd put the snatch on you! What the hell's going on here? (*Gesturing angrily toward the girls*) What's the matter with them? Are they dumb? Can't they talk for themselves?

TRACHALIO Sure. But they're keeping quiet because they know that's what makes a good woman—knowing how to keep quiet and not talk.

GRIPUS So help me, by that token you don't make either a good man or a good woman.

TRACHALIO Why?

GRIPUS Because you're no good whether you talk or keep quiet. (*To Daemones*) Please! Am I going to get a chance to speak today?

DAEMONES (*turning on him*) One more word out of you today and I'll have your head!

TRACHALIO (*to Daemones*) As I was saying, would you please make him give the box back to the girls? If he insists on some sort of reward, he can have one: let him keep whatever else is in the satchel for himself.

GRIPUS Finally you said it! And you know why? Because you know very well what my rights in the matter are. A few minutes ago you were out to get half for yourself.

TRACHALIO You know what? I still am.

GRIPUS I once saw a vulture out to get something, and you know what? He didn't get away with a thing.

DAEMONES (*to Gripus, angrily*) Do you need a beating to keep you quiet?

GRIPUS (*stubbornly*)   If he shuts up, I'll shut up. But if he's going to talk, let me talk too, and give my side of the story.

DAEMONES   Gripus, hand me that satchel.

GRIPUS   I'll trust you with it if you promise that, if there's nothing of theirs in it, I get it back.

DAEMONES   You'll get it back.

GRIPUS (*taking the satchel out of the net and handing it over*) Here it is.

DAEMONES   Now, Palaestra, and you too, Ampelisca, listen to me. Is this the satchel you say has your box in it?

PALAESTRA (*without hesitation*)   Yes, it is.

GRIPUS   Oh, my god in heaven, I haven't got a chance! She said it was hers before she even got a good look at it!

PALAESTRA (*earnestly*)   I know it's confusing, so let me clear things up for you. There should be a little wicker box in that satchel. Now, without your showing me a thing, I'll name every article that's in it. If I make a mistake, then I've wasted my breath and you people keep whatever's in there for yourselves. But if I don't, then please, please let me have my things back.

DAEMONES   Agreed. In my opinion, what you're asking for is plain and simple justice.

GRIPUS   And in mine, damn it all, plain and simple injustice. Supposing she's a witch or a fortuneteller and reels off the name of whatever's in there perfectly? Are we going to let some fortuneteller walk off with everything?

DAEMONES (*sharply*)   She's not walking off with a thing unless she names every item without a mistake. Fortune-telling won't get her anywhere. Now, unstrap that satchel so that I can find out who's right and who's wrong without wasting another minute.

TRACHALIO (*watching Gripus unstrap the satchel, aside with satisfaction*)   And that settles *his* hash.

GRIPUS (*to Daemones*)   The straps are off.

DAEMONES   Now open it.

PALAESTRA (*excitedly*)   I see the box!

DAEMONES (*taking it out and holding it*)   Is this it?

PALAESTRA   That's it! (*Extending her hand and touching it almost caressingly, to herself*) Dear parents, all I have of you I carry locked up here. Here are stored all my hopes, the only means I have of ever finding you.

GRIPUS (*to himself, growling*)   You deserve the wrath of god on your head, whoever you are, for squeezing your parents into something that small.

DAEMONES (*pointing to a spot at his side*)   Gripus, you stand here; this concerns you now. (*To Palaestra*) You stand over there and call off all the things in the box and tell us what each looks like. Mind you, don't leave anything out. And, believe me, if you make the slightest mistake, don't get any ideas about correcting it later. It'll be a sheer waste of time, my girl. (*Palaestra nods and steps a few paces away.*)

GRIPUS (*nodding approvingly*)   You're asking only for what's fair.

TRACHALIO   God knows he wouldn't ask anything like that of you. You don't know what it is to be fair.

DAEMONES (*to Palaestra*)   All right, my girl, you can start now. (*As Gripus opens his mouth*) Gripus! Shut up and pay attention.

PALAESTRA (*with her back to Daemones and Gripus*)   The box has my birth tokens.

DAEMONES (*holding the box open before him*)   I see them.

GRIPUS (*to himself*)   Knocked out in the first round! (*Grabbing Daemones' arm to bring the box closer to his chest*) Wait a second! Don't show them to her!

DAEMONES   Now tell me what each one of them looks like.

PALAESTRA   First there's a miniature gold sword. It's inscribed.

DAEMONES   What's the inscription say?

PALAESTRA   My father's name. Next, alongside the sword is

a miniature two-headed ax, also of gold and inscribed; this time it's my mother's name.

DAEMONES   Wait a second. What is your father's name? I mean the one on the sword?

PALAESTRA   Daemones.

(*Daemones holds the trinket in his hand and stares at the letters in amazement. Slowly he lifts his head to look toward the sky.*)

DAEMONES (*to himself, hoarsely*)   God in heaven! What is happening to all my hopes!

GRIPUS (*aside*)   You mean what's happening to all mine!

TRACHALIO (*to Palaestra and Daemones, eagerly*)   Please! Go on, don't stop!

GRIPUS (*turning on him*)   Either you take it easy or go straight to hell!

DAEMONES (*in a voice so full of emotion it is barely audible*)   Tell me, what's the name on the little ax, your mother's name?

PALAESTRA   Daedalis.

DAEMONES (*to himself, choking with emotion*)   It was heaven's will to rescue me!

GRIPUS (*aside*)   And throw me overboard!

DAEMONES (*sotto voce to Gripus*)   Gripus! This girl! She must be my daughter!

GRIPUS (*not exactly overcome by the news, sotto voce*)   It's all right with me. (*Looking toward Trachalio, under his breath*)   God damn you to hell for having gotten a look at me today—and me for being damned fool enough not to have looked around a hundred times to make sure no one was watching before I pulled that net out of the water!

PALAESTRA (*unaware of the excitement she is causing*)   Next a miniature silver sickle, and two clasped hands, and a miniature windlass—

GRIPUS (*aside*)   Windlass? I wish to hell you were windless.

PALAESTRA —and a gold medallion my father gave me on my birthday.

DAEMONES (*to himself, ecstatically*) It's she! I must take her in my arms! (*Rushing to her and taking her hands*) My daughter! I'm you own father! I'm Daemones! Daedalis —your mother—is right inside!

PALAESTRA (*throwing herself into his arms*) Oh, my father, my father! Who ever imagined this could happen!

DAEMONES (*holding her tightly*) What a joy it is to have you in my arms!

TRACHALIO (*beaming on them*) It's a joy to see how heaven has rewarded you both for being as good as you are.

DAEMONES Trachalio, pick up the satchel if you can and bring it inside. Hurry!

TRACHALIO (*to Gripus, grinning broadly*) See where all your dirty tricks got you? My heartiest congratulations on your bad luck.

DAEMONES (*to Palaestra*) Come, my daughter, let's go in to your mother. She'll be able to test you further about all this. She used to be with you more, and she's more familiar with these trinkets of yours.

PALAESTRA Let's all go in. Then we can do it all together. (*Turning to Ampelisca*) Follow me, Ampelisca.

AMPELISCA (*tearfully*) I'm so happy that god has been so good to you!

(*Daemones, Trachalio, and the two girls enter the cottage.*)

GRIPUS (*to himself*) Why the hell did I have to fish that satchel up today? Or, rather, why the hell didn't I stash it away in a safe spot after I fished it up? So help me, it was so rough out there when I found the thing, I knew I'd have a rough time with it. God, I'll bet that satchel's full of money. The best thing for me to do now is just sneak off and hang myself—at least for a while until the ache goes away! (*Exits, stage right.*)

(*The door of the cottage opens and Daemones emerges. He is radiant. He walks downstage and addresses the audience.*)

DAEMONES I swear I'm the luckiest man in the world! Suddenly, like a bolt from the blue, I found my daughter. (*Shaking his head wonderingly*) You know, when heaven wants to do well by a man, somehow he ends up getting his fondest wish—if he's been decent and god-fearing. Take me —today, like a bolt from the blue, I found my daughter, something I had given up hoping for, no longer believed could happen. And I'm going to marry her to a fine young fellow from one of the best families in Athens. What's more, I find that he's a relative of mine. I want him to come out here and see me just as soon as possible, so I've told his servant to step outside; I want to send him to town right away. (*Looking toward the door*) He hasn't come out yet. I wonder what's keeping him? I think I'd better take a look inside. (*Walks back to the entrance and peers in.*) What's this? My wife hanging on to my daughter's neck? All this hugging and loving is getting to be a silly nuisance. (*Calling through the doorway*) My dear wife, it's time to stop the kissing and start getting things ready for me. As soon as I come in I want to give a thank offering to our guardian angel for having added to our family the way he has. The lambs and pigs for the sacrifice are all ready. (*Impatiently*) What are you women keeping Trachalio for? (*Stepping back from the door*) Good. He's coming out now.

TRACHALIO (*as he hurries out the door, breathlessly*) I don't care where he is, I'll track him down and bring him back here with me. Plesidippus, I mean.

DAEMONES (*nodding approval*) And tell him what happened about my daughter. Ask him to drop everything and come right out here.

TRACHALIO Right.

DAEMONES Tell him he has my permission to marry her.

TRACHALIO Right.

DAEMONES   And that I know his father; he's a relative of mine.

TRACHALIO   Right.

DAEMONES   And hurry.

TRACHALIO   Right.

DAEMONES   Bring him here right away, so we can start preparing dinner.

TRACHALIO   Right.

DAEMONES   (*somewhat irritated*) Everything I say is "right," eh?

TRACHALIO   Right. But do you know what I'd like from you? That you remember the promise you made about my getting my freedom today.

DAEMONES   Right.

TRACHALIO   You get Plesidippus to agree to set me free.

DAEMONES   Right.

TRACHALIO   And get your daughter to ask him; she'll get it out of him without any trouble.

DAEMONES   Right.

TRACHALIO   And arrange to have Ampelisca marry me as soon as I'm free.

DAEMONES   Right.

TRACHALIO   I want to see some tangible appreciation for all I've done for you.

DAEMONES   Right.

TRACHALIO   Everything I say is "right," eh?

DAEMONES   Right—I'm just returning the favor. Now, off to the city this minute, on the double, and then come back here.

TRACHALIO   Right. I won't take long. In the meantime you get everything ready that we need.

DAEMONES   Right. (*To himself as Trachalio dashes off, stage left*) The devil take him with his "rights"! My ears are ringing: whatever I said, it was nothing but "right," "right," "right."

(*Enter Gripus, stage right.*)

GRIPUS (*determinedly*) Daemones, when will it be all right to have a word with you?

DAEMONES (*wincing at still another "right"*) What's on your mind, Gripus?

GRIPUS It's about that satchel. If you've got any sense, you'll have the sense to hold onto something heaven's dropped right in your lap.

DAEMONES (*reproachfully*) Do you think it's right for me to claim somebody else's property as my own?

GRIPUS (*exasperated*) But it's something I found in the sea!

DAEMONES So much the better for the man who lost it. But that doesn't make it any more your satchel.

GRIPUS (*disgustedly*) That's why you're so poor. It's that sanctified goodness of yours.

DAEMONES (*gently*) Gripus, Gripus, there are so many traps set for men during their lifetime to trick and fool them! What's more, the traps are often baited; if a man's avaricious and goes after the bait greedily, he gets trapped by his own greed. The man who's careful and experienced and astute in watching his step can live a long and honest life on what he's honestly earned. If you ask me, this prize you're so wedded to will fall prize to its owner—and the divorce will cost us money. (*In shocked tones*) I hide something brought to me that I know isn't mine? None of that for your old master Daemones, no, sir! The one thing any man of intelligence is always on guard against is consciously taking part in wrongdoing. I'll have nothing whatsoever to do with making any gains by collusion.

GRIPUS (*eying him pityingly*) I've often seen actors in a play deliver themselves of gems of wisdom of this sort—and seen them get a round of applause for having mouthed for the audience all these rules of good behavior. Then, when the audience left and everybody was back in his own home, there wasn't a one who behaved the way he had been told to.

DAEMONES (*impatiently*) Oh, go inside and stop bothering me. And watch that tongue of yours. Make no mistake about it—I'm not going to give you a thing.

(*Gripus, without a word, marches up to the door, opens it, then turns to deliver a parting shot.*)

GRIPUS (*bitterly*) I hope to god whatever's in that satchel— gold or silver or what not—turns into ashes! (*Ducks into the cottage, slamming the door.*)

DAEMONES (*to the audience, shaking his head sadly*) See that attitude? That's the reason we have such bad servants. Now if that Gripus of mine had gotten together with some other servant, he'd have involved the two of them in grand larceny. He'd have been thinking he had his hands on a prize, and he'd have turned out to be the prize himself. What he caught would have caught him. Well, I'll go in now and attend to the offering. And then I'll give orders to have dinner ready immediately.

(*Daemones goes into the cottage. A moment later Trachalio and Plesidippus enter, stage left. One glance at the latter is enough to reveal that he has gotten the news.*)

PLESIDIPPUS (*ecstatically*) Trachalio, my friend, my freed-man-to-be, no, my patron—more than that, the founder of my household! Tell me that whole story over again. So Palaestra found her mother and father?

TRACHALIO (*smiling indulgently*) Yes, she did.

PLESIDIPPUS And she's an Athenian like me?

TRACHALIO I think so.

PLESIDIPPUS And she's going to marry me?

TRACHALIO I suspect so.

PLESIDIPPUS What do you think, will we become engaged today?

TRACHALIO (*pretending, indulgently, to be under formal interrogation*) Yes, Mr. Chairman.

PLESIDIPPUS What do you say, should I congratulate her father on having found her?

TRACHALIO Yes, Mr. Chairman.

PLESIDIPPUS How about her mother?

TRACHALIO Yes, Mr. Chairman.

PLESIDIPPUS Have you anything to tell the chair?

TRACHALIO Yes, Mr. Chairman: yes to whatever the chair asks.

PLESIDIPPUS (*slyly*) All right, can you estimate the chair's net worth?

TRACHALIO (*taken aback*) Me? (*Recovering*) Yes, Mr. Chairman—

PLESIDIPPUS (*interrupting*) Look, I'm standing; forget about this "chair" business.

TRACHALIO Yes, Mr. Chairman.

PLESIDIPPUS Should I rush up to her?

TRACHALIO Yes, Mr. Chairman.

PLESIDIPPUS Or should I go up to her quietly, like this? (*Demonstrates.*)

TRACHALIO Yes, Mr. Chairman.

PLESIDIPPUS Should I shake her hand when I go up to her?

TRACHALIO Yes, Mr. Chairman.

PLESIDIPPUS Her father's too?

TRACHALIO Yes, Mr. Chairman.

PLESIDIPPUS And then her mother's?

TRACHALIO Yes, Mr. Chairman.

PLESIDIPPUS Should I embrace her father when I go up to him?

TRACHALIO No, Mr. Chairman.

PLESIDIPPUS How about her mother?

TRACHALIO No, Mr. Chairman.

PLESIDIPPUS (*eagerly*) How about her?

TRACHALIO No, Mr. Chairman. (*Starts walking toward the cottage.*)

PLESIDIPPUS Oh, lord! He votes Nay just when I want Aye —and walks out on the meeting.

TRACHALIO (*calling*) You're crazy. Come on!

PLESIDIPPUS Lead on, my patron, whither thou will.

(*The two enter the cottage, and the stage is now empty.*)

ACT V

(Enter Labrax, stage left.)

LABRAX *(to the audience)* Is there another man alive right now who's worse off than I am? I've just come from court; Plesidippus got them to condemn me, and they made me give Palaestra up. I'm ruined! *(Bitterly)* If you ask me, pimps were put on this earth just to make people laugh—that's the way it looks, judging from the general hilarity whenever a poor pimp has to suffer. *(Turning and walking toward the shrine)* I'm going to see to that other girl of mine in the shrine here. At least I'll take her away with me—the only remnant left of all my property.

(The door of the cottage opens and Gripus comes out. He is holding a spit encrusted with rust—eloquent testimony as to how long it's been since Daemones last held a party. He turns to speak to those inside.)

GRIPUS *(through the doorway)* By god, you're not going to lay eyes on me alive after tonight—unless I get that satchel back!

LABRAX *(to himself)* Oh, god! Whenever I hear anyone mention a satchel, it's like the stab of a sword through my heart.

GRIPUS *(as before)* That damned Trachalio gets his freedom and you refuse to give a single thing to the man who fished the satchel up in his net!

LABRAX *(his attention arrested, to himself)* So help me, what this fellow is saying sounds very, very interesting.

GRIPUS *(as before)* I'm going right out and post notices everywhere in letters a foot and a half high: "Found. One satchel full of gold and silver. For information see Gripus." You think you're going to get away with my satchel, don't you? Well, you're not.

LABRAX (*to himself*) By god, I think this fellow knows who has my satchel! I'd better have a talk with him. Lord in heaven, help me now!

GRIPUS (*as someone calls him to come back inside*) What are you calling me back for? I want to clean this outside here. (*Turns away from the door and starts scraping the spit; to himself*) My god! You'd think this spit's made of rust instead of iron. The more I scrape it, the redder and skinnier it gets. I think there's a curse on it: the thing's dying of old age right in my hands.

LABRAX (*in his most affable manner*) Hello there.

GRIPUS (*eying him distastefully*) Hello yourself, dirty face.

LABRAX (*as before*) What are you doing with yourself these days?

GRIPUS (*scraping away industriously*) Cleaning a spit.

LABRAX Business good around here?

GRIPUS What's it to you? You a broker?

LABRAX Oh, no. I'm one letter short of that.

GRIPUS Broke, eh?

LABRAX You hit the nail on the head.

GRIPUS I know. You look it. What happened to you?

LABRAX My ship was wrecked last night. Lost everything I had in it.

GRIPUS What did you lose?

LABRAX (*pointedly*) A satchel full of gold and silver.

GRIPUS (*his attention caught*) Do you remember any of the things in this satchel you lost?

LABRAX (*evasively*) What difference does it make? It's lost, isn't it? Forget it. Let's talk about something else.

GRIPUS What if I know who found it? I just want to see if you can prove it's your property.

LABRAX Well, there were eight hundred gold pieces in a pouch. Then another hundred gold eagles in a separate leather sack.

GRIPUS (*aside*) God almighty, what a haul! I'm in for a fat reward. There is a providence after all: I'm going to get a load of loot out of this fellow. It's his satchel, no question about it. (*To Labrax*) Go on, tell me what else was in it.

LABRAX Thirty thousand dollars in silver in a sack, all good coin. And some silverware—a bowl, a bucket, a pitcher, a jug, and a cup.

GRIPUS Wow! That's quite a fortune you had there.

LABRAX I "had"; now I don't have a thing. Saddest and worst word in the language, "had."

GRIPUS (*eying him narrowly*) What are you willing to pay the fellow who brings you information about its whereabouts? (*As Labrax hesitates*) Come on, speak up!

LABRAX Fifteen hundred dollars.

GRIPUS (*snorting*) Stop kidding.

LABRAX Two thousand.

GRIPUS That's a laugh.

LABRAX Two thousand, five hundred.

GRIPUS Peanuts.

LABRAX Three thousand.

GRIPUS Chicken feed.

LABRAX I'll give you three thousand, five hundred.

GRIPUS What's the matter? Your mouth hot and you want to air it out?

LABRAX I'll give you five thousand dollars.

GRIPUS Wake up.

LABRAX Not another cent.

GRIPUS All right then, beat it!

LABRAX Listen—

GRIPUS (*heading for the door*) Once I leave here, my friend, I'm gone for good.

LABRAX Will you take five thousand, five hundred?

GRIPUS (*walking away*) You're dreaming.

LABRAX (*calling after him*)   Name your price.

GRIPUS (*stopping*)   Fifteen thousand dollars and you don't have to give me a penny more. But not a penny less! That's it; take it or leave it.

LABRAX (*shrugging*)   What can I say? I've got to take it. All right, I'll give you fifteen thousand.

GRIPUS (*walking over to the altar*)   Come on over here; I want Venus to be a party to this deal.

LABRAX (*following him*)   Anything you want; just tell me what it is.

GRIPUS   Put your hand on this altar.

LABRAX   It's on.

GRIPUS (*grimly*)   You've got to swear by Venus here.

LABRAX   What should I swear?

GRIPUS   What I tell you to.

LABRAX   You say it; I'll swear it. (*Aside, sardonically*) The old master being told what to swear!

GRIPUS   Got hold of the altar?

LABRAX   Right.

GRIPUS   Give me your solemn oath you'll pay me the money the day you get your satchel back.

LABRAX   So be it. (*Raising his eyes to heaven and intoning*) I solemnly swear in the name of Venus of Cyrene that, if I find the satchel I lost in the shipwreck and regain possession of it with the gold and silver safe inside, I will pay to this man—

GRIPUS (*interrupting*)   Say "I will pay to this man Gripus" and touch me at the same time.

LABRAX (*sardonically*)   To make it absolutely clear to you, Venus, I will pay to this man Gripus fifteen thousand dollars on the spot.

GRIPUS   Now say that, if you should welsh, Venus should ruin your body, your soul, and your business. (*Aside*) And once you've done swearing it, I hope she does it to you anyway.

LABRAX (*intoning*) If I go back on anything I have sworn, may all pimps suffer a life of misery.

GRIPUS Don't worry, that'll happen even if you keep your word. (*Walking toward the door*) You wait there. I'll bring the old man outside right away. As soon as I do, you ask him for your satchel. (*Hurries into the cottage.*)

LABRAX (*looking after him scornfully, to himself*) Even if he gets the satchel back for me, I don't owe him a dime. *I'm* the one who decides what I do about what I swear. (*The door opens and Gripus and Daemones come out lugging the satchel.*) Here he comes with the old man. I'd better shut up.

GRIPUS (*to Daemones*) Follow me. This way.

DAEMONES Where is that pimp of yours?

GRIPUS (*calling to Labrax*) Hey, you! (*Pointing to Daemones*) Here he is. This fellow's got your satchel.

DAEMONES (*to Labrax*) Yes, I have it and I don't mind telling you that I do. What's more, if it's yours, you're welcome to it. You'll find everything that was in it still there, safe and sound. Here, take it if it's yours.

LABRAX (*unable to believe his eyes*) Well, what do you know! My satchel! (*Going up to it and fingering it lovingly*) Greetings, old satchel, greetings!

DAEMONES Is it yours?

LABRAX (*getting a firm grip on it*) What a question! I don't care if it belonged to god almighty himself; it's mine now.

DAEMONES Everything in it is safe and sound—with one exception: I took out a little box of trinkets I used in finding my daughter today.

LABRAX Who's that?

DAEMONES Palaestra, the girl you used to own. I found out she's my daughter.

LABRAX (*assuming his heartiest manner*) Well, that's just fine! Things have turned out beautifully for you. Just what you hoped for. I'm delighted.

DAEMONES (*dryly*)   I find it a little hard to believe that.

LABRAX (*as before*)   It's the god's honest truth. (*Slyly*) And just to prove my feelings are genuine, you don't have to pay me a cent for her. She's a gift.

DAEMONES (*as before*)   So kind of you.

LABRAX   Oh, no, nothing at all, really.

GRIPUS (*pointedly*)   All right you, you have your satchel now.

LABRAX   That's right.

GRIPUS   Well, let's get on with it.

LABRAX (*producing his blankest look*)   Get on with what?

GRIPUS   Paying me my money.

LABRAX   I'm not paying you any money. I don't owe you a cent.

GRIPUS   Hey, what's going on here! (*Disbelievingly*) You don't owe me a cent?

LABRAX   That's right. Not a cent.

GRIPUS   But you gave me your oath.

LABRAX (*blandly*)   I know I did. I'll give you another right now if I feel like it. This oath business is strictly for holding on to property, not letting it go.

GRIPUS (*shouting*)   You hand over that fifteen thousand dollars, you dirty liar!

DAEMONES (*to Gripus*)   Gripus, what's this fifteen thousand you're asking him for?

GRIPUS   He gave me his oath he'd pay it to me.

LABRAX (*to Gripus, as before*)   I get fun out of giving oaths. What are you, the chief justice? Going to try me for perjury?

DAEMONES (*to Gripus*)   What did he promise you the money for?

GRIPUS   He swore he'd give me fifteen thousand dollars if I got his satchel back for him.

LABRAX (*to Gripus, scornfully*)   Pick some free man to represent you and let's go to court. (*Grinning*) I'll prove you made me a party to a fraudulent contract, (*the grin widening*) and that I'm still a minor.

GRIPUS (*pointing to Daemones*) He'll represent me.

LABRAX (*losing his grin*) No. You'll have to get someone else.

DAEMONES (*to Labrax, firmly*) I'm not going to let you take a penny away from this boy—unless I find he's done something wrong. Now then, did you promise him the money?

LABRAX (*unabashed*) Sure I did.

DAEMONES (*promptly*) What you promised a servant of mine is by rights mine. (*As Labrax opens his mouth*) Don't get the idea you can pull any of your pimp's tricks on me; you won't get away with it.

GRIPUS (*to Labrax, jubilantly*) So you thought you had gotten your hands on some poor devil you could swindle, eh? You'll pay—and in good money, too. And the minute I get it I'm giving it to this man here (*pointing to Daemones*) to pay for my freedom.

DAEMONES (*to Labrax, reproachfully*) When you think of how well I've treated you and that it was all because of me this money was kept safe for you—

GRIPUS (*interrupting angrily*) None of that—all because of me, not you.

DAEMONES (*turning on him*) If you've got any brains, you'll keep your mouth shut! (*To Labrax*) —the least you could do is act decently and reciprocate for all I've done for you.

LABRAX (*softened by Daemones' conciliatory tone*) I take it you're asking me this because you recognize my rights?

DAEMONES I'm not exactly asking you to use them against me, you know.

GRIPUS (*his eyes fixed on Labrax' face, aside*) I'm in! The pimp's weakening! My freedom's just around the corner!

DAEMONES (*gesturing toward Gripus*) First of all, this boy

who found that satchel of yours is my servant. Secondly, I kept it safe for you, money and all.

LABRAX (*nodding his head in agreement*) I'm really very grateful to you. About that fifteen thousand I swore to give that boy of yours—I see no reason why you shouldn't have it.

GRIPUS (*to Labrax, shouting*) Hey, you! You give it to me, not him! Haven't you got any brains?

DAEMONES (*turning on him*) Will you please shut up!

GRIPUS (*wildly*) You're just pretending to be working for my interests; you're really out for yourself. I may have lost all the rest of the swag in that satchel, but, by god, you're not going to screw me out of this!

DAEMONES (*angrily*) If you say another word, I'll have you whipped!

GRIPUS (*as before*) Go on, kill me! I'll only keep quiet if you gag me with fifteen thousand dollars. There's no other way to shut me up.

LABRAX (*to Gripus, disgustedly*) Oh, pipe down. He certainly is working for your best interests.

DAEMONES (*beckoning Labrax off to the side*) Step over here, will you?

LABRAX Sure.

GRIPUS (*calling to them as they move to one side*) Hey, let's keep it in the open! I don't want any of this whispering business.

DAEMONES (*sotto voce*) How much did you pay for that other girl? Ampelisca, I mean.

LABRAX (*sotto voce*) Five thousand dollars.

DAEMONES (*sotto voce*) How'd you like me to make you a good offer for her?

LABRAX (*sotto voce*) I sure would.

DAEMONES (*sotto voce*) I'll split that fifteen thousand with you.

LABRAX (*sotto voce, with pleased surprise*) Thanks!

DAEMONES (*sotto voce*) You take half for letting Ampelisca go free, and give me half.

LABRAX (*sotto voce*) It's a deal.

DAEMONES (*sotto voce*) The half I get will pay for Gripus' freedom. After all, it was because of him that you found your satchel and I my daughter.

LABRAX (*sotto voce*) Thanks very much. I'm much obliged to you.

GRIPUS (*calling*) Hey, how soon am I going to get my money?

DAEMONES It's all settled, Gripus. I've got it.

GRIPUS Damn it all, I want me to have it!

DAEMONES Well, damn it all, you're not getting it, so don't start getting your hopes up. And I want you to let him (*gesturing toward Labrax*) off his oath.

GRIPUS (*roaring*) Damn it all, that's the end of me. I'm a goner—unless I hang myself. And, damn it all, I'll do it right now—you won't get a second chance to swindle me, no sir!

DAEMONES (*to Labrax*) How about joining us for dinner?

LABRAX Thanks. Be glad to.

DAEMONES Follow me in, both of you. (*Walks downstage and addresses the audience.*) Ladies and gentlemen, I'd invite you to dinner too—except that I'm not serving anything, and there's nothing decent to eat in the house anyway; besides, I know you've all got other invitations to eat out tonight. But, if you'd care to give a hearty round of applause to our play, you can all come to a big party at my house—sixteen years from now. (*Turning to Labrax and Gripus*) You two come to dinner.

LABRAX AND GRIPUS Thank you.

DAEMONES (*to the audience*) Your applause, please.

BIOGRAPHY, AUTOBIOGRAPHY AND LETTERS

ANDRADE, E. N. da C. Sir Isaac Newton, A151
BEETHOVEN, LUDWIG VAN Beethoven: Letters, Journals and Conversations, Trans. & Ed. Hamburger, A206
BENDIX, REINHARD Max Weber: An Intellectual Portrait, A281
COLETTE My Mother's House and The Vagabond, A62
CONNOLLY, CYRIL Enemies of Promise and Other Essays, A194
CONRAD, JOSEPH The Mirror of the Sea and A Personal Record, A207
DICKINSON, EMILY Selected Poems and Letters of Emily Dickinson, Ed. Linscott, A192
DUPEE, F. W. Henry James: His Life and Writings, A68
ESSLIN, MARTIN Brecht: The Man and His Work, A245
GEIRINGER, KARL Brahms: His Life and Work, A245
GONCOURT, EDMOND & JULES DE The Goncourt Journals (1851–1870), A158
GRAVES, ROBERT Good-Bye to All That, A123
HIMMELFARB, GERTRUDE Darwin and the Darwinian Revolution, A325
JAMES, HENRY The Selected Letters of Henry James, Ed. Edel, A204
KEATS, JOHN The Selected Letters of John Keats, Ed. Trilling, A70
KROPOTKIN, PETER Memoirs of a Revolutionist, Ed. Rogers, A287
LAWRENCE, D. H. Selected Letters of D. H. Lawrence, Ed. Trilling, A236
LEWIS, D. B. WYNDHAM François Villon, A147
LOWRIE, WALTER A Short Life of Kierkegaard, A273
NEALE, J. E. Queen Elizabeth I, A105
NICOLSON, HAROLD Tennyson, A284
PHILLIPS, DR. HARLAN B., ed. Felix Frankfurter Reminisces, A310
RAHV, PHILIP, ed. Discovery of Europe, A208
RILKE, RAINER MARIA Selected Letters of Rainer Maria Rilke, Ed. Moore, A223
SHATTUCK, ROGER The Banquet Years, A238
STEEGMULLER, FRANCIS The Grand Mademoiselle, A205
TAYLOR, A. E. Socrates, A9
TRELAWNY, E. J. The Last Days of Shelley and Byron, A225
WILSON, EDMUND A Piece of My Mind, A143
YEATS, WILLIAM BUTLER The Autobiography of William Butler Yeats, A142

ESSAYS, BELLES LETTRES & LITERARY CRITICISM

AUERBACH, ERICH Mimesis, A107
BARZUN, JACQUES Classic, Romantic and Modern, A255
BATE, WALTER JACKSON Prefaces to Criticism, A165
BAUDELAIRE, CHARLES The Mirror of Art, A84
BEERBOHM, MAX A Selection from Around Theatres, A226
BERGSON, HENRI Laughter (with Meredith's Essay on Comedy) in Comedy, A87
BLACKMUR, R. P. Form and Value in Modern Poetry, A96
BRANDEIS, IRMA The Ladder of Vision, A320
BROOKS, VAN WYCK America's Coming-of-Age, A129
CARY, JOYCE Art and Reality, A260
CASTIGLIONE, BALDESAR The Book of the Courtier, A186
CHASE, RICHARD The American Novel and Its Tradition, A116
CONNOLLY, CYRIL Enemies of Promise and Other Essays, A194
DUMAS, ALEXANDRE Adventures in Spain, A211
DUPEE, F. W. Henry James: His Life and Writings, A68
EDEL, LEON Literary Biography, A188
FERGUSSON, FRANCIS The Human Image in Dramatic Literature, A124
——— The Idea of a Theater, A4

FORSTER, E. M. Alexandria: A History and a Guide, A231
GRANVILLE-BARKER, H. & HARRISON, G. B., eds. A Companion to Shakespeare Studies, A191
HOFFMAN, DANIEL, ed. American Poetry and Poetics, A304
HYTIER, JEAN Andre Gide, A307
JAMES, HENRY The Art of Travel, Ed. Zabel, A306
KAUFMANN, WALTER From Shakespeare to Existentialism, A213
KAZIN, ALFRED On Native Grounds, A69
KITTO, H. D. F. Greek Tragedy, A38
KRONENBERGER, LOUIS, ed. Novelists on Novelists, A293
LAWRENCE, D. H. Studies in Classic American Literature, A5
MC CORMICK, JOHN & MAC INNES, MAIRI, eds. Versions of Censorship, A297
MEREDITH, GEORGE Essay on Comedy (with Bergson's *Laughter*) in Comedy, A87
MONTAIGNE Complete Essays of Montaigne, Trans. Frame: 3 volumes A227a, A227b, A227c
MOORE, W. G. Moliere: A New Criticism, A291
MORRIS, WRIGHT, ed. A Mississippi River Reader, A299
NICOLSON, HAROLD Tennyson, A284
NIETZSCHE, FRIEDRICH The Birth of Tragedy and The Genealogy of Morals, A81
ORTEGA Y GASSET, JOSE The Dehumanization of Art and Other Writings on Art and Culture, A72
ORWELL, GEORGE A Collection of Essays, A29
ROURKE, CONSTANCE American Humor, A12
SHATTUCK, ROGER The Banquet Years, A238
SHAW, GEORGE BERNARD Shaw on Music, Ed. Bentley, A53
STENDHAL On Love, A103
SYPHER, WYLIE Four Stages of Renaissance Style, A45
TOKLAS, ALICE B. The Alice B. Toklas Cook Book, A196
TRAVERSI, D. A. An Approach to Shakespeare, A74
TRILLING, LIONEL The Liberal Imagination, A13
VAN DOREN, MARK Shakespeare, A11
WELSFORD, ENID The Fool: His Social and Literary History, A262
WILLEY, BASIL The Seventeenth Century Background, A19
WILSON, EDMUND A Literary Chronicle: 1920-1950, A85
——— A Piece of My Mind, A143